THE FLINT AND THE FLAME

THE YOUTHFUL DICKENS

THE FLINT AND THE FLAME

The Artistry of Charles Dickens

Earle Davis

UNIVERSITY OF MISSOURI PRESS

COLUMBIA

1963

Publication of this book
has been aided by the Ford Foundation program
to support publication,
through university presses, of work in the
humanities and social sciences.

*Library of Congress Catalog
Card No. 63-11882*

Manufactured in the United States of America

for
KAY

Table of Contents

Foreword

NY CRITIC who begins constructing a book about a popular and established novelist owes innumerable debts to those who have gone before. The Dickens scholar must be particularly grateful to Edgar Johnson's monumental biography and to the study of Dickens' reputation made by George H. Ford. The relatively modern shift in critical emphasis upon the value of Dickens' novels properly begins with Edmund Wilson, and George Orwell and Jack Lindsay have contributed immeasurably to an understanding of the depth of Dickens' picture of his world. Among the many introductions and studies of individual novels, one must mention the inspiration of George Bernard Shaw and Lionel Trilling. John Hagan and Monroe Engel add their own measure of serious critical dissection and interpretation. Behind all these critics are the old guard—Forster, Gissing, Chesterton—and innumerable others. The Dickens scholar should hail them all, even if he occasionally disagrees with them. Nor can his debts ever be properly paid, no matter how hard he tries.

There has long been a gnawing need for an intense study of the artistry and craftsmanship of Dickens. The complexity of the task defies any claim to its absolute completion, for additional influences, corrections, and developments will be discovered as long as the novels are read. This book is an effort to break many trails of scholarly examination, identification of sources, details of technique, and the pursuit of narrative intentions. Its thesis is that Dickens developed in his mastery of his craft, that he was not an unconscious genius ("an original"), and that his control of narrative technique progressed in importance and fulfillment. In contrast to considerable traditional evaluation this view implies that the great Dickens novels are the late ones, from *David Copperfield* on, particularly *Bleak House, Little Dorrit,* and *Our Mutual Friend.*

Herein are advanced many specific source discoveries and the evaluation of influences which either have not been previously suggested or have not been developed to relevance. These include the detailed study of the influence of Charles Mathews on Dickens' caricature and speech tags; the manner and matter of melodrama; the background for the sentimental and Gothic influences; the attitudes of Romantic dialectic; specific plot sources for *Bleak House* and *Our Mutual Friend,* as well as others; clarification of the supposed influence of Wilkie Collins upon Dickens; and episode by episode analysis of the construction of novels like *David Copperfield* and *A Tale of Two Cities*. There are innumerable small discoveries for which no special attention is claimed, although they could have been spread out in a number of brief scholarly articles and published in appropriate journals.

The important technical and critical contention of this study is that Dickens developed an artistic plan for the panoramic or telescopic novel, weaving a number of plots around a central theme, thus presenting a concept of art form at the opposite pole from the Henry James definition of artistry in fiction—that which depends upon assuming a point of view and concentrating microscopically upon a single character or situation. The breadthwise-cutting of life is also intensified by Dickens' suffusing symbolism in the later novels, and this symbolism has been presented in some detail in this book.

Early stages for certain sections of this study have been represented by the author's articles and monographs, the Charles Mathews influence in PMLA, and the analysis of *David Copperfield* and the relationship of Wilkie Collins in the *University of Wichita Studies*.

Sir Francis Meynell and the Nonesuch Press have graciously given permission to quote the many passages from the letters of Dickens, and all references to the novels are footnoted from this great standard edition of the Dickens novels. I am grateful to Leslie C. Staples and *The Dickensian* for permission to quote from the magazine of the Dickens Fellowship. The Public Trustee and The Society of Authors have granted permission for the quotation of the excerpts from George Bernard Shaw. I am also grateful to Harcourt Brace for permission to quote from George Orwell's essay on Dickens. Especial gratitude is due Edgar Johnson, not only for permission to quote from his biography but also for his many pertinent suggestions about the manuscript of this book. He is not responsible for errors or opinions, of course, but his comments were consistently helpful.

I should like to register thanks to many scholars who were kind enough to make suggestions and give aid. A debt that goes beyond gratitude stretches back through the years, to Gordon Hall Gerould and to J. Duncan Spaeth at Princeton for encouragement of initial studies in the works of Dickens; also to Fred Higginson, William C. Hummel, and Philip Young for untold criticisms of the manuscript.

Kansas State University   E. D.
January, 1963

CHAPTER I

Toward a Frame of Reference

HE WORDS of a dead man (as Auden said of Yeats) are modified in the guts of the living. Sometimes the process of modification produces new energy for succeeding generations. After all, historical criticism is the intellectual form in which readers of one age decide for themselves the meaning of another time. Scholars are often concerned with causes, but readers are usually interested in results. The ever-changing significance of results keeps criticism healthy from century to century. It also drives succeeding generations back to the enjoyment of the best books.

The novels of Charles Dickens, because of their wide range and universal variety, have spurred critics to amazing differences in interpretation and evaluation. In the perspective of the nineteenth century, these novels reflect laughter and tears, suspense and sympathy to an extraordinary degree. Dickens was popular in a sense which is hard to believe. Some of his original popularity waned as the years went by, and his books rested on the shelves of libraries alongside others which occasionally gave the illusion of greater artistry or importance. Readers forgot him, defended him, discovered him anew, even resurrected him.

Up until recent years—say, around 1940—Dickens appeared to be on the road to critical mummification. He was surrounded by Victorian wrappings and trappings and labeled as typical of his time, occasionally fascinating for his eccentrics and his comedy, a representative of sentiment and melodrama in fiction. Except among a stalwart band of enthusiasts, he was not classed with the greatest writers. The last twenty years have produced an about-face, not exactly unanimous, but occasionally positive, as illustrated by the opinion of Lionel Trilling, who said in 1952, "No one, I think, is

1

any longer under any illusion about Dickens. It is now manifest that he is one of the two greatest novelists of England (Jane Austen being the other)."[1]

There are several good reasons for this shift in evaluation, but any attempt to explain the reasons in simple terms depends upon knowledge of what has happened to the reputation of Dickens since he began publishing his fiction. The infinite variety of his novels has contributed much to the conflicting ways in which he has been judged. Since he wrote on a grand and rambling scale, with innumerable characters, incidents, and subjects, he has not been interpreted with complete consistency by any critic. For example, he followed the narrative methods of Fielding, Smollett, and Scott; he copied parts of his world with journalistic exactness; other parts he heightened and distorted in order to focus interest or arouse laughter. He organized incidents as his picaresque predecessors, Smollett particularly, had done before him. He arranged the conversation of his characters and the action of his plots as did those who wrote for the stage. He inserted materials which proclaimed definite opinions about social problems, political economy, and morals. He was naturally uneven and varied in his prose style, and in his first novels he neglected to supply motivation for his action. Incredible energy and vitality accompanied his varied effects. In the glittering fragments of his works one can find substantiation for extreme and conflicting opinions about his total accomplishment. Many critics have solved the problem of evaluation by praising what they like and ignoring the rest. His detractors operate in reverse gear.

There are three main schools of criticism for Dickens before 1940, and each school displays little kinship with the others in its emphasis on the importance of the novels. First there are the traditional worshippers who see Dickens as a "Romantic artist." They have garlanded his memory with books which range from stubborn admiration to idealistic idolatry. They begin with John Forster, reach a climax with Gilbert Keith Chesterton, and include such disparate personalities as Swinburne, Paul Elmer More, Santayana, Priestley, Sir Osbert Sitwell, Stephen Leacock, and most of The Dickens Fellowship. They include great scholars, little scholars, patriotic admirers of jolly old England, and the lovers of picturesque Christmas cards. Their most characteristic representative is probably Chesterton, some of whose reasons for admiring Dickens may disconcert the modern reader. Chesterton remarks, for example:

> Dickens was a very great man, and there are many ways of testing and stating this fact. But one permissible way is to say this, that he was an ignorant man, ill-read in the past, and often confused about the present. Yet he remains great and true, and even essentially reliable, if we suppose him to have known not only all that went before his lifetime, but also all that was to come after.[2]

This perspective assumes that Dickens, like all the greatest creative artists, was inspired—perhaps divinely so. The fact of inspiration establishes an effect which cannot be analyzed. The reader can take it or leave it. Some of this group, like More or Santayana, seem surprised that they desire to continue reading Dickens, and they avoid an analysis of his novels for fear they will lose the spell of pleasure. But Chesterton praises Dickens on the grounds of genius alone, not knowledge or artistry, and solves every difficulty in interpretation by an appeal to the regions of unfathomable inspiration. One is reminded of Milton's portrait of Shakespeare's natural but uneducated genius, a creator of "wood-notes wild." Shortly after Dickens died, a critic writing in *Cornhill Magazine* suggested that if Bacon wrote Shakespeare's plays, surely Gladstone had written the novels of Dickens, since "neither by position nor by training was he likely to become the author of works in which politics, science, art, and literature are dealt with confidently and boldly."[3]

In this view, it is surely better for Dickens that he never attended a university or read many books; his later association with Wilkie Collins is especially to be deplored because it supposedly resulted in Dickens' attempting to plan his novels, not allowing them to flow forth with sprawling effortlessness; his inspiration served him best when he wrote without need for study, practice, or development, thus striking a chord in the heart of the common reader by virtue of a God-given kinship of spirit; his great popularity was proof of his transcendental capacity. In this charismatic spirit several writers contributing to *The Dickensian* allowed their hero-worship to express itself in the designation of Dickens as "The Master."

A second and different perspective focuses on the humanitarian

3

aspects of Dickens' novels. According to this analysis, he was a great writer because he fought for justice for all men. Despite his dislike of human imperfections, he was essentially an optimist; he taught that things always turn out for the best if we live up to our Christian capacities. Evil and good are appropriately rewarded in this life, and even if this is not exactly true, an author should be praised for thinking so. This attitude makes Dickens especially attractive to adolescent readers, and besides Dickens never propagated a morally offensive notion or presented a scene which might even begin to lead an innocent astray. His efforts toward the reform of abuses in law, education, and social theory materially aided the advance of his era to conditions which can be vaguely described as "better." He continually attacked selfishness, pride, hypocrisy, and kindred personal vices. Any novelist who contributes services of this nature is great, and since Dickens reached moral heights in the over-all sense, questions of technical excellence in artistic detail are beside the point.

Fittingly, or peculiarly, according to your attitude in such matters, this group of critics includes the liberal and socialist writers of the twentieth century. For a little while Dickens was hailed also by the Marxists. George Bernard Shaw, although he liked most of the later novels of Dickens, praised *Hard Times* particularly, because it is devoted to a study of the weaknesses of capital in its relations with labor.[4] The proletarian view is easy to understand, since Dickens was concerned with the problems and sorrows of the masses. He had a tendency to picture the rich man as being unhappy with his ill-gotten gains, while the poor but noble workingman, if society permitted, had joys in the love of his home and children which the upper classes rarely knew. Dickens praised those few rich men who gave cheerfully to the needy and sympathized wholeheartedly with the plight of unfortunates. In this view Dickens depicted Victorianism as essentially capitalistic and therefore hypocritical; accordingly he is praised because he was a critic, perhaps a revolutionist, against Victorian values.

The extremist of this group goes further; he sees Dickens as an unconscious Communist, who, unable to admit his real beliefs publicly or to hold his readers if he did, "bored from within" and spread propaganda for the rights of the common man in all his novels. T. A. Jackson in a book called *Charles Dickens: The Progress of a*

Radical (1937) thus insists that Dickens was always on the side of labor against capital; he portrayed conditions similar to those cited by Marx and Engels; he was in sympathy with the poor against the rich: therefore he was a Communist. The fact that Dickens' beliefs in the realm of economics and politics included opinions diametrically opposed to those of Marx can be conveniently ignored. In any case these critics find little point in referring to artistic matters like plot or motivation; to be finicky about aesthetic standards smacks of class distinction.

A third school of criticism might be described as the aesthetic school. It includes all those who value artistry and skill in narration above other considerations. Generally it has attracted everyone who dislikes Dickens for any reason whatever, but it also includes those who think he had faults which are not so important as his virtues. This group is likely to argue that Dickens was not a craftsman, or at least not a consistent or good one. In Dickens' own day the London *Times* consistently dismissed his novels as "a twaddling manifestation of silliness," or as books in which "there is no spark of originality, of truth, of probability, of nature, of beauty."[5] G. H. Lewes was the first critic to sum up arguments against Dickens which have been repeated since his time in different degrees by such varied writers as George Saintsbury, Bechhofer Roberts, Hugh Kingsmill Lunn, and Robert Graves. In some sense all these critics assert that Dickens' criticism of society is childish or misinformed: he avoided study of the inner lives of his characters; he ignored all standards of art to achieve entertainment and sell his novels; he omitted sex; he made no appeal to sensitive or educated readers; and at his worst he bathed in the tears of completely unbearable sentimental extremes.[6] "The Death of Little Nell," for example, has become a catch phrase in ridicule, encompassing the lowest standards of melodrama or of ineffective entertainment for intelligent readers.

The so-called New Critics of our time tend to implement this judgment. T. S. Eliot praises *Bleak House* offhandedly because he says it gives the most perfect balance among Dickens' novels of his artistic weaknesses and his strength. Eliot argues that the novel presents interesting characters which are larger than life at the same time that the author maintains a proper but unusual interest in plot structure and narrative artistry.[7] Robert Graves goes to the length of rewriting *David Copperfield* in order to leave out whatever Dickens did that was inartistic and add what he conceives a really good novelist ought to have put in. Among other things, he tried to omit the melodrama and the sentimentality while inserting sex. The result gives the impression of emasculation in reverse, David being supplied with a kind of hormone extract.[8]

The most satisfying exponent of this attitude is George Gissing, who admired realism in fiction. Despite the fact that he found Dickens to be lacking in faithfulness to life, despite his horror of excessive coincidences and sensational exaggerations, Gissing liked Dickens. He solved his mixed feelings by praising Dickens whenever his heightening suggested basic reality, and by abandoning whatever parts of the novels he could not defend. The Gissing point of view has long seemed most acceptable to the average student who enjoys Dickens, and his criticism has been required reading along with Forster and Chesterton for anyone who goes beyond the novels themselves to the biographers and the older critics.[9]

All three of these contradictory critical attitudes have been in some measure dependent upon the information which has been available concerning Dickens himself. No very exacting scholarship was devoted to him through the first hundred years following the publication of *Pickwick Papers* in 1836, although numerous laudatory articles and books appeared.[10] It is clear that the idealistic believers in Dickens as a Romantic artist rather shied away from scholarly dissection, either on the grounds that his novels would not stand analysis, or because they thought such study relatively futile. Part of the reason for this neglect by professorial critics was that much of their usual job had apparently been done by the first biographer, John Forster. Forster's *Life of Dickens* was an unusual book, since he had been Dickens' friend from the days before *Pickwick* and had advised Dickens in the writing of almost every one of his novels. Rarely does a man of letters have the opportunity to construct the definitive life of an author from personal contacts as wide and thorough as Forster's were. For many scholars there did not seem to be much left to do but fill in some small points which might have been missed, or to add a reinterpretation of judgment.

6

It was universally admitted that Forster had neglected some important facts in his account of the life of Dickens, notably the influence of Wilkie Collins. But The Dickens Fellowship in general harbored the idea that Wilkie had not been a very good influence anyway. Even though Collins was reputed to be dissatisfied with Forster's biography, he did not publish anything about Dickens himself. A few foreign scholars evolved studies of the influence of Smollett on Dickens, his borrowings from drama and the stage, and the like,[11] but the impression persisted that Dickens was "an original," and that everything he wrote came out of his own invention. Most of the non-biographical books about him traced the models for his characters taken from life, the topography of his novels, and the authenticity of his backgrounds.

Accordingly it was a great shock to those who revered the idealistic memory of Dickens to read in the April 3, 1934, edition of the London *Daily Express* the revelations of a certain Reverend Thomas Wright that Dickens had left his wife for an actress named Ellen Ternan, and that their relationship had continued for the rest of his life. Wright subsequently incorporated his information in a biography (1935), a book which had little merit except its new information, and a great hullabaloo ensued. The new biographical fact was established after a number of years, but the main result of this revelation was that more writers were stimulated to publish new biographies and critical works on Dickens. It is obvious that Dickens' novels are the same whether or not he kept a mistress, but the disclosure certainly had something to do with the sudden rush into print of a great number of new books, including those by Kingsmill Lunn, Una Pope-Hennessy, Hesketh Pearson, Jack Lindsay, Julian Symons, and eventually the monumental two-volume study by Edgar Johnson in 1952, the last book establishing itself as the biography which ought to be finally definitive.[12]

Perhaps coincidentally with the breaking of the scandal there appeared in 1941 the first important study of Dickens' novels to come from an American critic. This was Edmund Wilson's "The Two Scrooges," incorporated in a book entitled *The Wound and the Bow*. This long essay, based upon lectures Wilson had given at the University of Chicago, emphasizes the complexity and depth of Dickens' novels. Underneath the face value of the stories Wilson probes the bitterness of Dickens, his awareness of evil, all the qualities which had passed unnoticed or had been neglected by so many critics. At about the same time George Orwell published an essay on Dickens which must rank as the finest study of the Victorian novelist by any modern of like reputation.[13]

The Wilson essay stimulated a flood of new interpretations of Dickens, with the net result that critics began to discover evidences of artistry, secret meanings, symbolism, and all kinds of unsuspected intentions. Generally they found important values in the novels Dickens wrote *after David Copperfield;* some of them began to look at the manuscripts and the notes Dickens had left and which Forster had preserved; here and there a scholar suggested that Dickens was striving toward a new concept of artistry in a kind of panoramic or large-scale novel at the opposite extreme from the concepts of Henry James and his school. Eventually an American scholar, George H. Ford, published a book-length study of Dickens scholarship, *Dickens and His Readers*, in 1955. This book opened many vistas and paved the way for still more studies of the novelist who was now belatedly on his way to general acclaim from critics of all kinds. Jack Lindsay's exhaustive study of Dickens and his novels, a work marred by excesses of Freudian interpretation and pseudo-Marxian emphasis, is nevertheless full of information about Dickens' narrative sources and his aesthetic ideals.[14] The Edgar Johnson biography incorporates much of the material which has begun to intrigue scholars on both sides of the Atlantic, particularly stressing Dickens' symbolism and the underlying motifs which distinguished the later novels.

What does all this new study do to the three schools of criticism which have been interpreting Dickens in the past? Each of them presented partial truth based upon evidence which is still valid. Each of them achieved a total perspective which puts the real Dickens out of focus, the part masquerading as the whole. If Dickens is indeed one of England's two greatest novelists, as Trilling states rather categorically, the fact must be substantiated by more than the assumption of unusual inspiration, humanitarian intention, or the explaining away of mistakes in craftsmanship. No one-sided approach will serve, since Dickens was a mixture of methods and purposes in fiction.

Let us examine the remark of Chesterton about the ignorance of Dickens as a case in point.[15] Modern research makes it more and more evident that Dickens was not an ignorant man, unless one assumes some special Chestertonian definition of the term. It is true that Dickens was never exposed to a university curriculum; it is certain that he was sentimental; it is clear that he occasionally lacked a certain kind of judgment. But he was well-read, and he associated with the most cultured men of his time. He refers to hundreds of books and plays in his novels. These references do not include Plato, Aristotle, Homer, Dante, Chaucer, Kant, or certain other literary or philosophical names of great reputation, but any examination of his letters shows pertinent and mature comment about art, education, philosophy, politics, and history. The magazines he edited cover a wide field of information usually classed as knowledge. We are unlikely to agree with Dickens all of the time, but disagreement is not the same thing as the awareness of ignorance. Chesterton was saying that Dickens was wise without knowledge. This judgment is obviously false.

Go another step forward. From the proof now available, it is perfectly clear that Dickens studied the art of writing with enthusiasm and zeal. Therefore he was not an ignorant genius who achieved mastery unconsciously. In his style of narration, tending to cumulative excitement, using action in contrast, and introducing symbolic overtones, he is one of the most painstaking of English novelists. He was, indeed, a *conscious* artist, however one judges unexpected flashes of inspiration, and one cannot dismiss his occasional inability in the early novels to get his effects under artistic control by saying that he did not know what he was doing, but whatever he did proved to be right. The most that can be argued is that he was less mature in the early works.

If the critic begins to examine the methods by which Dickens got his narrative effects, he immediately finds overwhelming evidence of careful craftsmanship. Characters and episodes did not always spring full-fashioned into his mind. Dickens remembered how other writers handled similar effects, he used sources constantly, and he attempted to improve upon his inspiration—an inspiration which can be traced and compared. For many years critics have centered upon the people, the places, and the "things" which Dickens observed and which he put into his novels; but the books and the plays were there too. It is part of our purpose to examine these sources, and it is amazing how many of them are just now beginning to be noticed and identified.

In order to judge the circumstances which produced the novels, one needs to go back and remind himself of how Dickens began to write. The story is not commonplace, and knowledge of the circumstances of creation is of prime importance for essential interpretation. Dickens was a normal, slightly precocious boy who came from a lower-middle-class home. His parents' financial difficulties put them in a debtors' prison for a time, and their general circumstances of life allowed the youth little schooling of a formal nature. He worked in a law office in his teens; he taught himself the difficult shorthand system of the period in order to make more money; he drifted naturally into newspaper work and became a good reporter. He had tremendous energy and found time for a great deal of reading on his own, most of it in the English essays and fiction of the preceding century. He loved the stage and was ambitious to act. Self-education is not easily defined and it often has grave limitations, but Dickens achieved it to a remarkable degree.

Like most young men he desired independence and a happy marriage. Writing became his profession. He wrote farces for the stage; he created feature stories and sketches to make more money, signing them "Boz" after a younger brother's nickname; to his superiors he was an ambitious hack-journalist who could turn his hand to anything. He was twenty-four years old when the chance came to furnish copy for some drawings of a sporting nature. Sudden fame and popularity arrived miraculously with Mr. Pickwick, Mr. Jingle, and Sam Weller. But this is not the whole story; it is only the beginning.

He wrote *Pickwick Papers* in monthly installments; never did he publish a novel in book length until it had run for weeks or months in serial form. Except for small details he never rewrote or revised the serial versions of his novels. From 1836 to 1842 he finished five novels, working part of the time on two—even three for a short period—at once. Most of the planning for these novels was done from month to month, and it is certain that there could be little vision which looked very far ahead. Where then did he get his materials? The general answer has been from his experiences as a reporter wandering around London and the vicinity, plus some kind of miraculous inspiration.

But Dickens himself said that he adapted his stories from the books he read and from the plays he saw. What were these books and plays? The best evidence available stems from the well-known passage in *David Copperfield* in which the youthful Dickens, reincarnated in David, tells of the books he read for escape while he was suffering from Mr. Murdstone's principles of child psychology. Smollett, Fielding, Le Sage, Cervantes, and Defoe were his chief comforters, plus *The Arabian Nights* and *The Tales of the Genii*. Because these books were few, because the boy liked to read at an early age, because his peculiar sense of visualization made him play games with the imaginary characters he read about, the few books available to him had a much greater influence than the many books accessible to children in more fortunate circumstances. To dream of these books, he says,

> . . . was my only and my constant comfort. When I think of it, the picture always rises to my mind, of a summer evening, the boys at play in the churchyard, and I sitting on my bed, reading as if for life. Every barn in the neighborhood, every stone in the church, and every foot of the churchyard, had some association of its own, in my mind, connected with these books, and stood for some locality made famous in them. I have seen Tom Pipes go climbing up the church-steeple; I have watched Strap, with the knapsack on his back, stopping to rest himself upon the wicketgate; and I *know* that Commodore Trunnion held that club with Mr. Pickle, in the parlor of our little village alehouse.[16]

It is not generally recognized that Dickens began to write in direct imitation of the materials and styles suggested by this passage—all the characters and scenes are out of novels by Smollett. The growth from boyish enjoyment to serious study and direct imitation came very fast. Some of it happened under the forced growth of the necessities of *Pickwick* and the other early novels. Dickens continued to study novels and plays all his life, his later works again and again giving evidence of his use or adaptation of some admired narrative device or sequence of action which he had observed in his serious or relaxed reading. He seems never to have forgotten anything he read, and he attempted to duplicate or improve upon almost every technique which had been used by his predecessors. Along with Smollett and Fielding came the sentimental novelists, the Gothic novelists, the humanitarian writers like Holcroft and Godwin, the historical novelists like Scott; and after the novelists came the plays he loved and borrowed from, the farces, the tragedies, the melodramas—even the special mannerisms of certain actors. Dickens tried every narrative device which had worked in the past, and the circumstances surrounding the creation of his first five novels forced him to try all these conglomerate techniques rather experimentally.

An additional factor which influenced the artistry of his first novels comes under the heading of commercial pressure. Probably all novelists write to make money, but surely Dickens did. Commonplace romances in the circulating library tradition were being produced in great numbers. The repeal of the law which exorbitantly taxed paper and which up till 1821 virtually choked off magazines had permitted the sudden expansion of periodical publications. Pierce Egan, a writer of modest capacities, produced the best-selling farce studies of London life in the twenties; Theodore Hook contrived attractive rogues who rambled through society managing to get into constant amorous difficulties and comic situations; Robert Surtees constructed tales of sporting adventures and misadventures with gun, rod, and reel. These writers were published in weekly or monthly installments. They depended greatly upon illustrations and comic drawings, having kinship with the comic strip serial writers of the twentieth century, or even the so-called comic books. It was Egan, Hook, and Surtees that Dickens first surpassed. He did what they did, consciously, but better. He wrote novels to sell, and the scholar remembers that Trollope called him "Mr. Popular Sentiment."[17]

The easiest way to judge what Dickens was doing in these early novels is to separate the various styles he imitated, examining his farce-caricature technique (inherited from Smollett and Fielding), following his debt to the stage, and assessing his experiments in sentiment, horror, melodrama, and all the other individual manners of writing which he imitated. Obviously he changed his technique on occasion, although farce and caricature are the basic ingredients of *Pickwick Papers*. He developed a structural plan which might be called alternation or contrast, and it is easy to see how naturally he fell into the habit of

12

broad-scale narration, using many characters and styles. At first this shifting from one mannerism to another was dictated by the demands of whatever characters and action occurred to him at the moment. The only over-all planning observable in the first novels is organized around the occasional lengthy plot sequences he was developing. Since he was utilizing many characters, he tended to invent more than one plot in order to involve as many characters as possible. Much of his distinctive accomplishment can be attributed to inspiration or luck or genius, but it is also possible to say that he was not constantly or continuously masterful, even that he was learning his craftsmanship. The reader who enjoys the early novels overlooks occasional lapses and apprentice-like handling of certain techniques used by the author. Dickens' remarkable gifts in farce and caricature have pleasantly obscured the accompanying weaknesses of these first novels.

Another factor which influences the judgment of Dickens' accomplishment in the early novels is his innate ability to mix and mingle his various techniques so that they do not give the impression of being separate styles. His attitude toward the writing of fiction may be explained rather simply. It was an understanding of the novel form as implying a realism of detail spread thinly over an unreality of action which was part of the model handed down to him by the tradition established by his predecessors. In this view, a novel is primarily a story, and its action must be limited, selected, arranged, and heightened in order to achieve interest. It is not an attempt to copy or analyze the happenings of everyday life. Dickens assumed that this process of limiting, arranging, and heightening represented truth if his action *suggested* and *emphasized* what was true. He knew that the stage utilized stereotyped plot formulas in plays; he knew that Smollett and his school had heightened and caricatured individuals in order to make them more interesting; he knew that humanitarian reformers were accustomed to present real issues in "unreal stories"; he knew that he had to appeal to common unliterary taste in order to sell stories to readers who desired to escape from some degree of unpleasant actuality. It is essential to remember that Dickens always considered realism to be a matter of detail and atmosphere rather than plot or action, even though the events he described had their roots in fact. In spite of continued contact with everyday existence he persisted in viewing life as literary tradition viewed it: a place where the best ought to triumph and poetic justice should double for fate or insurance. Santayana phrased this attitude admirably when he said that "the secret of this new world of Dickens lies . . . in the combination of the strictest realism of detail with a fairy-tale unrealism of general atmosphere."[18]

There is a generally unnoticed passage in *David Copperfield* which bears directly upon Dickens' approach to fiction. David refers to Mr. Micawber in the Marshalsea thus:

> By way of going in for anything that might be on the cards, I call to mind that Mr. Micawber, about this time, composed a petition to the House of Commons, praying for an alteration in the law of imprisonment for debt. I set down this remembrance here, because it is an instance to myself of the manner in which I fitted old books to my altered life, and made stories for myself, out of the streets, and out of men and women; and how some main points in the character I shall unconsciously develop, I suppose, in writing my life, were gradually forming all this while.[19]

The situation referred to here in real life concerned a petition Dickens' father had composed—not about the alteration of the law for debt, but about a proposal to drink the King's health. All the facts of Dickens' own life are altered, selected, heightened, and arranged in order to make *David Copperfield* more interesting. But the real point concerns what Dickens says in the latter part of this passage. He says that he made stories out of the streets, out of men and women, *while he fitted his old books to his altered concept of life.* Forster apparently referred to this practice when he said:

> Here was but another proof how thoroughly Dickens understood his calling, and that to weave fact with fiction unskilfully would be only to make the truth less true.[20]

Dickens' habit of weaving fact with fiction is based upon his use of the people and events he saw in life, but narrated according to the styles and techniques he appropriated from the novelists and playwrights who served as his masters.

In his first period, therefore, Dickens developed several specific techniques of narration: farce and caricature, speech mannerisms with elocutionary devices and tags of expression repeated every time the

14

character appeared, action derived from the melodramatic stage and from romantic novels in some form of plot arrangement, sequences designed to appeal to the tender emotions of sentiment, and episodes which utilized suspense or horror in the tradition fostered by the Gothic novelists. For all these techniques there are demonstrable literary models and influences which need to be examined in detail.

After finishing his fifth novel, *Barnaby Rudge,* Dickens took a vacation and went to America. When he returned to fiction he wrote *Martin Chuzzlewit,* a novel which he had planned carefully, with several plots arranged around a central purpose. By this device he intended to alternate his various technical devices, securing planned contrast. From *Martin Chuzzlewit* on, his moral or social purpose was the *nucleus* for each novel. Under the influence of the teachings of Carlyle he embarked upon social propaganda, and as new novels appeared he attempted a number of definite narrative plans which were adapted to the particular subject, plot, or circumstance which inspired the succeeding stories. What the critics have begun to discern in the later novels of Dickens is his tendency toward a kind of revolving plot arrangement, with several strands of action woven around a central theme. When he could manage it, Dickens emphasized a different technique of narration for each of these separate sequences, thereby securing contrast and alternation, but still getting a unified plan by the central intention of his novel. Eventually his central inspiration added a kind of *suffusing symbolism* built around his theme, the symbolism decorating the action, but never being obtrusive. It is the identification of his symbols which has so attracted modern critics, for it now appears that these symbolic overtones add a dimension which has been almost completely unsuspected before the last few years. With *David Copperfield* he achieved a sustained development of the technique seen dimly for the first time in *Martin Chuzzlewit,* combining his varied technical powers in presenting a number of characters, incidents, and plot situations which are unified by their reference to the circumstances of romantic and unromantic love.

By this time he was intellectually mature and his opinions concerning Victorian society had crystallized. He had much that he wanted to say about what was wrong with his world. He wanted to launch a measured but artistic attack on the abuses he saw in law, education, politics, economics, social theory, the caste system, religion, and individual incapacity in the world about him. In his first five novels he had indulged in separate and individual attacks on abuses, from the prison system to the Poor Law to bad boarding schools to bad conditions in mills and factories and so on. But from *Bleak House* to *Our Mutual Friend* he made this kind of attack on a cumulative basis, building most of his late novels around a central purpose and organizing all his sequences and techniques to move his purpose forward.

This new concept of fictional artistry was a view of the broad-scale panoramic novel unified by a central purpose, developed by a number of revolving plots, and distinguished by suffusing symbolism. His concept, now apparent in the perspective of a later time, allows us to see that his varied techniques—developed and combined in the casual necessities of his first writing—supplement and complement each other in the more mature masterpieces. This conclusion argues that *Bleak House, Little Dorrit,* and *Our Mutual Friend* are his greatest novels, and that all the late masterpieces exceed the earlier works in *total* effect.

This critical perspective needs to be examined in detail in order to be understood or accepted, to show how Dickens developed artistically from his first accomplishments to the mastery of his last and greatest period. The early techniques must be identified so that their combination may show itself in his later revolving arrangement. It is imperative to trace his sources of inspiration, his borrowing and improvement of incident and plot, and his practice of narrative contrast and alternation. Eventually it will be important to add his suffusing symbolism. Criticism at the last judgment must be aware of all the circumstances of creation, as if a kind of eschatalogical relativity were involved. Certainly the last judgment will find that the original one-sided and limited perspectives of the early critical schools do not supply enough information to estimate the enduring accomplishment of Dickens. Only by detailed study of the whole artistic record can an adequate frame of reference be provided. In the light of that detailed record the novels of Dickens seem to be born again so that they illuminate a new age of readers. The examination is a demanding but exciting study.

CHAPTER II

Humor in Motion
The Farce-Caricature Technique

F YOU are inclined to laugh at life, you must see that our world is composed of human beings who possess ridiculous flaws. If you are a writer of comedy, your task is to expose those flaws. The essence of comic narration depends upon selection of the unusual and exaggeration of the normal. Dickens had an unerring sense for exposing eccentricity, but basically his comedy depends upon his attention to qualities of feature, dress, and behavior which are ridiculous because they are exhibited in the extreme. This, of course, is the kind of insight possessed in some degree by all great masters of humor, from Chaucer to Molière to Fielding. It has been called "the comic spirit" by Meredith, and it depends upon the assumption that a little ego, or a little pride, or a little selfishness, or a moderate amount of acquisitiveness is normal, but that a great amount of any perfectly natural quality is ridiculous.

When Dickens began to write *Pickwick Papers*, his basic narrative technique was a combination of caricature and farce. Caricature may be defined as the exaggeration of appearance, farce as the exaggeration of behavior. Exaggeration may be achieved by selection of the unusual and omission of the ordinary, or it may depend upon deliberate heightening of the normal and the real. Dickens' creative process is uncomplicated. He begins by describing a character, giving him ridiculous traits, and heightening whatever qualities of dress, feature, or behavior will amuse the reader. He records the typical talk of this person, accentuating some mannerism of speech, and he puts him in contact with other similarly caricatured individuals. He then proceeds to enmesh his characters in embarrassing and uproarious situations. Description, talk, and action are intentionally overdrawn, and the trick is to provide contrast by seizing upon different kinds

17

of eccentricities so that the reader gets a combination of extraordinary but varied people, conversation, and action. This technique is constant in *Pickwick Papers;* it is used sparingly in *Oliver Twist;* it has major force in *Nicholas Nickleby;* it is always present in the later novels in some degree. Whenever Dickens permits it to vivify his materials, he reaches great heights of humor.

The particular models which Dickens used in developing this technique have long been recognized as Smollett and Fielding. He is on record as saying that Smollett's *Humphry Clinker* was his favorite novel, and he also expressed high regard for *Roderick Random* and *Peregrine Pickle.*[1] Usually joined with Smollett in his comments about eighteenth-century fiction is some reference to Fielding's *Tom Jones* and *Joseph Andrews.* These five novels were Dickens' first textbooks in creative writing. His admiration for Fielding increased with the years, eventually surpassing his regard for Smollett. It reached its height about the time he wrote *David Copperfield,* for he named one of his children after Henry Fielding and deliberately imitated *Tom Jones* in the creation of the novel based upon his own life.

It is illuminating to see how Smollett drew a character and how exactly Dickens followed in his footsteps. One must remember that Dickens was an able reporter and had collected materials for feature stories and narrative sketches all over London. He had learned shorthand and was keenly aware of the necessity for accurate but selected description of all kinds. The reporter's first skill is to get down what is important, and Dickens possessed an uncanny sense for the unusual and amusing.

Smollett leaned toward the extreme of drawing parts of the body or dress which he heightened beyond reality, but generally his descriptions center on picturesque detail, marking the striking at the expense of the ordinary and the natural. His most famous description is of Commodore Trunnion in *Peregrine Pickle,* a description inserted at the moment when the retired sea captain is starting out on horseback to the church where he is to be married.

> He had put on in honour of his nuptials his best coat of blue broad cloth, cut by a taylor of Ramsgate, and trimmed with five dozen of brass buttons, large and small; his breeches were of the same piece, fastened at the knees with large bunches of tape; his waistcoat was of

red plush lapelled with green velvet, and garnished with vellum holes; his boots bore an intimate resemblance both in colour and shape to a pair of leathern buckets; his shoulder was graced with a broad buff belt, from whence depended a huge hanger with a hilt like that of a backsword; and on each side of his pummel appeared a rusty pistol rammed in a case covered with bearskin. The loss of his tye-periwig and laced hat, which were curiosities of the kind, did not at all contribute to the improvement of the picture, but on the contrary, by exhibiting his bald pate, and the natural extension of his lanthorn jaws, added to the peculiarity and extravagance of the whole.[2]

Smollett, following this description, shows the Commodore proceeding to church after the manner of a ship tacking against an unfavorable wind. His trip is interrupted by a hunting party which crosses in front of him. The Commodore's horse, being a hunting horse, joins the party, carrying the protesting rider along.

A) Description

This description is a classical example of the implications of caricature. Occasionally Smollett went into the realm of distortion as well as the selection of unusual detail. His description of Lismahago, in *Humphry Clinker,* emphasizes a face which is said to be "at least half a yard in length." The artists Hogarth in Smollett's century and Cruikshank in Dickens' day followed this manner, an art which continues in the practice of the twentieth-century cartoonist.

Dickens' description of Sam Weller's father in *Pickwick Papers* is in the exact tone set by Smollett. Note that Dickens never copies the details, only the manner.

It is very possible that at some earlier period of his career, Mr. Weller's profile might have presented a bold and determined outline. His face, however, had expanded under the influence of good living, and a disposition remarkable for resignation; and its bold fleshy curves had so far extended beyond the limits originally assigned them, that unless you took a full view of his countenance in front, it was difficult to distinguish more than the extreme tip of a very rubicund nose. His chin, from the same cause, had acquired the grave and imposing form which is generally described by prefixing the word "double" to that expressive feature, and his complexion exhibited that peculiarly mottled combination of colours which is only to be seen in gentlemen of his profession, and underdone roast beef. Round his neck he wore a crimson travelling shawl, which merged into his chin by such imperceptible gradations, that it was difficult to distinguish the folds of the one, from the folds of the other. Over this, he mounted a long waistcoat of a broad pink-

striped pattern, and over that again, a wide-skirted green coat, orna-
mented with large brass buttons, whereof the two which garnished the
waist, were so far apart, that no man had ever beheld them both, at the
same time. His hair, which was short, sleek, and black, was just visible
beneath the capacious brim of a low-crowned brown hat. His legs were
encased in knee-cord breeches, and painted top-boots: and a copper
watch-chain terminating in one seal, and a key of the same material,
dangled loosely from his capacious waist-band.[3]

Lengthy portrayal of a character in this fashion is rare in both
authors. Smollett does it for special scenes, and in *Pickwick Papers* the
only other long illustration of this exact kind of caricature is in
the early description of Mr. Jingle. But the lengthy description will
serve as typical of the manner which both use in some degree in
presenting all their characters. The Pickwickians themselves are good
examples. The "Club" idea, originally supplied by the artist Seymour
for the publication, included the central figure (who became Mr.
Pickwick) and three companions. The drawings showed a fat, elderly,
bald-headed man, so that Dickens had a body furnished him. It
was no great leap to the concept of the well-meaning, addle-headed,
opinionated bachelor. Smollett had created such a character in
Matthew Bramble (*Humphry Clinker*); Fielding's Parson Adams
(*Joseph Andrews*) was married, but otherwise he fitted the pattern;
one could even go back to Don Quixote, if necessary, in order to find
a general model for inspiration. And so Mr. Pickwick in the beginning
is easily imposed upon; he always means well, even though he is
pedantic, absent-minded, and kind-hearted.

The other three members of the Pickwick Club started out as
rapidly sketched characters, and they are remembered at the end of
the story for a few exaggerated traits. Tupman is the fat, middle-
aged, well-dressed simpleton who ogles the ladies and never succeeds
in getting anywhere. Winkle is the sporting type, put in originally to
furnish a foil for all the jokes about guns and games which Seymour
wanted to draw. Snodgrass is the Byronic, poetic, and romantic fool,
not generally distinguished for brains. This kind of description is
repeated for most of the people in the novel, the features and appearance of some being more detailed than others. Obviously we remember
best those who, like Mr. Weller, are most spectacular in feature and
dress.

Smollett, Fielding, and Dickens advance their action by conversation and dialogue. On the simplest level this means that seeing is believing, but hearing is endearing. Most of the caricatured individuals encountered by the Pickwickians talk like the people Dickens had met in the streets, in the inns, and on the roads of England—but usually a little better. Fielding is the master of supplying characters who speak in a garrulous manner which advances action as well as understanding of character. In *Tom Jones,* Squire Western, Mrs. Honour, and Partridge are most easily distinguished by what they say. Dickens' habit of giving vocal mannerisms and speech devices to his characters was accentuated by the examples furnished by the stage, and particularly from the model supplied by the actor, Charles Mathews. This influence will be considered separately.

Certainly Dickens rises to boisterous heights in imaginative monologue and dialogue in his first novels. Whether it is in the talk of Sam Weller, or the lamentations of Job Trotter, or the maunderings of dozens of relatively minor characters, he gained a major part of his first public popularity by the constantly amusing conversation which accompanied the action. When Sam says, "There's nothin' so refreshin' as sleep, Sir, as the servant-girl said afore she drank the egg-cup-full o' laudanum," thousands of readers bought their monthly copies. By the time they read, "He's the wictim o' connubiality, as Blue Beard's domestic chaplain said, with a tear of pity, ven he buried him," everybody wanted to know what Sam would say next. They were sure to find something like, "Business first, pleasure arterwards, as King Richard the Third said ven he stabbed the t'other king in the Tower, afore he smothered the babbies."

This art is not confined to tag ends of speeches. Sometimes the story moves for pages on a fairly even but appealing level. Then one will run across a conversation like the one which occurred after the death of Sam's stepmother.

> "Vell, gov'ner, ve must all come to it, one day or another."
> "So we must, Sammy," said Mr. Weller the elder.
> "There's a providence in it all," said Sam.
> "O' course there is," replied his father with a nod of grave approval. "Wot 'ud become of the undertakers vithout it, Sammy?"[4]

21

This manner is occasionally more than inspired foolishness. It sparkles and flashes with the wit which is Dickens' own stock in trade. More than any other device, it illustrates the kind of genius which Dickens had from the beginning, which miraculously had no need for development in order to be effective. At the end of an amusing conversation between Mr. Pickwick and Sam, one finds:

> "You are quite a philosopher, Sam," said Mr. Pickwick.
> "It runs in the family, I b'lieve Sir," replied Mr. Weller. "My father's very much in that line, now. If my mother-in-law blows him up, he whistles. She flies in a passion, and breaks his pipe; he steps out, and gets another. Then she screams wery loud, and falls into 'sterics; and he smokes wery comfortably 'till she comes to again. That's philosophy Sir, ain't it?"[5]

Farcical action was also the basic comic technique of both Smollett and Fielding. The effect of farce often derives from placing a character in some situation which is distasteful to him. The narrative method of a book like Smollett's *Peregrine Pickle* is to provide one good embarrassing situation or amusing predicament for each chapter. The only exception to this rule occurs when the general plot is being advanced. Dickens naturally followed this scheme in *Pickwick,* for he too needed one good laughable incident or embarrassing situation for each installment (every three chapters as the book is printed). He used many suggestions for these farcical incidents, reaching into his reading and his experience for inspiration, but it is amazing how many of these incidents resemble a situation first developed by Smollett or Fielding.

Of all Smollett's characters, Peregrine is the most ingenious in thinking up devilment which will annoy other people or put them in some laughable predicament. In one episode, Peregrine lures his friend, the painter, into a duel in which this perfectly cowardly person is placed in the position of fighting for his honor. The prospect paralyzes the painter. He pretends that he wants to fight at all costs, but keeps throwing out hints, hoping they will encourage someone to stop the duel before anyone—especially the painter—is hurt. Pipes, one of his seconds, evinces a completely callous lack of interest in the health of his principal, and by his conversation materially increases the agony of mind undergone by the painter as he approaches his ordeal. The duel is stopped at the last moment, and the amusement of the reader depends upon his enjoyment of the painter's cowardice in his predicament.

This episode must have been one of the youthful Dickens' favorites. He wrote a sketch called "The Great Winglebury Duel," which was included in *Sketches by Boz,* based directly on this source and he later wrote a farce for stage production from it called *The Strange Gentleman.* One of the earliest adventures of the Pickwickians leads them to a ball at which Mr. Jingle, in the evening clothes borrowed from the completely inebriated Mr. Winkle, insults a certain Dr. Slammer. When Mr. Winkle is challenged the next day by Dr. Slammer's seconds, he has no clear recollection of what he may have done or said on the previous evening. He therefore prepares to fight the duel in the place of the real culprit, Mr. Jingle, who has disappeared. Mr. Snodgrass, Winkle's second, does nothing to relieve the poor fellow's mind in their conversation and blandly misses all hints at telling the story to anyone who will stop the affair without Winkle's having to admit his cowardice. At the climax, when Winkle has just about decided to accept certain death, Dr. Slammer sees that his opponent is not the man who insulted him, and the duel is halted.

In this instance Dickens took an initial idea from Smollett, adapted it to his own purposes by preparing for it in an entirely original way, and embroidered it with his own variety of witty conversation. This was his general way of achieving his farcical effects. Smollett supplied a model by inventing a series of practical jokes which continually inspired Dickens. Smollett's characters were likely to get in the wrong beds, or be caught in some kind of undress in public places, or be exposed to some situation in which their perfectly honest intentions are made to appear in the worst light imaginable. Fielding's Parson Adams was also prone to get himself befouled with filth, or suspected of moral turpitude, or chased by dogs in the most common difficulties experienced by actors in farces.

In like manner Mr. Pickwick, after watching some highly burlesqued hunting scenes, imbibes too much cold punch, falls asleep, is deposited in the pound for trespassing by an irate landowner, and is pelted with ripe vegetables by the onlookers. Mr. Stiggins, the ministerial shepherd who haunts the Weller tavern and who always seems to be drinking pineapple brandy, is made very intoxicated just before

23

he appears to address the Brick Lane Branch of the United Grand Junction Ebenezer Temperance Association. Mr. Pickwick, in attempting to stop an elopement, finds himself in the yard of a girls' boarding school late at night, and is discovered in a pouring rain apparently intending some kind of assault on the inmates who discover him. This latter episode is the result of a practical joke perpetrated by Mr. Jingle's servant, the weeping Job Trotter, who hoaxes Sam Weller as well as Mr. Pickwick.

There are many more of these instances of farce, but perhaps the best example is the episode in which Mr. Pickwick leaves his room to recover his watch and manages to get into the wrong room on his return. He is disrobing in the shadow of the bed-curtains (the good old four-poster bed of Victorian days) when the old maid enters. It is her room. She does not see Mr. Pickwick, and his natural reticence prevents him from emerging. His confusion reaches a climax when the lady makes her first direct preparations for bed. He coughs, reveals himself hurriedly, and gets out of the room, a feat which he accomplishes without making a satisfactory explanation. This leaves him in inexplicable difficulty the next day when he is introduced to the lady by her jealous fiancé.

Smollett's farcical scenes often involve some element of the vulgar or risqué. Dickens unquestionably enjoyed this kind of humor, but had difficulty in imitating it because of the canons of taste enforced in his time. One cannot help wondering what he would have invented had he lived in Smollett's day. Another tendency of Smollett's was in the direction of cruelty and nausea. His novels have been described as "unvarnished." He loved to present people whose stomachs are upset, and in several instances he manages to endanger the digestion of his readers. When Peregrine plays a joke on Pallet, his first intention had been to give him the idea that he had eaten cat meat instead of rabbit. Some claws are discovered in the dish, and Pallet is very ill. The distinctive Smollett touch comes in the remarks of the physician who hated Pallet. He suggests:

> That the flesh of a cat was as nourishing and delicious as veal or mutton, provided they could prove, that the said cat was not of the boar-kind, and had fed chiefly on vegetable diet, or even confined its carnivorous appetite to rats and mice, which he affirmed to be dainties

24

of exquisite taste and flavor. He said, it was a vulgar mistake to think that all flesh-devouring creatures were unfit to be eaten; witness the consumption of swine and ducks, animals that delight in carnage, as well as fish, that prey upon each other, and feed on bait and carrion; together with the demand for bear, of which the best hams in the world are made. He then observed, that the Negroes on the coast of Guinea, who are a healthy and vigorous people, prefer cats and dogs to all other fare; and mentioned from history several sieges, during which the inhabitants, who were blocked up, lived upon these animals, and had recourse even to human flesh, which, to his certain knowledge, was in all respects preferable to pork; for, in the course of his studies, he had, for the experiment's sake, eaten a steak cut from the buttock of a person who had been hanged.[6]

This speech makes sure that Pallet will be unable to retain his dinner.

There was no taboo on humor of this kind in Victorian times. Dickens made the most of Smollett's example in *Pickwick Papers,* and it is interesting to see how far in this direction he went. For example, Sam Weller discourses on veal pie for the benefit of the Pickwickians and tells the story of the butcher who kept prices down by seasoning kittens "for beefsteak, weal, or kidney, 'cording to the demand." On a later occasion Mr. Pickwick joins Bob Sawyer and Benjamin Allen for breakfast, and the two young medical students begin discussing dissection.

"By the bye," said Mr. Allen, "have you finished that leg yet?"

"Nearly," replied Sawyer, helping himself to half a fowl as he spoke. "It's a very muscular one for a child's."

"Is it?" inquired Mr. Allen, carelessly.

"Very," said Bob Sawyer, with his mouth full.

"I've put down my name for an arm, at our place," said Mr. Allen. "We're clubbing for a subject, and the list is nearly full, only we can't get hold of any fellow that wants a head. I wish you'd take it."

"No," replied Bob Sawyer; "can't afford expensive luxuries."

"Nonsense!" said Allen.

"Can't indeed," rejoined Bob Sawyer. "I wouldn't mind a brain, but I couldn't stand a whole head."[7]

Mr. Pickwick manages to stop this interesting subject of conversation on the plea that the ladies are coming.

Perhaps the nicest Dickensian example is Sam Weller's story of the man who ran a sausage shop and had a machine to grind the sausages. The man was extremely unhappy with a wife who berated him unmercifully at every opportunity. He had always threatened to run away to "Merriker," and after a horrible scene one evening, he disappeared. No body or trace of him turned up, but several months later a customer called to protest that he found trouser buttons in the sausage he had bought.

> " 'They're my husband's buttons,' says the widder, beginning to faint. 'What!' screams the little old gen'lm'n, turnin' wery pale. 'I see it all,' says the widder; 'in a fit of temporary insanity he rashly converted himself into sassages!' and so he had, Sir," said Mr. Weller, looking steadily into Mr. Pickwick's horror-stricken countenance, "or else he'd been draw'd into the ingine, but however that might ha' been, the little old gen'lm'n, who had been remarkably partial to sassages all his life, rushed out o' the shop in a wild state, and was never heerd on artervards."[8]

Dickens continued to use this kind of humor all through his books, and one needs only to be reminded of Quilp in *The Old Curiosity Shop* (who chews tobacco and eats prawns at the same time), or Dennis in *Barnaby Rudge* (Dennis is the hangman who is interested in necks according to their capacity for being stretched), or Mrs. Gamp in *Martin Chuzzlewit* (the practical nurse who officiates when people enter this world and when they leave it, as well as doing little odd jobs in between), or the undertakers in various novels, or Jerry in *A Tale of Two Cities* (the grave-robbing body-snatcher who beats his wife because she flops while he is at work, and by her prayers interferes with his success), or Mr. Venus in *Our Mutual Friend* (whose shop contains a weird and horrible collection of anatomical monstrosities). Smollett's models are forceful, but those of Dickens have more variety in inducing nausea. If the reader thinks grotesque humor is funny, Dickens surpasses any model.

Another distinctive farce-caricature device in narration is based upon letter-writing. Smollett and Fielding depended upon a well-worn but sure-fire stage convention which achieved humor by the misuse of words. The famous model for this diction who gave her name to the type is Mrs. Malaprop in Sheridan's *Rivals*. When Smollett chose the narrative device of letters to tell the entire story of *Humphry Clinker*, he used at least two characters, Tabitha Bramble and Winifred Jenkins, to convey this kind of comedy. Their misuse of

2) farce— caricature in letter— writing

26

words is complicated by their extraordinary misspellings, many of which have the secondary virtue of becoming vulgar *double-entendres*.

Dickens' characters misuse words, and sometimes they do so in letters. Mr. Weller, senior, sends a letter to Sam to inform him of the death of Mrs. Weller, beginning "I am wery sorry to have the plessure of bein a Bear of ill news," and ending "Infernally yours." This device also illuminates the valentine which Sam writes to Mary. Curiously, Dickens did not invent many such letter-writing opportunities in the early novels, apparently feeling that the advantages were limited. He gives us one full-length illustration in *Nicholas Nickleby* when Fanny Squeers writes to Ralph Nickleby:

DOTHEBOYS HALL
Thursday Morning

SIR,

My Pa requests me to write to you, the doctors considering it doubtful whether he will ever recuvver the use of his legs which prevents his holding a pen.

We are in a state of mind beyond anything, and my pa is one mask of brooses both blue and green likewise two forms are steepled in his goar. We are kimpelled to have him carried down into the kitchen where he now lays. You will judge from this that he has been brought very low.

When your nevew that you recommended for a teacher had done this to my pa and jumped upon his body with his feet and also langwedge which I will not pollewt my pen with describing, he assaulted my ma with dreadful violence, dashed her to the earth, and drove her back comb several inches into her head. A very little more and it must have entered her skull. We have a medical certificket that if it had, the tortershell would have affected the brain. . . .[9]

One notes that by the time Dickens got to the letters of Wilkins Micawber in *David Copperfield* the humorous effect is more subtle.

The influence of Smollett and Fielding extended to the broad scope of Dickens' first novels. How far can the novelist go in making the entire story depend upon farce and caricature? Will the eventual total effect be a compilation of farcical scenes, each of which may be considered complete in itself? Smollett and Fielding wrote novels which fall into the picaresque tradition, derived from the famous older

27

examples of Cervantes' *Don Quixote* and Le Sage's *Gil Blas*. Smollett himself described this kind of writing as "a large diffused picture, comprehending the characters of life, disposed in different groups, and exhibited in various attitudes." Each individual, according to this definition, should be subservient to a general plan, there being a central character "to attract the attention, unite the incidents, unwind the clue of the labyrinth, and at last close the scene by virtue of his own importance."[10]

Generally speaking, this means that a central character, usually accompanied by a servant who acts as a comic foil, travels from place to place, having adventures in each locality, meeting completely different sets of characters as well as events, and eventually marrying and settling down when enough pages have been filled. If the hero is young, he is called a *picaro*, roughly meaning a rogue, probably implying an attractive young man with a heart of gold and a body of clay. His body usually gets him into difficulties with women, and many other things happen to him because he is not a model of rectitude. If the hero is old or middle-aged, he is a well-meaning but impractical fool. Specifically Dickens followed the picaresque structure in *Pickwick Papers,* in which Mr. Pickwick is the elderly fool, and in *Nicholas Nickleby,* in which Nicholas is the youthful rogue, even if watered down.

The action of this type of novel is advanced by having the main character travel from place to place. Parson Adams, Tom Jones, Roderick Random, Peregrine Pickle, and the Matthew Bramble party do this automatically in Dickens' models. So he naturally sent the Pickwickians from London to Rochester, Dingley Dell, Bath, and other places on the highroad. In the novels which followed, Oliver Twist runs away from his apprenticeship and falls into the hands of Fagin in London; Nicholas Nickleby leaves Dotheboys School after his defense of Smike, goes to London, then sets out to make his fortune, but is interrupted by the highly entertaining group of provincial actors led by the immortal Vincent Crummles; Little Nell and her grandfather wander from London to the village where Mrs. Jarley's waxwork caravan affords them momentary shelter, then they go on through the factory district to the healthful open country of the north, where they find refuge and Nell dies; Martin Chuzzlewit travels extensively in America. After these novels Dickens began to advance his action in different ways, but in the early works his structure is essentially picaresque.

The broad, diffused picture of life implies a casual, over-all romance "plot," an intrigue which must be introduced or developed toward the end of the tale, but which plays second fiddle to the farce-caricature scenes which are interesting and relatively complete in themselves. Fielding, in *Tom Jones,* supplies an exception to this practice by his reference to the epic form, but the other picaresque novels introduce the plot toward the end. The pattern is filled with the perambulations of a company or of a hero and squire from place to place, continuous farce-caricature episodes, characters who constantly get into difficulties and finally into prison, adventurers who often redeem themselves and get a new start in life, coaches which are overturned, duels prevented in the nick of time, and finally—after many pages have been filled—a satisfactory marriage or two, after which the hero settles down. After *Pickwick Papers* had gone on for a number of farce-filled installments, Dickens involved Mr. Winkle in a love affair, tieing up the Bob Sawyer scenes by marrying Arabella Allen to Winkle and introducing a small intrigue by having Arabella's brother oppose the marriage to the last. The same sort of intrigue is assigned to Mr. Snodgrass, who finally marries Emily Wardle. This was the manner in which Smollett and Fielding brought their picaresque stories to a close.

Percy Lubbock has pointed out Dickens' technique of presenting a wide variety of characters, treating them humorously or realistically, involving them in inconsequential episodes, but effectively convincing the reader of their resemblance to life.[11] This may constitute half the book and is usually good reading. Then the author feels it necessary to insert a plot, whereupon he thinks of something that is typical of traditional fiction, romance, or the stage; his real, amusing, and beloved characters begin to do things which we are willing to believe because we like them. No matter how strange or how hackneyed the plot, it is made effective by the preparation of the earlier scenes and by the believable characters who have already won our regard before they become involved in any intrigue.

29

E.
INTERPOLATED
STORIES.

This analysis applies mostly to the novels which follow the picaresque formula, certainly not to the mature late books which depend upon an organized plan from the first pages. Dickens always felt the need for contrast; he always wanted to insert episodes which by contrast would make his farce-caricature scenes more effective. The example of Fielding and Smollett did not serve him well in supplying models for contrast. The best illustration of this point is the use of "interpolated stories" in the picaresque structure.

Peregrine Pickle has one very large insertion, a completely separate tale told by one of the characters, called "The Memoirs of a Lady of Quality," which interrupts the main story for a large part of the novel. Roderick Random listens to the misfortunes of a lady of the town, Miss Williams, and later Mr. Melpoyn recounts in the Marshalsea his attempts to get his tragedy performed on the stage. In *Joseph Andrews*, Mr. Wilson discloses his misguided youth, downfall, reformation, and retirement to a life of natural freedom and innocence. A lady riding in a coach tells a long tale about Leonora, the unfortunate jilt. *Tom Jones* has a windy insertion known as the tale of the man of the hill. In fact, picaresque fiction reserves to itself a dubious right to stop all relevant action and substitute extraneous contrasting matter at any convenient point in the narrative. It took Dickens quite a while to see that such insertion was bad narrative practice unless there was some particularly good reason for it. An inserted story or subplot may underline or intensify the main action, and Dickens is on record as arguing that this intention may justify its inclusion.[12]

SEE;
Dickensian
Vol. LXIV
Part III
No. 356
pp 141-151.

Pickwick Papers is full of interpolated stories. They give the impression of being filler—materials the author used whenever he ran out of good farcical ideas. The inserted tales center for the most part on themes of horror. They are gloomy and concerned with revenge, insanity, and persecution—at the opposite pole from farce and caricature. *Nicholas Nickleby* also has two such filler stories early in the novel, but after this novel Dickens abandoned an unsatisfactory narrative idea. He achieved balance and contrast by the use of other technical devices.

When the critic studies the typical narrative styles being developed by a great novelist, he begins with identifiable sources and influences. The essential question in examining Dickens' work, however, is: What did Dickens accomplish with his farce-caricature technique? The answer is almost the only easy one available to anyone reading his novels: He carried the farce-caricature technique further than any other writer in fiction, and he still seems consistently amusing and entertaining. He builds humor in motion. *"Human in motion"*

Readers react to farce in different degrees, since this is a type of entertainment which encourages you to roll down a hill of laughter, *FARCE* gathering mass and momentum like a snowball. If you never start to roll, nothing in the scene is funny. But the caricatured individuals in Dickens' stories have a tendency toward pushing every reader over the brow of the hill. This is the reason why it has become natural to say of any sufficiently eccentric person, "He's just like a character out of Dickens."

Given the caricatured subjects, farce reaches its climax in scenes which build one upon another. Dickens' great success in *Pickwick Papers* depends upon the multiplicity of the situations which make up his humor and the cumulative effect which derives therefrom. There are three sequences which illustrate the principle of extension in farce, each successive incident being tied to its predecessors and gaining additional humor from its connection. *THREE EXAMPLE OF EXTENDED FARCE IN PICKWICK*

The first extended farce sequence is the Wardle-Jingle pursuit ① scenes. In the beginning it depends upon the fact that Mr. Jingle is able to fool Mr. Tupman, even to the extent of borrowing money from his rival suitor so that he may elope with the lady. This is comic in itself, but moderately so. Then the scene proceeds to the chase and to the place where the pursuing coach breaks down. It continues by introducing Sam Weller as the boots of the hotel to which the runaway couple flee. And it ends with Wardle buying Jingle off. Each successive scene gains from its connection with the preceding one, and the final effect is greater than the sum of the parts.[13]

The second cumulative sequence begins with Mr. Pickwick and ② Mr. Peter Magnus in a coach on the way to Ipswich. It presents Mr. Magnus as an insanely jealous man getting ready to propose to a lady. It then puts Mr. Pickwick in a room in the Great White Horse hostelry. There follows the incident in which Mr. Pickwick retrieves his watch and gets into the wrong room. After he escapes from the

lady's presence, Sam directs him back to his own room, and like most
people he is a little suspicious of Mr. Pickwick's explanation. There
intervenes a chapter in which the humor is divided between Tony
Weller's advice to Sam concerning widows and Sam's second meeting
with Job Trotter. This lets us know that Mr. Jingle is in the neighbor·
hood, a fact which will be important in the final scene. Then Mr
Pickwick accompanies Mr. Magnus to visit the lady Magnus intends
to ask to be his wife. She turns out to be the old maid Mr. Pickwick
had encountered in the wrong room. A scene of outrageous misunderstanding follows, and the lady, Miss Witherfield, fears that
violence will result. She informs the magistrate, Mr. Nupkins, that Mr.
Pickwick is proposing to engage in a duel, and so Mr. Pickwick and
Mr. Tupman are arrested. Mr. Nupkins is a squire who, in brief
fashion, behaves as an illustrious ancestor, Squire Western, would
have conducted himself in *Tom Jones*. The trial is grossly unfair,
the squire depends on a clerk for points of law, but manages to do as
he pleases just the same. Mr. Pickwick is saved by the fact that he
discovers Mr. Jingle to be paying attention to the Nupkins daughter.
He exposes Mr. Jingle to the judge, and the procedure of the trial is
reversed. The Pickwick party is invited to dinner. Sam meets the
housemaid, Mary, and in a kind of afterscene shows the first signs of
passion which will lead him eventually to matrimony.[14]

Various influences are manifest in this extended series of episodes.
There is the situation in which the wrong people get into the same
hotel room. There is the business of the worst possible interpretation
being put upon an innocent mistake. There is the unjust but riotous
trial, with judgment of guilt or innocence depending upon completely extraneous reasons. Smollett and Fielding present models for
each of these situations as well as for some of the characters involved.
But Dickens mixes them all up, combines several strands of action,
and turns out a cumulative effect which materially aids the reader to
start with a chuckle and end with a guffaw. The single parts of the
whole sequence may be traced back to individual sources, but the
joining together is pure Dickens.

The third illustration is the best one. It reveals the suit for breach
of promise instituted by Mrs. Bardell against Mr. Pickwick. The first
scene of this sequence is fine low comedy in itself, for it allows Mr.

Pickwick to give a completely false impression through his oblique manner of speech. In trying to tell Mrs. Bardell that he is hiring a manservant, he seems to tell her that he wants to add a new member to his family and take on new responsibilities. She hopes and believes he is proposing to her. So she faints in his arms, joyfully, and the other Pickwickians come in at the inappropriate moment to find Mr. Pickwick apparently embracing her. Obviously he can never explain this circumstance. The following part of the sequence develops when Mr. Pickwick is lecturing the other members of his group for their amorous folly. He is interrupted by a letter from the shyster lawyers, Dodson and Fogg, serving notice of the lawsuit, and everyone suspects that he is slightly hypocritical. Next a moderately funny scene follows his visit to Dodson and Fogg during which he gets very angry because his predicament begins to look dangerous. While other episodes progress, Mr. Pickwick hires a lawyer. Sam goes to the Bardell rooming house to terminate his master's tenancy and has a laughable encounter with the landlady and her friends. Dodson and Fogg then subpoena the other Pickwickians for the trial, obviously to get their testimony about seeing Mr. Pickwick holding Mrs. Bardell in his arms. Mr. Pickwick also has a highly unsatisfactory meeting with the lawyer, Serjeant Snubbin, who will defend him in court.

All this is preparation for the great trial itself and for the priceless legal foolishness engineered by Serjeant Buzfuz for the plaintiff. Mr. Pickwick is made to appear completely in the wrong, and Buzfuz reads extraordinarily suggestive meanings into two simple and innocent letters Mr. Pickwick had sent to Mrs. Bardell. The whole delightful parody of the trial, including the ecstatic scene in which Sam testifies, marks the high point of the novel.[15]

This is Dickens at his farce-caricature best. In this manner he surpasses every other novelist, and this sequence is a major reason for the fact that the readers who value humor more than any other quality in fiction still find *Pickwick* to be their favorite novel. The trial by itself would be funny, but it comes as a climax to a number of prepared episodes which multiply its farcical effect. The well-meaning hero has never been more exposed to circumstances which defeat him at every turn, leaving him the victim of jesting fate and fickle misunderstanding. Satire upon legal absurdity keeps the reader laughing

33

at the same time that he recognizes the abuse which furnishes the amusement.

USE OF A VARIETY OF IRONY

It is this last point which also indicates a typical Dickensian trait: a variety of irony which often distinguishes his farcical scenes. It may be described as primarily indirect. Irony occurs when the reader understands the point of what is happening, even though the characters involved are completely unaware of the implications of their experiences. Fielding is usually considered to be the English novelist most skilled in the use of absolute and measured irony. Dickens never gets quite the effect Fielding does in a scene like the one in which Parson Adams lectures Joseph and Fanny on controlling their desires and passions. They want to get married in a hurry. His sermon is interrupted by the news that his favorite child has just drowned. He naturally descends into uncontrolled expressions of grief and sorrow, and even when Joseph tries to calm him down by reminding him of his advice about controlling his emotions, he defends himself by saying that it was his *favorite* child.[16]

FIELDING IS THE MASTER IN THE USE OF IRONY

Fielding's irony is unusually direct, and his point never has to be explained. There is the famous occasion when Partridge accompanies Tom Jones to the theater and sees a performance of *Hamlet*. He is extremely excited by the play, comments loudly, and vocally encourages the performance in progress. Afterwards when he is asked to express his choice of the best actor, he names the King. Tom suggests that the part of Hamlet had been performed by one of the great actors of all time (presumably David Garrick). This choice Partridge cannot understand, for he says that the man acting Hamlet was behaving naturally. It was the King who recited his lines the way an actor should.[17]

DICKENS TENDS TO RUIN HIS IRONY AT TIMES.

It is fair to point out that Dickens was occasionally subject to the Victorian habit of explaining his effects. This either ruins the irony or insults the reader's intelligence. But he often used a kind of symbolic irony in his farcical effects, a sign that his sure touch in humorous action relieved him of the necessity for explaining why his readers should laugh. One might say that irony in this sense serves as a subjective correlative for his farcical action.

E.G.

For example, Mr. Pickwick always means well, always wants to do good, but never manages to control the circumstances which plague

34

him. The irony is indirect; that is, it is in the concept of the character as he is exposed in the various incidents of the story. Every reader understands why Mr. Pickwick gets in trouble, even if he does not feel like blaming Mr. Pickwick for his impracticality. Tony Weller censures widows as being responsible for unhappy marriages, but you and I know whose fault it is. The partisanship of Mr. Potts, the jealousy of Mr. Magnus, the stupidity of Mr. Dowler, the righteousness of Mr. Stiggins—these are characteristics which shine brightly because the individuals themselves are so completely unaware of their own weaknesses. It is certainly ironic that everyone concerned with the Pickwick-Bardell trial accepts ridiculous legal procedures as part of normal human behavior. If the reader disagrees he finds himself in a lovely but unreal world.

All the early novels of Dickens illustrate some of his best and also some of his weakest effects. The modern reader is likely to wish that *Pickwick* was completely taken up with the remarkable farce and caricature which is present most of the time, and that the book did not contain the filler stories or the mawkish romantic love stories. We can also wish that Dickens' irony was always as forceful as it is when he is being farcical. When Oliver Twist asks for "more," meaning another helping of gruel in the Poor House, there should have been a wonderful opportunity for irony. But Dickens found it appropriate to go into an oratorical discourse explaining to the reader the boy's need for decent food. This is making a point and explaining it.[18] When he wanted to show, in the same book, that the new Poor Law was cruel and unjust, he doubled and tripled his explanations of the "irony" to explain his point. The Beadle says, "What have paupers to do with soul or spirit? It's quite enough that we let 'em have live bodies."[19] This is twisting what a real beadle would never have said to what Dickens thinks he meant. In *Nicholas Nickleby,* Mr. Gregsbury harangues a committee of the irate constituents who have elected him to Parliament. He tells them exactly what he has used his office for and how little he has really represented them. Again, for pseudoironic purposes, Dickens makes a character say what he would never say in real life, but what his words and actions would imply if one could read them truly.[20]

[handwritten margin note: EXAMPLE OF NOT USING IRONIC SITUATION]

35

These are differences between direct and indirect irony, between implication and explanation. So much of *Pickwick* is marvelous that the modern reader may join the romantic lovers of the inspired Dickens and ignore the contrasts which do not always come off. The farce-caricature technique served him well, and he had reason to be grateful to his first literary models. Never after *Pickwick* did he depend so completely upon this technique. In *Oliver Twist* the ridiculous scenes are overwhelmed by the criminal characters and the moral point; farce wars with melodrama in *Nicholas Nickleby,* but in that novel Dickens accomplishes great comic effects, especially in the monologues of Mrs. Nickleby and in the almost perfect Vincent Crummles episodes; *The Old Curiosity Shop* is a conglomeration of techniques, mostly sentiment and tears, with a few flashes of caricature; the heavy historical plot of *Barnaby Rudge* shifts the emphasis completely away from humor.

But Dickens utilized farce and caricature in all of the later novels, even if his general purpose was conveyed by another technique and a separate emphasis. *Martin Chuzzlewit* has Pecksniff and Mrs. Gamp; *David Copperfield* has a host of caricatured immortals; *Great Expectations* gives us Jaggers, Wemmick, Wopsle, and Pumblechook. Every novel supplies its examples, and every reader must have his own favorites. One must conclude, quite simply, that in this style of writing, in the technique of caricature and farce, Dickens has no peers.

CHAPTER III

Mimicry: The Technique of Monologue

HE WAY of all flesh is vocal. The characters of Dickens re- DICKENS
veal themselves in speech, rather than by their thoughts. REVEALS
The psychology of an individual may be studied through CHARACTERS
speech, action, or thought, but Dickens depended mostly THROUGH
upon the way his characters talk. He presented them as actors speaking SPEECH
to an imaginary audience, and their speeches are adjusted to necessities of fiction, which is not quite the same art as drama. It is the process of adjustment which distinguishes Dickens' narrative style. In tragic
scenes, his characters use the dilated devices of elocution characteristic
of the stage of his day; in comic scenes, they explore peculiar grammar, mannerisms of speech, and tags or catch phrases of expression. It
is the manner of their speech which is of first importance in evaluating
Dickens' narrative artistry.

Dickens served two dramatic apprenticeships. Appropriately
enough, one was in the field of tragedy, the other in comedy. William MACREADY
Macready provided the main influence which decorated the serious (TRAGIC)
and melodramatic scenes of Dickens' novels; Charles Mathews fur- MATHEWS
nished the model for the comic speech devices and mimicry. The name (COMIC)
and reputation of Macready have come down to our time, since he is
listed in stage history with Kean and Kemble among the greatest
actors of the early nineteenth century. The reputation of Mathews,
the comedian, has been more or less obscured. Yet it was Mathews who
was of first importance to the young Dickens, who imparted the spark
and the variety of speech mannerisms which the novelist developed in
such a remarkable way throughout his career.

Charles Mathews (the elder) began in 1818 to present London's CHARLES
theater-going public with a series of entertainments conducted en- MATHEWS
tirely by himself. He continued until his death in 1833 the practice SR.

of performing one-man shows, which he called "Programs at Home," in imitation of the example of Samuel Foote in the preceding century. Foote, forbidden by law to charge admission for public performances because of his ridicule of political figures belonging to the party in power, evaded the statutes by "inviting" people, for a fee of course, to be his guests "at home," where he entertained them. His home was the theater.

At this distance it appears that Charles Mathews had extraordinary powers in mimicry and comic variety. In 1818 he was a veteran, having performed the important roles offered by the stock repertory of comedy during his lifetime. On occasion his reputation takes on shades of the effects we associate with such varied talents as those of Charlie Chaplin, W. C. Fields, and Alec Guinness in our own century.

In the one-man shows—and after 1818 Mathews limited himself to this form of entertainment—he drew upon the comic mannerisms, the peculiarities of dialect, the characteristic jokes, and the surprising situations which had been effective in the various comedies and farces he had encountered during his stage career. Since there was no copyright protection in this era, any good characterization, stunt, or scene was stolen or adapted at will. Mathews appropriated so many characters, so many stunts and scenes from the farce-comedy productions of his time that he epitomized the best moments of the comic drama of the early nineteenth century. In his desire to prevent imitation he he did not publish his scripts. They have survived in pirated editions, taken down by stenographers in the audience, and preserved (so far as I have been able to discover) only in cheaply printed pamphlets illustrated by George Cruikshank.[1]

Mathews offered a variety of skits or acts in his one-man performances. He began with a scene which brought contrasting eccentrics together, his first script centering upon individuals riding in a coach. He then let his characters talk, gave a separate speech mannerism to each one, and reproduced by mimicry the ensuing conversation. His characters argued, reminisced, discussed politics, social questions, or their relatives. They also told funny stories. He drew for speech mannerisms upon a wide range of dialect and elocutionary reserves. The cockney presented obvious opportunities, but Mathews added

38

Scotch, Welsh, and Irish, plus occasional foreign and broken-English characterizations. He also delved into the jargon of various professions, mimicking florid and formal asses as well as ungrammatical fools.

He followed his first act with a rapid succession of shorter skits, most of which have not been preserved. He could sing songs with patter choruses, and he used the humor of dialect to make his patter amusing. In the early twentieth century Sir Harry Lauder did this kind of act with his Scotch kilt routine, and famous vaudeville actors like Van and Schenck entertained countless American audiences with contrasting dialect peculiarities set to music. Mathews was also a ventriloquist and a magician. His entertainment was completely versatile.

The climax for his performance was called a monopolylogue. This was a short play in which he acted all the parts. It was so constructed that it became a series of monologues, with Mathews entering in the dress and character of each person in the playlet, exiting at the end of his speech, then suddenly appearing in another costume and with another mannerism. He used lightning changes of make-up, and an occasional stage trick like the one in which he sat in a chair with his back to the audience, managed to vanish through a trap door, leaving a dummy on the stage, then entered from the wings in the guise of another character. He wrote a new opening skit and a new monopolylogue for each season, but from 1818 to 1833 he repeated parts of his repertory from night to night.

One remembers that Dickens was born in 1812. He apparently first saw Mathews in 1828. One of his letters to Forster says:

> When I was about twenty, and knew three or four successive years of Mathews' At Homes from sitting in the pit to hear them [this would be from 1828 or 1829 to 1832], I wrote to Bartley who was stage-manager at Covent-Garden, and told him how young I was and exactly what I thought I could do; and that I believed I had strong perception of character and oddity, and a natural power of reproducing in my own person what I observed in others. This was at the time when I was at Doctors' commons as a shorthand writer for the proctors. And I recollect I wrote the letter from a little office I had there, where the answer came also. There must have been something in my letter that struck the authorities, for Bartley wrote to me almost immediately to say that they were busy getting up the Hunchback (so they were), but that they would communicate with me again, in a fortnight. Punctual

39

> to the time another letter came, with an appointment to do anything of Mathews' I pleased, before him and Charles Kemble, on a certain day at the theatre. . . .[2]

Subsequently, Dickens tells of having a cold in his face so that he never kept the appointment. He may have lost his nerve, although he usually had self-confidence enough to try anything. In any case it is interesting to inquire what he proposed to do at that tryout. He planned to take his sister Fanny to play accompaniments, so he was going to do something like Mathews' patter songs. In direct imitation, he must have been prepared to mimic various characters with peculiarities of dialect and speech. Certainly he had copied those opening and closing skits of Mathews, since he had recently become proficient in shorthand. He says he studied the comic devices of Mathews over a period of years:

> I went to some theatre every night, with a very few exceptions, for at least three years: really studying the bills first, and going where there was the best acting: and always to see Mathews whenever he played.[3]

DICKENS ENTERTAINS AT HOME

Any student of the biographical details of Dickens' life comes upon countless references to the way in which he entertained his companions at social affairs. He mimicked conversations as he told jokes. As the years went by, he acted in many plays, and he arranged for an extraordinary number of performances with amateur actors for charity. At Christmastime he invited friends to his home and put on some kind of drama for the main celebration. At one time he rehearsed magic stunts and, according to the audience, became extremely proficient in the magician's art. In 1851 he followed an amateur performance of Bulwer's *Not So Bad As We Seem* with a skit called "Mr. Nightingale's Diary," written originally by Mark Lemon, but reconstructed by Dickens himself. In this version of a monopolylogue he acted all the parts: a lawyer, a waiter, a pedestrian, a hypochondriac, an old woman, and a deaf sexton.

PUBLIC READINGS

When he began to do his public readings he put his lifelong talent to practical financial advantage. By this time there was no need to imitate or remember Mathews. The material was all in his own novels, and he had only to choose from *Pickwick,* from *Oliver Twist,* from *Nicholas Nickleby,* from *A Christmas Carol,* and from the later stories for the most effective scenes. The illuminating deduction one

40

draws from this utilization of his novels concerns his approach to dramatic narrative. His daughter, Mamie Dickens, tells of the day when a rule was broken because everybody had to be away from home on some business or other except her father and herself. No one was supposed to be in her father's study when a story was being written, but a monthly installment was due, and Mamie was recovering from an illness. She was allowed to rest in the study under strict instructions not to speak, move, or bother the author. She says:

> I was lying on the sofa endeavoring to keep perfectly quiet, while my father wrote busily and rapidly at his desk, when he suddenly jumped from his chair and rushed to a mirror which hung near and in which I could see the reflection of some extraordinary facial contortions which he was making. He returned rapidly to his desk, wrote furiously for a few moments, and then went again to the mirror. The facial pantomime was resumed, and then turning toward, but evidently not seeing me, he began talking in a low voice. Ceasing this soon, however, he returned once more to his desk, where he remained silently writing until luncheon time.[4]

This is a clear description of the creative process by means of mimicry, as Dickens reproduced the way in which his characters spoke, looked, or acted. He wrote for his readers to see and hear action on a fictional stage.

The mimicry of peculiarities of gesture, posture, walk, and talk was the essence of Mathews' acting. Contrasting mannerisms were heavily emphasized, and each character was assigned a way of speaking which would impress itself upon the audience. This process was necessary to make sure the audience would keep the characters separate. Most noticeable of Mathews' mannerisms was the assignment of tags of speech to his characters: the little phrase which recurred every time a person spoke served to fix that individual's identity in the attention of the listeners. This device was particularly helpful to his monopolylogues. Dickens' use of such tags is one of his most individual characteristics in fiction.

Mathews invented eccentric speech tags for all the characters he mimicked. For example, Drainemdry keeps saying, "That's moderate, ain't it, hey?" Sir Harry Skelter ends each remark with, "I'm very much disappointed." Mr. Sassafras finds himself in several discouraging situations, after each of which he says sourly, "I'm not jealous, but

41

I'll be revenged." Mr. Waglington continually observes with hesitation, "It might be so—and then again it might not." Major Longbow, the most interesting of Mathews' personations, climaxes the tales which rival the adventures of Baron Munchausen with "'Pon my soul it's true; what'll you lay it's a lie?" A character called Smart uses Sam Weller's comparisons, although they do not threaten Sam's figures of speech in quality. Smart says, "Well, some folks have curious tastes, as my grandmother said, when I used to eat the cinders."[5]

NB.

The development of the tag-line catch phrase is a striking part of Dickens' narrative technique. Most students of Dickens have realized this, but there has been no clear understanding of exactly where he got the mannerism. The pirated editions of Mathews' scripts have not been generally available for study. There is no tag-line habit in the works of Smollett and Fielding, or indeed in any of the standard writers who preceded Dickens. The comedy and farce tradition of the stage before the time of Dickens occasionally utilized the tag line, but it was the peculiar necessity of the one-man performances which encouraged Mathews to develop it to the extreme. Other novelists of the time, including Egan and Hook, show signs of the Mathews influence, but it was Dickens who took this particular symbol of individualism and gave it to so many of the characters who enliven his novels.

DICKENS' "TAG LINES"

The collection of persons possessing tags begins in *Pickwick* with Mr. Wardle, who is always addressing the Fat Boy, "Joe, Joe! Damn that boy, he's gone to sleep again." Mr. Grimwig in *Oliver Twist* says, "I'll be content to eat my own head, sir!" Fagin persuades his juvenile delinquents to evil activity with a simpering "My dears." Mr. Mantalini, in *Nicholas Nickleby*, is always consigning something or somebody to "the demnition bow-wows." Dennis, the hangman in *Barnaby Rudge*, is perpetually willing to "work people off," a remarkable euphemism for fixing and pulling the rope. Major Bagstock, in *Dombey and Son*, refers to himself as "Old Joe Bagstock, tough and devilish sly." Captain Cuttle in the same novel, when reminded of something he cannot quite pin down in memory, suggests, "When found, make a note of." There is also Mr. Toots, who insists that "It is of no consequence." The list can be multiplied by anyone familiar with the Dickens canon.

For most readers, the catch phrase reached fruition in *David Copperfield,* since a host of characters have tags in that novel. Mrs. Gummidge is "a lone, lorn creetur, and everythink goes contrairy with her"; Barkis is always remembered because "Barkis is willin' "; Aunt Betsey Trotwood at Dover interrupts almost any conversation by calling to her servant, "Janet, donkeys!" because of her phobia concerning the animals driven past her front door by mischievous or careless boys and her desire to preserve the grass; Uriah Heep finds the word "'umble" in everything he wants to say; Traddles is romantically obsessed by his fiancee: "She's the dearest girl"; Mrs. Micawber can be talked into most things, but always insists that she "will never leave Mr. Micawber."

These particular tags explain a part of Dickens' creative processes: He took a manner of talking, invented or developed his own tags, and fitted them to the characters and situations of his stories. The case of Sam Weller is in point. Sam's tag is variable in that it involves a different comparison each time it is used. Sam also owes a debt to a source other than Mathews, a farce called *The Boarding House* in which a character called Splatterdash entertained countless audiences in the 1820's with a similar form of humor. Most remarkable in this source is the fact that the actor who made such a hit with it was named Sam Vale. Weller and Vale in cockney pronunciation are very close to the same name, and remembering that there was an argument over the spelling of Sam's name in the Bardell-Pickwick trial, one concludes that Dickens, as usual, made little effort to hide his inspiration.[6] From the days of his early study of Mathews—perhaps one should say from the days of his success with Sam Weller—Dickens took distinguishing phrases for his tag lines from many sources— literature, life, or the stage, wherever they attracted his attention— and attached them to characters of his own and for his own purposes. The point worth emphasis here is that he often took the tag or the peculiarity without necessarily meaning to associate the whole character in his own story with the original. The other traits of his character might have no resemblance to the source which had supplied the speech device or tag.

It is also important to understand that Dickens made Sam so much better than Splatterdash or Smart that there is no vital similarity in humorous accomplishment. Splatterdash's best similes include: "Let everyone take care of themselves, as the jackass said when he danced among the chickens"; "Where shall we fly? as the bullet said to the trigger"; and "Nibbled to death by ducks, as the worm said to the fisherman." If one wishes a kind of specific proof of the genius of Dickens, one has only to compare him with his sources of inspiration.

Even more important to Dickens in the long run were the speech *mannerisms* of Mathews. The actor called on all the resources of elocutionary extremes in mimicking his contrasted characters. This point is most easily illustrated by studying Mr. Jingle in *Pickwick,* the character who possesses the speech device of one of Mathews' most famous impersonations.[7]

Mathews had once acted the part of Goldfinch in Holcroft's *Road to Ruin* and had made a great hit with the broken-staccato-start-stop manner of telling a story. The excuse in the original play for this speech mannerism was that Goldfinch had been a jockey before he acquired money and became a man about town. Whenever horses entered the conversation, he became excited and talked in a galloping, full-speed, jerky rhythm, as if he were riding a horse as he told the story of which he was always reminded.

> "To be sure! know the odds—hold four in hand—turn a corner in style—reins in form—elbows square—wrist pliant—hayait—drive the Coventry stage twice a week all summer—pay for an inside place—mount the box—tip the coachy a crown—beat the mail—come in full speed—rattle down the gateway—take care of your heads—never killed but one woman and a child all my life—that's your sort!"[8]

"That's your sort!" is also Goldfinch's tag line.

Mathews acted in several later plays in which this staccato device was given to some comic character who had no horsey past as excuse, but who talked this way just the same. By the time he came to invent his "At Home" characterizations, he had learned to use the mannerism for telling any kind of tall tale. His first character to do so was Major Longbow, in *Travels in Air, Earth, and Water* (1821). The Major recounts a typical experience in a balloon thus:

> "Know all about it, to be sure I do—went up myself with Rosiere and Romaine from Boulogne, forty years ago—Montgolfier balloon—fire as large as the kitchen fire at the Thatched House tavern—three miles high took fire—there was a blaze—all Paris saw us—down we came slap-bang—like a cannon-ball, 2840 yards high, French measure—down

we came like a thunderbolt—Rosiere and Romaine, they both killed on the spot, I not hurt a bit—forty years ago—not a bit older now—Pon my life it's true—what'll you lay it's a lie?"[9]

This mannerism is so distinctive that it can be seen a long way off. Mathews found it an unfailing laugh-getter; accordingly he created new characters in succeeding programs, all of whom talk the same way, and all of whom tell unbelievable stories. I find at least three major characters besides Major Longbow: Brigadier General Babington, Mr. Popper, and Commodore Cosmogony. Their only variation is that they center respectively on impossible military adventures, sporting tales, and yarns of travel. The Commodore tells of his adventures on the Nile:

> "Seen the River Nile, if you mean that—something like a river—thousand miles long—swam down it many a time—eat part of a crocodile there, that wanted to eat me—saw him cry with vexation as I kill'd him—tears big as marrowfat peas—bottled one of them, for the curiosity of the thing. True tale—pos—I'm not joking."[10]

When Dickens planned to emulate Mathews in his tryout before the famous Charles Kemble, we can be sure that he had Mr. Jingle all ready, for Mr. Jingle was the first eccentric with a speech mannerism introduced into *Pickwick*. That he could hold his own with Major Longbow in the construction of tall tales is illustrated by one of Mr. Jingle's first stories:

[handwritten marginal note: MR. JINGLE'S SPEECH CHARISTIC IS ALSO FROM MATHEWS.]

> "Don Bolaro Fizzgig—grandee—only daughter—Donna Christina—splendid creature—loved me to distraction—jealous father—high-souled creature—handsome Englishman—Donna Christina in despair—prussic acid—stomach pump in my portmanteau—operation performed—old Bolaro in ecstasies—consent to our union—join hands and floods of tears—romantic story—very."[11]

The staccato speech device has one limitation. Whatever Mathews could do with it on the stage, it could only be used once in a novel; once used it was used up. Also there is another difficulty: if Mr. Jingle says anything at all which is ordinary or normal in content, the device is awkward and accomplishes nothing at all. But Mr. Jingle proves one thing about Dickens' narrative habits. He is irrefutable evidence of Dickens' development of the habit of depending upon speech mannerisms for comic purposes. The technique has little effectiveness in tragic or serious fiction. But whenever Dickens used one of these distinctive devices for farcical effect, he seemed inspired. Mr. Jingle has relatively few speeches, but they are extraordinarily effective. Nothing of Mathews compares with:

> "Heads, heads—take care of your heads! [the Pickwickians are going under a bridge in the stagecoach]—terrible place—dangerous work—other day—five children—mother—tall lady—eating sandwich—forgot the arch—knock—children look round—mother's head off—sandwich in her hand—no mouth to put it in—head of family off—shocking—shocking!"[12]

MIXED SENTENCES

Most of Mathews' impersonated characters talk a lot. Several of his female inventions mix sentences together and get their connectives all tangled. In the *Comic Annual for 1830,* Mrs. Eleanor Neverend wanders on and on from this beginning:

> "I wonder how your head can contain so much—you must have a large head, Mr. Mathews, to hold such a lot. Well how's all your family? I should like my daughter to play the piano. Bless me! My dog had his tail run over. Dear me, your coat is all over flue!"[13]

It takes no exercise of the memory to recall that almost any character who talks endlessly in a Dickens novel is funnier than this, but Dickens usually gave this device to eccentric women. Garrulous females are scattered through his novels. Their manner of speaking takes on individuality, depending on the place assigned them in their stories, but the essential device is the same. One can trace a growing complexity as the years go by, the later women being more and more incoherent.

EXAMPLES! ①

Mrs. Nickleby is the first sparkling example of the female who keeps shifting her subject-matter by a kind of free association of ideas:

> "Roast pig—let me see. On the day five weeks after you were christened, we had a roast—no that couldn't have been a pig, either, because I recollect there were a pair of them to carve, and your poor papa and I could never have thought of sitting down to two pigs—they must have been partridges. Roast pig! I hardly think we ever could have had one, now I come to remember, for your papa could never bear the sight of them in the shops, and used to say that they always put him in mind of very little babies, only the pigs had much fairer complexions; and he had a horror of little babies, too, because he couldn't very well afford any increase to his family, and had a natural dislike to the

subject. It's very odd now, what can have put that in my head! I recollect dining once at Mrs. Bevan's in that broad street round the corner by the coachmaker's, where the tipsy man fell through the cellar-flap of an empty house nearly a week before the quarter-day, and wasn't found till the new tenant went in—and we had roast pig there. It must be that, I think, that reminds me of it, especially as there was a little bird in the room that would keep on singing all the time of the dinner—at least, not a little bird, for it was a parrot, and he didn't sing exactly, for he talked and swore dreadfully; but I think it must be that. Shouldn't you say so, my dear?"[14]

Mrs. Nickleby is supposed to derive from the example of Dickens' own mother, but one realizes that she talks better in the novel than in real life. Her way of speaking, like that of Mrs. Neverend, allows her first subject to suggest something incongruous, which in turn leads to another shift whose relationship to the beginning is increasingly ridiculous. This device is also assigned to Mrs. Gamp in *Martin* *Chuzzlewit,* with the variation that she reports endless conversations with a mythical Mrs. Harris whom she is always quoting. A choice between Mrs. Nickleby and Mrs. Gamp is hard to make.

"As a good friend of mine has frequent made remark to me, which her name, my love, is Harris, Mrs. Harris through square and up the steps a turnin' round by the tobacker shop, 'Oh Sairey, Sairey, little do we know wot lays afore us!' 'Mrs. Harris, Ma'am,' I says, 'not much, it's true, but more than you suppose. Our calcilations, ma'am,' I says, 'respectin' wot the number of a family will be, comes most times within one, and oftener than you would suppose, exact.' 'Sairey,' says Mrs. Harris, in a awful way, 'Tell me wot is my indiwidge number.' 'No, Mrs. Harris,' I says to her, 'ex-cuge me, if you please. My own,' I says, 'has fallen out of three-pair backs, and had damp doorsteps settled on their lungs, and one was turned up smilin' in a bedstead, unbeknown. Therefore, ma'am,' I says, 'seek not to proticipate, but take 'em as they come and as they go.' Mine," said Mrs. Gamp, "mine is all gone, my dear young chick. And as to husbands, there's a wooden leg gone likeways home to its account, which in its constancy of walkin' into wine vaults, and never comin' out again 'till fetched by force, was quite as weak as flesh, if not weaker."[15]

The rapid-shift-in-subject-matter type of talking found a later expression in the speech of Flora Finching in *Little Dorrit,* showing that Dickens could play upon many stops and vary his organ tones with the same tune. Flora is more extreme in her jumps than either of the other two predecessors, impossible as that sometimes appears:

"You must know, my dear," said Flora, "But that I have no doubt you know already not only because I have already thrown it out in a general way but because I feel I carry it stamped in burning what's-his-names upon my brow that before I was introduced to the late Mr. F. I had been engaged to Arthur Clennam—Mr. Clennam in public where reserve is necessary Arthur here—we were all in all to one another it was the morning of life it was bliss it was frenzy it was everything else of that sort in the highest degree, when rent asunder we turned to stone in which capacity Arthur went to China and I became the statue bride of the late Mr. F. . . . To paint," said she, "the emotions of that morning when all was marble within and Mr. F's Aunt followed in a glass-coach which it stands to reason must have been in shameful disrepair or it never could have broken down two streets from the house and Mr. F's Aunt brought home like the fifth of November in a rush-bottomed chair I will not attempt, suffice it to say that the hollow form of breakfast took place in the dining-room downstairs that papa partaking too freely of pickled salmon was ill for weeks and that Mr. F. and myself went upon a continental tour to Calais where the people fought for us on the pier until they separated us though not for ever that was not yet to be. . . ."[16]

Flora, according to all authorities, resembles Dickens' youthful sweet-heart, Maria Beadnell, as she appeared to him years later, shockingly different from the idealized person Dickens remembered. But the reader wagers that her lack of punctuation and breathless rambling were again funnier on Dickens' stage than in real life.

The last extreme of this never-ending garrulousness is little known, for it occurs in a minor Christmas story written for *All the Year Round* in 1864. Mrs. Lirriper tells her own story, and since she rambles more than any of her predecessors, the tale wanders considerably. There is a foreshadowing of Joyce's Molly Bloom in Mrs. Lirriper's speech, and the normal connectives have almost vanished. Stream-of-consciousness is just around the corner.

Mentioning my poor Lirriper brings into my head his own youngest brother the Doctor though Doctor of what I am sure it would be hard to say unless Liquor, for neither Physic nor Music nor yet Law does Joseph Lirriper know a morsel of except continually being summoned to the County Court and having orders made upon him which he runs away from, and once was taken in the passage of this very house with an umbrella up and the Major's hat on, giving his name with the door-mat round him as Sir Johnson Jones K.C.B. in spectacles residing at the Horse Guards. On which occasion he had got into the house not a minute before, through the girl letting him on the mat when he sent in a piece of paper twisted more like one of those spills for lighting candles than a note, offering me the choice between thirty shillings in hand and his brains on the premises marked immediate and waiting for an answer. My dear it gave me such a dreadful turn to think of the brains of my poor dear Lirriper's own flesh and blood flying about the new oilcloth however unworthy to be so assisted, that I went out of my room here to ask him what he would take once for all not to do it for life when I found him in the custody of two gentlemen. . . .[17]

This speech mannerism goes on all through the tale.

It is clear that Mathews' influence on Dickens' artistry supplied the habit of using distinguishing vocal mannerisms or tags of speech for practically every eccentric character created by Dickens. He carried the example far beyond the influence, naturally. One runs across many characters in the "At Home" scripts which remind us that Dickens appears never to have forgotten any peculiar traits of character when he needed inspiration in his later novels. There is a Mr. Lavolta, who laughs whenever he finds something unfortunate or unpleasant to discuss, making it praiseworthy to be happy when it is hard to be so.[18] Mark Tapley also has this faculty in *Martin Chuzzlewit*. Mathews' Mr. Chyle has a wife who makes her husband uncomfortable in his own home while she prepares soup for the poor and lets her own children run about half-naked while she makes baby-linen for the County Hospital and changes for meritorious convicts.[19] Mrs. Jellyby in *Bleak House* also forgets her home for aid to foreign missions in Africa. In the 1825 *Memorandum Book,* Mathews created a Mr. Alum, "a sort of poisoner of the pantry," who keeps interrupting the attempts of everyone to eat by saying, "Beware, that's poisonous! I've analyzed it, I've tried it, and I know it." Further details about the ingredients in various dishes usually stop all consumption of the food in question.[20] Dickens, in *Our Mutual Friend,* gives this trait to the Veneering's butler.

> "Dinner is on the table!"
> Thus the melancholy retainer, as who would say, "Come down and be poisoned, ye unhappy children of men!"
> Meantime the retainer goes round, like a gloomy Analytical Chemist; always seeming to say, after "Chablis, sir?"—"You wouldn't if you knew what it's made of."[21]

[handwritten margin note: DICKENS ACHIEVES MORE SUCCESS + WORKS THESE MANNERISMS MUCH FURTHER]

49

To anyone who has examined the original scripts of Mathews, even in the poorly transcribed pirated editions, there is clear evidence of the opportunity for entertainment; but it must have been materially aided by the actor in his delivery on the stage. Dickens goes so much further and manages to create so many more mannerisms than Mathews, that his material achieves comic effectiveness even when it is read rather than heard. The flow of extreme speech devices continues as the novels pour out their contrasts. The elocutionary and high-flown language of the stage comes out of the mouth of Vincent Crummles in *Nicholas Nickleby*. At another extreme is the baby talk of Mr. Mantalini, along with the reminiscences of Mrs. Nickleby in that novel. Dick Swiveller, in *The Old Curiosity Shop,* calls upon wild figures of speech in order to make sure that "the fire of soul is kindled at the taper of conwiviality, and the wing of friendship never moults a feather."

Martin Chuzzlewit contains, besides the fascinating Mrs. Gamp, the pompous and hypocritical Mr. Pecksniff, whose manner of speech is always offensive. Scrooge's "Bah! Humbug!" delivery bedecks *A Christmas Carol. Dombey and Son* shows several speech devices, from the almost incoherently stupid Captain Jack Bunsby, to Mrs. Mac-Stinger who pursues and browbeats her lodgers, to tough old Major Joseph Bagstock, to Captain Cuttle, to the artificially natural Mrs. Skewton. All of these characters, and many more, gain essential impetus of character from the way Dickens manages on paper to mimic the delivery of the words they speak. This fact accounts for the ease with which Dickens' novels adapt themselves to stage performances, to readings in costume, and to motion picture production in the twentieth century. The comic scenes come over when characters talk, even if the melodramatic plot may seem hazardous on occasion.

MICAWBER

Dickens' finest utilization of a speech device decorated with tag lines is in the character of Micawber. Micawber contrasts formal and decorative prose with a sudden summation in concise terms, introduced by "in short—". When he first meets David, he says:

"Under the impression . . . that your peregrinations in this metropolis have not as yet been extensive, and that you might have some difficulty in penetrating the arcana of the Modern Babylon in the direction of the City Road—in short . . . that you might lose yourself—I shall be happy to call this evening, and instal you in the knowledge of the nearest way."[22]

The "in short" manner is distinctive in itself. In addition, Micawber is "always expecting something to turn up." His florid phrases are studded with philosophical jewels, almost always appropriate to the occasion, but oddly applied.

Before leaving London for Plymouth, Mr. Micawber gives David some advice, advice which has served as a precise picture of that gentleman's own character for all who read *David Copperfield:*

> "My dear young friend," said Mr. Micawber, "I am older than you; a man of some experience in life, and—and—of some experience, in short, in difficulties, generally speaking. At present, and until something turns up (which I am, I may say, hourly expecting), I have nothing to bestow but advice. Still my advice is so far worth taking, that—in short, that I have never taken it myself, and am the"—here Mr. Micawber, who had been beaming and smiling all over his head and face, up to the present moment, checked himself, and frowned,— "the miserable wretch you behold. . . . My advice is, never do tomorrow what you can do to-day. Procrastination is the thief of time. Collar him!"[23]

It is hard to praise this scene too highly. Anyone who has read Dickens remembers that it goes on to the famous advice about spending a little less rather than a little more than one's income. Every particle of the effect gained depends upon the speech mannerisms given Micawber, illustrating Dickens' supreme accomplishment in making his best characters talk like comic actors on a stage in heaven.

When Dickens came to do the readings from his novels, it should be noted that almost all his reading script was speech. Examination of his personal copy for these readings, corrected from the published text, shows how he noted in the margins a mass of hints as to byplay and gesture, a kind of stage-direction guide for himself. Generally the descriptive parts of his text were acted whenever possible, and often they were crossed out. For instance, beside the copy for his reading of *Oliver Twist* is the word *Action*:

> Fagin raised his right hand, and shook his trembling forefinger in the air.[24]

As Dickens performed it, he *did* what the text said; he did not read the words.

Looking at the artistry of Dickens in an over-all sense, we can see that the essential context of the dramatic scenes in his novels was conversation or monologue; his characters were differentiated as much as possible by speech devices and individual vocal mannerisms. He thought of his scenes, particularly the comic ones, as imaginary stage performances intended to entertain an audience; in order to make his characters vivid or individualistic he fancied how they would act and mimicked them in his mind's eye before he described on paper what they did and said. This practice is an intensification of the farce-caricature technique which he developed after the example of Smollett and Fielding; it reinforces that technique at every point. Its only disadvantage is that it also exposed his art to the charge of having created only eccentrics and stage figures, not real people. The charge is dependent upon whether his concept of the stage imitated or symbolized reality. In any case, it achieved entertainment.

Mathews, in his introductory address given on the occasion of his first "At Home," defended his art reasonably. He said:

> The best authorities have characterized the drama by the title of the mimic art; and I humbly conceive, that, without mimicry, there can be no acting. It is the very essence of personation, and he who cannot personate the character imagined by the author, in my mind can never be an actor. If this argument, which I have presumed to advance, be admitted, it is surely a strange deduction, that a man ceases to be an actor because he personated half a dozen characters in a drama instead of one.[25]

The art of the actor is to produce the illusion of comparative reality, says Mathews, and such illusion must assume the persons mimicked are justly conceived. Since Dickens did not often attempt to present intricate analyses of characters, but portrayed a number of partially displayed individuals in contrast to each other, he had to depend for effectiveness upon what he selected or exaggerated as representative of the essential traits of his characters. His success for his age and for future generations rests upon the vitality of the values one recognizes in his selected qualities and mannerisms. The part symbolizes the whole. If his heightening or caricature emphasizes what is true and important, he succeeded; if he selected that which distorts truth, he failed.

IS CARICATURE REAL?

There is no outright judgment possible with artistry of this nature. Some of Dickens' characters may always be limited to their outward manifestations, and in the minds of some readers no ecdysis ever occurs. These characters will remain partially unreal. At his best Dickens gained force by emphasizing what was essential; at his worst he left out characteristics which seem necessary to many readers. George Gissing, in his fine study of Dickens' novels, said that Mrs. Gamp is made effective by omitting part of the whole picture of her as she might have been in real life. Who cares about the rest? The essential Mrs. Gamp is as Dickens portrayed her.[26] She is more real than real life because the reader can see her more clearly than if he met her on the street. Caricature in this sense becomes a step to symbolic artistry and is completely satisfying if it centers the reader's attention on the essential, the real, the permanent, and the true.

Any novel which is so real that it seems to be a "piece of life" may include detail which in extreme quantities adds nothing but boredom to the course of the story. That which is real should also seem important in fiction. Dickens thought that the real must be entertaining. Since his art deliberately scattered its attention while it depicted large scenes and masses of people in contrast with each other, he chose a remarkable narrative device in his utilization of speech mannerisms and repetitive tags to help achieve his purpose. The technique of mimicry makes one see and hear his characters, and the effect is likely to last in memory long after the novel is laid aside. The unforgettable character, like Sam Weller, or Mrs. Nickleby, or Mr. Pecksniff, or Mr. Micawber, is one that has a mannerism of speech which will not vanish or a tag that will not come off.

CHAPTER IV

Conflict in Action:
The Technique of Plot Arrangement

HE EARLY novels of Dickens are concerned—not at first, but eventually—with action which follows some plan: with love and hate, with life and death, with wealth and poverty, with long-lost relatives and evil companions, with passion and desire, with mischance and divine justice—in short, with a plot. Dickens derived and developed his plots from the example of traditional fiction and from stage plays. The first of them tend to be melodramatic and occasionally sentimental. Often they are so involved and complex in their development that they avoid the necessities of reasonable motivation. The fact that they are superimposed upon interesting characters who have established interest in the reader's consciousness by virtue of caricature and farce keeps their coincidental tendencies from being too conspicuous. In addition they often illustrate some humanitarian purpose or criticism of social and moral evil, so that the point of the story impels sympathetic readers to accept the plot along with the purpose. Dickens improved rapidly in his planning, motivation, and development of the action of his plots, so that the later novels eventually become expert in these matters.

The main influence upon Dickens' plot arrangement was the stage. One should not be surprised that the writer who was impressed by the mimicry and comedy of Mathews should also enjoy the serious dramatic productions of his day. The early nineteenth-century stage fascinated Dickens in all its forms. The tragic or melodramatic productions furnished him with models which we tend to criticize or even laugh at in the twentieth century. The main reason for our contempt is that the language and the manner of producing the serious speeches of melodrama became highly elocutionary and occasionally hackneyed. Dramatic language at its worst is artificial, and in this

THIS IS WHAT SAVAGE WOULD CALL "SENTIMENTAL"

54

period it could become so unnatural that it escaped all connection with conviction, even by way of stage illusion.

Beyond the problems of melodramatic speech and gesture, plays in a period of questionable dramatic taste tend to patterns of action which may distort life or make it unrecognizable. Characters that were all black or all white, customary intrigues repeated from play to play, standard peculiarities of behavior which lose effectiveness with repetition, excessive coincidences and manipulated climaxes—all these features of melodrama plague the early novels of Dickens whenever they imitate the theater of their time.

IN OTHER WORDS D.'S IMITATION WAS A MISTAKE OF STYLE.

In one sense it is easy to see why the stage attracted Dickens. As a novelist he was aiming at entertainment for his readers. Stage plots furnished devices which aroused interest; sensational action presented the effect most likely to appeal to the taste of his time. His interest turned naturally to scenes of excitement, passion, and sentiment; he brought intrigue, stimulating conflict, love stories, and idealistic complications into every novel. His aim was to tell a story and to be essentially true to reality. His action was not primarily intended to expose character or the details of cause and effect in human psychology; he intended to present life through a dramatic examination of mysteries and complications. He always showed two or more forces in conflict, and his stories were arranged to reveal the eventual triumph of one over the other.

Whenever a critic has voiced disapproval of Dickens, his main reason has been dependent upon the manner in which Dickens handled his plots. He developed his action as dramatists approach the art of organizing a play. A successful play produces suspension of disbelief; the onlooker is persuaded that stage, scenery, footlights, and actors have transferred their pretense to imaginary reality; imitation becomes illusion. In farce and caricature Dickens succeeded in achieving satisfactory illusion by means of heightening, partially because one's judgment is relaxed by laughter. Serious scenes demand a different kind of artistry, and the stage models available to the young author did not automatically provide it.

PLOT IS WEAKEST PART

If one examines the way in which Dickens organized his first five novels, it is easy to see that the plots are the most tenuous part of his narrative accomplishment. In his approach to *Pickwick Papers*, ①

55

circumstances provided him with no opportunity for an original plan or outline of intention. He was given some drawings, a central set of characters, and a purpose which required the creation of a series of ridiculous incidents. He made up his story as he went along, using the techniques of caricature and farce. Mr. Pickwick grew upon him as a person, and his comic sequences became more involved. His genius in the development of farce and caricature produced the unexpected success of the novel. His artistic sense required him to try some form of contrast for the farce materials. He therefore used the filler stories which illustrate sensational materials. Eventually he inserted a love plot, added two more, and after marrying some of the characters off and temporarily putting Mr. Pickwick in prison, he brought things to a satisfactory conclusion. Mr. Pickwick's difficulties with fate developed into the central plot. The love stories are ordinary stage conflicts, usually referred to as "boy-meets-girl" type, with simple obstacles temporarily interfering with marriage.

In _Oliver Twist_ he had an opportunity to plan what he was doing. He began with a serious purpose and had his main intrigue in mind from the outset. His idea is not complicated; it depends upon a traditional stage gambit. The illegitimate son is hated and pursued by the legitimate one, and all sympathy is directed to the illegitimate child; the inheritance of a fortune is at stake. The plot is then arranged to permit Dickens to criticize the Poor Law and attack the centers of juvenile delinquency, the schools for thieves in the city of London. At some time or other, probably in the course of creation, it occurred to Dickens that he could build a climax through the gruesome murder of Nancy by Bill Sikes. This action is almost all melodrama, with only a few rare touches of the farce-caricature technique. Without question the novel has a challenging humanitarian purpose.

Nicholas Nickleby was organized on the picaresque model, with a youthful hero instead of the Pickwick Club carrying the action. This plan allowed Dickens to utilize farce and caricature, and also to experiment with a number of contrasting techniques and episodes. He intended to expose the bad boarding schools for boys run by masters like Squeers; he could let himself go in satirizing provincial acting companies led by directors like Vincent Crummles; he could portray a host of caricatured eccentrics like the Kenwigses, the Mantalinis,

Mrs. Nickleby, and her mad neighbor; he could introduce a number of plot sequences like the Ralph Nickleby-Smike story, Kate's difficulties with her would-be seducer, and the love story of Nicholas and Madeline Bray. He achieved contrast in this novel, which comes close to illustrating practically every virtue and defect in Dickens' artistic capacity.

The Old Curiosity Shop was conceived as a short serial. It was (4) written initially in the first person, then changed unceremoniously to the third at the end of the third chapter when the decision was made to turn the periodical, *Master Humphrey's Clock* (in which it was appearing), into a novel rather than a collection of shorter pieces. The main plot depends upon a gambling grandfather and the little girl who suffers from his financial difficulties and tries to save him. Dickens called upon the method of travel to advance his story, following the picaresque example, so he sent Nell and her grandfather north, giving them varied adventures as they travel. He used caricature for some of his variety, introduced a mysterious relative, and concentrated on a hunchbacked, deformed villain called Quilp. He inserted a contrasting plot around Kit, the youth who was unjustly accused of crime and convicted. He managed a few farcical scenes involving Dick Swiveller and the Marchioness. But he achieved great popular appeal by having Nell die.

Barnaby Rudge underwent several changes in planning, but (5) it probably contained two simple boy-meets-girl plots at the start. This beginning was sidetracked effectively by the historical setting, and the boys depart, are absent through most of the story, then return at the last to marry their girls. Dickens added two other melodramatic plots for his historical story, apparently seeing the first signs of the novel which would depend upon a number of alternating or balancing plots conceived around a central theme. These plots have stage origins, the Rudge supposedly-dead-murderer-with-half-witted-son plot and the Sir John Chester-Hugh plot playing upon well-worn emotions. These two sequences are superimposed on history, and the various strands of action jostle each other as the pages fill up.

As the later novels were written, Dickens became more and more concerned with motivating his action. Several disagreements in criticism should be noted, for his accomplishment can hardly be judged exclusively by the plot development of the early novels. Nor is it completely accurate to say, as many critics do, that Dickens began his novels with some entertaining eccentrics, that he carried on with some amusing episodes, then saw that he needed some action, so inserted a stage plot, then ended by marrying every available person off. This judgment might fit *Pickwick Papers,* it may apply to *Nicholas Nickleby,* but it does not resemble the other three at all, and it has little reference to the later novels, with the possible exception of *David Copperfield.* Further, one can dismiss the plots in *Pickwick* as having little to do one way or the other with the effect of the book. But in the stories that he began with a plan, the plots are integral parts of the end Dickens aimed at and must be taken into serious account. In each of the novels of his first period, his plots are arranged according to the tradition of the stage, and they are subject to the kind of manipulation of reality we call *melodrama.*

THESIS!

One must point out in passing that the result is surprising. The stage gave Dickens the example of farce and the particular example of Mathews in mimicry, the net effect being some of his finest writing in comedy; but the stage also gave Dickens the serious pattern of melodrama that exposed him to artistic accomplishment which is doubtful or arguable.

THEATERS
IN DICKENS
DAY

In order to see just how influential the impact of melodrama was on Dickens, the modern reader must look closely at the stage productions of his time. The theater in his youth was at a low ebb in standards of presentation. Drury Lane and Covent Garden produced plays by the best English dramatists from Shakespeare on down, but the Haymarket, the Adelphi, and dozens of other playhouses put on spectacles, operas, burlettas, extravaganzas, and "shows" whose artistic ideals were aesthetically inferior. This judgment, to be sure, can be made on any age when one looks below the top level, but at its best there is not much to be said for this period beyond the accomplishments of a few great actors and an occasional rare performance. The star system was just coming into prominence; the theaters were being increased in size in order to meet growing expenses; stage displays, animals, and novelties were featured to attract crowds; acting became broad, exaggerated, and used conventional motions and gestures for particular effects—all because of the decline of a tradition—a condi-

in which right triumphed and villainy met its just reward, he instinctively imitated on paper the stage mannerisms of Macready, just as he mimicked Mathews in comedy and farce. He wrote to Forster about his conceiving *The Chimes* in a dream:

> Observe that throughout I was as real, animated, and full of passion as Macready (God bless him) in the last scene of Macbeth.[3]

Overacting has many ramifications when transferred from the stage to the page. It is simpler to make exaggerated feelings convincing in drama than it is in novels; that which is on paper has to stand the possibility of unimpassioned reading. Highly charged language is assisted by the speaking voice, the lights, the scenery, the atmosphere of the theater to move those who listen rather than read. In the early novels Dickens seems always to be struggling for the necessary theatrical atmosphere.

The example of Mathews allows a precise and neat discussion, but not the example of Macready. Not every melodramatic mannerism of the author can be traced to this one actor, of course. Dickens saw many tragedies and melodramas; he admired other actors in some measure. The list of plays he refers to in his writings and his letters comes to more than a hundred titles. Besides the traditional tragedies of the poetic or Shakespearan kind, he enjoyed domestic tragedy; Lillo's *George Barnwell* and Moore's *The Gamester* illustrate this kind of play. Sentimental comedy on all levels of artistic accomplishment attracted his comment, from Sheridan and Goldsmith to the pathetic and trite company who followed Steele and Cibber. In these plays right always triumphs, and wrong always suffers. Jerrold's *Black-Eyed Susan* is a very popular but almost simple-minded example of this kind of drama, written, produced, and played over and over in Dickens' time, complete with hero, heroine, villain, and eventual poetic justice after escape from evil and mischance. The list of plays is so long that it is convenient to lump the influences into as many general trends as possible, referring specifically to Holcroft or Morton, Colman or Jerrold, Knowles or Bulwer-Lytton whenever some definite plot or scene resembles accurately what Dickens used in one of his novels.[4]

The influence of the stage on Dickens' plots is comprised in our understanding of what is meant by *melodrama*. For melodrama is not the same thing as tragedy. Tragedy is exact, it is convincing, it is absolute. It lives in a different world from vile villains, seduced or unseduced maidens, heroic revenge, unsubdued hope, and deathbed repentances. When death occurs in a melodrama, death may be horrible, but only because it is not inevitable. The maiden might so easily have lived; she usually did. Fate or the author might save the situation at any point in the story. Melodrama grows with coincidence, but tragedy is destiny. There is no hope in tragedy; you cannot escape.[5]

This is the reason that William Archer defines *melodrama* as "tragedy without logic." The implication of the word in this sense is inferior workmanship, since the action is not completely convincing because of improper motivation, unbelievable coincidence, or illogical expression. In this sense, the early novels of Dickens contain melodrama. One recalls that Chesterton says flatly:

> Dickens was meant by heaven to be the great melodramatist; so that even his literary end was melodramatic.[6]

This implies, since it is intended as praise, that melodrama is a satisfactory art form, like opera, fantasy, or ballet, and is not to be judged by the same rules as narrative which pretends to the illusion of real life. If Dickens deserves a place in the ranks of great novelists, this opinion must be rejected fiercely. Melodrama is always artistically inferior to authentic tragedy.

What are the unfailing signs of melodrama? They usually appear in stilted, hackneyed language which actors speak on the stage but never off it. Words of this vocabulary are bombastic, figured, unreal, rhetorical, or archaically poetic. Their tradition has worn thin, but the groove is still there. If the hero says:

> "Have I been nursing a viper in my bosom? You insufferable villain!
> I will tread you into a paste. Never darken my doors again,"[7]

the language is melodramatic. It is also completely ineffective when read in the next century.

Now this is the way Dickens occasionally writes. Inadequate and trite phrases accompany his dramatic climaxes in *Oliver Twist* and *Nicholas Nickleby*. Kate Nickleby indignantly says to the villain, "Unhand me sir, this instant."[8] Nicholas concludes a scene with his uncle by promising, "It will be long, very long, before I darken these doors again."[9] Later he discusses the evil scheming of Ralph with the words, "He is my uncle, but he is a villain, and has done me wrong."[10] After he has attempted to force Sir Mulberry Hawk to an explanation of his intentions toward his sister Kate, Nicholas comes home injured and wants to know the facts of the situation which are unfamiliar to him. He says to Newman Noggs, "But before I remove one jot of these stains, I must hear the whole from you."[11] When Bray, the father of Nicholas' love, Madeline, dies just at the opportune moment to prevent Madeline from having to marry Gride, Nicholas says, "Stand off! . . . if this is what I scarcely dare hope it is, you are caught, villains, in your own toils."[12]

This language is recognizable, obviously melodramatic. It is not natural or believable speech, and much more of this variety of rhetorical fluff can be found in early scenes in which an emotional crisis is described. For example, Fagin's last moments are well recorded as long as Dickens sticks to narration and description. Then Oliver begins to speak:

> "Let me say a prayer. Do! Let me say one prayer. Say only one, upon your knees, with me, and we will talk till morning."[13]

There we are, back behind the gaslights, not only in the world of make-believe but in the company of ham actors.

Perhaps one might believe that Oliver could talk as he does under emotional stress were it not for his previous speeches. His language has no resemblance to reality. Eventually every reader recognizes this fact. The boy has been brought up in a workhouse; he has never been educated, nor has he heard educated people speak except on rare occasions. Yet he, and Nancy the prostitute too, converse with due regard for copybook maxims of technical grammar. They speak, as stage actors enunciate, with emotional flourishes. When Oliver's thievish companions carry him off from Mr. Brownlow's, he protests because they are taking from him the books he is returning:

> "They belong to the old gentleman," said Oliver, wringing his hands; "to the good, kind, old gentleman who took me into the house, and had me nursed, when I was near dying of the fever. Oh, pray, send them back; send them back; send him back the books and money. Keep me here all my life long, but pray, pray, send them back. He'll

think I stole them; the old lady: all of them who were so kind to me: will think I stole them. Oh, do have mercy upon me, and send them back."[14]

On occasion, the understandable emotions of Oliver become completely entangled with the word "pray." When Sikes tries to make the boy aid him in robbing a house, Oliver falls to the ground:

> "Get up," murmured Sikes, trembling with rage, and drawing the pistol from his pocket; "get up, or I'll strew your brains upon the grass."
>
> "Oh! For God's sake let me go," cried Oliver; "let me run away and die in the fields. I will never come near London; never, never! Oh! pray have mercy upon me, and do not make me steal. For the love of all the bright angels that rest in heaven, have mercy upon me!"[15]

The evidence can be carried much further. One of the most recognizable types of melodramatic speech occurs when a lady repels the villain who is making some improper proposal to her. Douglas Jerrold's *Black-Eyed Susan* has a fine example of this kind of language. The heroine, Susan, speaks to the villain:

> "Sir, scorn has no words, contempt no voice to speak my loathing of your insinuations. Take sir, all that is here; satisfy your avarice—but dare not indulge your malice at the cost of one who has nothing left her in her misery but the sweet consciousness of virtue." [*Exit*.][16]

The nineteenth-century audience was wont to cheer loudly at this emotional outburst, while the evil seducer cringed in understanding that he had been told off.

Kate Nickleby is the first of Dickens' heroines to send away a potential seducer. She says:

> "I hold you in the bitterest detestation and contempt, sir," said Kate. "If you find any attraction in looks of disgust and aversion, you—let me rejoin my friends, sir, instantly. Whatever considerations may have withheld me thus far, I will disregard them all, and take a course that even *you* might feel, if you do not immediately suffer me to proceed."[17]

Mary Graham in *Martin Chuzzlewit* has to reject an unwelcome suit from Mr. Pecksniff. Her language is trying if not true:

> "Pray, pray, release me, Mr. Pecksniff. I cannot listen to your proposal. I cannot receive it. There are many to whom it may be acceptable,

but it is not so to me. As an act of kindness and an act of pity, leave
me! . . . I hold you in the deepest abhorrence. I know your real
nature and I despise it."[18]

Dickens occasionally reaches into realms that Macready would
have enjoyed inhabiting, in other examples of extreme emotional
passion. There are climaxes to several of his plot situations in the
early novels in which the figured rhetoric resembles a species of blank
verse. It does not reach Shakespearean standards, and it is often
inserted in narrative spots where it contrasts with normal and realistic
description. The narrative and the dialogue are in two different
manners, the one natural, the other stagey. The father of Barnaby
Rudge, for example, surprises his wife and demands money from her.
His harangue is the kind of talk which Macready would read with
menacing elocutionary eloquence on the stage:

"I, that in the form of a man live the life of a hunted beast! that in
the body am a spirit, a ghost upon the earth, a thing from which all
creatures shrink, save those curst beings of another world, who will not
leave me;—I am, in my desperation of this night, past all fear but
that of the hell in which I exist from day to day. Give the alarm,
cry out, refuse to shelter me. I will not hurt you. But I will not be
taken alive; and so surely as you threaten me above your breath, I
fall a dead man upon this floor. The blood with which I sprinkle it,
be on you and yours, in the name of the Evil Spirit that tempts men
to their ruin."[19]

The list of examples could easily be multiplied. The young Dickens
used melodramatic language as a device which was intended to intensify his serious action. When these speeches are separated from the rest
of the novel and examined by themselves, they develop "action without
logic."

Even more important than the manner of melodrama is the
matter. Dickens introduced many characters into the action, the
intrigues, and the plot situations which came from the stage. Because
of his abilities in caricature and distinguishing speech mannerisms,
these characters have given the impression of absolute individuality, so
much so that Stefan Zweig once said, "Though they are legion, not one
resembles the other."[20] Yet often among the caricatured eccentrics
and the individualized actors Dickens inserted some stock characters
out of melodrama—characters which have little individuality. These

stock characters naturally behave as they should in stock plots and sequences of action which resemble that which was normal only on the stage of his time.

Remarkably enough, Dickens *knew* from the beginning what was convincing and what was not convincing on the stage. This is, of course, the reason why he eventually overcame his tendencies to distort the action of his novels. The surest indication for this conclusion is the sequence in *Nicholas Nickleby* in which he depicts the adventures of his hero with Vincent Crummles' stock company of provincial actors. This passage is one of his finest examples of sustained ironic caricature. The Crummles troupe stage sentimental comedy and standard melodrama of questionable merits. Each member of the company has a particular type of role which he plays in almost every performance. Mrs. Crummles is the tragic actress who speaks in a sepulchral voice; Mr. Lenville does first tragedy with Mr. Crummles; Mr. Folair helps the infant phenomenon; Tommy plays the low-spirited lovers; an inebriated elderly gentleman acts the calm and virtuous old men; another plays the irascible elders who try to force their unwilling sons to marry heiresses; another does the swaggering hero in comedy; and Miss Snevellicci plays anything or everything, being versatile. This is a delightful company, and the reason for its success is that each character is a burlesque of some melodramatic original.[21]

Dickens often created characters who could have been satirized by the Crummles company. His heroes are good examples. In melodrama a hero is a youthful, romantic, remarkably good and innocent person. His actions are impeccable because his heart is pure. Come what fate presents, he will be sinless still. His gaze is warm because his faults are frozen. Oliver Twist and Harry Maylie are perfect; Nicholas Nickleby is the ordinary romantic hero, possessing only a hot head; Kit represents the lower classes, but never does anything that can be considered questionable; Joe Willet and Edward Chester are absent from the scene of action for many pages, but they too are heroes in the stock melodramatic sense. In general they resemble each other a great deal, and Kit might substitute for Oliver, Edward Chester for Harry Maylie, and so on. Nicholas is perhaps an exception, but he would be at home in most melodramas.

66

Then there are the heroines. They are even more in the tradition. They are sexless, ignorant, and faultless, perpetually on guard against evils they can only suspect, alert to motives which they instinctively repel, possessing heads and hands attached to clothing under which are nameless bodily organs, having mouths that talk and lips that taste food, but after the talk, the rest is silence. Every one of Dickens' early heroines suffers as a personality from an excess of unconscious goodness. Rose Maylie, Madeline Bray, Kate Nickleby, Dolly Varden, Emma Haredale, Mary Graham:—they certainly could be shuffled and dealt out to any novel without danger of the reader's noticing the substitution. The slight exception may be Dolly Varden, who is flirtatious and fickle. Little Nell achieves individuality by dying; but Nell's role could have been acted by the same member of the company that played all the other heroine roles in the early Dickens novels.

The most interesting stock characters are the villains. Dickens put so much vitality into them that even the very stagey ones achieve energy which occasionally transforms them from the norm. The influence of the stage with regard to evil characters is not exactly a pale one. The best acting of Macready was done in such parts. For the villain who commits murder and is tormented by conscience, there was Macbeth; for the suave, smooth, smiling scoundrel, there was Stukely, in *The Gamester,* or Joseph Surface, in *The School for Scandal.* The early nineteenth-century plays began to feature a mustached, smartly-dressed-in-black, knavish, leering villain with gleaming smile, shining teeth, and crafty eyes. He doffed his hat when he acted Appius pursuing the daughter of Virginius, but he donned it when he was Doggrass making passes at Black-eyed Susan.

Character without logic or reality! Surely such an individual is Monks, who causes so much trouble for Oliver Twist! There has been some very special pleading for Monks by loyal Dickensians. Walter Dexter in his book, *Some Rogues and Vagabonds of Dickens,* defends him passionately:

> The character of Monks may travel on conventional lines: it savours much of the theatre, but we must not condemn either the character or the story as they are both true to type and more than ever in those early days was Dickens permeated (not to say obsessed) with a love and desire for the stage: and of all the stage figures he drew, none was

67

truer to the type beloved of the dramatist of the day, than was Monks, the villain of the piece.[22]

Monks deserves special attention. If he is unreal, it is because he acts as no one in real life could act. This is true, even if one removes his exaggerated behavior and melodramatic speech. His psychology is all wrong. Dickens had never met a person like him on the street or in any social contact; he had seen him on the stage in bad plays. He had also read about him in Lewis' novel called *The Monk*. Like his melodramatic relatives, Monks is an evil creature who vindictively pursues the hero without cause. Following in his footsteps are Ralph Nickleby and Gride; Quilp is a kind of distorted Richard III; John Chester and Gashford contribute their own stock behavior. But Monks is the clearest case. He grinds his teeth and curses when he is foiled. When he is unmasked, he says:

> "He came in my way at last. I began well; and, but for babbling drabs, I would have finished as I began."
>   As the villain folded his arms tight together, and muttered curses on himself in the impotence of baffled malice, Mr. Brownlow turned . . .[23]

Ralph Nickleby hears of a temporary setback to his plans with similar reactions:

> "There is some spell about that boy," said Ralph, grinding his teeth. "Circumstances conspire to help him. Talk of fortune's favours! What is even money to such Devil's luck as this?"[24]

However, Dickens' villains derive from Macbeth and Richard III as well as from Doggrass and his relatives. Ralph Nickleby has some convincing moments, and the greater intensity of Dickens' character portrayals tends to remove his villains from a part of the pattern of melodramatic falsehood. Sometimes they take off their grease paint. Bill Sikes commits a realistic murder which is vivid enough to horrify a reader accustomed to pale melodrama. Fagin is sinuously evil in his criminal role. Both of these individuals demand more than a character actor to depict their capacities for malice on the stage. Yet they are in the same novel with Monks, who wilts when Mr. Brownlow tells him off, and accepts his moral castigation in the worst tradition of the stage. Remember that Mr. Brownlow goes over all Monks's misdeeds in phrases which reek with well-worn language:

"Unworthy son, coward, liar,—you who hold your councils with thieves and murderers in dark rooms at night,—you whose plots and wiles have brought a violent death upon the head of one worth millions such as you,—you, who from your cradle were gall and bitterness to your own father's heart, and in whom all evil passions, vice, and profligacy festered, till they found a vent in a hideous disease which has made your face an index even to your mind,—you, Edward Leeford, do you still brave me!"

And Monks collapses, according to form:

"No, no, no!" returned the coward, overwhelmed by these accumulated charges.[25]

The *total* effect of these early novels must not be confused with the temporary manifestations of melodrama, but stock heroes, heroines, and villains were part of Dickens' plots, and their participation has a corresponding part in the effect of the whole. Many of Dickens' plots use the time-honored convention of conflict between parent and child over a love affair, the boy-meets-girl complication. The romantic plots of *Pickwick Papers, Barnaby Rudge, Martin Chuzzlewit,* and even *Dombey and Son* illustrate this type of action in Dickens' stories.

The plot most often seen in sentimental drama concerns the seduction of a girl by the villain. The situation is modified when the girl retains her virtue and saves herself to marry the hero. This is a staple intrigue for most of Dickens' novels, and it is treated traditionally in the early examples. The presence of little Oliver in the world is the result of a seduction, with some modifying sympathy for the difficult situation in which the parents found themselves; Kate Nickleby has to defend herself from Sir Mulberry Hawk; the fair ladies are carried off in *Barnaby Rudge,* to be rescued from the villain at the last moment; Pecksniff makes advances to Mary Graham; Carker elopes with Edith Dombey, falling under a train to incur just punishment when fleeing from her husband; Steerforth tempts little Emily away from the straight and narrow path; Lady Dedlock's secret in *Bleak House* is a love affair before her marriage; there are more. Situations of this sort in melodrama are legion.

A plot conflict which has become inextricably associated with nineteenth-century plays is that wherein the villain attempts to force the heroine to marry him by some power he has over her or over one she holds dear. This is sometimes facetiously called "the mortgage on the home" plot. Dickens appropriated it for his operetta, *The Village Coquettes,* and based the love story in *Nicholas Nickleby* on it. Ralph Nickleby and Gride attempt to force Madeline to marry Gride by means of the hold they have over her father. The situation is most familiar to Dickens lovers in the well-laid plans of Uriah Heep to gain control over Mr. Wickfield and thereby the lovely Agnes, in *David Copperfield.*

Another time-worn situation is the one in which a relative plots against the noble hero, as in *Oliver Twist* and *Nicholas Nickleby.* A variation of this motif involves the hero in a situation in which he is wrongfully accused of crime and narrowly escapes punishment at the very last moment. This idea furnishes the central reason for Kit's difficulties in *The Old Curiosity Shop,* it was used to plague Oliver, and it climaxes the troubles of the half-witted Barnaby Rudge.

A favorite romance theme, easily distorted in melodrama, presents parents and children lost to each other, miraculously restored at the end of the story. Thus Oliver's relatives show up after he successfully fends off all attempts to make him a criminal; Hugh goes to the gallows in *Barnaby Rudge* after learning that he is really the son of Sir John Chester; Smike's relationship to Ralph Nickleby is discovered too late to save the boy's life; and *Bleak House* contains a central plot situation dependent upon a mother's discovery of the existence of a daughter whom she had thought to be dead. A variant upon this theme, which Dickens uses twice, is to have the villainous father persecute his son unwittingly. Ralph Nickleby and Chester suffer this misfortune, although Chester is callous about it.

There are several more typical situations: a girl will not marry her lover because of the difference in their caste or rank—or vice-versa—(Steerforth and Emily, Lizzie Hexam and Eugene Wrayburn); one lover self-sacrificingly gives up the other because he thinks a third person is beloved (Tom Pinch, Rose Maylie, Walter Gay, Nicholas Nickleby, Clennam, Jarndyce, etc.); an elderly man has difficulties with his young wife, either doubting her love or attempting to subjugate her (Mr. Dombey, John Peerybingle in *The Cricket on the Hearth,* old Dr. Strong in *David Copperfield*); or a relative disguises himself in order to find out whether a loved one is worthy (*The Old Curiosity Shop, Martin Chuzzlewit,* and *Our Mutual Friend*).

70

Nothing in the world is likely to be entirely new, certainly not the action illustrated in fiction. Seduction, the pitfalls of true love, and the jealousies of relatives have graced the action of good and bad plays and novels. Careful motivation and development can make any time-worn plot fresh and convincing, and in these matters Dickens began to be more convincing from *David Copperfield* on. He prepared his climaxes carefully in the later novels; he built motivation as his skill grew; but not at first.

A few specific instances may serve to illuminate the argument. There is the abduction episode in *Barnaby Rudge*. The idea of an inflamed mob's carefully carrying off several women in a coach, leering at them from the outside, and then shutting them up for several days until there is time to do something to them, is so improbable that it escapes all comparison with reality. It is true that Dickens' audience would hardly accept a scene which showed a real mob attacking women. But the reason Dickens invented the episode was to prepare for the melodramatic climax in which Gashford finally arrives to carry off Emma Haredale. As on the stage, the rescuers appear in the nick of time.

Carefully constructed coincidence is the strong arm of melodrama. Dickens had a theory about coincidence which led him to imagine many scenes which have little but fortuitous sensation to justify them. The history of sensation for its own sake shows that it too often fails to stimulate readers in succeeding generations. Dickens once argued about his theory with Forster, who had objected to—of all things— the culmination of events which supplies the death of Madame Defarge at the hands of Miss Pross in *A Tale of Two Cities*. Dickens felt that there were plenty of people dying in Paris at the moment, and that one way was as good as another. He might as well select, from the coincidences at his disposal, one which fitted the general intention of his plot. He wrote:

> I am not clear, and I never have been clear, respecting the canon of fiction which forbids the interposition of accident in such a case as Madame Defarge's death. Where the accident is inseparable from the action and passion of the character; where it is strictly consistent with the entire design, and arises out of some culminating proceeding on the part of the individual which the whole story has led up to; it seems to me to become, as it were, an act of divine justice. And when I use

71

Miss Pross (though this is quite another question) to bring about such a catastrophe, I have the positive intention of making that half-comic intervention a part of the desperate woman's failure; and of opposing that mean death, instead of a desperate one in the streets, which she wouldn't have minded, to the dignity of Carton's. Wrong or right, this was my design, and seemed to me to be in the fitness of things.[26]

Dickens is either right or essentially on the right track in this instance. Occasional and climactic coincidence merits any author's defense, because a certain number of coincidences happen in real life. The *deus ex machina* who solves plot difficulties should not be a bad actor, however, or a novelist who can think of no better way to resolve his conflict at the moment. When Ham Peggotty and Steerforth die in the famous storm scene in *David Copperfield,* the reader usually feels that the climax happens in exact harmony with the novel's design. It is coincidence, unlikely but barely possible. Many readers will be sympathetic with the climactic coincidences of either *A Tale of Two Cities* or *David Copperfield* because, as Dickens says, "the accident is inseparable from the action and passion of the character." We are willing to believe that it might have happened so, and is it not interesting that it did?

These accidents are in the later novels; the more doubtful coincidences occur early. There is the love crisis faced by Nicholas Nickleby and Madeline Bray. Nicholas walks the streets all night trying to think of some way of preventing Madeline's marriage to Gride. Apparently nothing but an act of God, or the author, can save her. Both come to the rescue. Just before the marriage ceremony, Madeline's father drops dead, thus releasing her from the need of marrying a man she does not love. Nicholas welcomes this stroke of fate with understandable surprise, even though Madeline's feelings must be mixed. This coincidence is not quite the same thing as Madame Defarge's death in *A Tale of Two Cities.* People were not dying all about in the streets.

Other signs of less important melodramatic manipulation of action illuminate Dickens' practice of explaining antecedent circumstances to the reader. This recapitulation is handled as on the stage, by dialogue. He often solved awkward situations by having one character overhear another, and on occasion he even depended upon the overhearing of thoughts spoken out loud in some form of soliloquy.

Extremely coincidental overhearing occurs at four important moments in *Nicholas Nickleby,* as well as in several other novels.[27]

Several instances may be cited briefly to show how he overcame the excesses of melodrama, and this development can be substantiated as the later novels are examined in more detail. In *David Copperfield* Aunt Betsey and Mr. Dick discuss David's future with the Murdstones, after David had run away from London to Dover. Aunt Betsey asks David whether he wants to go back to his stepfather. This is how Dickens describes the feelings of his hero:

> I answered no, and entreated her not to let me go. I said that neither Mr. or Miss Murdstone had ever liked me, or had ever been kind to me. That they had made my mama, who always loved me dearly, unhappy about me, and that I knew it well, and that Peggotty knew it. I said that I had been more miserable than I thought any could believe who only knew how young I was. And I begged and prayed my aunt—I forget in what terms now, but I remember that they affected me very much then—to befriend and protect me, for my father's sake.[28]

If this passage had been in *Oliver Twist,* it would have been in melodramatic and elocutionary terms, perhaps like these:

> "Oh! for God's sake, do not make me go back with them! Let me run away and die in the fields. Pray, pray, pray, have mercy upon me, and let me stay. For the sake of my dear, dear father in heaven, have mercy upon me!"

An excellent example of artistry occurs in *David Copperfield* when the villainous Uriah Heep is exposed. In the early novels, this kind of climax suffers from the fact that Dickens has not found opportunity for much preparation for his emotional scene. He needs to explain a great deal of the intrigue, and his characters speak in high-flown periods of rhetorical speech. But Mr. Micawber is an elocutionary person by nature. He has endeared himself through many pages by talking in an alternately flowery and concise manner. Therefore it is perfectly natural for him to expose Uriah Heep in the same fashion. His bewildering array of verbal flourishes adds a comic but convincing touch to the very serious proceedings. In this climax, the effect has been prepared for; it depends upon a character who has talked bombastically all through the tale, not just for the occasion.

In the earlier novels, the characters often assumed melodramatic mannerisms for special moments; Mr. Micawber is Mr. Melodrama himself.

The heroes of Dickens progress in intricacy and complexity from pale stock characters to human beings, from flat to round studies. Beginning with Nicholas Nickleby, he tried to show a hero who was a mixture of good and bad, an individual who learned to overcome his weaknesses in order to achieve stature by the end of the tale. He scratched the surface with Nicholas, and he did a little better with Martin Chuzzlewit; then he came closer to a full portrait with David Copperfield. He experimented with the reformation of Sidney Carton and reached his best study of the developing, completely individualized hero in Pip, in *Great Expectations*. His heroines follow a similar development, Little Dorrit being a great improvement over Little Nell, and Estella and Bella Wilfer, toward the close of his career, achieving lifelike qualities.

When a novelist attempts several contrasting ways of telling a story, he aims at a more complex effect than the novelist who confines himself to a carefully studied portrayal of a single character by a single technique of narration. Dickens' problems as an artistic craftsman were dependent upon learning to bring all the techniques at his command under control. Farce and caricature blossomed early; the effective development of conflicting actions in plot structure bore fruit late.

CHAPTER V

Tears and Terror:
The Techniques of Sentiment and
Sensation

HE EPISODES and the atmosphere of a plot may be so arranged that the novelist appeals to a special emotion in his readers. Wilkie Collins tried to sum up the writer's creed when he said, "Make 'em laugh; make 'em cry; make 'em wait." Dickens would have added, "Make 'em shiver." Two of his most important narrative resources aimed at the evocation of sympathetic sorrow and convulsive horror. These techniques added immeasurably to his immediate popularity, for his readers wept and shivered in great numbers. But no part of his attempt to secure constant narrative contrast achieved greater disparity of effect for later generations than these devices.

Dickens has often been charged with being sentimental. It is evident that he was. From some readers this is a compliment, but for the vast majority in the twentieth century it is a complaint. A definition of sentimentality provides two conflicting interpretations. The positive one describes sentimentality as susceptibility to the tender emotions, sympathy for any unfortunate victim, and dissatisfaction with triumphant injustice. The negative meaning suggests weak or mawkish emotion, the tendency to take refuge in tears rather than action, and unheroic self-pity.

In the fiction of Dickens, the artistic effect depends upon which kind of sentimentality is present. To cry may mean that one possesses lubricated tear ducts, nothing more. The twentieth-century reader feels that one should weep for the right reasons and in season; great and sincere sorrow expresses itself in heartbreak. The other face of laughter is tears; Dickens believed that the whole man is two-faced.

75

The reader who does not understand this premise has never turned around. The simplest way to state this contention is to say that positive sentiment may be defended, negative sentiment deplored. Dickens used the negative kind in his early novels, but turned more and more to the positive variety in his late work.

An examination of Dickens' craftsmanship shows how he tried to arouse the tender feelings of his readers. Inevitably a question of fashion comes into the discussion. It is not now as proper—from the standpoint of etiquette—to weep openly. The twentieth century theoretically praises restraint. Accordingly, a modern reader may reasonably ask: Did Dickens intend to stir emotions of sympathy in passages which no longer have verity? Did he ever, when he asked his audience to cry, discover that some section of his readers stubbornly refused to reach for handkerchiefs? In his day thousands of people cried at the death of little Nell or little Paul Dombey; few adults weep today.

The difference between yesterday and today is not only in fashion, it is also in workmanship. One supposes that essential sympathy remains the same in any age. Many adults still fight back tears when Sidney Carton goes to the guillotine. Surely the climactic scene of *A Tale of Two Cities* is more effective writing than the chapters which describe the death of little Nell. The result depends not only on degree, but absolute effect. We do not cry a little for Nell and more for Carton. Modern readers tend to be moved or nauseated.

If we assume that an appeal to sympathy is subject to the principle of tragic katharsis, the whole problem resolves itself into a matter of artistry. The sentimental models which Dickens knew were not always distinguished, and it is natural that he would imitate them at first. The mawkish emotional novels he mentions in his writings include Goldsmith's *Vicar of Wakefield,* Mackenzie's *Man of Feeling,* and Brooke's *Fool of Quality.* On a higher level he found Richardson uninteresting, but he enjoyed Sterne. He was familiar with many sentimental stage plays. The plays particularly directed themselves to themes like the death of a loved one, recovery from sickness, the problems of childhood, unselfish charity, humble loyalty, gift-giving, devotion, and general sorrow. In all these models the tradition required that the characters themselves cry either occasionally or constantly.

The basic narrative method employed by the sentimental tradition was to cry so that the observers should be encouraged to join in. Rarely did one of these authors restrain himself so that he showed something so moving that his readers cried spontaneously. One is tempted to say that the first method caused most of Dickens' difficulties, exposing him to the criticism of those who dislike sentimentality. His predecessors enjoyed weeping, they presented characters who wept constantly, and they established patterns of action which made readers weep in their time. When Sterne sympathizes with Maria in *The Sentimental Journey,* he says:

> I sat down close to her; and Maria let me wipe them [her tears] away as they fell with my handkerchief.—I then steep'd it in my own —and then in hers—and then in mine—and then I wip'd hers again— and as I did it, I felt such undescribable emotions within me, as I am sure could not be accounted for from any combination of matter and emotion.[1]

Sterne, dripping as this sounds, was far from being at the extreme of the tradition. Besides he alternated his sentiment with suggestive references to situations which induce a kind of snort or snicker. But most sentimental authors confined themselves to tears. A certain Mr. Villiers, in *The Adventures of a Bank-Note,* by Thomas Bridges, finds that:

> The tears cours'd one another down his manly cheeks, and form'd a rapid current o'er his garments.[2]

Colman, at the height of the popularity of sentimental drama, makes one of his characters say, in *The Heir-At-Law*:

> I believe I've been drowned myself, for the salt-water runs out of my eyes by pails-full.[3]

The crying habit attacks the characters of Dickens on many occasions. The most moderate example one can find in *Pickwick Papers* appears in a conversation between the Pickwickians after Mr. Jingle has eloped with Rachel Wardle, leaving Mr. Tupman at the post:

> "Snodgrass," said Mr. Pickwick earnestly, "how is our friend—he is not ill?"
> "No," replied Mr. Snodgrass; and a tear trembled on his sentimental eyelid, like a raindrop on a window-frame. "No; he is not ill."[4]

The single raindrop might serve as an argument for extraordinary restraint in Dickens, except that it becomes a genuine cloudburst later. In *Nicholas Nickleby* there is weeping at what seems every opportunity, even the stolid John Browdie joining in at the end. Someone cries at least once every ten pages in *The Old Curiosity Shop,* and the grand total is reached in *Dombey and Son,* in which Florence alone has eighty-eight separate weeping spells.

For the intelligent reader, emotion cannot be turned on like a water faucet. The tradition expected sympathetic tears whenever the source was mentioned or the process described. Whatever sentiment is present usually descends to mawkish self-pity and destroys whatever sympathy the modern reader might normally feel. The method depends upon extremes, as did so many of Dickens' devices. For example, all humanitarian sentimentalists are interested in kindness to animals. Uncle Toby was concerned, in Sterne's *Tristram Shandy,* even for the safety of a fly, and Brooke's love for animals in the late eighteenth century established a cult. There are shades of Uncle Toby in the prayer Dickens wrote for his children:

> Make me kind to my nurses and servants and to all beggars and poor people and let me never be cruel to any dumb creature, for if I am cruel to anything, even to a poor little fly, you, who are so good, will never love me.[5]

There were obviously no fly-swatters in the Dickens household, and pests must have found sanctuary.

In *Barnaby Rudge,* during the No-Popery Riots, some houses are burned:

> At one house near Moorfields, they found in one of the rooms some canary birds in cages, and these they cast into the fire alive. The poor little creatures screamed, it was said, like infants, when they were flung upon the blaze; and one man was so touched that he tried in vain to save them, which roused the indignation of the crowd, and nearly cost him his life.[6]

Dickens loved dogs, but it is probably optimistic to expect every reader to share his excessive affection for them. Florence Dombey's dog, Diogenes, takes over some of the characteristics of humanitarian sentimentality in his sympathy for his mistress. There is the passage in which the dog rose up on his hind legs, with his awkward fore paws on her shoulders, licked her face and hands, nestled his great head against her heart, and wagged his tail till he was tired.[7]

In contrast to this picture one needs to look at Dora's dog Jip in *David Copperfield;* the ludicrous pet achieves the stature of high comedy. At least, Dickens *occasionally* laughed at mawkish sentimentality.

Lovers and dogs follow one another in expressing their emotions. The behavior of heroes and heroines under the influence of the divine passion is startling at most times in fiction, never more so than when Smollett's lovers succumb to their feelings. Peregrine Pickle parts from Emily in this abandoned fashion:

> "My charming Emily," cried the impatient lover, throwing himself at her feet, "Why will you deal out my happiness in such scanty portions? Why will you thus mince the declaration which would overwhelm me with pleasure, and cheer my lonely reflection while I sigh amid the solitude of separation?" His fair mistress, melted by this image, replied with the tears gushing from her eyes, "I'm afraid I shall feel that separation more severely than you imagine." Transported by this flattering concession, he pressed her to his breast, and while her head reclined upon his neck, mingled his tears with hers in great abundance, breathing the most tender vows of eternal fidelity. The gentle heart of Sophy could not bear this scene unmoved; she wept with sympathy, and encouraged the lovers to resign themselves to the will of fate, and support their spirits with the hope of meeting again on happier terms. Finally, after mutual promises, exhortations, and endearments, Peregrine took his leave, his heart being so full that he could scarcely pronounce the word Adieu.[8]

Peregrine's lack of self-control is notorious, and there are many other reasons for disliking him. But the following scene clinches the case against his character. Emily is dancing with someone else:

> His endeavours to conceal the situation of his thoughts were so violent, that his constitution could not endure the shock; the sweat ran down his forehead in a stream, the colour vanished from his cheeks, his knees began to totter, and his eyesight to fail; so that he must have fallen at his full length upon the floor had he not retired very abruptly into another room, where he threw himself upon a couch, and fainted.[9]

Examination of the habits of Dickens' predecessors in sentimentality is valuable if it shows that Dickens is often restrained if only in comparison. When Harry Maylie proposes to Rose in *Oliver Twist* and is refused, he gives way to despair. But Peregrine outdoes him by a comfortable margin. When Nicholas Nickleby argues with Madeline about her feeling of duty to her father, a duty which will force her to marry Gride, he reaches heights of irrepressible agony. But he retains consciousness. By the time Dickens wrote *David Copperfield,* he was able to present a normal, balanced story of David's love for Dora. Knowing the hero's character, the reader understands that he is in love, that his passion can be amusing, sincere, and sentimental at the same time—something which was not present in Dickens' models or in *Nicholas Nickleby.* It is noteworthy that Dickens gives no evidence of having read Jane Austen.

The numerous death scenes in Dickens' novels constitute his most concentrated appeals to tears. In the story of little Nell, whose pathetic death started him on experimentation with occasional unhappy events to contrast with the pleasant endings he was accustomed to invent, Forster argued that Nell was destined to death, that sorrow was her lot. He says:

> I was responsible for its tragic ending. He had not thought of killing her, when, about half-way through, I asked him to consider whether it did not necessarily belong to his own conception, after taking so mere a child through such a tragedy of sorrow, to lift her out of the commonplace of ordinary happy endings, so that the gentle pure little figure and form should never change to the fancy. All that I meant he seized at once, and never turned aside from it again.[10]

Up to the writing of *Bleak House,* Dickens seemed always ready to accept Forster's suggestions as a kind of Victorian chorus. The pompous critic knew unerringly what the public would admire, and what readers would buy. This particular idea of Forster's paid off in sales, but its logic is open to question. He says that a child who goes through "a tragedy of sorrow" is destined to death. This depends, naturally, upon the sorrows encountered, and many a child has suffered as much as Nell and remained alive longer than Nell did. Disease entered into the circumstances, but the exact illness is left indefinite. Obviously she died from *some* cause, but the point is that her death is not inevitable from the premises of the story. Dickens might have saved her, as in any melodrama; he did not intend to "kill her" when he began. From the viewpoint of tragic katharsis, the narrative effect depends upon the circumstances which produce the illusion of being inescapable or inevitable. The mannerisms of the sentimental tradition interfere also with Forster's logic. The action thus gives the impression of unfortunate coincidence rather than fate or punishment which derives from something the character did. It is easier to conclude that Forster and Dickens decided, in effect, "A death scene will draw tears from sympathetic readers; they will buy more copies of the book; therefore I will insert a death scene and lay it on thick." This conclusion is clearer in examining the death of little Paul Dombey, for necessity is even less certain in the later novel.

Loyal Dickensians have argued in harmony with Forster that Nell *was* born to sorrow. The mood of the story contributes to the death scene, and Dickens was so fond of his character that he hated to let her die. When she finally did, he suffered almost as much as if he had lost a member of his own family—perhaps more. He had to delay the following installment until he could get over some portion of his own sorrow and finish the novel. For him, at least, her death arose out of the necessities of fiction according to Forster—which doubled for fate at the moment. His memories of his wife's beloved sister Mary unquestionably contributed to his own reactions. Modern psychoanalysts have had a field day with this circumstance.

However, judgment of the artistic effect of the heroine's death does not rest entirely upon the author's evident sincerity. Dickens related the details of her decease with all the heightened rhetoric at his command. He declaimed while he eulogized her. Heaven spreads its golden wings over Nell, hatching her tender soul so that it takes wings and flies away with the angels of sorrow. Or if you do not like that, listen to Dickens himself:

> She was dead. No sleep so beautiful and calm, so free from trace of pain, so fair to look upon. She seemed a creature fresh from the hand of God, and waiting for the breath of life; not one who had lived and suffered death.
>
> Her couch was dressed with here and there some winter berries and green leaves, gathered in a spot she had been used to favour. "When I die, put near me something that has loved the light, and had the sky above it always." Those were her words.
>
> She was dead. Dear, gentle, patient, noble Nell was dead. Her little bird—a poor slight thing the pressure of a finger would have

81

crushed—was stirring nimbly in its cage; and the strong heart of its child-mistress was mute and motionless forever.

Where were the traces of her early cares, her sufferings, and fatigues? All gone. Sorrow was dead indeed in her, but peace and perfect happiness were born; imaged in her tranquil beauty and profound repose.

And still her former self lay there, unaltered in this change. Yes. The old fireside had smiled upon that same sweet face; it had passed like a dream through haunts of misery and care; at the door of the poor schoolmaster on the summer evening, before the furnace fire upon the cold wet night, at the still bedside of the dying boy, there had been the same mild lovely look. So shall we know the angels in their majesty, after death.[11]

It is excruciatingly overwritten, but it has served many a preacher in a funeral oration. Nor does any writer before Dickens come up to this mark, whatever you think of the mark. Dickens dissects every small portion of Nell's character which would add to the effect of tears; he squeezes out every sigh. But if you think the scene can be defended, what about the chapters which follow and which say over and over again much the same thing?

This kind of writing sold so well that it was natural for Dickens to try it again with little Paul Dombey. Here there is more evidence than in the previous case that Dickens planned the death from a commercial angle. The purpose of *Dombey and Son* was to illustrate Mr. Dombey's questionable philosophy of life. He was all business enterprise, with no sympathetic understanding of his fellowmen. He loved his son because he thought the boy should continue the father's way of life; Paul would inherit the business and carry on. Dickens, to prove to the world that such a man was wrong, that his philosophy of life was evil, had to kill Paul to punish the father. If one agrees with his premises, the death is coincidentally fortuitous, but not inevitable. Little Paul was really too good to live, even if little Nell was too good to die. But Dickens and God loved them both.

The most extreme attack on Dickens' sentimentality is argued in a book by Kingsmill Lunn entitled *The Sentimental Journey*. The case is that Dickens deteriorated as he grew older, his sentiment became more maudlin, and his character decayed so much that he finally left his wife for Ellen Ternan. There is not much point in denying a thesis which can be easily destroyed in any one of a number of ways, but artistically it is completely wrong. Dickens was still sentimental when he died, but from *David Copperfield* on, his novels show more restraint and control of the means by which he appealed to tears. His characters weep less and less. Furthermore, it would be very difficult to criticize him for mawkish sentimentality in the latter half of his career on the basis of his death scenes.

Dora dies, for example, and her death affects David as any reader will admit that it should. But Dora had never been described as a majestic angel, like little Nell. She was in some measure human, with weaknesses which contribute to her normality. David, as he waits for Agnes to come back from the death chamber, wonders:

> Would it, indeed, have been better if we had loved each other as a boy and girl, and forgotten it?[12]

Since in real life he had never married the prototype of Dora, this question is illuminating. And yet, when Dora dies, Jip dies too. There is sentiment present, of course, but it cannot be accurately described as weak or mawkish:

> It is over. Darkness comes before my eyes, and, for a time, all things are blotted out of my remembrance.[13]

In *The Old Curiosity Shop* discussion of Nell's death goes on for two more chapters. Dickens begins the next one in *David Copperfield*:

> This is not the time at which I am to enter on the state of my mind beneath its load of sorrow. I came to think that the Future was walled up before me, that the energy and action of my life were at an end, that I never could find any refuge but in the grave. I came to think so, I say, but not in the first shock of my grief. It slowly grew to that.[14]

In its measure this is brief, reasonable, and restrained, still effective in the twentieth century in contrast to Nell's death.

The characters in succeeding novels are also portrayed with progressive restraint, even if the word must be understood in a comparative sense, whether they live or die. Thus Esther Summerson is an advance upon previous heroines, although for some readers she has not made the full journey from artificial perfection to humanity. Sissy, in *Hard Times,* retains some but not all of the qualities of sentimental allegory. Little Dorrit is many times superior to little Nell as

83

a real individual. Estella and Bella are Dickens' most human and least sentimental heroines, perhaps because they had some of the characteristics of Ellen Ternan. This latter fact alone completely demolishes the arguments of a critic like Kingsmill Lunn.

The greatest *emotional* death scene in a Dickens novel is the guillotine episode in *A Tale of Two Cities*. Here there is an argument for enduring tragic effect. Someone was fated to die through circumstances which seem completely beyond his or the author's control. The curse of the St. Evremondes and the cumulation of their sins plague Charles Darnay so that he must suffer for the wrongs committed by his ancestors and his class. Darnay symbolizes unwittingly the corrupt aristocracy of old France, even though as an individual he has not merited punishment. His conviction and sentence are inevitable. That Carton would substitute himself for Darnay provides sympathy and admiration for the hero who achieves nobility by a last effort at atonement for his own previous incapacity. He dies for Darnay so that Lucy may be happy.

The artistry of the climactic scene is admirable. There is no excessive maundering about the horror and pity of death. It is told with care for detail. The scene is prepared by Carton's previous memory of the burial service and the resurrection theme. There is the beautiful touch of the little milliner who is terribly afraid to die. Carton comforts her and strengthens his own resolution in the act. The knitting women sit about and count stitches and heads. The crowd roars; the great knife falls steadily, crashing as it comes down; it is the little milliner's turn, just before Carton's:

> She kisses his lips; he kisses hers; they solemnly bless each other. The spare hand does not tremble as he releases it; nothing worse than a sweet, bright constancy is in the patient face. She goes next before him—is gone; the knitting-women count twenty-two.
>
> "I am the Resurrection and the Life, saith the Lord: he that believeth in me, though he were dead, yet shall he live: and whosoever liveth and believeth in me shall never die."
>
> The murmuring of many voices, the uplifting of many faces, the pressing on of many footsteps in the outskirts of the crowd, so that it swells forward in a mass, like one great heave of water, all flashes away. Twenty-three.[15]

84

Aristotle would have found the tragedy more pervasive if Darnay had died instead of Carton. But still, the Defense rests. . . .

The building of an effect of sensation and horror so that the reader will shudder and shiver is a related narrative device, psychologically allied to weeping. Its background in fiction is represented by the strong Gothic tradition which influenced the young Dickens. The chilling, grotesque atmosphere of terror derived principally from Walpole, Mrs. Ann Radcliffe, Monk Lewis, and Sir Walter Scott. To these writers one must add Dickens' first literary friend, William Harrison Ainsworth, who professed to model his novels on those of Mrs. Radcliffe.

Ainsworth in his preface to *Rookwood,* which appeared just before *Pickwick,* gives some hint of what he felt were the most important features of the Radcliffe technique:

> I resolved to attempt a story in the bygone style of Mrs. Radcliffe (which had always inexpressible charms for me), substituting an old English squire, an old English manorial residence, and an old English highwayman for the Italian marchese, the castle, and the brigand of the great mistress of Romance.[16]

The Gothic scene, which originally came from the French model of Prévost and Baculard d'Arnaud, reflected exciting adventure, violent emotions, gloomy atmosphere, forests, castles, dungeons, graveyards, and secret passageways. The grosser sensations inspired by terror and crime aimed to make the flesh of the reader creep. This kind of narrative purpose serves as an ugly twin to sentimentality, stirring reactions which are not always wholesome.

The most specific influence upon Dickens which can be discerned in this genre is that of Scott. Scott's tales of terror are included in his historical panorama, but *The Bride of Lammermoor* and *Kenilworth,* among others, illustrate also the original Gothic tradition. Dickens is on record as admiring both these novels, and he mentions *Rob Roy* more frequently than any other Scott tale. This influence shows most clearly in the way he described gloomy atmosphere in architecture, landscape, and weather. It also underlies his dependence upon exciting conflict which ends in violence or murder. Like Ainsworth, Dickens and

Scott transferred menacing scenes from other lands and set them in the British Isles.

The functional inspiration of the horror novelist is inherent in the word *Gothic*. One of Dickens' most interesting debts to Gothic sensationalism centers about the style of architecture, the pseudo-medieval setting which presents the mysterious old house or building as a substitute for the original castle. He was particularly struck by the fictional possibilities of that mysterious type of mansion which contains dark corridors and dimly lighted rooms, and in which all manner of appropriately evil deeds might happen.

A typical setting with corresponding action was established by Mrs. Radcliffe in *The Mysteries of Udolpho*. When Emily comes to Montoni's castle in the Apennines, she is deeply affected by her first view of the forbidding structure, gloom shrouding the ramparts, mystery frowning from the mouldering turrets, and evil hovering over the desolate gateway.[17] In this same manner Scott was likely to describe a ruined castle set on precipitous rocks, with a tower "like the sheeted specter of some huge giant."[18] Wild and disconsolate were the words for these buildings, and Dickens took over the habit of describing such places whenever he needed a mysterious and evil background for the action of his more sensational plot sequences.

There is an actual Gothic castle in the interpolated story of the Bagman's Uncle in *Pickwick*. Ghostly and macabre dwellings haunt much of his apprentice writing, in *Sketches by Boz* and several filler stories in *Pickwick*. This influence even stretches as far as the undertakers' shops in his various novels, although these scenes may be grotesquely comic too. One of his most interesting descriptions is the house to which Monks summons Mr. and Mrs. Bumble for the interview which adds suspense to the secret of Oliver Twist's parentage. Monks was named for Lewis's avenging Monk, who pursues the hero tirelessly in the sinister novel of the same name. The ghostly old building in *Oliver Twist* has all the furnishings of the tale of terror:

> In the heart of this cluster of huts; and skirting the river, which its upper stories overhung; stood a large building, formerly used as a manufactory of some kind: and which had, in its day, probably furnished employment to the inhabitants of the surrounding tenements. But it had long since gone to ruin. The rat, the worm, and the action of the damp, had weakened and rotted the piles on which it stood;

86

and a considerable portion of the building had already sunk down into the water beneath; while the remainder, tottering and bending over the dark stream, seemed to wait a favourable opportunity of following its old companion, and involving itself in the same fate.[19]

The castle has been modernized, simplified, and removed from the romantic and distant past to the realizable present. Quilp's summer home, half-ruined and propped up to the tavern close to the Thames, is another pseudo-Gothic structure. The old cathedral where Nell and her grandfather find refuge furnishes an appropriate setting for her death. Probably the most emphatic use of Gothic atmosphere is in *Barnaby Rudge;* Barnaby in his idiot costume, carrying his ugly raven, lives in several buildings which might have graced a scene from Scott or Mrs. Radcliffe.

In this last novel, Haredale's residence has everything but the towering precipices and the mighty but mysterious forests:

> It was a dreary, silent building, with echoing courtyards, desolate turret-chambers, and whole suites of rooms shut up and mouldering to ruin.
> The terrace-garden, dark with the shade of overhanging trees, had an air of melancholy that was quite oppressive. Great iron gates, disused for many years, and red with rust, drooping on their hinges and overgrown with long rank grass, seemed as though they tried to sink into the ground, and hide their fallen state among the friendly weeds. The fantastic monsters on the walls, green with age and damp, and covered here and there with moss, looked grim and desolate. There was a sombre aspect even on that part of the mansion which was inhabited and kept in good repair, that struck the beholder with a sense of sadness; of something forlorn and failing, whence cheerfulness was banished. . . . The very ghost of a house, haunting the old spot in its outward form, and that was all.[20]

This description is derived from and squarely in the tradition. With it are all the trappings: the shadowy fugitive who menaces Mrs. Rudge, the mysterious forces which threaten her happiness and the well-being of her idiot son. Later in the tale Haredale spends many nights in the Rudge house from which Mrs. Rudge has been forced to flee by the murderer, waiting and watching, hoping to catch the mysterious visitant when next he returns to plague his wife.

The list of ghostly and ghastly buildings in Dickens' novels is a fairly long one, and some of them are quite impressive. There is the chemist's school in *The Haunted Man* (which is a Gothic tale in itself); there is Krook's house and shop in *Bleak House* (which serves as a proper setting for the old man's death by spontaneous combustion); there is the old Clennam mansion in *Little Dorrit* (with its melancholy, mysterious air, strange visitors going hither and yon, hints of secret passageways, noises in the walls, and the final collapse of the old place); there is Miss Havisham's Satis House (with its unused rooms, dark passages, even the uncleared wedding feast left to decay through the years); and there is the old cathedral in *Edwin Drood* (where a murder may have taken place and where a body may have been buried with quicklime).

One of the pregnant signs of the Gothic sensational plot is the mysterious and pursuing villain. When Emily first "thought she saw a shadow gliding between the pillars," in *The Mysteries of Udolpho,* she suffers the beginning of a series of shadowy visitations contrived to wear her out and drive the reader to nervous frenzy. Lewis's Monk became the prototype for this kind of menacing fiend in all the novels which followed. Only a few of Dickens' villains possess this haunting evil, but one naturally remembers Monks, Barnaby's father, and Compeyson in *Great Expectations.*

Weather is also a Gothic factor in narration. The elements in a tale of terror cooperate whenever anything awful is about to happen. This enveloping air is usually stormy; it may be limited to mist and fog. Dickens states the argument for such atmosphere in *Barnaby Rudge,* as if he were writing a textbook on creative style:

> There are times when, the elements being in unusual commotion, those who are bent on daring enterprises, or agitated by great thoughts, whether of good or evil, feel a mysterious sympathy with the tumult of nature, and are roused into corresponding violence. In the midst of thunder, lightning, and storm, many tremendous deeds have been committed; men, self-possessed before, have given a sudden loose to passions they could no longer control. The demons of wrath and despair have striven to emulate those who ride the whirlwind and direct the storm; and man, lashed into madness with the roaring winds and boiling waters, has become for the time as wild and merciless as the elements themselves.[21]

The first attempt at building such atmosphere in Dickens' novels comes in *Pickwick* when the reader is prepared for Mr. Pickwick's reading of "The Madman's Manuscript" by typical cooperation from stormy weather. *Oliver Twist* and *The Old Curiosity Shop* utilize the assistance of aroused nature, and storms rise and abate throughout *Barnaby Rudge*. The first really masterful use of atmosphere for a terrible deed occurs in *Martin Chuzzlewit* when Jonas rides down in a coach with Tigg to see Pecksniff and plans to murder him while the storm rages outside. At the time the actual deed is done, nature is particularly vicious, and Dickens begins, "It is a common fancy that nature seems to sleep at night. It is a false fancy, as who should know better than he?" The reader realizes that everything is watching Jonas: the fishes, the streams, the rivers, the birds, the trees, the moon, the stars, the grass—perhaps a stalk of corn.

The climactic storm in *David Copperfield* is more than accompanying atmosphere, for it wrecks the ship which allows Ham to perish in attempting to save the stranger who turns out to be Steerforth. The spontaneous combustion scene in *Bleak House* has overtones which transcend the forces of nature in sympathy with violence. But as an example of what Dickens could do in this manner, the finest instance occurs in his last book, *Edwin Drood,* when a violent storm shakes the cathedral town on the night Edwin disappears:

> The darkness is augmented and confused, by flying dust from the earth, dry twigs from the trees, and great ragged fragments from the rooks' nests up in the tower. The trees themselves so toss and creak, as this tangible part of the darkness whirls madly about, that again a crack, and a rushing fall, denote that some large branch has yielded to the storm. . . . Not such power of wind has blown for many a winter night. Chimneys topple in the streets, and people hold to posts and corners, and to one another, to keep themselves upon their feet. The violent rushes abate not, but increase in frequency and fury until at midnight, when the streets are empty, the storm goes thundering along them, rattling at all the latches, and tearing at all the shutters, as if warning people to get up and fly with it, rather than have the roofs brought down upon their brains.[22]

Sensational action in horror stories has a tendency to follow selected plot developments. There is likely to be a curse on a family or a house; or foul fiends persecute a hero or heroine for reasons which are vile or inhuman; or suffering and torture continuously threaten loved ones; or passion culminates in murder. Sometimes there is mystery as well as suspense. Mrs. Radcliffe always explained her mysterious sequences eventually, but early Gothic novelists left some of their explanations to supernatural forces or even forgot to explain things which needed illumination. In *Barnaby Rudge* Dickens gives us the murderer who is forced through influences beyond his control to return to the scene of his crime on its anniversary; in *Bleak House* he sets an ancestral curse on Sir Leicester Dedlock's estate, centered about the Ghost's Walk; in *Martin Chuzzlewit* he calls up Tigg's dream in which the dreamer tries to keep a terrible being out of his room and awakens to find Jonas Chuzzlewit standing beside his bed.

This last incident was used many times by "the great mistress of Romance." Emily, in *The Mysteries of Udolpho,* is assigned to a room in a ruined part of the old castle, and people who do not belong there insist upon disturbing her late at night. She is always half-asleep, it would seem, and coming awake to watch a latch slip, or to hear a noise and see a dim form enter the room and approach her bed. She nearly faints with terror, pretends to be asleep, and hopes till the last moment that the fiend will go away. Eventually she loses the power to scream. Nothing ever happens in these nocturnal encounters. If the visitor intends harm, he changes his mind and retreats. But if the reader does not know that the author is watching, he may fear the worst until the moment of release. He may also be relieved to know that Emily fortuitously neglected to take off her clothes before she pulled up the covers. The modern reader has a tendency to find such effects contrived rather than terrible, since he may have been scared by experts who have written since that time.

A similar scene in *The Old Curiosity Shop* is the most interesting case of exact borrowing which can be identified. Little Nell is on the point of going to sleep in an inn, a rambling old hostelry with long dull corridors and wide gloomy staircases:

> At last, sleep gradually stole upon her—a broken fitful sleep, troubled by dreams of falling down from high towers, and waking with a start and in great terror. A deeper slumber followed this—and then—What! That figure in the room!
>
> A figure was there. Yes, she had drawn up the blind to admit the light when it should dawn, and there, between the foot of the bed and the dark casement, it crouched and slunk along, groping its way with noiseless hands, and stealing round the bed. She had no voice to cry for help, no power to move, but lay still, watching it.
>
> On it came—on, silently and stealthily, to the bed's head. The breath so near her pillow, that she shrunk back into it, lest those

wandering hands should light upon her face. Back again it stole to
the window—then turned its head toward her . . .[23]

The outcome is anticlimax, for it is Nell's grandfather, not Quilp, who
has come to rob her.

All in all, the Gothic technique added another narrative device
to the arsenal of dramatic weapons in Dickens' possession. It is not
a weapon that served him unfailingly, yet it hit many marks. The
much-praised atmosphere of *Bleak House* derives from this technique,
and the background of the Marshalsea Prison fixes the symbolism of
Little Dorrit. Satis House provides a reminder that "great expectations" may come to something like the dying old remnant of living
things which have lost contact with eternal hope. Early in *Great
Expectations* Dickens makes miraculous use of the atmosphere of
terror in the graveyard scenes in which Magwitch catches Pip. Certainly Dickens had achieved complete mastery of the best Gothic
manner when he got to *Edwin Drood*.

Like the other techniques—after caricature and farce—this one
became more and more effective as Dickens continued to use it—
at first for its own sake, later as part of his over-all plan. The effect
of horror merely accentuates the melodramatic plot situations being
developed in *Oliver Twist* or *Barnaby Rudge*. In the beginning Dickens
was likely to leave motivation or explanation of a mysterious plot
sequence till he came to a sudden, revealing climax. Some readers are
not quite sure, unless they read more than once, exactly what happened
to Oliver Twist's parents or why Monks acts as he does. Even in a
late tale like *Great Expectations,* the details of the Compeyson-Mag-
witch-Havisham intrigue remain misty.

As the novels poured forth their contrasts, Dickens saw more and
more clearly the possibilities of fiction which developed the broad,
diffused panorama of life. He alternated and contrasted his characters
and his plots. He turned from one technique to another. At his best
he surpassed other novelists because of this versatility whenever his
effects came off and whenever his contrasts fell into their proper places
in his picture of life. When the sentimentality and the atmosphere of
horror came under control he was ready to write his telescopic novels,
to approach life from many angles, and to make his artistic progression
geometrical rather than arithmetical in intention.

CHAPTER VI

Dialectic Romanticism: Techniques in Fusion

ITH ALL his interest in characterization and action, in comedy and sentiment, Dickens believed that great fiction is about something, that it has important content. As he developed his narrative devices and styles, he directed his attention to propaganda and purpose. He hid idealism behind the salesman's mask; he wanted to improve the world by his fiction.

The artistry of a novelist rarely lends itself to systematic analysis of his ideas. What he believes must show itself in action; the most convincing theses are better implied than expounded. However, certain abuses may also be attacked openly, and Dickens felt that the scheme of human affairs is subject to many abuses. He lived by writing fiction, he made money by selling what he wrote, and he made concessions to public taste; but he held his art in lofty esteem and believed its highest purpose is to rise above entertainment and escape. Novels in this sense are means to an end; the value of his stories gained inner importance to him as they superseded farce, sentiment, horror, or suspense. His aims stretched as high as the farthest reaches of man's destiny, and Dickens saw the explanation for existence in some variety of Dialectic Romanticism—an argumentative belief in man's perfectibility. This kind of dialectic requires analysis.

For specific reasons he attacked prisons, poorhouses, schools, laws, churches, business in general, the government, unions, working conditions, slums, intolerance, tolerance, state officials, members of Parliament, politics, pride, hypocrisy, statisticians, teachers, lawyers, preachers, economists, laborers, rich men, Americans, doctors, nurses, capitalists, Tories, and people he did not like. His attacks were far from haphazard, all-inclusive as they appear. Behind them were definite philosophical, moral, political, and economic principles.

From the standpoint of narrative technique, Dickens approached the serious purposes of his novels from the logic of deductive reasoning. That is, he began with a premise, a decided opinion. Like a debater or political orator, he expounded one side of his thesis and eliminated any evidence or arguments which would contradict his conclusions arrived at in advance. This approach had been the method of the novelists he admired, of Fielding and Smollett, of Holcroft and Godwin. He organized most of his tales in part or in entirety to prove some point. Artistically speaking, he thought of his action as evidence which would support his opinions.

The advantages and disadvantages of turning one's philosophy into a dialectic are more than usually obvious in Dickens' case. He was a Romanticist; he followed what had been taught by Rousseau and Godwin as he understood their doctrines. Basically, this meant to him that man should trust his instincts because his instincts are naturally good. If man lets Nature take its course, happiness will result. Nature, according to this doctrine, will always achieve perfection if unhampered by decaying, man-made traditions which interfere with progress. Artificial institutions which hamper Nature offer the best subjects for attack if a novelist wishes to improve the world.

There is a curious comparison between the reasoning of Dickens and Thomas Jefferson. This fact may explain why the novels have appealed so consistently to Americans, despite Dickens' attacks on American institutions following his visit in 1842. Both men felt that Nature was a divine force on the side of deserving mankind. The poetry and prose of the early nineteenth century are full of passages extolling the good influences of Nature and the beautiful soul of the natural man when unpolluted by urban civilization and general social decay. Class distinctions were decried, and the rising commercial prosperity of the few at the expense of the many was viewed with alarm by all righteous Romanticists. To a certain extent the liberal Whigs shared this viewpoint. The French Revolution had been hailed by early enthusiasts, including the youthful Wordsworth, as a step toward the regeneration of man, and the march of the people toward natural freedom, liberty, and equality started as a noble crusade. When it turned into something else, with Robespierre and Napoleon, the enthusiasts were stunned. A period of readjustment set in, much

93

like the modern retreat from Communism experienced by a segment of idealists who first hailed it as a reform movement. The readjustment of Dickens' time expressed itself in confusion and differences of opinion, but in the mind of Dickens the basic idea of natural good and institutional bad persisted.

Dickens' connection with the other famous Romantics was not close. He had little interest in Romantic poetry. Even his enthusiasm for Shakespeare depended upon his interest in drama, as did his attention to Byron. Burns's homely and earthy poetry appealed to him, and he had enthusiastic respect for Tennyson, a feeling which was not exactly reciprocated. Wordsworth as a writer attracted him mildly—probably an overstatement—although he expressed ideas which the earlier Wordsworth would have praised wholeheartedly. There is no mention in any of Dickens' writings of Coleridge, Shelley, or Keats, but he was acquainted with Leigh Hunt, Landor, Haydon, and Bulwer-Lytton.

The theory that life is better in the country than in the city was also part of the philosophy of Fielding, Smollett, and Goldsmith. They too had argued for social reform. Matthew Bramble defended the country at the expense of the city in *Humphry Clinker,* and a propagandistic insertion in that novel has as its point the contention that a man can live on an estate in the country—actually live *on* it—and make money, besides being happier than if he were living in town beyond his means. Holcroft, Mackenzie, and Godwin were of course in the main line of humanitarian reform. Dickens was particularly fond of Holcroft.

Belief in the essential good of Nature shows itself in Dickens' novels early. Several apostrophes to Nature are scattered through the first books. In *Oliver Twist,* the hero is recovering from his adventure at the Maylie house where Sikes had attempted to force him into the housebreaking profession. The effect of his natural surroundings is beneficent, and Dickens stops to remark upon the philosophy involved:

> Who can describe the pleasure and delight, the peace of mind and soft tranquillity, the sickly boy felt in the balmy air, and among the green hills and rich woods, of an inland village! Who can tell how scenes of peace and quietude sink into the minds of painworn dwellers in close and noisy places, and carry their own freshness, deep into their

jaded hearts! Men who have lived in crowded, pent-up streets, through lives of toil, and never wished for change; men, to whom custom has indeed been second nature, and who have come almost to love each brick and stone that formed the narrow boundaries of their daily walks; even they, with the hand of death upon them, have been known to yearn at last for one short glimpse of Nature's face; and, carried far from the scenes of their old pains and pleasures, have seemed to pass at once into a new state of being; and crawling forth from day to day, to some sunny spot, have had such memories wakened up within them by the mere sight of sky, and hill, and plain, and glistening water, that a foretaste of heaven itself has soothed their quick decline, and they have sunk into their tombs, as peacefully as the sun, whose setting they watched from their lonely chamber window but a few hours before, faded from their dim and feeble sight. The memories which peaceful country scenes call up, are not of this world, nor its thoughts and hopes. Their gentle influence may teach us how to weave fresh garlands for the graves of those we loved: may purify our thoughts, and bear down before it old enmity and hatred; but beneath all this, there lingers, in the least reflective mind, a vague and half-formed consciousness of having held such feelings long before, in some remote and distant time, which calls up solemn thoughts of distant times to come, and bends down pride and worldliness beneath it.[1]

This lengthy quotation is remarkable in that it contains practically every copybook maxim attributed to the early Wordsworth, including the pre-existence of the soul. There are plenty of similar passages in *Oliver Twist* alone. At every opportunity Dickens was wont to proclaim the favorable influence of the countryside and the pure open air on sick and suffering people. In *Nicholas Nickleby* the country atmosphere brings a few last days of happiness to the slowly dying Smike. In *The Old Curiosity Shop* there is meticulous praise of Nature while little Nell journeys away from urban wickedness into the beautiful valleys and meadows outside London. Her grandfather tells her, as they start their journey:

"We will travel . . . afoot through the fields and woods, and by the side of rivers, and trust ourselves to God and the places where He dwells. It is far better to lie down at night beneath an open sky like that yonder—see how bright it is!—than to rest in close rooms which are always full of care and weary dreams."[2]

Nell continues to think in such fashion during several soliloquies, nor does the hope held forth by Nature fail them. Despite the suffering

95

they might have encountered had not Mrs. Jarley taken them in, they feel revived and comforted:

> As they passed onward, parting the boughs that clustered in their way, the serenity which the child had first assumed, stole into her breast in earnest; the old man cast no longer fearful looks behind, but felt at ease, and cheerful, for the farther they passed into the deep green shade, the more they felt the tranquil mind of God was there, and shed its peace on them.[3]

In these passages Dickens sees life through the tinted glasses of the early Romanticists, with the extreme approach to the doctrine which was summarized by Hegel, that any bad in Nature is a matter of distorted perspective; everything results eventually in good; the whole picture, if we could see it, would justify what seems harmful at the moment. Dickens in his youth was a cosmic optimist, believing that the future is or should be certain. He appropriated the standard religious belief that evil is put into the world to test us, but it can never do real harm to the good man who has the fortitude to resist temptation or temporary malice on the part of fate. Dickens easily reconciled such a belief, when presented with natural catastrophes and accidents, with his hopes for man's perfectibility, even before he could have been expected to work out a systematic philosophical position. Thus he manipulated happy and just endings to his books without feeling that he was distorting life. Since Nature is on the side of justice, he had the power to help her in his capacity as author by inventing the fortuitous circumstances which would aid right to triumph and wrong to meet its due reward.

He was particularly enchanted with the phase of Romanticism which concerns childhood and its instinctive nobility. Wordsworth had outlined this principle for the Romanticists. The belief that the child is good and pure, that his task in life is to keep himself as near as possible to the spiritual condition in which he was born, that he has intimations of immortality and of a previous existence in God's unknown before he grows up and the "shades of the prison-house" close about him is familiar in all its implications. Dickens, like the early Wordsworth, believed that children are noble in their innocence before they mature and learn evil from their surroundings and other men. Oliver Twist and little Nell are his first character studies in this mold.

How can the innocent soul retain its primal freshness as it grows in the physical body? The Romanticists differed in their answers to this question. Says Dickens, "If we all had hearts like those which beat so lightly in the bosoms of the young and beautiful, what a heaven this world would be." But our rough struggles with the civilized world rub off the early "faint image of Eden" and leave us individually and the world in general in a state of "mournful blank."[4] Naturally, Dickens attacked those institutions and customs which aid the world to injure innocence and to interfere with humanity's progress toward a state of natural perfection.

In the light of this doctrine, little Oliver becomes an allegorical or symbolical character rather than a real person. He is one of those ideally good individuals who retain their primal nobility instinctively. Says Dickens: The innocence which is ours at birth ought not to be spoiled; to protect this innocence is man's responsibility in life. False social customs, the squalor of surroundings, city slums, the inhumanity of the law, hypocritical religion, a hidebound system of education, commercial greed, intolerance—all these forces in opposition to natural good must be fought at all times and on all occasions. Oliver's particular enemies are the Poor Law and Big City Crime Schools.

The assumption of inherent goodness in Oliver also explains Dickens' attitude toward those other characters who are not in complete control of their faculties. The simple-minded people he describes are not real, in the manner of a modern psychological novelist's diagnosis of insanity, idiocy, or abnormality. Dickens' psychological cases are children who never grew up. They retain their connection with innocence, refuse any association with the evils of a world they do not understand, and accordingly are to be envied in most respects, despite their lack of mental capacities and understanding. Smike and Barnaby, especially, are examples of this general thesis, and among those whom the world considers not exactly smart are Tom Pinch, Mr. Toots, and Mr. Dick, although these are partially farcical characters.

The instinctive good that resides in the heart of the idiot Barnaby is a perfect illustration of Dickens' Romantic beliefs. God and Nature ally themselves in taking care of the boy:

It is something to look upon enjoyment, so that it be free and wild and in the face of nature, though it is but the enjoyment of an idiot. It is something to know that Heaven has left the capacity of gladness in such a creature's breast; it is something to be assured that, however lightly men may crush that faculty in their fellows, the Great Creator of mankind imparts it even to his despised and slighted work. Who would not rather see a poor idiot happy in the sunlight, than a wise man pining in a darkened jail.[5]

Barnaby was a noble idiot, serving also as a living reminder to his father of the latter's act of murder, yet the boy who lacks the faculties others possess is filled with a spirit which degenerate or more normal creatures are unlikely to retain in their state of sane depravity.

This position explains Barnaby's actions when he becomes entangled with the group which is directing the crowds in the No-Popery Riots. The conspirators use him to help them lead the wanton mobs, but it is necessary to fool him completely and to keep from him any hint as to their real purpose: that of directing the riots against Haredale's house. Barnaby is instinctively opposed to evil and astonishingly quick, considering his mentality, to understand any careless word which might give some indication of what is beneath the surface. There is the incident in which Gashford comes to the rendezvous to make arrangements for raiding Haredale's country estate. While he is discussing the matter with Hugh and the others, he mentions the name of Haredale so that Barnaby can hear him. The idiot turns around quickly, and his more intelligent companions have to rush him back to his place to divert his attention. Dickens wants the reader to know that Barnaby would not consent to the harming of his friends, and that his instinctive sense of good, with a little luck, would have prevented the catastrophe. Just what Barnaby would have been able to do had he understood is not clear. But Hugh says:

> "You might have spoiled our plans, master. . . . *You,* too of all men!"
>
> "Who would have supposed that *he* would be so quick?" urged Gashford.[6]

Who indeed? Why, Dickens.

It is this instinctive innocence which later accounts for Barnaby's attitude in the death cell. Certainly he has done no intentional harm; he is a naturally good character victimized by circumstances and his surroundings. Dickens would not defend a murderer, and he makes no attempt to excuse Hugh, although the exact point at which a man ceases to be responsible for his deeds because of lack of mentality remains undemonstrated. Barnaby is an idiot, and he—like an innocent child—cannot be held accountable for what he has done. His instincts have been distorted by others. It is a clear case, says Dickens, but similar reasoning should not be applied to real criminals. Therefore Dickens can make a hero out of Barnaby as he goes to his death—or supposes that he is going—at the same time that he would exult in the proper punishment Hugh and Dennis suffer.

> His [Barnaby's] kindling eye, his firm step, his proud and resolute bearing, might have graced some lofty act of heroism; some voluntary sacrifice, born of a noble cause and pure enthusiasm; rather than that felon's death.
> But all these things increased his guilt. They were mere assumptions. The law had declared it so, and so it must be. The good minister had been greatly shocked, not a quarter of an hour before, at his parting with Grip. For one in his condition, to fondle a bird![7]

In *Martin Chuzzlewit* the author makes his most earnest attempt to create the simple good person in contrast to the worldly-wise man. He loved Tom Pinch so much that he continually comments upon some action of Tom's which illustrates his thesis: that worldly wisdom is an idiot's folly, weighed against a pure and simple heart. The modern reader is willing to make many allowances for idiocy, whatever the term may mean. That Heaven would protect anyone as simple as Tom Pinch seems extremely unlikely. Yet Barnaby is just as much dependent upon the author's general premise.

That the Golden Age is in the future rather than in the past was the turn given to Romantic thinking by Godwin and Holcroft. The perfectibility of man by rational education was, for these thinkers, a more practical proposal than what seemed to them the impossible suggestion of having everyone return to a state of nature. The concept of the "noble savage" was ridiculed by these writers. Godwin describes in *Caleb Williams* a certain Mr. Grimes, a natural, boorish farmer selected by Tyrrel as a husband for the frail Miss Melville:

> His complexion was scarcely human; his features were coarse, and strangely discordant and disjointed from each other. His lips were

> thick, and the tone of his voice broad and unmodulated. . . . He
> could not feel for those refinements in others of which he had no
> experience in himself.[8]

This general dislike of the savage, whether in pagan lands or in England, is perfectly in accord with Dickens' own rationalization of the situation. He interpreted the present as being much better than the past, no matter how much was wrong with the present. It looked toward a more perfect future, and it was the business of politicians, thinkers, and novelists to help the world along the right track as far as possible from savagery. He hated lamentations for the good old days. Mrs. Skewton, Edith Dombey's mother, says:

> "Those darling, by-gone times, Mr. Carker, with their delicious
> fortresses, and their dear old dungeons, and their delightful places of
> torture, and their romantic vengeances, and their picturesque assaults
> and sieges, and everything that makes life truly charming! How dread-
> fully we have degenerated."[9]

Dickens, like many humanitarian thinkers who were repelled by what they considered the hypocrisy and stagnation of orthodox religion in its institutional form, was able to carry over Christian doctrine to his view of personal degeneration, an approximation of good old-fashioned sin in *his* mind. Perfection is available to our imperfect or *fallen* nature either in this world or the next. When little Nell weeps in sympathy with the girl she meets at Miss Monflathers' school, he comments:

> Let us not believe that any selfish reference—unconscious though it
> might have been—to her own trials awoke this sympathy, but thank
> God that the innocent joys of others can strongly move us, and that
> we, even in our fallen nature, have one source of pure emotion which
> must be prized in Heaven![10]

The hope of perfectibility, even if it is only a moment of atonement, as in the case of Sidney Carton, is open to all; God, the spirit of eternal good, like Nature, remains to help us if we intend aright, and to guide us in every trial, no matter what we have done to depart from our original state of innocence.

The fall from grace is a fall from our individual childhood purity rather than from a perfect historical or racial past. Dickens, despite his interest in the noble child and the noble idiot, hated the noble savage. He comments on the impossibility of anyone's going back to a desert island to live as the savages do. One of the idiosyncrasies of Mrs. Merdle in *Little Dorrit* is to lament our social state today and wish we were living in savagery somewhere:

> "A more primitive state of society would be delicious to me! There used to be a poem when I learnt lessons, something about Lo the poor Indian whose something mind! If a few thousand persons moving in Society could only go and be Indians, I would put my name down directly; but as, moving in society, we can't be Indians, unfortunately— Good morning."[11]

This satire implies that a rotten social regime can be cured only by changing the people concerned; perfectibility can be attained by bringing individuals to a state of nobility which depends upon tolerance, understanding, benevolence, and unselfishness. Mrs. Merdle, says Dickens, would not be helped by living on a desert island or among Indians; her trouble is in herself, not where she lives in society.

Dickens once wrote an article for *Household Words* about the noble savage, the gist of which is a violent denunciation of such a concept.[12] Most followers of the Romantic movement at some time or other came up against a certain contradiction in terms. If they admired Rousseau, they looked for perfection in Nature and the unfettered instincts; if they followed Godwin, they expected perfection to come from gradual development of man and from social betterment. The Rousseauite may be said to have believed in the noble savage, the noble idiot, and the noble child; the Godwinian objected to the noble savage.

In an age which has generally rejected many of the arguments of Romanticism, the reader may be forgiven for being confused when he reads the early novels of Dickens. For example, why should the author hate the noble savage and still believe that Oliver Twist has an instinctive nobility which wards off all evil? If Oliver does what is right by instinct, why would not a savage, presumably closer to Nature, have the same instincts? Later in life Dickens would have argued—indeed he did in *Little Dorrit,* that man may remain good if he exercises his free will and resists the temptations of his environment. This is what Oliver must have done. The same opportunity could

101

be seized by a noble savage, a noble cockney, a noble lord, or a noble laborer, each of whom could retain his early innocence if he desired to do so. What Dickens apparently resented in his attacks on the noble savage was the assumption that a man who lived close to Nature was *bound* to be perfect just because of his environment.

He portrayed the savage at some length in *Barnaby Rudge*. Hugh is his idea of the man born and reared close to Nature, akin to the animals. John Willet says of him when Hugh is introduced:

> "He's not often in the house, you know. He's more at his ease among the horses than men. I look upon him as a animal himself."[13]

Dickens took his plot idea for Hugh's story from the old tale of Valentine and Orson which he had read as a child in chapbook form. It is a romantic, Tarzan-like fairy tale of two brothers, one brought up at court, the other reared as a wild man by a bear—the wild brother, Orson, eventually being captured and taken to court by his brother Valentine. Dickens makes Hugh the Orson and his father (who did not know he was the father), Sir Chester, the Valentine. The father ruins the boy as he civilizes him. Evil institutions and sophistication overcome Nature.

In the original edition of *Barnaby Rudge,* Chapter XXIII has a drawing at the beginning entitled "Orson Tamed," showing Hugh in Chester's rooms. Chester continually treats Hugh as a bear, even addressing him as "Bruin" when it is plain that he has completely mastered the animal. The theme is preserved to the last, for Hugh dies "more brute than man." Dickens' desire to attack the noble savage makes him pull the strings on Hugh as if he were a marionette, and to the thoughtful reader it must seem that Dickens is producing evidence against the assumption that a man is responsible for his own deeds. Hugh lacks stamina, and is led astray by Chester's practical philosophy. At the end Hugh makes a grandiloquent prefuneral oration cursing his newly discovered father. Dickens' intention must have been to show that both Hugh and Chester are responsible for what happens to Hugh, but one wonders whether the father should not bear most of the blame. If Dickens intended Hugh to have freedom of will, he does not completely succeed in convincing us of the fact. Since he defends Barnaby because he is an idiot who knows no better, the result is inconsistent. Barnaby, the noble idiot, and Hugh, the ignoble savage, are in the same book. Dickens' premise and his plot are in contradiction, and one must suppose that the author did not realize that he derived different conclusions from similar evidence.

Immediately after writing this book Dickens went to America. The visit occurred at a turning point in his artistic development and served to bring out several traits in his character which might have remained inactive in other circumstances. The justice or injustice of Dickens' reaction to America in 1842 was argued acrimoniously in his day, but the point of interest is the influence of the visit on his ideas. The early Romantics had thought of America as a free, natural country where human instincts would more easily reach perfection than in decadent Europe.

Dickens found America to be much like Europe, or even worse. America in the roaring forties was unrefined; Dickens was particularly disgusted by promiscuous tobacco-spitting. What he expected must have been an imaginary land that was less burdened by class struggles than England, a democracy where the goodness of human nature had an unusual chance. He wrote to Macready, "This is not the republic I came to see; this is not the republic of my imagination."[14]

That Dickens should discover America to be a country of ignoble savages seems amusing to the modern American. Unquestionably, plenty was wrong with America in 1842. Dickens proved that he was culture-conscious as well as English. His disillusion caused him temporarily to doubt the beneficence of Nature which he had espoused so passionately in *Oliver Twist*. When, in his next novel, he conducts Martin Chuzzlewit to America and that awful place near Cairo, Illinois, which he calls Eden, the selfish Martin experiences no regeneration under the influence of his surroundings. Instead, American Nature comes near killing Martin as well as Mark Tapley. Martin's change of heart occurs when he suddenly realizes Mark's unselfishness; Nature has nothing to do with it.

The matter of understanding America's pretensions to freedom and natural simplicity as a guide to the regeneration of man is discussed by General Choke, talking with Martin (note the connection of "choke" with "vomit"):

> "What are the great United States for, sir?" pursued the general,
> "if not for the regeneration of man? But it is nat'ral in you to make

such an enquerry, for you come from England, and you do not know my country."[15]

Regeneration! snorts Dickens, and calls up the character of Major Chollop as an example of what the regenerated man in America really is. Major Chollop might have been Hugh in the previous book. It is Pogram who describes Chollop:

> "Our fellow-countryman is a model of a man, quite fresh from Natur's mould! . . . He is a true-born child of this free hemisphere! Verdant as the mountains of our country; bright and flowing as our mineral licks; unspiled by withering conventionalities as air our broad and boundless perearer! Rough he may be. So air our Barrs. Wild he may be. So air our Buffalers. But he is a child of Natur', and a child of Freedom; and his boastful answer to the Despot and the Tyrant is, that his bright home is the Settin' Sun."[16]

The American trip clinched Dickens' attitude toward the noble savage, if it needed clinching. Americans who were close to Nature could stay there for all of Dickens; he admired civilization, progress, and culture.

Dickens was annoyed with America because of the lack of international copyright laws, a condition which permitted American publishers to reprint his novels without paying the author. His criticism of Americans was put into *Martin Chuzzlewit* for commercial as well as philosophical reasons. It is fair to point out that his essential criticism applied to people and conditions both in England and America. He continued his attacks upon whatever he felt was interfering with the advance of human perfection wherever he noticed a target. He came back from America with a desire to assail artificiality, a condition which included in its generous scope hypocrisy, selfishness, and pride. *Martin Chuzzlewit* and *Dombey and Son* both bombard some degree of artificiality and hold up for praise individuals like the naturally good and unsophisticated Tom Pinch. Much of this broad purpose is revealed in his caricature of Mrs. Skewton, the "Cleopatra" of *Dombey and Son*. This fine satire on a character who is artificial to the limit and pretends to extreme simplicity has not always been praised. It is delightful caricature, almost the best thing in the novel. It symbolizes one of the author's most interesting theses, for Mrs. Skewton talks of Nature constantly:

"I do assure you, Mr. Dombey, Nature intended me for an Arcadian. I am thrown away in society. Cows are my passion. What I have ever sighed for, has been to retreat to a Swiss farm, and live entirely surrounded by cows—and china . . . . What I want . . . is heart. What I want is frankness, confidence, less conventionality, and freer play of soul. We are so dreadfully artificial."[17]

Dickens by now was sure that people were responsible for artificiality. Nature needed man's help.

"We could be more natural if we tried?" said Mrs. Skewton. Mr. Dombey thought it possible.

"Devil a bit, ma'am," said the major. "We couldn't afford it. Unless the world was peopled with J. B.'s—tough and blunt old Joes, ma'am, plain red herrings with hard roes, sir—we couldn't afford it. It wouldn't do. . . ."

But Mrs. Skewton says:

"I would have my world all heart: and Faith is so excessively charming, that I won't allow you to disturb it, do you hear?"[18]

Dickens had thus satisfactorily reached a compromise in attitude, a condition which is like that assumed by the average human being who is not a professional logician. Many people believe that man's destiny is dependent upon his environment, but that his will exercises sufficient control over environment to make him responsible for what he does. Dickens began to say that men must be judged according to their conflicts with their surroundings, each one according to what he encounters. There is no arbitrary way to define sin, or right, or wrong. Certainly all men would find it easier to resist temptation if there were less temptation, if their environment aided them instead of hindering them. But man will always have some obstacles to overcome.

Consequently Dickens attacked artificial society, unjust laws, and outworn customs; but he also exposed the man who permitted these forces to defeat him. Dickens' main difficulty came when he examined extreme instances of unfortunate environmental influence upon his characters. For example, Godwin had denounced prisons as makers of criminals. The cruelty of solitary confinement which grates the iron of slavery upon the tender soul of the sufferer and changes his entire philosophy of life, the ignorance of so-called justice which ruins the lives of innocent people or punishes out of all proportion to the offense, Godwin argued, turned the well-meaning man from the condition he might otherwise have reached, all without his being at fault. But Dickens disagreed violently with this argument. Whatever the environment, he held the individual responsible. It is the development of his emphasis upon individual responsibility in conflict with environment which eventually becomes the most important part of his dialectic.

His original treatment of this point came in *Oliver Twist,* long before his visit to America; he conceived this early novel as an answer to the novelists who had argued for criminal irresponsibility. Godwin, the first of these writers, had commented forcefully upon prison maladministration and unjust punishment in *Caleb Williams.* These evils were attributed to the ruling classes.

> Wealth and despotism easily know how to engage those laws as the coadjutors of their oppression, which were perhaps at first intended . . . for the safeguards of the poor.[19]

Caleb Williams loses much of its force by its sentimental and sensational study of the reasons for Falkland's implacable pursuit of the hero, Caleb. It impressed succeeding generations, particularly the novelist Bulwer-Lytton, as a tale of unfair imprisonment, relentless pursuit, and remorse for murder.

Several years before Dickens began *Pickwick,* Bulwer published *Paul Clifford,* a novel about the influence of environment and prisons upon crime. He described a boy brought up in evil surroundings, made criminal despite himself by circumstances beyond his control. This book established a vogue for stories about worthy criminals, usually called "Newgate novels," because of the heroes who served sentences in the famous prison of that name. *Paul Clifford* has many brilliantly written episodes and two priceless, humorous characters in Augustus Tomlinson and Squire Brandon. Furthermore, Bulwer understood something of criminal psychology in a modern sense, and he was a far better storyteller than Godwin. There is much that is convincing about his view of legal injustice, and he draws a vivid picture of the prison to which Paul is sent, "a place where, let him be ever so innocent at present, he was certain to come out as much inclined to be guilty as his friends could desire." The author was bitter against

106

laws which make "no fine-drawn nonsensical shades of difference between vice and misfortune."[20]

The example of Bulwer moved Dickens to choose for his second novel the subject matter of *Oliver Twist*. It is true that Dickens refers in the preface to his second novel to Gay's *Beggar's Opera*, an eighteenth-century production which, he says, illustrates what is wrong with writing about criminals. This opinion is not usually accepted today, since Gay's operatic satire strikes us as good moral and artistic entertainment; however, Dickens thought Gay did not put vice in the right light, that he unconsciously glorified the criminal by painting him in attractive colors. Macheath, the idealized highwayman, is popular and handsome; the leader of the thieves who "peaches" and sends his dupes to prison or the hangman when it suits his purpose, is an amusing stage villain; the woman who for love of her outlaw will dare anything, no matter where her passion leads her, is probably too much a picture of what is rather than what Dickens thought should be. These three prototypes became typical of all the Newgate novels, eventually finding reincarnation in Bill Sikes, Fagin, and Nancy in *Oliver Twist*.

Bulwer was alive, so Dickens did not criticize *Paul Clifford* in his preface. Bulwer later defended himself against the charge of praising the heroic criminal in a preface of his own (1840), complaining that of all his novels he had made the robber a hero in only this one. He declares that the object of this novel was first "to draw attention to two errors in our penal institutions, viz., a vicious prison-discipline, and a sanguinary Criminal Code,—the habit of corrupting the boy by the very punishment that ought to redeem him, and then hanging the man, at the first occasion, as the easiest way of getting rid of our own blunders." He insists that his secondary purpose was a burlesque one, "to show that there is nothing essentially different between vulgar vice and fashionable vice."[21]

Paul Clifford has some of the components of impressive tragedy. A boy brought up in unfavorable surroundings in the heart of London's "flash" underworld, meeting with an unjust prison sentence through no fault of his own, associating with thieves, joining them, distinguishing himself to become their leader, falling in love with a pure and beautiful girl, eventually being captured and sentenced to death by a judge who turns out to be his own father—all these incidents have force, except the last one. The thesis of the book lies in Paul's argument concerning the attitude the world takes toward crime and the criminal:

> "Repent! that is the idlest word in our language. . . . From my birth to this hour, I have received no single favour from its [society's] customs and its laws; openly I war against it, and patiently will I meet its revenge. . . . I come into the world friendless and poor—I find a body of laws hostile to me, then, I acknowledge hostility in my turn. Between us are the conditions of war. Let them expose a weakness— I insist on my right to seize the advantage; let them defeat me, and I allow their right to destroy."[22]

Bulwer later denied that these views were his own, but the point of the book is lacking without them. He felt that the injustice of laws ought not to deprive a man of an honest chance to oppose them when he had been a victim of those laws, or if he had succumbed to his environment under great pressure. Bulwer's next novel was *Eugene Aram,* in which a noble character commits a murder, is undetected, and lives a good life for many years. He is eventually exposed just as he is about to be happily married. The argument apparently is that Aram had either atoned for his crime by long years of reform, or circumstance had driven him to it in the first place. In either case it is unjust to punish him as society automatically does.

Dickens wrote *Oliver Twist* in protest against the Newgate novels' depiction of the heroic criminal. In his story the criminal, Bill Sikes, was to be the villain, not the hero. He says:

> Here are no canterings upon moonlit heaths, no merrymakings in the snuggest of all possible caverns, none of the attractions of dress, no embroidery, no lace, no jack-boots, no crimson coats and ruffles, none of the dash and freedom with which "the road" has been, time out of mind, invested.[23]

His purpose was to take characters and plot of somewhat similar outlines to Bulwer's but to prove the opposite moral point. Oliver falls among criminals, but he—unlike Clifford—does not succumb to evil or become the leader of the gang. He fights against his evil surroundings and stands for virtue against impossible odds.

Paul Clifford and *Oliver Twist* both present curious examples of mixed effectiveness. Bulwer's analysis of the influence of environment in forming criminals is more acceptable today than is Dickens' stubborn portrait of the allegorical Oliver. Yet few of us would accept the thesis that because environment tends to mold criminals it is proper to make heroes of those who fight against all law. Dickens' intent to praise the boy who stands fast against temptation is admirable, but the modern world suspects that circumstances can conquer any resolution on occasion, and the reader is unlikely to believe that Oliver as he is presented would be the person who would hold out against the forces which beset him. Hitler said and often demonstrated that no ideals can withstand a rubber truncheon, and Communist terrorism and torture have altered a great many noble characters in our century.

There is another important influence to be considered. The novel which has the closest connection with *Oliver Twist* is not *Paul Clifford,* but *Jack Sheppard,* written by Dickens' first literary friend and patron, William Harrison Ainsworth. Ainsworth's influence on Dickens is important in this period; it antedates that of Forster, and the fact that it faded rapidly can probably be attributed to the sharp difference of opinion the two novelists took toward the heroic criminal. After achieving a modest success with *Rookwood* in 1834, Ainsworth decided to canonize all the Newgate saints in separate novels, the stories to be based freely upon the lives of the most spectacular of these criminals. The first to be so honored was *Jack Sheppard,* who had repeatedly in the previous century escaped from Newgate. This novel was written and published concurrently with *Oliver Twist.* Its attitude toward crime is at the opposite extreme from Dickens'.

In *Rookwood* Ainsworth had claimed that the real robber "never maltreated anyone, except in self-defense."[24] In *Jack Sheppard* he defends the glorious death of hanging. The comparison between the plot of his novel and *Oliver Twist* is most interesting. Ainsworth describes a school of thieves called "The Old Mint," where the inhabitants speak the lingo of the criminals, called "flash." Thames Darrell (the character parallel to Oliver) has a villainous uncle who schemes against him, and with the connivance of Jonathan Wild (the Fagin) wrongfully accuses him of theft. Darrell's parentage is obscure, and it is supposed during most of the story that he is illegitimate. Jack Sheppard is made a criminal by the earnest and continued efforts of Wild, and he is finally tempted to steal in church, thus coming irrevocably under the power of the gang of thieves. Jack goes to prison when he is discovered stealing, and later helps to lead a housebreaking expedition on the home of a certain Mr. Wood. When one of Wild's gang breaks into the Wood household and murders Mrs. Wood, a bloody scene ensues which is second only to the Nancy-Sikes episode and of the same quality.

Environment will do it to you every time, argued Ainsworth—and Dickens must have heard him before he started on *Oliver Twist.* Ainsworth went further than any of his contemporaries were willing to go when he described the woman who was forced to prostitution by poverty. Jonathan Wild defends Mrs. Sheppard:

> "In the first place she had no knowledge of her birth; and, consequently, no false pride to get rid of. In the second, she was wretchedly poor, and assailed by temptations of which you can form no idea. Distress like hers might palliate far greater offences than she ever committed. With the same inducements we should all do the same thing."[25]

This opinion must have shocked Dickens beyond words. He was always willing to offer the possibility of repentance to sinners like Nancy, as he does for Emily in *David Copperfield,* but his sinners are generally responsible for their misdeeds, not excused by their environment.

Yet as time went by he saw more and more clearly the power that outside forces exercised in leading men astray. He sympathized particularly with the lower classes, the poverty-stricken and underprivileged, those who deserve better because they try to do the best they can. Poverty was, and is, a breeder of vice, he said. It causes sin in general, although he could never admit that it excuses sin in particular. When he recounts his own experiences in the warehouse, he expresses horror at what might have been done to him had he not been lucky enough to escape. The background, even the education, may mold the man. Jonas Chuzzlewit illustrates this conclusion. In the Preface to *Martin Chuzzlewit* Dickens describes the forces of environment as they overwhelm individual resolution:

> I conceive that the sordid coarseness and brutality of Jonas Chuzzlewit would be unnatural, if there had been nothing in his early education, and in the precept and example always before him, to engender and develop the vices that made him odious. But, so born and bred; ad-

mired for that which made him hateful, and justified from his cradle. in cunning, treachery, and avarice; I claim him as the legitimate issue of the father upon whom these vices are seen to recoil. And I submit that their recoil upon that old man, in his unhonored age, is not a mere piece of poetical justice, but is the extreme exposition of a plain truth.[26]

Yet Dickens had to feel, in the last analysis, that Jonas was responsible for his own deeds. One is reminded of a non-Presbyterian minister's definition of foreordination: something a man can't help which is his fault anyway.

This conclusion may be verified by examining the recurring theses of Dickens' novels, theses which always deal with characters who fight against environment that sometimes leads them astray. His best novel of purpose, *Little Dorrit,* is partially devoted to a study of the effect of prison atmosphere upon character. He had originally intended to call it *Nobody's Fault,* a satiric statement of the point opposite to the one he wanted to make. He wove several sequences around the same theme which was: No matter what your environment, you can be what you choose to be. Clennam, for example, complains that he never had a chance, but Dickens shows how he manages to escape his environmental influences eventually, even though they cause him much unhappiness and suffering. Little Dorrit herself is the same person whether she lives in a debtors' prison or in possession of great wealth. Difference in social and financial status merely gives her and the other members of her family opportunity for revealing their essential natures: the fault is not in their stars. Environment is fate, but man is master of it if he wills to be.

The eventual course of Dickens' Dialectic Romanticism is now clear. Man must fight to keep his original innocence and his instincts pure; he must overcome adverse surroundings in order to become admirable; the main duty of intelligence is to attack adverse circumstances and evil institutions. In novel after novel Dickens assaulted the forces which man had built up contrary to Nature. So he exposed the Poor Law in *Oliver Twist,* the incompetent boarding schools in *Nicholas Nickleby,* debtors' prisons, poverty-stricken slums, bad working conditions, and all the other social evils which enter into his later novels. He also studied at length the reasons why his characters do or do not overcome the circumstances which plague them. *Martin*

Chuzzlewit awards praise for sincerity and disgust for hypocrisy; *Dombey and Son* stresses the ideals of humility and understanding at the same time that it holds up pride to scorn; the later novels become more and more concerned with man's fight against the evil forces inherent in our world—man-made forces, not natural ones.

In the early novels his Dialectic Romanticism is not completely defensible. Some of Dickens' first theses have become threadbare. Few of us would say that the influence of Nature as Dickens portrays it is all for the best. Nor do we believe that poetic justice always operates. Nor will we admit that if man's instincts are unhampered by social stagnation or the degeneration of institutions they will automatically direct themselves in the right pathway. Cosmic optimism implies limited experience. Modern pathologists would hardly agree that an idiot is a naturally good person, luckier than normal but unwise individuals. Dickens' early novels suffer in proportion to the degree in which they depend upon these concepts.

Yet when Dickens roused all his narrative resources in fighting against artificiality, selfishness, pride, inhuman laws, unjust punishment, inadequate education, and hypocritical religion he was allied with all the powers of good. As he continued writing, as he grew in knowledge, as he adapted his theses to experience, he learned how to select from reality the evidence which would make his viewpoint convincing; his novels became better organized and planned in respect to plot and his purposes more impressive. The crucible of experience improved him as an artist of propaganda. In *Bleak House, Hard Times,* and *Little Dorrit* he also began to expand his concept of Dialectic Romanticism to include political and economic theory.

From the standpoint of artistry it is of vital importance to discover and understand the purposes which directed the course of Dickens' intentions in constructing his novels. He proceeded from entertainment for its own sake to the exploration of the reasons for existence. Eventually his aims in writing depended upon his utilization of all the techniques at his command in order to illustrate and develop his theses. He began to fuse these narrative resources by the time he came to write *David Copperfield*. In the novels preceding *David Copperfield* his success is dependent upon how far the modern reader is willing to go with him in accepting the doctrines he had inherited from the Romanticists.

CHAPTER VII

Economic Theory

HE HIGHEST point of tension reached in the fiction of Dickens results from the stress of conflicting economic and political ideas. He began writing under the spell of the dialectic he formed from the heritage of Romanticism; gradually he went on to mature consideration of the relationship of man to his economic surroundings, to capital and labor, and to the political factors which affect the welfare of society. This area of his fiction challenges his twentieth-century readers even more than it did the audience of his own time, for the issues live on—indeed, they may seem to be more important than any other issues in the world of today.

Approximately three attitudes toward economic theory were open to Dickens, any one of which he might have adopted. The first is the basic doctrine of capitalism usually associated with Adam Smith and his followers. Dickens did not accept this doctrine, and it is important to understand why. Smith had stated in *The Wealth of Nations* that self-interest is the most important law of social action. Along with this premise goes the corollary that the law of God sets up a "natural order," that man working with complete freedom within the limits of competition laid down by Providence will "naturally" achieve economic stability if he deserves it and works for it. The business of government is to avoid interference, but to protect life, liberty, and property; the individual moving without restraint will act more in harmony with universal law than would the government or any monopolistic organization. God intends that man should struggle for a living; accordingly, the best and most practical way to prosperity and the perfectibility of society is complete economic and competitive freedom: *laissez faire, laissez passer, leave-business-alone.*

Dickens thought, as do a number of economists, that this doctrine works very well, but only for the business class. When business is let alone, it naturally exploits labor. This, of course, is the heart of whatever argument there is about capitalism. Dickens felt that self-interest, uncontrolled, subject to the passions and desires of unworthy men, was responsible for the mess in which Victorian society found itself. Even when the followers of Adam Smith campaigned for social reform, Dickens objected to their motives. In the first half of the nineteenth century these followers were called utilitarians, and they were led by Jeremy Bentham and James Mill. They argued that laws which interfere with free competition add to human misery; the way to reform is to get rid of such laws. The utilitarians accordingly placed themselves in partial alliance with the "liberal" thinkers of Dickens' day and supported the great political reform movements of the time.

Utilitarianism derived originally from the doctrines of Hume, who had said that the ultimate motive for obedience to the state is self-interest or utility. Bentham's first premise was the assumption that there is no such thing as moral or immoral action; everything is either *useful* or *not useful*. The ends of utilitarian doctrine are encompassed in practicality. Dickens defined this as selfishness. The doctrine assumes that universal law somehow or other makes the practical right and good; individuals are therefore conditioned by heredity and environment; ideal conditions would allow everybody to live in some degree of competitive freedom or, as has often been said, to be free without interfering with the freedom and happiness of others.

Theoretically this system depends upon its comparative effectiveness; it is argued that it is good because it is better than any other system. If a man works for what is useful to himself, he will help grease the wheels of industry and speed the greatest good for the greatest number; if his environment aids him to work and to prosper, he will be more likely to find economic stability and personal comfort. Bentham and Mill objected to whatever interfered with man's opportunity to work and prosper; they saw hindrances to economic freedom in outmoded laws and prison conditions; they considered bad working conditions to be bad for business; they disliked unequal parliamentary representation, hampering tariffs, and class-favoring legislation. Utilitarians helped pass the Poor Law of 1834, aided the establishment of free trade in 1846, and campaigned for the adoption of universal suffrage. They believed that their system of economic freedom would make deserving workers prosperous and happy.

Even in Dickens' day the economists who preferred the doctrines of Adam Smith to any other analysis of the social order did not argue that it set up an ideal society. No system could supply employment and happiness automatically, they said. In this way they explained the alternate periods of economic expansion and depression which plague most nations at some time or other. One of the followers of Adam Smith, Malthus (in 1798), held that since population increases in geometrical progression and the means of subsistence in arithmetical progression, jobs and workers can never stay parallel in numbers. Even with free competition working smoothly, the poor are likely to be with us always. To Malthus this result was a matter of fate and destiny; man could do little about it. He suggested that the pressure of population could be relieved by certain checks: foresight in avoiding parentage (he did not argue for birth control, merely foresight), emigration or the opening up of new industry, and—Dickens said—what he really meant was poverty unrestrained, disease unhampered, and war encouraged.

Dickens constantly attacked Adam Smith, Bentham, Malthus, and the utilitarian point of view. The core of his objections was his disagreement with the fundamental assumption that utility is the basis for all action. He saw no improvement of the world unless human beings were to recognize and practice sympathy and understanding for other human beings. Competition had to be limited by something which took all the people into account. Up to this point what Dickens was *against* is clear; the problem in understanding his economic ideas comes from identifying exactly what he was *for*.

Between 1837 and 1850, a time coinciding with Dickens' early literary development, conditions in England reached political and economic crisis. After passing the Great Reform Bill, the liberal Whig leadership struck a snag. Several years of depression put the conservative Tories back in power in 1841. Wages and living conditions grew steadily worse as the industrial revolution permitted the rise of great fortunes for owners and employers along with starvation and poverty for great numbers of the working classes. Spokesmen for the underprivileged masses argued that the laissez-faire system would have to be modified or even overthrown to produce satisfactory living wages for the majority of the people. Extremists urged revolution, and many of them joined a movement which eventually centered around Karl Marx in Germany and Friedrich Engels in England, a movement which came to be called *communism*. This is the second possible economic position which Dickens might have embraced, and several modern critics have argued that it is what he believed, even though he never openly espoused the doctrines of Marx and Engels.[1] One of the great fallacies of twentieth-century misinformation is the assumption that whoever is opposed to the weaknesses of capitalism is automatically for communism. In the early days of Dickens' fictional development the pseudoradical Chartist movement gained momentum in England, causing many sober people to fear that the country might suffer a revolution comparable to the horrible experience of France in the 1790's. The Chartists summed up their demands in the publication of "The People's Charter" in 1838, asking for universal manhood suffrage, annual parliamentary elections, electoral districts equal in population, abolition of property qualifications for Parliament, and payment of salaries to members of Parliament. They stopped there, but the business class feared that the workers, organized, might seize control of property for themselves. There was general worry about a doctrine called *socialism* in this connection, some form of cooperative control of the means of industry in the interest of all the people.

The depression of the forties increased the numbers of Chartists in England; trade unions began to form; agitation grew for centralization of capital in communal control, for state ownership and management of business, and for the abolition of laws which favored wealth and property. Engels in England and Marx in Germany preached the theory of cooperative organization and equal rewards. In 1848 agitation reached a boiling point, and the *Communist Manifesto* was published. All over Europe revolts broke out, and the English government feared that the Chartists in England would aid a general European explosion.

Revolution did not succeed on the Continent, and the commercial crisis passed. Whether it was the discovery of gold in California and Australia, the opening of a period of expanding trade and emigration, the alternate rise of the fluctuating capitalistic system following a decline—whatever the reason, Victorian prosperity set in, and the problems of the working classes, while still acute in individual cases, were not so pressing as to cause an English uprising. Strife continued between capital and labor, trade unions gradually gained power enough to bargain with capital, strikes occurred in many districts from year to year, and long hours in combination with bad working conditions decreased slowly—the utilitarians said "surely." But Dickens did not think that economic conditions were improving very much or that people understood the issues involved.

No novel of Dickens argues for revolution, but again and again he attacked capitalistic selfishness and political indifference to the welfare of all the people. He was always on the side of the lower and middle classes against the businessman who makes money at the expense of general human happiness. He was also opposed to the hereditary aristocracy because it showed no signs of understanding its responsibilities in terms of leadership which would help the lower classes. He attacked Smith and Bentham constantly; he never mentions Marx or Engels in his writings. The discerning reader senses that his position was somewhere between the extremes of Smith and Marx: a bitter critic of the weaknesses of capitalism as an economic theory, but not an advocate of its overthrow. Improvement or reform is preferable to destruction.

The best statement of a "middle position," and the third attitude toward economic and political theory available to Dickens, was advocated by Thomas Carlyle. This individualistic and spectacular essayist, like Dickens, disliked the selfish ethics inherent in utilitarianism; he also voiced the fears of many men that communism would foster anarchy and dispose the able individual to lower himself to the level of the average man. Carlyle constantly preached the doctrine of *work* and the necessity for a just reward for work. He believed that the common man cannot be trusted to control or improve his conditions of life, principally because he does not possess enough intelligence or information. Giving the suffrage to ignorant men was as ridiculous to Carlyle as refusing to remedy their grievances. Education would eventually help the comman man—say, in about two centuries—but the only present hope was in some political and economic organization controlled by intelligent and kindly leaders.

Carlyle's basic assumption is that the laissez-faire doctrine of economics will not work equitably or smoothly without intelligent direction and unselfish control. Since, according to this assumption, it is obvious that unintelligent men cannot direct the fair operation of business as individuals, they must be regulated into "fair practices" in competition; employers must sometimes pay higher wages and impose fewer working hours than the laws of supply and demand permit— for the good of the country and humanity as a whole; in the interests of social welfare, business must admit a standard of right and wrong in the payment of a living wage rather than a measure of practical utility and ruthless or irresponsible business enterprise.

The problem for Carlyle was that of securing proper regulation. The individual businessman can hardly be expected to regulate himself. Government control is untrustworthy unless directed by a benevolent leader—a "hero." Because Carlyle argued for centralized government direction of industry under a kindly disposed and brainy prime minister (someone like a dictator), because he praised benevolent feudalism in the past and heroic leadership in any age, he is often hailed as an advocate of some system similar to national socialism. He has been claimed by such divergent groups as the fascists, the British labor leaders, and by the Hitlerites in the twentieth century. It can also be argued that his viewpoint has spiritual kinship with the economic theories of the American New Deal or with those of John Maynard Keynes.

The opinions of Dickens coincide with these arguments of Carlyle at practically every point of reference. In the beginning—before he was acquainted with Carlyle—he attacked the utilitarians. His theories are all in the category of objection to the wrongs as he saw them. In *Oliver Twist* he assaulted the new Poor Law which had been fostered by the utilitarians. Ostensibly this law was a step in the direction of reform, but Dickens thought it was the wrong step. For decades the poor in England had been supported on a kind of dole. The Benthamites argued that under free competition there ought to be work for everybody. A man out of work deserved little relief, for he could obtain a job if he wanted one badly enough. The Poor Law established

118

workhouses where the poor and needy could be cared for but were treated so badly that nobody would want to go to the Poor House. This measure was intended to encourage every able-bodied man to find work and to discourage the man who was lazily willing to let the Government support him.

Carlyle later argued that the idea behind the Poor Law was a good one; people should be encouraged to work. The only trouble was the perfectly obvious one that the law needed a balance; the Government should be sure that sufficient work was available and that the offered wages would support men at work. Otherwise the Poor Law would merely aggravate suffering and hardship for thousands of people. Dickens asserted savagely that the utilitarian needed to proceed several steps beyond the Poor Law, for it and Malthus' law of population were in conflict.[2]

In episodes scattered through the first five novels Dickens exposed various abuses which have their roots in economic troubles. In *Pickwick Papers* he protested against prison conditions and legal injustice, particularly in connection with debtors. He thought that many men were punished in debtors' prisons through economic conditions which no amount of individual initiative could conquer. In *The Old Curiosity Shop* he assailed the general working conditions in Manchester, an industrial center where long hours and short pay oppressed the workers. In *Nicholas Nickleby* he praised the Cheerybles, a pair of capitalists who bear some resemblance to men like Robert Owen, the benevolent Socialist employer who had run his business for the good of the laborer as well as of the owner. The Cheerybles are feudal, but paternal. In *Barnaby Rudge* he pictures the dangerous results which followed when the lower classes rioted and got out of hand. This last novel was written during the period of early Chartist agitation and clearly is not in sympathy with revolution. The direct cause of the riots was religious rather than economic, but the novel includes a minor sequence involving Tappertit and a very silly trade union which shows Dickens' initial distrust of organized labor.

Dickens met Carlyle for the first time at a dinner party in 1840. They expressed liking and regard for each other soon after, and if Dickens had not already studied *The French Revolution* and *Chartism*, he did so immediately. He claimed to have read *The French Revolution* an unusual number of times, and it served as his main source for *A Tale of Two Cities* in later years. The gradually growing friendship between the two men was furthered by Carlyle's support of Dickens in his agitation for an international copyright law about the time the younger man went to America. His letter to Dickens in 1842 was published to aid the cause. Forster says concerning Dickens' feeling for this man and his ideas:

> Admiration of Carlyle increased in him with his years; and there was no one whom in later life he honored so much, or had a more profound regard for.[3]

Carlyle published *Past and Present* in 1843. This book and *Chartism* furnished the core of inspiration for the first two Christmas books by Dickens, *A Christmas Carol* (1843) and *The Chimes* (1844). Most readers, familiar as they are with the *Carol,* recall it as a fairy story of the regeneration of a crabbed old man at Christmastime through a vision of ghosts. The political and economic implications are nevertheless distinct. Scrooge is Mr. Laissez-faire with a "Bah! Humbug!" personality and an un-Christmas spirit. He serves as an allegorical example of all Dickens hated in the free-competition system:

> Oh! But he was a tight-fisted hand at the grindstone, Scrooge! A squeezing, wrenching, grasping, scraping, clutching, covetous old sinner! Hard and sharp as flint, from which no steel had ever struck out generous fire; secret, and self-contained, and solitary as an oyster . . . he iced his office in the dog-days; and didn't thaw it one degree at Christmas.[4]

When solicitors for charity approach Scrooge, he asks about prisons, Union workhouses, and whether the treadmill and Poor Law are in full vigor. Why should the people ask for charity?

> Do we not pass what Acts of Parliament are needful; as many as thirty-nine for the shooting of partridges alone? Are there not treadmills, gibbets; even hospitals, poor-rates, New Poor-Law? So answers Aristocracy, astonishment in every feature.[5]

These are Carlyle's words. What Scrooge actually says is:

> I help support the establishments I have mentioned [prisons, workhouses, treadmill, and Poor Law]—they cost enough; and those who

are badly off must go there. . . . If they would rather die, they had better do it, and decrease the surplus population.[6]

Dickens later introduces the lovable, lame Tiny Tim as an example of the person most likely to die off and deplete the surplus. Carlyle had jested mournfully in *Chartism* about the various humane ways of killing off excess population.

The implication of Scrooge's sins and those of his dead partner Marley follows directly in the main track of Carlyle's opinions. Scrooge and Marley are worshippers of Mammon, the God of Cash-payment. When the ghostly apparition of Marley appears to Scrooge, the latter says:

> "But you were always a good man of business, Jacob" . . .
> "Business!" cried the Ghost, wringing his hands again. "Mankind was my business. The common welfare was my business; charity, mercy, forbearance, and benevolence, were, all, my business. The dealings of my trade were but a drop of water in the comprehensive ocean of my business!"[7]

Scrooge's activities are all on the principle of financial gain at the cost of everything else. He does what is useful to him and avoids what is not useful. He is the sharp-dealing, merciless-creditor type, a point which emerges when the Ghost of Christmas Yet to Come shows him the couple who are saved by the hypothetical death of Scrooge and thereby given time to pay their note.

Yet Scrooge has paid the wages fixed by the supply-and-demand principle of Smith-Benthamite economics. Dickens brings in other wage earners: Martha Cratchit, milliner's apprentice; workers in the mining district; the children Ignorance and Want—all fostered by the laissez-faire doctrine of unhampered competition. The implication is that despite this doctrine men are not being paid enough for their labor. Says Carlyle, in *Past and Present:*

> True, it must be owned, we for the present, with our Mammon-Gospel, have come to strange conclusions. We call it a Society; and go about professing openly the totalest separation, isolation. Our life is not a mutual helpfulness; but rather, cloaked under due laws-of-war, named "fair competition" and so forth, it is mutual hostility. We have profoundly forgotten everywhere that Cash-payment is not the sole relation of human beings; we think, nothing doubting, that *it* absolves and liquidates all engagements of men. "My starving workers?" answers

the rich mill-owner: "Did I not hire them fairly in the market? Did I not pay them, to the last sixpence, the sum covenanted for? What have I to do with them more?"—Verily, Mammon-worship is a melancholy creed.[8]

Carlyle's general argument is that wages should be "justly apportioned," and not determined on the basis of supply and demand. "A fair day's wages for a fair day's work" meant to Carlyle a reasonable and sufficient living wage. He even suggests a kind of permanent contract between employers and workers instead of a temporary one, a concept which is usually called *paternalistic* in the relationship between capital and labor.

Dickens contrasts Scrooge, "excellent man of business," with old Fezziwig, the master of his apprentice days. Fezziwig was a "reasonable" employer; he worked his men hard and fairly, but he was able to play occasionally, and he did not hesitate to spend money at Christmastime for the entertainment and jollification of his employees. Part of the problem could be solved, says Dickens, if employers were in direct contact with their workers and sympathetic with them. At the end of the fable, when Scrooge changes, most of the reform is a shift in attitude. No revolution is envisaged, of course. Cratchit is not supposed to take the place of his master or become his economic equal. But Scrooge sends him a turkey for his dinner and the next day raises his salary so that his bare existence may be made a little more comfortable. Presumably he pays Cratchit a "living wage," even though supply and demand do not force him to do so.

The Chimes carries the war to the governing classes, who manage to avoid doing anything constructive for the poor. In *Chartism* Carlyle had argued that the ignorant desire to be ruled by the wise, but complained because the ruling classes are rarely wise. He used the term *dilettantism* to designate the aristocratic habit of misunderstanding economic problems on a national scale and of doing nothing to remedy them. So Dickens' Toby Veck, cockney errand man, comments on Parliament's habit of "obserwation." The newspapers are full of such "obserwations," but they don't *do* anything for poor people. As the various officials introduced into the story manage to do nothing or the wrong thing for the poor, Dickens builds the tale up to an appeal for the reader to do something himself; then the chimes will really ring out the old year and ring in the new. Intelligent government regulation is just around the corner if individuals are unwilling to solve the problem.

Dickens criticizes four distinct attitudes toward the poor in *The Chimes*. Three gentlemen come out of an aristocratic dwelling house to find Toby eating his lunch of tripe. The first of these is Filer, the man of statistics. Carlyle, in *Chartism*, waxed violent about the kind of economist or politician who was always able to quote statistics in order to prove that things were either all right or not too bad:

> With what serene conclusiveness a member of some Useful-Knowledge Society stops your mouth with a figure of arithmetic! To him it seems he has there extracted the elixir of the matter, on which now nothing more can be said. . . . Twice or three times have we heard the lamentations of a humane Jeremiah, mourner for the poor, cut short by a statistic fact of the most decisive nature: How can the condition of the poor be other than good, be other than better; has not the average duration of life in England, and therefore among the most numerous class in England, been proven to have increased? If life last longer, life must be less worn upon, by outward suffering, by inward discontent, by hardship of any kind; the general condition of the poor must be bettering instead of worsening.[9]

So Filer in *The Chimes* examines Toby's tripe and reads him a lecture upon how well he is being fed, how much above the average he is, and what a generally wasteful food tripe is for the poor.

The second gentleman is Alderman Cute, an allegorical representation of Malthus. There was a real London alderman named Sir Peter Laurie who held these views. Cute strenuously advises Richard and Meg, who are with Toby, not to get married, holding up before them pictures of unemployed days, suffering children, and general poverty. Their natural desire for happiness would lead to nothing but more misery and "increase the excess population." Here Dickens criticizes not only Malthus but the politician who uses the doctrines of Malthus to justify his unwillingness to cure the economic conditions which grind down the poor. The third gentleman, like the alderman, thinks nothing can be done, and laments the good old days when things must have been better and people did not suggest doing anything.[10]

The fourth attitude is expressed by Sir Joseph Bowley, the man to whom Toby carries Alderman Cute's letter. Bowley, like Bentham, sums up the utilitarian attitude toward the poor as both Carlyle and Dickens saw it. Sir Joseph refers piously to the sacred relationship between a man and his banker, carries no unpaid accounts over into the new year, and tells the poor that it is their own fault if they do not work harder or make more money:

> "Now, the design of your creation is—not that you should swill, and guzzle, and associate your enjoyments, brutally, with food . . . but that you should feel the Dignity of Labour. Go forth erect into the cheerful morning air, and—stop there. Live hard and temperately, be respectful, exercise your self-denial, bring up your family on next to nothing, pay your rent as regularly as the clock strikes, be punctual in your dealings . . . and you may trust to me to be your Friend and Father."[11]

Sir Joseph is a self-appointed Father, assuming a paternal attitude toward the poor, but possessing no sympathetic understanding. Dickens considers this kind of hypocrisy in high places to be worse than complete neglect. It leads to dangerous conflict between classes. Alderman Cute, Sir Joseph, Adam Smith, or Malthus all argue that the poor are getting as much as supply and demand assign them. Therefore, if they want more, "Put 'em down!"

Dickens experimented with the technique which presented two endings to his tale, one bad and one good. This had the advantage of implying the happy ending which would satisfy the romantic demands of his readers but at the same time put the problem of doing something for the poor up to the general public. His unhappy ending is the realistic one which Engels was writing about in the same year.[12] In this section, Will Fern is jailed again and again, finally becoming a vandal and setting fire to the property of the hated upper classes; Lillian goes on the streets and dies prematurely; Meg works herself into ill health and unhappy old-maidhood; and Richard falls easily into the evils of bad companionship, drinking, and idleness. When Meg is driven almost to suicide, Toby wakes up to find it all a dream. The world, says Dickens, is really too intelligent and kindhearted to let such things happen when people are informed about conditions.

When Dickens had finished *The Chimes* in manuscript, he made a special trip from the Continent to England to read his story to a dinner party. Carlyle was the guest of honor. Apparently Carlyle was somewhat taken aback at the idea that kind hearts might solve national economic problems. Gavan Duffy reports a conversation with Carlyle, presumably after he had listened to *The Chimes:*

> Dickens is a good little fellow, one of the most cheery, innocent natures I have ever encountered, and maintains something of his old reporter independence . . . his theory of life is entirely wrong. He thinks men ought to be buttered up, and the world made soft and accommodating for them, and all sorts of fellows have turkey for their Christmas dinner. Commanding and controlling and punishing them he would give up without any misgivings, in order to coax and soothe and delude them into doing right.[13]

Whether Dickens sensed this reaction at the time we do not know, but from this period on he experimented with ways and means of putting the serious ideas he and Carlyle held in common into the propagandistic parts of his longer novels. He wrote three more Christmas books, but they have nothing to do with economic theory. However, every novel he wrote subsequently—from *Dombey and Son* to *Our Mutual Friend*—reflects his attempts to use in some way the serious economic theories he admired in terms of story-telling.

Artistic craftsmanship and propaganda do not always live together happily. Fiction which gives the impression of being organized and arranged to prove a point tends to lose conviction in proportion to the degree of manipulation which is apparent to the reader. Novelists of purpose before Dickens propagandized by telling a story which illustrated a thesis; then they explained the thesis to the reader. Dickens sometimes followed this hazardous practice, but his narrative experimentation led him eventually to a more subtle scheme.

Dombey and Son is an attempt to combine an appealing and exciting story with an attack upon a hardhearted utilitarian businessman. Mr. Dombey is Scrooge in another form, excessively selfish and proud, so greedy and obsessed with buying cheap and selling dear that he has no sympathy for those about him. His love for his son is based entirely on the idea of bringing up a family representative to carry on the business. Dickens' plan is in the simplest tradition of straightforward propaganda: Show how wrong such a man and his economic philosophy can be. Mr. Dombey loses his son and his wife; strangely enough his daughter loves him and saves him when he reforms at the last.

The experiment with propaganda in *Dombey and Son* produced a number of peculiar results: The effect of the novel depends upon the sentiment and suspense of the plot rather than upon the economic thesis. Dickens' various narrative abilities tended to war with the purpose. He introduced funny characters, then deliberately tried to restrain his caricature and farce. The death of little Paul visits poetic justice upon Mr. Dombey, but the impression made on the reader depends upon the natural sympathy felt at the death of an attractive child.

The novel did allow him to develop a minor thesis derived from Carlyle. In *Chartism* several suggestions are made for aiding the nation to escape the current depression. Two of these are Universal Education and General Emigration. *Past and Present* also suggests the need for a Right-Education Bill and the development of an effective teaching service for the country as a whole. The subject of education always aroused Dickens, and in *Dombey and Son* he made his first serious criticism of the inadequate education offered the poorer classes in England. Mr. Dombey says:

> "I am far from being friendly . . . to what is called by persons of level-
> ling sentiments, general education. But it is necessary that the inferior
> classes should continue to be taught to know their position, and to
> conduct themselves properly. So far I approve of schools. Having the
> power of nominating a child on the foundation of an ancient establish-
> ment, called (from a worshipful company) the Charitable Grinders;
> where not only is a wholesome education bestowed upon the scholars,
> but where a dress and badge is likewise provided for them."[14]

So Richards' eldest son goes to the charitable school and turns out badly. The master of the school, like the more familiar Creakle in *David Copperfield*, knows nothing and spends most of his time caning his students on some pretext or other. Dickens was very bitter about such schools as examples of the education provided for the poorer classes:

> But they never taught honor at the Grinders' School, where the system
> that prevailed was particularly strong in the engendering of hypocrisy.
> Insomuch, that many of the friends and masters of past Grinders said,
> if this were what came of education for the common people, let us
> have none. Some more rational said, let us have a better one. But the

governing power of the Grinders' Company were always ready for *them,* by picking out a few boys who had turned out well, in spite of the system, and roundly asserted that they could have only turned out well because of it. Which settled the business of those objectors out of hand, and established the glory of the Grinders' Institution.[15]

In contrast to the Grinders' School, Dickens portrays one which would normally be considered the best available. However, he does not like Doctor Blimber's school any better. This is the old-fashioned grammar school where Paul is educated, and where the aims are cultural rather than practical. Dickens objects not so much to the teaching of subjects like Latin as to the system of teaching too much too fast. This school, he says:

> ... was a great hot-house, in which there was a forcing apparatus incessantly at work. All the boys blew before their time. Mental green-peas were produced at Christmas, and intellectual asparagus all the year round. Mathematical gooseberries (very sour ones too) were common at untimely seasons, and from mere sprouts of bushes, under Doctor Blimber's cultivation. Every description of Greek and Latin vegetable was got off the driest twigs of boys, under the frostiest circumstances. Nature was of no consequence at all. No matter what a young gentleman was intended to bear, Doctor Blimber made him bear to pattern, somehow or other.[16]

It is quite modern to say that education should be adapted to the particular needs of the student. Dickens is—as usual—much better at showing what was wrong than in suggesting what might be right. One supposes that Paul's death was attributable to natural causes, but the general implication of the story is that this forcing education hastened his death, if indeed it was not directly responsible. Observe what happened to young Toots, another student:

> There was not the right taste about the premature productions, and they didn't keep well. Moreover, one young gentleman, with a swollen nose and an excessively large head (the oldest of ten who had "gone through" everything), suddenly left off blowing one day, and remained in the establishment a mere stalk. And people did say that the doctor had rather overdone it with young Toots, and that when he began to have whiskers he left off having brains.[17]

The forcing system in education makes Mr. Toots a farce character with a few ridiculous scenes, but Paul Dombey dies. Many a schoolmaster has been known to say, sometimes almost regretfully, that education has never been known to kill anyone.

The next novel, *David Copperfield,* is an adaptation of Dickens' own life story to fiction; only a minor sequence or two refers to economic theory. From here on it is more convenient to examine the influence of Carlyle and the development of Dickens' theories in conjunction with his over-all purposes in fiction. In *David Copperfield* he introduced references to emigration and objections to model prisons which pampered criminals; in *Bleak House* he attacked aristocrats and bureaucratic mismanagement of government, as well as slum conditions which spread fever and disease through the community; in *Hard Times* he proceeded to a full-scale examination of Carlyle's theories in a study of capital-labor relations in the manufacturing center of Coketown; in *Little Dorrit* he pilloried governmental red tape in the Circumlocution Office and pyramiding speculating capitalists and bankers in Mr. Merdle; in *A Tale of Two Cities*—following Carlyle's *French Revolution*—he studied the evil results of revolution in a country where nothing was done about the demands of the downtrodden masses; in *Great Expectations* he examined the effect of undeserved inherited money on the character of the recipient; in *Our Mutual Friend* he made his final charge against a civilization dominated by utilitarian, laissez-faire economy. Each of these novels was an experiment in adjusting his major purposes to fictional artistry, and each demands detailed examination in conjunction with other technical considerations.

But in the matter of economic and political theory Dickens' general position is plain. The examination of his major and minor theses from *A Christmas Carol* on indicates that he was violently antiutilitarian, violently anti-Adam Smith. Certainly he was antirevolutionary, and there is no indication that he discussed or favored any communist remedy. He followed a determined but middle ground, assailing the evils of the capitalistic system and arguing, like Carlyle, for paternalistic understanding on the part of capital and efficient government supervision on the part of Parliament. His attitude toward trade unions was negative, and no argument against economic strife could be more lucid than *A Tale of Two Cities,* in which the Defarges are first shown sympathetically and later as the villains of the story

128

after the revolution gets out of hand. He believed that a class war should be avoided at any cost, but that it is the duty of society to remedy the faults of the capitalist system so that no revolution is necessary or possible.

The positive part of his political theory depended upon legislative action and intelligent leadership. Dickens went through several periods of disillusion about England's legislative processes. He seems to have been much less sanguine than Carlyle about heroic dictatorship, although he dedicated *A Tale of Two Cities* to Lord John Russell. Carlyle had high hopes for the intelligence of Lord Peel, whose term as prime minister was quite short. Dickens hated Lord Palmerston with vindictive contempt, and although he mentions Gladstone more favorably, he could hardly be called his supporter. *Household Words* and *All the Year Round* offer a number of outright statements about his later positive beliefs. His letters also contribute to our knowledge of his disgust with Parliamentary procedures. He wrote to Forster in 1854, saying he wished "every man in England [could] feel something of the contempt for the House of Commons that I have."[18] To the actor Macready he wrote, "As to the suffrage, I have lost hope even in the ballot. We appear to me to have proved the failure of representative institutions without an educated and advanced people to support them."[19] But these expressions came from the lowest depths of his blackest moments. Just before he died he wrote what appears to be the final and classic statement of his beliefs:

> My faith in the people governing is on the whole infinitesimal; my faith in the people governed, is, on the whole, illimitable.[20]

Among the positive social measures he supported in his magazines were the formation of provident societies, post-office savings banks, cooperative insurance companies, annuities and insurance for sickness and old age, and the use of tax money to establish something like social security for all workers. He wanted wage-hour legislation and better working conditions enforced by law. His essential democracy led him to believe that no reform would work before the people in general understood the reform. One concludes that he would be a vocal member of Britain's Labour party if he were alive today. His fiction reflects his feeling that England's only hope was an enlightened and aroused

129

public conscience, and he devoted his novels to arousing that conscience.[21]

Artistically, the record shows that Dickens leaned more and more to novels which were dominated and unified by some variety of social thesis; the farce-caricature technique took a secondary place after *Pickwick Papers.* His main artistic impulses began to depend upon organizing his plots and arranging them to throw light on some serious criticism of society which went far beyond mere entertainment. He turned more and more away from melodrama, excitement, and suspense for their own sakes. Since his writing developed from a scattered emphasis upon characters and short episodes to unified broad-scale novels, the next step in the study of his narrative craft is to examine his handling of action from the standpoint of multiple-plot structure.

CHAPTER VIII

From Alternation to Pattern: The Technique of Contrast

CUMENICAL prototypes and invigorating activity do not in themselves constitute artistry. Dickens came gradually to a perception of fiction as an art form. Up to his time the novel had developed no exact aesthetic rules which distinguished the style or limited the manner of developing the action portrayed. Fiction was the last of the great literary types of expression to assume any consciousness of formal design. Poetry had rules of rhythm, rhyme, and stanza arrangement which crystallized epic, dramatic, and lyric composition; drama was subservient to ideals of unity or concentration of action in act and scene division which furnished the playwright with standards, a form on which to build and contain his dramatic arrangement of action. But fiction ordinarily progressed as it pleased, casually dividing its development by chapters, following no law but the author's preference in exposing character and action.

From the time of Defoe, novelists had solved their artistic problems according to their genius or their individual luck. Defoe himself limited his tales to a biographical narrative, achieving a kind of unity by the confining use of the first person. Richardson revealed his action entirely by letters, balancing his main characters against diverse personalities in correspondence. Fielding and Smollett used a picaresque organization, the loose form which revolved around the unconnected adventures of the hero. *Tom Jones,* the great exception, stands out like an artistic obelisk among all the novels before those of Dickens. Fielding in that book deliberately borrowed—and satirized in the process—the artistic ideals and strictures of the poetic epic. His masterpiece profits greatly from this alliance, but it was a single effort and did not set a model which could be readily imitated or formalized.

After Fielding, Scott adjusted his tales around a body of historical fact and atmosphere. Various other novelists organized their stories by presenting their characters in contention with each other, developing a scheme of action which was arranged like the plots of plays, but not limited by act or scene division. These stories began when the conflict was introduced and came to a conclusion after the event which resolved the conflict: the climax. Whatever artistry was involved depended on the logical and essential development of the action. Complex novels utilizing more than one plot were related in an omniscient manner, the narrator leaping from place to place and scene to scene according to his judgment or whim. He often created an interesting story without any particular design or pattern. Occasionally, as in the novels of Jane Austen, the action was concentrated on a small community or social group, achieving compact artistry and unity of effect by careful and pertinent selection of detail and incident.

The modern novel, since the day of Dickens, has reached out toward artistic form in two separate directions. One road has concentrated more and more upon a single individual and, following the varied tests and trials of Henry James, has experimented with deliberately narrow points of view in telling the story. Previously this had been done more or less by accident when the author told his tale in the first person, but James also suppressed extraneous explanations and interruptions, argued for erasing the author himself from any part of the action, and achieved artistry by strict limitation according to a self-imposed approach to the manner of narration. Artistry in this sense may be called *microscopic*. It depends upon sticking to an arbitrary narrative point of view and reaches its best results when the character studied in minute detail is completely revealed. After James come those novels which benefit by the careful observation of thought processes or stream of consciousness.

The opposite road to artistry has dealt with a wide variety of characters in action, usually with the breadthwise intent of portraying a representative cross section of society, or a district, or a nation, or an era. This approach is *panoramic* or *telescopic*. It sets forth a number of characters in contrast to each other and balances them either in representative action or alternative behavior as their stories are told. Tolstoi's *War and Peace,* Conrad's *Nostromo,* and Dos Passos' *U. S. A.*

132

illustrate variations on this artistic approach. The handling of several themes simultaneously is extraordinarily difficult in narration, posing problems similar to those of counterpoint in music. The reader expects to be told selected but important things about many characters rather than everything about one individual. A great deal of experimentation with narrative counterpoint has been carried on in our century, particularly by Huxley and Gide.

Dickens had no historical part in developing the use of a microscopic point of view or in telling a story according to principles which concentrated on a single character in detail. This is true even when he used the first person, as in *David Copperfield, Bleak House,* and *Great Expectations*. His abilities demanded action on a grand scale. He was always fascinated by the antithetical variables of human behavior and got his effects by contrasting them. A single plot or sequence of action never satisfied him when he was past the second or third installment of his tale. Since he inherited no rules or sense of restrictive form, he felt his way toward a planned pattern in the direction of panoramic narration. He developed many techniques, as has been demonstrated. His great abilities in farce-caricature, in speech devices, in conflicting and exciting action, in the use of sentiment, horror, and purpose worked to his advantage, since he was able to set a variety of narrative effects side by side, thereby appealing to a larger audience. Still, he found it easy to allow some one technique to get out of focus. From *Pickwick Papers* to *David Copperfield* he fought against a tendency to ramble and to allow his novels to develop loose ends. Satisfactory balance eluded him in the early stories. Writing and publishing his tales in installments kept him from rewriting and polishing at the same time that this necessity encouraged him to depend more and more upon variety of manner and matter. He needed a striking effect in each installment, and—if possible—a type different from the last striking effect.

Oddly enough, his interest in propaganda and his desire to prove a moral or politico-economic point eventually came to his aid. When his novel had a thesis, he intended to organize his action around it. The consciousness of integral pattern dependent on his thesis grew slowly. His polymorphous components of society were always stopping to entertain the reader; his varied techniques, like papers filed in the pigeonholes of his writing desk, were always popping out at some propitious moment to run off with the plan of the story. At first he merely experimented with contrast and alternation of materials and techniques. He produced marvelous single episodes and sequences. As his art matured, he proceeded from alternation to synthesis, from contrast to pattern, from panorama to cyclorama. Finally all his techniques began to gather around his purpose—the thesis—each in its appropriate place. *The balance and contrast of several plots and techniques, so that each intensifies the others, the entire action arranged around a central pattern—this is his original contribution to the development of fiction as an art form.*

The manner in which Dickens arrived at this telescopic concept provides a great deal of comment upon experimentation in narration. The first novel, *Pickwick Papers,* had no form except the organization dependent upon a series of episodes that revolved around Mr. Pickwick and his companions. This style followed the picaresque model, depended upon the farce-caricature technique, attempted contrast in the filler stories which were inserted from time to time, and eventually ended with an inconsequential love story or two.

The plot development of the second novel, *Oliver Twist,* was planned. Here Dickens called upon suspense and intrigue to advance the action of his story, rather than the picaresque method inherited from Smollett and Fielding. His theme was: *Crime does not pay!* or *Criminals are not heroes!* A major part of his thesis included his attack on the Poor Law and the circumstances which produced juvenile delinquency in big cities. The plot he imagined in order to further his purpose went something like this: man separated from wife—loves girl—has illegitimate child—mother dies giving birth—father dies soon after—will leaving fortune to bastard son is suppressed—legitimate son pursues brother in relentless hatred—boy raised in Poor House—runs off to city—adopted by criminal gang—attempts made to teach him the art of crime—resists—finds relatives and friends of his parents—is saved—villainous half brother exposed and inheritance restored.

The way in which Dickens worked out this plot—whatever one thinks of it—is not entirely successful. The Poor House scenes are heightened, but not hampered by the original plot plan. Nor is the story of Fagin's gang in any conflict with the central theme, that of the persecution of Oliver by Monks, his half brother. In fact, the Poor House scenes and the criminal gang sequence carry the action very successfully without any help from the plot at all. When the intrigue does enter, rather spasmodically, the reader is asked to believe that a half brother would make a lifework of persecuting the young boy who stands for his father's defection from Monks's mother. This is not improbable, but to make it entirely convincing Dickens needed to show either more evidence for psychotic obsession or financial greed. Monks may have been deranged, but he acts like a villain in a melodrama; money is involved, but the facts do not make this point clear. After all, the will was suppressed; Monks and his mother already have the fortune. The means of getting to the plot climax are also devious. We are asked to believe that the old midwife would have kept up interest on a pawn ticket for years and that Mr. Bumble's wife would have redeemed the pledge. The pawn ticket contains the evidence for Oliver's parentage and inheritance.

The plot therefore does not help the main effect of the novel very much. It does not take a complicated intrigue to make Oliver's struggle with his environment, with the Poor House and Fagin's gang, interesting and important. Fagin and Sikes would have attempted to make a criminal out of Oliver just the same, Monks or no Monks. The subplot which presents Rose and Harry Maylie with typical difficulties before they get married also does not matter much one way or the other. It provides contrast, but better contrast enters the story with the murder of Nancy by Bill Sikes; Dickens also found an outlet for his comic sense by way of Mr. Bumble's courtship and unhappy marriage. Nancy's murder is a by-product of the Monks-Oliver intrigue; it adds suspense, horror, and a sensational lift to the ending while Oliver is working out his destiny.

This novel is "organized" in a limited sense. Dickens began with an outlined plot and attempted to arrange that plot to coincide with his propagandistic purpose. The propaganda ran away from the plot. As the tale progressed he managed to place his main characters in different locations, Oliver here, Fagin and Sikes there, Mr. Bumble somewhere else, so that he had to alternate his narrative chronology to follow his separate courses of action. The principle of alternation is to skip from one set of characters to another whenever it seems convenient. Dickens explains this in the course of the novel—showing that he had thought about it:

> It is the custom of the stage, in all good murderous melodramas, to present the tragic and the comic scenes, in as regular alternation, as the layers of red and white in a side of streaky, well-cured bacon. The hero sinks upon his straw bed, weighed down by fetters and misfortunes; and, in the next scene, his faithful but unconscious squire regales the audience with comic song. We behold, with throbbing bosoms, the heroine in the grasp of a proud and ruthless baron: her virtue and her life are alike in danger: drawing forth her dagger to preserve the one at the cost of the other; and, just as our expectations are wrought up to the highest pitch, a whistle is heard: and we are straightway transported to the great hall of the castle: where a gray-headed seneschal sings a funny chorus with a funnier body of vassals, who are free of all sorts of places, from church vaults to palaces, and roam about in company, carolling perpetually.
>
> Such changes appear absurd; but they are not so unnatural as they would appear at first sight. The transitions in real life from well-spread boards to death-beds, and from mourning-weeds to holiday garments, are not a whit less startling.[1]

He continues by appealing to books and critics of the past; everybody does it, he says. Therefore he whisks the reader back to the town where Oliver was born, "the reader taking it for granted that there are good and substantial reasons for making the journey."

When this leaping from place to place and from one sequence to another occurs, Dickens gets his best results by leaving the reader in suspense. This is the later motion-picture-serial technique: desert the audience at a breath-taking climax, then resolve it next week and do it all over again. Once Dickens leaves Oliver just after Mr. Brownlow notices the similarity between the boy's face and the expression in a portrait on the wall. Oliver has fainted, and while attempts are made to revive him, the author shifts in the middle of the installment back to the point in the narrative at which the Artful Dodger has escaped and Oliver has been caught for stealing the handkerchief. The story centers on the Dodger for some pages; eventually it returns to Oliver.[2]

In another instance Oliver is shot while housebreaking with Sikes. The next chapter returns for Mr. Bumble's courtship to the workhouse where Oliver was born. Five chapters later we return to Oliver, Dickens saying:

Let us set on foot a few inquiries after young Oliver Twist; and ascertain whether he be still lying in the ditch where Toby Crackit left him.[3]

In this novel, then, Dickens may be said to have used contrast in a tentative fashion and also capriciously. His main plot got lost, and when he came to the end of his story there was still much of it to be explained to the reader. So he introduced the ending which exposes Monks and brings the mystery of Oliver's birth to light. The explanation bursts upon the reader, floods over him, and is gone. But the conclusion indicates that the virtues of this novel are not dependent upon the plot sequence with which the tale begins and ends.

Nicholas Nickleby follows a different structure entirely. Derived from the picaresque model of *Roderick Random* and *Peregrine Pickle,* it centers on the goodhearted hero rather than on a club, as had *Pickwick Papers.* This form cries out for effective contrasting scenes and techniques. So Dickens used everything he had, farce, propagandistic attacks, stage plots, extended parody, a little sentiment, a little horror, and a lot of melodrama. Some of it is very good; some of it seems unlikely to have been written by a great author. But no other novel of Dickens illustrates greater profusion of contrast and alternation. The small intrigues are many and varied. After one looks at Smike and the attack on the bad boarding schools, at Vincent Crummles and his company, and at Mrs. Nickleby's extraordinary monologues, one finds a heterogeneous combination of contrasting complications. The main plot is meant to intensify our impression of Ralph Nickleby and to show his villainous character. We are already sure of this at the beginning, from his treatment of Nicholas, so that there is little compelling reason for making him the father of Smike except that this is another surprising complication Dickens admired and thought his readers would enjoy.

This plot must be examined several times to be appreciated. Ralph had secretly married an heiress whose fortune depended on her brother's consent to her marriage. Neither wanted to buy off the brother, and his consent is never secured. The marriage and the child are kept secret, and the lady finally runs off with someone else after a seven-year interval. The father does not know what happened to the boy, who turns out to be Smike, someone he has coincidentally been persecuting. Dickens must have had this intrigue worked out when he started the novel, but as in *Oliver Twist* it is lost as the tale progresses, and the novel goes merrily on without it.

The main love story concerns Nicholas and Madeline Bray, who escapes being forced to marry the odious Gride when her father drops dead. But there are many other full-blown intrigues. They include: the troubles suffered by the Mantalinis; the Kenwigs family which hopes to inherit money from Mr. Lillyvick, who sneaks off to marry an actress, who eventually leaves him and lets him go back to his hungry relatives; the pursuit of Kate by Lord Frederick Verisopht and Sir Mulberry Hawk; her eventual marriage to Frank Cheeryble; the persecution of Smike which ends in his death; Mrs. Nickleby's mad lover who throws cucumbers at her instead of roses; the ruin and suicide of Ralph at the end of the story. There are several more that might be mentioned, but the point ought to be clear. All these themes represent a combination of generally unrelated circumstances and events, typical of the picaresque model for a mounting number of episodes, separated in effect, but supposedly centering about the hero. An examination of the intrigues will indicate that many of them have nothing to do with Nicholas. The scene shifts from Dotheboys Hall to London, back to Nicholas, then to the Kenwigses, then to the Crummles Company, then to the Mantalinis; from Nicholas to Ralph to Kate to Newman Noggs to the Brays and always from here to there. True, it stays with Nicholas more than with anyone else. The total effect of the story is accordingly scattered, perhaps kaleidoscopic; its accomplishment in artistry is fragmentary. There is no discernible plan in the order of its contrast or alternation of technique.

In the novels which followed, Dickens began to experiment with the idea of deliberately balancing several plots against each other. The main technical problem was to keep the chronology straight when he was following more than one strand of action. His characters had a tendency to separate from each other, so he naturally alternated in following them. He had to learn how far to develop one plot sequence before he turned to its counterpart.

The Old Curiosity Shop has certain unique qualities. It developed without initial plan—this we know for certain—except that Dickens had intended a tale of medium length about a young girl and her grandfather. Dickens had recently seen Lemaitre, one of his favorite actors, in a melodrama called *Thirty Years of a Gambler's Life*. The plot of this play involved an old man who had a mania for gambling; it also presented a beautiful young granddaughter who tried to save him from his vice and his doom.[4] Little Nell and her grandfather reflect this basic situation, although Dickens allows his heroine more success than her prototype in the play; the original girl could not keep her grandfather from murder and ruin.

When—for commercial reasons—Dickens decided to enlarge the tale to a full-length novel (beginning in Chapter IV), he must have had to do some rapid planning. The grandfather-Nell sequence involves the villainous Quilp, who lends money to the old man, seizes his shop in payment, and makes amorous suggestions to Nell; Nell and her grandfather leave London and travel north. Forster suggested that Dickens allow Nell to die eventually, and the sentimental technique took over most of this plot. The journey northward is varied by their encounter with the Jarley waxwork caravan and by the picture of the industrial hell of Manchester. For contrast Dickens turned to Quilp, Swiveller, and Brass back in London. He introduced an additional intrigue which revolves about Kit and the Garlands, eventually placing Kit in jeopardy because of a false charge of stealing. After a time three separate courses of action are going more or less simultaneously: Nell and her grandfather on their way north; Swiveller, Brass, and Quilp in one part of London; Kit and the Garlands in another. Dickens starts a chapter, for example:

> Kit—for it happens at this juncture, not only that we have breathing time to follow his fortunes, but that the necessities of these adventures so adapt themselves to our ease and inclination as to call upon us imperatively to pursue the track we most desire to take—Kit, while the matters of the last fifteen chapters were yet in progress, was, as the reader may suppose, gradually familiarizing himself more and more with Mr. and Mrs. Garland.[5]

This sounds as capricious as his practice in *Oliver Twist*, but the three-fold plot arrangement really goes much better. There is only one completely unprepared-for intrigue, which appears at the finish of the tale. If Dickens intended to motivate this, he neglected it till the last

139

moment. Nell's great-uncle appears, and the reader finds that: he and Nell's grandfather had loved the same girl; her great-uncle had withdrawn from the competition and left the girl to his brother; the daughter from this marriage had married a worthless man, leaving eventually two orphaned daughters, one wild (she disappeared) and the other (Nell) like her mother; then the great-uncle finally returns to England, discovers what has happened, and resolves to do something to help Nell and her grandfather. Like so many of the romance-intrigues of Dickens' early novels, this one barely beats the closing chapters to the reader's attention. The great-uncle is too late, too.

The strange case of *Barnaby Rudge* is Dickens' most elaborate attempt at panorama up to this time. The novel, under the title of *Gabriel Vardon, the Locksmith of London,* was advertised for publication by Macrone as early as 1834, two years before the appearance of *Pickwick.* It is probable that this novel comprises Dickens' first vision of a full-length story. The advertisements continued till 1837, when Macrone went bankrupt. About three years later Dickens transferred whatever had been his original plan to the tale of Barnaby. Following the example of Scott and Ainsworth, he went to history and settled on the No-Popery Riots of 1780 for his main action. In this case he did some factual research before writing. He visited the British Museum and found the most usable source to be a pamphlet (now known to have been written by Holcroft) entitled: *A Plain and Succinct Narrative of the Late Riots and Disturbances with an Account of the Commitment of Lord George Gordon to the Tower and Anecdotes of his Life.*[6] He also looked at newspaper accounts and consulted some other historical reference works for minor details. From his sources he derived the story of Gordon, well-meaning fanatic, invented the rascally follower Gashford, and depicted the Protestant-Catholic explosion which culminated in the riots. Dickens explained the contradictions in Gordon's character by blaming them on Gashford's villainous influence, changing or manipulating the historical account in minor details whenever he desired.[7]

Forster says of this novel:

Begun during the progress of *Oliver Twist,* it had been for some time laid aside; the form it ultimately took had been comprised only partially within its first design; and the story in its finished shape presented strongly a special purpose, the characteristic of all but his very earliest writings.[8]

Dickens' Preface explains what this "special purpose" was. He says succinctly that the riots "teach a good lesson," that religious persecution and intolerance lead to terrible results. This purpose did interesting things to the climax of the story. Dickens felt that there was little real difference between Gordon's fanaticism and insanity, so he wanted to make this leader of intolerance a lunatic. He also desired to bring in three new characters to lead the mob scenes, men who should later turn out to have escaped from the asylum at Bedlam.[9] Forster dissuaded him from these touches with some difficulty, apparently because Forster thought they would lead some people to resent the idea that extreme religious feeling could encompass insanity. Modern readers are likely to have as much difficulty as Dickens in seeing Forster's point, for such a solution of Gordon's character is most likely. The exact nature of his complex could be determined by almost any modern psychiatrist. The scene which Dickens proposed concerning the other madmen would be improbable, but was surely in the same vein symbolically as his later handling of Krook's death by spontaneous combustion in *Bleak House*. The idea is fantastic, not real; the riots partake of the nature of unbelievable fantasy come true. But Forster won; he was Dickens' commercial conscience.

The historical action in *Barnaby Rudge* eventually has to take into account three separate and distinct plots. The one Dickens began with (judging from the earlier title *Gabriel Vardon*) is the least important of them. It concerns Vardon, a henpecked husband with a beautiful flirtatious daughter, the latter loved by a young man whose development is held back by his father. One can guess that Dickens intended to send Joe Willet off on a journey to make his fortune, and he might have encountered some of the adventures of Nicholas Nickleby if this story had been written earlier. As the plot stands, Joe's adventures are not described, but he comes back to marry Dolly, after the pattern of the love story common to sentimental romance.

The Haredale-Rudge mystery comes to the center of the stage early. It presents the murder of the elder Haredale's brother years before the tale begins. Barnaby's father had been Haredale's steward,

141

and his supposed dead body was also found after the murder of his master. But the murderer is still alive. On anniversaries of his deed he returns to haunt his wife and idiot son. Dickens became much interested in young Barnaby and devoted many pages to following his adventures. Haredale, whose niece Emma attracts the villainous Gashford, is a Catholic. This circumstance allows the Haredale household to become more thoroughly embroiled in the historical events narrated toward the last of the novel.

The third main plot is based on a man's persecution of a younger person who turns out to be his son. Dickens' Sir John Chester is partially a general satire on snobbery, but refers specifically to Lord Chesterfield, the eighteenth-century aristocrat who worshiped the god of practical selfishness. Chesterfield's famous advice to his son in letters told him just how to get along in love, politics, and society.[10] Dickens put this type in the fairy-tale Valentine-Orson situation; the civilized father ruins the uncivilized son by his evil philosophy of life. Dickens' explanation for the existence of the son reminds one of a previous plot or two. Chester had enticed a gypsy maid and abandoned her with her son, and later she was sentenced to death for passing forged notes. Hugh was reared in ignorance of his parentage. All becomes known in true romance tradition through the hangman, Dennis; the gypsy's former sweetheart told him the name of Hugh's father just before he himself was hanged. This plot is tied to the previous one by having Edward Chester, Sir John's legitimate son, love Emma Haredale. At the end Haredale kills Sir John in a duel.

There are thus three plot sequences in the novel, the Haredale-Rudge, the Chester-Hugh, and the Varden-Willet stories. They all merge into and are more or less swallowed up by the historical events which culminate in the riots. Several minor motifs supply more contrast, particularly the Tappertit apprentice incidents and the conduct of Dennis, the hangman. Grotesque atmosphere is aided by Grip, Barnaby's raven. This novel contains the most complex plot pattern Dickens had attempted, and since each sequence is full of complications, he managed to write more pages than for any other novel in weekly installments. He continually complained in his letters to Forster of his troubles with the small portions—difficulties which were aggravated by the broad canvas appropriate to the riot scenes themselves and by the involutions of the three main plot sequences he had to develop. He was forced to skip nimbly from Barnaby to Joe Willet to Gashford to Haredale to Gordon to Dennis to Tappertit to Chester to history—and sometimes to a place just short of confusion. The book contains many excellent passages, although its rambling pattern has made it in later generations the least popular of Dickens' novels. Forster notes this:

> But, as the story went on, it was incident to such designs that what had been accomplished in its predecessor could hardly be attained here, in singleness of purpose, unity of idea, or harmony of treatment; and other defects supervened in the management of the plot. The interest with which the tale begins has ceased to be its interest before the close; and what has chiefly taken the reader's fancy at the outset, almost wholly disappears in the power and passion with which, in the later chapters, the great riots are described.[11]

This judgment comes from the person closest to Dickens' narrative intentions, and it explains the difficulties he experienced in carrying on a number of plots simultaneously. The ideal of a guiding pattern was still in the future.

The first five novels show marked development in handling contrasting action. Dickens' best writing was done in the farce-caricature scenes of *Pickwick Papers* and in the various similar technical sequences in *Nicholas Nickleby*. All the early novels demonstrate a lack of sustained plan or motivation, a degree of melodramatic unreality, and incidental shifts in intention. From this time on he deliberately tried to be more certain of the main course of his story, and his veerings in purpose or in treatment were subsidiary to the general plan which he had set from the beginning of his tale. He continued to experiment with the multiple-plot idea, holding before himself the ideal of controlled contrast. He drifted further and further from the practice of introducing a multitude of entertaining personalities, following their eccentricities in a variety of relatively unconnected scenes, then finally entwining them in whatever romance plot occurred to him.

Martin Chuzzlewit surpasses in total effect all the earlier novels. Most of the reason for this success comes from the fact that Dickens outlined and arranged several plots around a unified frame of reference. Forster says that Dickens originated his novel with the picture of Pecksniff, a character who should epitomize *selfishness* or *hypocrisy*. Every additional character introduced was to show "the number and variety of humours and vices that have their root in selfishness."[12] By this plan, Dickens intended to present contrasting characters and plot sequences, but the recurrent theme was to be the same. This is his first sustained effort at writing a broad-scale novel which would be subservient to a concept of over-all artistry. He was not able to stick to this concept completely, and he was more successful with it in later novels; but in artistic design *Martin Chuzzlewit* is a great step forward.

There are three important courses of action which develop the theme of selfishness. The first concerns the efforts of Mr. Pecksniff to improve his position in the world. He cheats his apprentices, makes halfhearted advances to Mary, and fawns over old Martin in an effort to install himself as his heir. He invests his fortune and loses his money in a gold-brick speculation promoted by Tigg. His other plans are circumvented by old Martin's guile in pretending to be fooled. The old man, like Ben Jonson's Volpone, leads the hypocritical victim on, refuses to forgive the grandson he had disinherited, but eventually shows in a surprising denouement that he has changed, so he kicks out Pecksniff and settles his fortune on young Martin.

The second sequence sustains most of the action. It introduces young Martin, whose love for Mary is opposed by his grandfather, this opposition leading to his being disinherited. There is no compelling reason for delaying his marriage to Mary, since he has lost his inheritance anyway. But Dickens motivates the delay reasonably. Young Martin is selfish; he needs a lot of money in order to be happy; therefore he goes off to make his fortune. The Peregrine Pickle type of hero would have returned with his pot of gold or would have found a wealthy inheritance elsewhere, but Martin discovers spiritual regeneration in America, in spite of the people and conditions he encounters. He does not make his fortune, and it is the self-sacrificing spirit of Mark which finally changes his character. When he comes back to Mary he is worthy of her, and the reader feels pleased when Martin's grandfather finally gives him the money he wanted all the time. This is the finest example of sustained character study and plot development Dickens had created up to this time. Before Martin leaves for America, the narrative technique assumes a degree of convincing reality unattained previously. The American scenes tend to break the spell with their stinging satire, and their heightened quality does not entirely fit the rest of the novel. Still, the complete effect is generally admirable.

The third sequence concerns Jonas Chuzzlewit, brought up by his father in a frigid atmosphere of business selfishness. He is desirous of having his inheritance before his time. Therefore he apparently murders his father by a cleverly conceived plan, is blackmailed by Tigg, and commits a second but more spectacular crime to get rid of the blackmailer. This plot provides sensation in its contrast, displaying itself expertly against the comedy, the adventure, and the suspense of the other two sequences.

Additional minor parts of the story revolve about selfishness or its opposite. Tom Pinch wins his way by simple honesty, or unselfishness; his attractive sister, who is similarly unselfish, gains the heart of John Westlake because she deserves happiness; the Pecksniff daughters try matrimony, but resembling their father in character, they do not have much luck. Merry secures Jonas as a husband, and Cherry loses her affianced groom at the altar. Mrs. Gamp was added purely for entertainment, and surely everybody is happy that Dickens invented her, even if she departs from the pattern. One can stretch the facts and say that she too is grotesquely selfish.

There are many expertly conceived passages in *Martin Chuzzlewit*, and most of them are subservient to the purpose of the tale. The scenes in which Mr. Pecksniff's hypocrisy is revealed are uniformly superb. In the wonderful episode in which he goes after Mrs. Gamp to procure her services as a nurse and everyone thinks he is a frantic husband in need of a midwife, Dickens manages to use his comic touch to develop an incident which is important to his plot. Nor is there any better use of farce to illustrate his purpose than in Jonas Chuzzlewit's proposal of marriage. It is part of this man's character to disappoint the elder sister in wanting to marry the younger one. Even though the reader may laugh immoderately at his proposing to the younger sister through the elder, the effect is in perfect harmony with the author's general exposition of selfishness. In this novel Dickens came very close to making his various techniques serve his purpose on a phylogenetic scale. Especially is this true in the first quarter of the novel.

Several touches are less effective. Forster tells how very early in the composition of the story, Dickens sent him the outline of old Martin's trick to expose and torture Pecksniff. He continues:

> And the difficulties he encountered in departing from other portions of his scheme were such as to render him, in his subsequent stories more bent upon constructive care at the outset, and adherence as far as might be to any design he had formed.[13]

What happened is clear. Dickens knew at the start where he intended to go. Then, despite his feeling that he was writing well and achieving a better artistic effect than in anything he had previously created, the installments did not sell as well as the other books had done. One fourth of the way along he and Forster decided there was something wrong, at least from a commercial standpoint. They concluded that the plot was not sensational enough; there was no sentimental death in the offing; the characters were not getting enough laughs.

Dickens decided to bring in Mrs. Gamp and to heighten the farce scenes. He also built up the murder episodes. But his main shift was to send Martin to America. Presumably Martin would have traveled somewhere, but whatever Dickens had planned previously went out the window. The attack on America was supposed to bring sales up, although they never did rise very much. The American scenes shift the emphasis of the story, even though they are not entirely antagonistic to the original theme.

This novel shows Dickens dropping into a questionable rhetorical habit. When he felt deeply about something, he wanted to exclaim about it in order to emphasize it. *Martin Chuzzlewit* has numerous examples of this declamatory style, something which reached its height in *Dombey and Son*. For some readers, this manner damages the style irretrievably. There is the portrait of Jonas Chuzzlewit; Dickens never lets the reader forget he is selfish, the irony and the emphasis being explained from scene to scene. Jonas and his wife do not get along, and Dickens shows Jonas being cruel to her; he treats her badly through sheer perversity, and even beats her—hush!

> He answered with an imprecation, and—
> Not with a blow? Stern truth against the base-souled villain: with a blow.

Then the chapter ends:

> Oh woman, God beloved in old Jerusalem! The best among us need deal lightly with thy faults, if only for the punishment thy nature will endure, in bearing heavy evidence against us, on the Day of Judgment![14]

This heightened rhetorical verbiage involves Dickens in explaining the point of his moral purpose, a practice he did not indulge in when he found better ways of emphasizing his point. Exclamations creep into Mark's speeches and make his comments on the boorish Americans painfully plain; they involve the author in sentimental apostrophes to Tom Pinch, for whose honest simplicity and unselfishness he has a great weakness; they make Jonas rave wildly while suffering agonies of remorse for his deeds.

The handling of the Jonas Chuzzlewit murders also deserves some small notice. It is very easy for the modern reader to fall into several misunderstandings of the death of Jonas' father because he is used to having a puzzle to solve. Jonas intended to commit murder, and Dickens made little effort to mislead us. The surprise was to come when it was disclosed that the old man had died of natural causes after all. The detective story tradition has intervened since this novel was written. Readers of mystery tales expect to be misled as to the identity of the murderer or the solution of the mystery; they like to match wits with a fictional detective or with the author. This sequence is treated by Dickens as any other sensational part of his plot would be. In later novels (*Bleak House,* for example) he emphasized the intellectual puzzles inherent in his mysterious plot situations. By the time he came to *Edwin Drood,* he had learned to present a mystery so as to get the full challenge that comes from misdirection. He did it so well in his last novel that no one has ever solved the mystery of that uncompleted book.

The happy ending to *Martin Chuzzlewit* includes poetic justice for everybody, all being rewarded according to their relationship to selfishness. Dickens even brought in the starving neighbors from Eden so that they might be settled comfortably, a touch which necessitates their journeying all the way from America and turning up astonishingly at the right moment. They travel just fast enough to arrive before the final pages.

147

Even with the shiftings from the original plan, and making allowance for the weaknesses, *Martin Chuzzlewit* must be judged an artistic advance. Such judgment includes a consideration of all Dickens' technical accomplishments, not farce-caricature alone. This book has two of the greatest comic characters in literature in Pecksniff and Mrs. Gamp, so that even in the field of comedy the novel takes second place to *Pickwick* only in quantity. The strong points of the story surely outweigh the flaws. If there were no later book which reached greater heights, this one would stand as effective accomplishment of the broad-scale novel with multiple plots developing a central theme, the first such masterpiece in the history of English fiction.

Following *Martin Chuzzlewit* it is appropriate and convenient to examine a diversion. The shorter Christmas Books (written between 1843 and 1847) helped Dickens toward the telling of a story unified by a purpose. The ordinary Christmas Book was about twice the length of a monthly installment of a novel, and the idea was a good financial venture at first. The length of the tales puts them in the long short-story class. There was no short-story form established by tradition, at least as we understand the type, and Dickens was influenced more by the chapbooks of his childhood than by anything else in the form and design he essayed in *A Christmas Carol*.

The history of chapbooks is a little-known development of minor literary interest. From late in the seventeenth century until about 1820, the underprivileged and uneducated classes received much of their limited literary experience from chapbooks and hornbooks. These little volumes, sixteen or twenty-four pages in length, were hawked about the country by peddlers and sold for anything from a penny to sixpence. They included the old fairy tales about Jack the Giant-Killer, Bluebeard, Beauty and the Beast, Valentine and Orson, Wat Tyler, Tom Thumb, Cinderella, Richard Whittington, Friar Bacon, the Wandering Jew, and endless others. Famous plays and novels were sometimes shortened and printed in digest form in the chapbooks, *Robinson Crusoe, Gil Blas, Don Quixote,* and *Gulliver's Travels* finding wide circulation in this way. All these titles are referred to at some time or other in Dickens' novels, his references to chapbooks being more numerous than to any other book or author, with the exception of Shakespeare.[15] It is possible and even probable that Dickens became

148

acquainted with eighteenth-century fiction in shortened form before the full texts were given to him.

Many of these chapbooks were written for fantasy and fun, the level being simple enough to appeal to the commonest taste and particularly to children. They were used for moral purposes, too, the widespread compositions of Perrault giving rules of conduct which derived from the best-known fairy tales. Thus Red Riding Hood points out to the reader that there are wolves of every sort and character; Bluebeard imprints the lesson that one should not be too curious; and so on. Mrs. Sherwood, Maria Edgeworth, and Jane Marcet were among the established authors who wrote moral fables for the chapbook trade. Production of these small publications declined after 1820, when cheap magazines and illustrated periodicals ousted them from public favor.

Dickens' idea in writing the first Christmas Books was to provide a higher form for the old chapbook manner. He appropriated the fairytale atmosphere and intended to preach a moral. As has been shown, *A Christmas Carol* had as its purpose a criticism of utilitarian selfishness and an appeal to return to the good old-fashioned virtues of Christian sympathy at Christmastime. There are several technical reasons why the first of these Christmas Books is an artistic success. Primarily the narrative manner fits the way of saying, "Children, let me tell you a story." Dickens assumes a confidential style and gives the impression of extemporizing the tale; when he pounds home the moral, it fits the manner of the story, for he is writing a moral fairy tale, one which should appeal to children and adults for different reasons.

Having three ghosts visit Scrooge at the behest of Marley's troubled spirit allows further latitude in technique. Since ghosts pass over space and time at will, Dickens could shift from scene to scene and from one set of characters to another without straining the patience of the reader. No artistic design could be better adapted to his manipulation of event and personality to prove a thesis. The fairly-tale technique and the real background live in happy wedlock in *A Christmas Carol;* the reader leaps easily from Scrooge's childhood to his funeral or reformation, from Fezziwig to Bob Cratchit, from the sufferings of the needy to the true spirit of the nephew's Christmas dinner, without

149

noticing any creakings of the plot hinges. It is possible to prefer other types of writing, but within the limits of this one, the artistic effect is quite perfect.

The Chimes is not so successful in seizing the glorified chapbook manner, but its politico-economic point is even clearer. The subsequent three Christmas Books lost the style gradually, *The Cricket on the Hearth* achieving sentimental appeal and *The Battle of Life* and *The Haunted Man* coming close to being the least effective stories Dickens ever published.

After the interlude of the Christmas Books, when Dickens approached the planning of his next novel, he was at a difficult crossroads in his artistic development. The reception of *Martin Chuzzlewit*, judged by serious critics to be his best novel to date, but not nearly so profitable as some of the earlier works, had naturally complicated his motives. He wanted to write a book which would be artistic and have a high moral purpose; his interest in the problems of the poor and the stimulus of Carlyle's writings aided this desire. But he also wanted the book to sell. Surely he could find a way to combine serious and salable materials. He was not the first or the last novelist to be confronted with this problem.

He and Forster argued a great deal about *Dombey and Son*. This close friend, a professional critic of wide renown, was loyal, well-meaning, and not exactly superficial. But he was very positive in his views, and he was hard to move in a debate. He records in his biography of Dickens more corrections, more arguments (all of which he apparently won, causing Dickens to change what he intended or had already written) about *Dombey and Son* than about any other novel. The gist of his advice to Dickens was to stick to his original plan this time and be sure to put in what would sell the book.

Dickens based his outlined plot on Mr. Dombey, symbol of capitalistic selfishness and pride. He wrote jubilantly to Forster when he had conceived the essential action:

> I will now go on to give you an outline of my immediate intentions in reference to Dombey. I design to show Mr. Dombey with that one idea of the Son taking firmer and firmer possession of him, and swelling and bloating his pride to a prodigious extent. As the boy begins to grow up, I shall show him quite impatient for his getting on, and

urging his masters to set him great tasks, and the like. But the natural affection of the boy will turn towards the despised sister; and I purpose showing her learning all sorts of things, of her own application and determination, to assist him in his lessons; and helping him always. When the boy is about ten years old (in the fourth number), he will be taken ill, and will die; and when he is ill, and when he is dying, I mean to make him turn always for refuge to the sister still, and keep the stern affection of the father at a distance. . . .[16]

The rest of the outline, which Dickens had apparently set down in enough detail to know by installments what was to be in each one, shows his plan to have Mr. Dombey react to the death of his favorite child by growing to hate his daughter, and to have Florence love her father more and more because of her compassion for his sorrow; the business house will decay and bankrupt Mr. Dombey, but this will merely increase his hostility toward Florence because he realizes his injustice and will not admit any error in his pride. After mentioning Polly and Susan Nipper as part of the initial plan, Dickens says:

This is what cooks call "the stock of the soup." All kinds of things will be added to it, of course.[17]

The compromise between artistry and salability resulted in the plan for Paul's death. It was tied to the central theme, and readers were expected to weep in sympathy at the same time that they saw the justice of the catastrophe which punished Mr. Dombey's pride. Or so Dickens thought. The sentimental death scenes did cause the novel to make more money than *Martin Chuzzlewit,* but somehow or other there were no balancing major plots as in the previous novel. The additions, subplots, characterization, and atmosphere were all intended, as in the earlier book, to illustrate some variation of pride. The search for contrast began early. Dickens knew that when Paul died he would have to devise something else to keep up interest. So he invented Edith Skewton, brought up by her mother to artificial pride in social position, ripe to be bought in marriage by Mr. Dombey, who wants another son to replace Paul. The Dombeys' incompatibility becomes intolerable to Edith, and she elopes with Carker, Mr. Dombey's business manager. Losing Edith and his business—two shocks which coincide—brings Mr. Dombey to despair, finally inducing his change of heart at the end of the novel.

This action is merely added to the basic plot, serving as a continuation of it. Apparently Dickens intended to use Walter Gay in a parallel sequence which would reinforce the effect of his main action. Walter was to be sent away from London to separate him from Florence, and his subsequent adventures were to show him making many mistakes dependent upon pride. Martin Chuzzlewit had gone away with the characteristic of selfishness, but Walter would not reform. In presenting his idea Dickens ran afoul of Forster, and an argument ensued. Dickens tells in a letter what he proposed to do with Walter:

> About the boy, who appears in the last chapter of the first number, I think it would be a good thing to disappoint all the expectations that chapter seems to raise of his happy connection with the story and the heroine, and to show him gradually and naturally trailing away, from the love of adventure and boyish light-heartedness, into negligence, idleness, dissipation, dishonesty, and ruin. To show, in short, that common, everyday, miserable declension of which we know so much in our ordinary life; to exhibit something of the philosophy of it, in great temptations and an easy nature; and to show how the good turns into the bad by degrees.[18]

Forster viewed this intention with horror, and after he argued that it would turn readers away from the novel, Dickens accepted his judgment. Perhaps he had already strained his sources of invention for a journeying hero; so out went Walter to narrative oblivion, except for his return to marry Florence at the end of the book.

The comic contrast in the story does not supply completely satisfactory foils for pride, except for Mrs. Skewton. Captain Cuttle, Mrs. MacStinger, and Captain Bunsby provide their measure of humor, but not exactly in the pattern. Dickens consciously kept his comic scenes down, apparently fearing that they would interfere with his thesis. He says:

> You can hardly imagine what infinite pains I take, or what extraordinary difficulty I find in getting on FAST. Invention, thank God, seems the easiest thing in the world; and I seem to have such a preposterous sense of the ridiculous after this long rest as to be constantly required to restrain myself from launching into extravagances in the height of my enjoyment.[19]

Conscious restraint may be responsible for the fact that none of these characters is as successfully comic as Pecksniff or Mrs. Gamp, who occasionally run away with their novel. In *Dombey and Son* Dickens intended to keep strictly to his purpose, allowing only materials which would provide what he felt to be necessary, but were definitely minor contrast and relief. The result does not sufficiently help the novel's purpose. Without proper contrast Dickens' fiction could easily become more and more moral in tone, achieving the status of narrative tracts and preachments, but not fiction.

The general effect of an extended single plot pounding home a moral also produced distortion in many scenes of the novel. Young Paul, because of the words he is given to say, always is open to the suspicion of being an allegorical character speaking for the author. This would be suitable to a short moral fairy tale like *A Christmas Carol*. Paul says wise things naturally, but it is hard to believe in their actuality:

> "Well!" retorted Mrs. Pipchin, shortly, "and there's nobody like me, I suppose."
> "A'n't there really though?" asked Paul, leaning forward in his chair, and looking at her very hard.
> "No," said the old lady.
> "I am glad of that," observed Paul, rubbing his hand thoughtfully. "That's a very good thing."[20]

Mrs. Pipchin's instruction is a prime example of bad teaching method, so that what Paul says is much to Dickens' point. His face is always varying between an expression of age and youth, the old aspect being connected with his father's remarks about the power of money.

The relationship between Mr. Dombey and his daughter also gives the impression of being contrived rather than reported. He grows in hatred toward her, and there has to be a reason for this unnatural feeling. A man might prefer a son to a daughter, but Dickens, in his desire to make the reader sympathetic with Florence, shows her absolutely blameless. According to what is set down, nobody in his right mind could *hate* his child as Dombey does. The lengths of his misunderstanding toward the end, especially when he orders his wife away from Florence's company, remind one of the similar trials of Elsie Dinsmore, than which nothing seems more unlikely.

153

Edith's behavior is also subject to charges of distortion rather than a heightening of reality. She has been brought up to marry wealth, a perfectly believable concept of character. But Dickens thinks of her as understanding perfectly—just as the author does—how evil such a marriage is. Still, she goes ahead. A girl would do this for security, because of financial necessity, or to get away from an unbearable environment. No such motive is stressed, Dickens preferring to show her as realizing that she is too far gone to object to her mother's upbringing. She is convinced that her marriage to Mr. Dombey is wrong.

> "But my education was completed long ago. I am too old now, and have fallen too low, by degrees, to take a new course, and to stop yours, and to help myself. The germ of all that purifies a woman's breast, and makes it true and good, has never stirred in mine, and I have nothing else to sustain me when I despise myself."[21]

This analysis is what the author thinks, but it is absolutely improbable that *she* would *say* it in real life. Her references to her "sale" have a continued moral tilt toward the reader, who must not be allowed to miss the point.

The marital unhappiness of Mr. Dombey and Edith might have come in real life from a difference in temperament. Mr. Dombey's pride prevents much sympathy with anyone, much less his wife. Any modern novelist would include some reference to sex, the forbidden Victorian subject. Avoiding this explanation for incompatibility, Dickens suggests that Mr. Dombey is jealous of his wife because she prefers the society of his hated daughter to his. He sends disciplinary messages to her through Carker. The author keeps sternly silent about the fact that Mr. Dombey has married Edith in order to get another son, and Edith has not obliged him. She probably found that she could not stand him; any reader can see that. But this conclusion is guesswork.

Many women, denied marital happiness or a separation, driven to the point of desperation, might leave their husbands. Dickens asks us to believe that Edith eloped with Carker, a man she hates. Apparently the author's first purpose was to show that there was no other way out for her. Even the despised Carker offered escape; she had sold herself to a man before, why not again?

When this much of the novel was published Dickens received a letter from his friend Jeffrey, the well-known critic, who was following the story with fervor. Dickens writes to Forster:

> Note from Jeffrey this morning, who won't believe (positively refuses) that Edith is Carker's mistress. What do you think of a kind of inverted Maid's Tragedy, and a tremendous scene of her undeceiving Carker, and giving him to know that she never meant that?[22]

The improbability had struck Jeffrey, but apparently for the wrong reasons. He liked Edith. So Dickens changed his mind and turned to a play by Beaumont and Fletcher, rather than to anything in actuality, for a concluding explanation.

The point is important; Dickens' last-minute changes are rarely for the better. *The Maid's Tragedy* concerned Evadne, a beautiful lady of the court, who was married by the King to young Amintor, the marriage serving as a cloak for his own love affair with the lady. Evadne's brother, Melantius, a great general and noble gentleman, discovers this deception and shameful trampling upon the honor of his family. He terrifies Evadne into repentance and a desire for expiation to wipe out her dishonor. Visiting the royal bedroom, as usual, Evadne ties down the arms of the sleeping king, wakens him, and charges him with his villainy and sin before she stabs him to death. Finding that this deed does not win back her husband—strangely enough—she kills herself. There is more to the play, but this is the part which concerned Dickens and his proposed solution of Edith's relations to Carker.

Obviously Edith, like Evadne, is betraying a husband for love of a paramour. What Dickens meant by "a kind of *inverted* Maid's Tragedy" is that she will be struck with remorse *before* she becomes Carker's mistress. In a climactic scene she will, like Evadne, charge him with his sin (in this case, an *intended* sin). She will tell him that she has never meant any suggestion of sex to be involved in their relationship. Unlike Evadne, Edith was not really Carker's mistress, so she does not have to murder her lover to expiate her shame; a railroad train will do the job for her. This is the ending that Dickens wrote. It apparently satisfied Jeffrey, but it leaves the rest of us mystified as to any reasonable explanation for Edith's behavior.

155

Even though we have been dwelling upon weaknesses in a novel which contains the usual Dickensian qualities of fine narration, it would seem to be obvious that *Dombey and Son* falls short of the total accomplishment of *Martin Chuzzlewit*. It is aimed at entertainment plus a propagandistic lesson; it subordinates all narrative elements to the main plot; it avoids the rambling and scattering effects of earlier stories; it achieves concentration. But it also acquires some painful distortion in forcing home the moral. It does not successfully build up a broad pattern of action which would intensify the main purpose —the castigation of pride. The contrasting characters and scenes are less inspired than is usual with Dickens. It has a sentimental death sequence, but this factor is not so impressive today as it was in his time. It has Mrs. Skewton, but she fights a hard battle. The conclusion is that in aiming at unity and trying to compromise between artistry and commercialism, Dickens wrote a dated novel—one which has limited appeal for many modern readers.

When he had finished *Dombey and Son* and was preparing to write the next book, *David Copperfield*, his artistic development was still in a state of flux. He was trying to bring his various techniques under absolute control, to integrate his devices of writing around a pattern for serious effect. He did achieve much of what he was striving for in *David Copperfield*, a novel which illustrates a neat balancing of creative powers. That his talents should come to full flower in this novel is partly luck, partly plan, but essentially genius. Exactly how it happened is worth minute study.

CHAPTER IX

First Person: David Copperfield

VERY MAN spends moments in self-admiration. Extreme cases—especially if the man in question is egotistic and a writer—sometimes result in autobiographies. There are other reasons for describing one's own experiences, and it was inevitable that Dickens should consider writing the story of his own life. The urge to do so came when he read Holcroft's autobiography. This happened while he was working on *Dombey and Son,* and the idea of producing something like this model struck him immediately. He wrote to Forster:

> Shall I leave you my life in MS. when I die? There are some things in it that would touch you very much, and that might go on the same shelf with the first volume of Holcroft's.[1]

Holcroft's first volume carries his life up to the time when he was about sixteen years of age. The narrative style is simple and unaffected, extraordinarily well-conceived for its purposes. The story concerns a neglected childhood, a struggle for an education, and a gradual rise from the humblest circumstances toward respectability and force of character. The style and the subject appealed to Dickens, both being akin to his own talents and experiences. He began an account of his early life, probably following the story up to about the time he met his "Dora," Maria Beadnell. But we do not know exactly how much of it he wrote.

Forster and Dickens discussed the proposed autobiography, as was their usual practice with anything Dickens wrote. Forster thought the use of the first person was unusually effective, and he advised Dickens to write his next novel in the first person, as a change.[2] Dickens received the recommendation "gravely," saw almost immediately

157

how he could weave parts of his own life into projected action, and began to plan "The Personal History" of the boy who was to be named "David Copperfield." At some time or other he destroyed whatever he had written of the autobiography.

A story which proposed to follow a hero, beginning with his youth and the adventures of his young manhood to happy marriage, fell naturally into the picaresque structure of Fielding and Smollett. *Roderick Random* was told in the first person and furnished an easy reference before Dickens began on a like tale. He had attempted something of this order in *Nicholas Nickleby*, but at that time he had been more concerned about gathering a great number of contrasting materials around the picaresque framework. He had progressed toward a controlled pattern of narration since that day; he had also grown tremendously in his understanding of artistry in fiction. Then, too, he had never tried the first person in such a tale.

Artistic ideals influenced his plans from the first. *David Copperfield* was to be no journeyman piece of work; it speedily became something special. He eventually said of it, "Of all my books, I like this the best."[3] As the story took shape in his fancy, he turned to the greatest model in biographical fiction available to him, Fielding's *Tom Jones*. He asked himself: What did Fielding mean by the "comic epic"? How were his effects achieved? What exactly was he trying to do?

There is adequate evidence that Fielding directly influenced his creative consciousness. When Dickens' eighth child was born in 1849 he had planned to call him "Oliver Goldsmith." Most of his children were named for literary friends or distinguished persons from the past. The choice of Goldsmith was made because Forster had just finished a biography of the eighteenth-century novelist, essayist, and dramatist —a book which was Forster's chief scholarly opus excepting his eventual biography of Dickens. At the last minute Dickens changed his mind and called the child "Henry Fielding," a change "which he had made in a kind of homage to the style of work he was now so bent on beginning."[4]

It is not hard to see what Dickens admired in *Tom Jones*, nor is there much difficulty in discerning what he tried to imitate. The novel, along with much that may be said about it, emphasizes minute observation of original and eccentric characters; it selects typical representatives from the passing show of society; it presents a panoramic view of life in its era; the center of the narrative design is a "hero" who comes from the common people; and the story itself moves around this hero rather than about an intrigue, although a carefully developed plot is involved.

Dickens was not particularly impressed with most of the satiric mannerisms by which Fielding made fun of poetic epics. A division into eighteen books with an introductory chapter parodying the "invocation" for each one—this was outside his interest. But the epic principle, defined as a painting of a broad and diffused picture of life, he had always liked. In *Tom Jones* all society is observed from the point of view of the main character. The author indulged in moral condemnation of hypocritical wickedness, but defended his hero's slips on the grounds of inexperience and good intentions. Tom also has many interesting adventures. All these potentialities were suited to Dickens' demonstrated talents in a tale of similar pattern. Further, Fielding's epic style did not encourage melodramatic plot development or excessive sentimentality, something which must have acted as an unconscious check upon Dickens.

In his two previous novels he had planned his action around a central theme. Dickens had several reservations about the moral tone of *Tom Jones*. Tom is attractive physically and does not allow his sincere love of Sophia to interfere with his pursuit of other members of the willing sex. There is some indication at the end of the novel that he is prepared to reform in marriage, but Dickens had difficulty imagining a hero—modelled on his own life and exposed to the public eye—quite so successfully amorous in fiction. He accordingly invented a foil for David, named him Steerforth, and gave him the attractive physical charm and the negative morals of the youthful Tom Jones. David would keep Tom's heart of gold and be a more admirable hero. This was a first step in the planning of his pattern, a pattern which naturally formed around the question of romantic and "proper" love.

David was not intended to be inhumanly good. Dickens was beyond the idea of an allegorically perfect hero like Oliver Twist. David would have weaknesses; he might drink to excess, but only once; he would fall in love unwisely and marry an attractive girl who would hardly be a good wife for him; but these mistakes would be obvious lessons to him, and he would learn by his errors. Steerforth, on the other hand, with all his physical charm, would lack stamina and go bad. The example of hundreds of stage plays made this sequence easy to plan. Steerforth would seduce a beautiful girl, ruin her life, and thus illustrate the evils of moral laxity. Little Emily, desiring to be a lady although coming from the lower classes, would help draw a moral which Fielding had neglected.

The outline for David's story used Dickens' own life as he had so often used other sources for his imagination. He invented a central character and decorated his experiences with whatever parts of his source he felt to be appropriate. He decided to use his own experiences in the bottling factory, his family's days in the debtors' prison, his legal training in Doctors' Commons, his youthful passion for Maria Beadnell, and his rise to fame as an author. As the plan began to take form in his mind, he found his first problem to be the arrangement of the life of David to include the bottling-factory episode. As he mingled fact with fiction he found himself wanting to avoid a direct confession of his family's experience in the Marshalsea. It is also clear that he remembered with horror his days in the factory. Therefore he gave David parents different from his own and put his hero into the factory by means which differed from his own experience. He imagined an orphaned David, brought up by a stepfather he hated, eventually rooming with people who lived in the debtors' prison while the child worked at the factory. The general model for this apparently came from the early days of Roderick Random.

Roderick's grandfather was a haughty and selfish man of wealth whose son fell in love with a poor relation, a housekeeper, married her, and begot Roderick, although the alliance was kept secret. When the old gentleman found out, he disinherited his son and treated the couple barbarously. After Roderick's mother died and his father had disappeared, the boy was brought up haphazardly. He was ill provided for at school, was taught badly by a tyrannous schoolmaster, and eventually left to shift for himself. From this unpromising beginning, Roderick set forth on his travels.

Dickens' hatred for the tyrannous parent or schoolmaster had found expression in *Nicholas Nickleby* and *Dombey and Son*. He gave to David's stepfather most of the inhuman qualities of Roderick's grandfather and manipulated the rest of his outline to fit the early trials of a mistreated child. His plan was: David's father would die before the birth of his child; the mother would marry again; the stepfather would make David's life unhappy; he would be sent to a school like Roderick's; after the death of his mother, he would be set to work in a factory; the family with whom he boarded in London would be made interesting eccentrics, and like Dickens' parents would live in fear of bill collectors.

Dickens had escaped from the horror of the factory when his father was released from prison, although his mother thought her son might as well continue in his job. This experience he resented even from the perspective of the years.[5] In planning his novel, he had to invent some logical reason for getting David out of the warehouse. He solved this by giving him a relative to whom he could run away, Aunt Betsey Trotwood, an eccentric. She could be introduced in the first chapter but remain offstage during the intervening action—an absence explained by her disappointment at David's birth: she wanted David to be a girl and to be named after her. All this course of action Dickens had well in mind before starting to write, and although he dressed up his first fourteen chapters with a collection of interesting characters—managing to introduce Steerforth at the school he attended, bringing in little Emily as a relative of his nurse, Peggotty— his main action was logically complete.

The point of view from which he approached this story was entirely different from that for any of his previous tales. In the first placc he identified himself with David more completely than he had ever done with his other heroes. His general manner of mimicking his actors led him naturally to the point where he lost himself in his epic hero, especially since that hero duplicated certain parts of his own experience. Telling the story in the first person added vitality and reality to the style. The author says that "no one can believe this Narrative in the reading more than I believed it in the writing." David Copperfield was his "favorite child."[6]

Dickens had often entered into the telling of a story in his capacity as author. On occasion he put words in the mouths of his characters that he might more fittingly have said himself. Nowhere could such tendencies be more appropriate than in a tale which assumed the air of autobiography. The "Let me tell you a story" manner also suits the first part of the novel in which he recounts his youthful experiences. One expects a child to be a little more sentimental or painfully direct than the adult. Dickens' manner in the early chapters of this book is his happiest attempt at achieving naturalness. All the eccentric characters are more acceptable as real persons because they are described as a child would see them, and any exaggeration can be attributed to the way they appear in David's memory. Even the farce-caricature method does not seem exaggerated because of this point of view. A child naturally heightens what he sees and does, especially if the child is really Dickens.

The first chapter of the novel recounts the circumstances of David's birth, a whimsical reconstruction which is properly entertaining. Much of the humor comes from the presence of David's Aunt Betsey, a lady who appears suddenly, terrifies the expectant mother into her first birth pangs, and mystifies the doctor in attendance. Dickens' invention sets a high level of ingenuity for the succeeding chapters. He begins by assuming that he is privileged to tell exactly what happened on his birthnight, as had Sterne's Tristram Shandy, a gentleman who managed to wander about the subject for more than two books of his tale before he succeeded in getting himself born. Despite the fact that David could not have known exactly the circumstances, he says that he was born at twelve o'clock at night, just as the clock began to strike, "as I have been informed and believe."[7] There is a different emphasis on the clock in *Tristram Shandy*, but Dickens wrote for a less ribald audience.

The comedy of the first chapter is of the sort that makes fun of the waiting relatives who suffer more than the mother does while the child is being born. Unlike Sterne, Dickens avoids giggling about the details of obstetrics, but he introduces the facts of David's parentage, his mother's place in life, and the presence of Aunt Betsey, who could now safely be dismissed from the action until David needs her as a refuge when he runs away years later.

David's earliest remembrances concern his mother's courtship and her marriage to Mr. Murdstone (the name suggesting "Murderer," or possibly "Merde"). They also present his nurse, Peggotty, her relatives at Yarmouth, and Mr. Barkis, the carrier. All the Yarmouth people are imagined with as much force and humor as Dickens was able to command by way of the farce-caricature technique or by means of the speech devices he was accustomed to create. Peggotty's popping buttons, Miss Murdstone's jail-like pocketbook, rough and ready Mr. Peggotty who is also "gormed" on occasion, Mrs. Gummidge's despair because she is thinking of "the old one," Barkis, and Ham—they are all examples of Dickens' delight in the ridiculous. Many other characters introduced later in the book have eccentricities and tags of speech which distinguish them, Dickens warming to the joy of imagination and finding new and interesting peculiarities in quantities never before lavished on one book. He held his farce down in *Dombey and Son*, but not here.

His invention in small things is delightful. There are few incidents from Dickens' novels which are remembered with more amusement than his recounting of the courtship of Barkis. The gentleman who proposed by asking young David to take a message to Peggotty, "Barkis is willing," is an inspired individual. Dickens had always enjoyed the comedy secured by having a proposal made through a second party, as illustrated by Jonas Chuzzlewit and the Pecksniff sisters. But Barkis is unique.

Part of the success of this scene is derived from David's innocent role in carrying the message. Dickens makes much of any incident in which he can inform his readers of all the facts necessary to enjoy the situation without the youthful David (who is recounting it all) knowing what he is talking about. There is the episode in which Mr. Murdstone takes him for a ride and is bantered by his companions concerning his courtship of the pretty widow. David is naturally interested, and Mr. Murdstone warns the company that "somebody is sharp." David wants to know who somebody is, and is told that the individual referred to is "Brooks of Sheffield," a stratagem which fools him, but leaves the reader entirely clear as to Mr. Murdstone's marital intentions.

For many people sentimentality is most effective when it concerns children. David falls childishly in love with Emily, and his innocent passion is just the kind to amuse a reader and excite his sympathy. Dickens later wrote one of his most touching short stories about young

Harry Walmers, an entertaining child who runs off with his tiny
sweetheart to marry her. The two are entertained with understanding
at Holly Tree Inn until the parents can arrive.[8] Dickens and the
reader observe in unison that it is too bad all passion cannot be as
innocent and sweet and perfect as that of children, an expression of
sentiment which is unlikely to turn sour in the sophisticated mouth,
inaccurate as it is and obvious as it sounds.

David's childish curiosity also helps routine matters of narration,
such as informing the reader of antecedent action in the Peggotty
family. David asks Mr. Peggotty all manner of embarrassing questions
concerning his exact relationship to the individuals in his ship-house,
most of the questions like those about the father of Ham and the
husband of Mrs. Gummidge receiving the answer: "Drowndead."

Mr. Murdstone contrasts with Mr. Peggotty, possessing all the
selfish qualities which are missing in the honest seaman's character.
He is extremely harsh to David after the manner of Mr. Dombey with
Florence, but he is seen through the eyes of the boy. Any alleviating
advantages he possesses would not be observed by the youthful storyteller. The first person singular, David speaking, can be expected to
present any character one-sidedly.

Because David loves to read he spends hours in acquainting himself with eighteenth-century fiction, this touch from his own life allowing the author to wax eloquent about his early infatuation with
Smollett and Fielding. Perhaps the best example of Dickens' many
comments about teaching method is the one presented here. David
loves the "crocodile book," a volume which Peggotty saves for him as
the years go by. The crocodile book was Day's *Sandford and Merton*,
a disgustingly moral book contrasting a good boy and a bad one, painfully explicit about questions of behavior. Dickens remembered the
book with scorn, as he shows in a later article written about it,[9] but
David's childhood fascination for the crocodile passage lasts because
he read the book under the pleasant encouragement of Peggotty. The
beginning of all learning is interest which turns into desire.

When David is sent from his home to school in London, the
invention of Dickens roams far afield. On the way the child is victimized by a waiter who imposes on him to the extent of eating a huge
dinner for him. This episode Dickens borrowed from Holcroft's similar

experience, related in his autobiography.[10] It illustrates the usual practice of Dickens in reworking a hint from a source even in his least important episodes.

The next sequence is also borrowed, but altered in greater detail. When David arrives in London, he is met by the usher from Mr. Creakle's school, Mr. Mell by name, and taken to his lodgings by way of Mr. Mell's mother's rooms in Poverty Lane. Mr. Mell steps out of the pages of Forster's *Life of Goldsmith*, and the episodes surrounding him are again indicative of the way Dickens used his sources of inspiration. Goldsmith's nickname was "Noll," and says Forster, one of his characteristic customs was to "sit in a window of his mother's lodgings, and amuse himself by playing the flute."[11] This habit is shared by Mr. Mell who, like the young Goldsmith, had spent days of absolute poverty and distress in London, sometimes haunted by bailiffs, but always carrying his flute.

Goldsmith's period of employment as an usher or junior teacher later showed itself in his bitterness about the plight of this poorly paid and badly treated employee in the school system. Dickens too realizes that the usher often knows more than the master, and Mr. Mell is no exception in teaching David all he learns at the academy. Dickens' own experiences at Wellington House must have added some details to his description of the school.[12]

The episode wherein Steerforth defies the authority of Mr. Mell, causing the latter's dismissal, comes directly from Forster's account of an anecdote concerning Goldsmith:

> When amusing his younger companions during play-hours with the flute and expatiating on the pleasures derived from music, in addition to its advantages in society as a gentleman-like acquirement, a pert boy, looking at his situation and personal disadvantages with something of contempt, rudely replied to the effect that he surely could not consider himself a gentleman.[13]

Mr. Mell has to keep school on a Saturday afternoon, and the boys are out of hand:

> Boys whirled about him, grinning, making faces, mimicking him behind his back and before his eyes; mimicking his poverty, his boots, his coat, his mother, everything belonging to him that they should have had consideration for.

165

Mr. Mell explodes finally in righteous indignation, and clashes with the defiant Steerforth, whose position as the wealthy boy has established him above the master, Mr. Creakle. Mr. Mell protests:

> "And when you make use of your position of favouritism here, sir . . . to insult a gentleman—"
> "A what?—where is he?" said Steerforth.[14]

Dickens uses this incident as one of a number to portray the thoughtless character of Steerforth, who has already fascinated David with his personal charm and his desire to hear David's collection of stories. Steerforth is selfish, just the sort to impose upon his friends later in life to their disadvantage and discomfort. Even though David will never have the chance to describe the details of the Steerforth-Emily love affair, Dickens prepares the characteristics of these principals so that the reader may be willing to imagine that the two could act as they do. Emily consistently desires to be a lady, and Steerforth is consistently willful.

The usher in *Roderick Random* had also been the teacher who provided whatever learning the hero received. Mr. Creakle's regular use of the cane upon his students had its model in Roderick's cruel master, and Dickens probably considered designing a scene such as Smollett's in which the master gets a touch of his own medicine with the help of Roderick's seagoing uncle. There is a similarity in type of punishment visited upon both Roderick and David. Roderick annoys his grandfather by writing letters; therefore he is prevented from writing by having a board with five holes in it fitted over his hand and drawn tight with a cord.[15] David has to carry a placard on his back which reads: "Take care of him. He bites."[16] This punishment follows his resistance to Mr. Murdstone when his stepfather attempted to whip him. Dickens rarely copied exactly; he invented something suggested by the materials supplied by his source.

The death of David's mother is handled with restraint. Dickens prepares for it at the end of Chapter VIII when David returns to school. As he drives away with Mr. Barkis he looks back at her and his baby half brother:

> So I lost her. So I saw her afterwards, in my sleep at school—a silent presence near my bed—looking at me with the same intent face—holding up her baby in her arms.[17]

The presence of the Murdstones would have interfered with the effect of a sentimental death scene had David been present. It is natural to have him informed of his mother's death at school and to get all the details a child could be told from the mouth of the sympathetic Peggotty after he goes home for the funeral. Dickens uses a morbid form of contrast for narrative relief in this episode by sending David to the undertaking establishment of Mr. Omer, where the child, waiting for transportation home, has the rare experience of watching the stitching of black clothes and hearing hammering on a coffin. The happiness of Minnie and the undertaker's apprentice Joram, who together make the funeral trip a sort of lovers' holiday, illustrates Dickens' deft touch in grotesquerie.[18]

Now the action is prepared for David's neglect and his eventual work in the bottling factory. Mr. Murdstone is represented as owning a part of this factory, and his friend, Mr. Quinion, suggests that the boy might work there, since he seems very unhappy at home and without prospects of any kind. This journey comes hard upon another study in contrast: David, while visiting the Peggotty family, has been part of the wedding expedition of Mr. Barkis and Peggotty. Episodic contrast continues to be a narrative concern of Dickens, faithfully followed throughout the novel.

The youthful David finds a room in London with the Micawber family. Mr. Micawber is Dickens' finest example of a caricatured eccentric, replete with peculiarities, speech mannerisms, and tags of expression. Alternately cheerful and in the depths of despair, his rolling periods and grandiose rhetoric often come to "in short—" and a plain summary. His verbosity reeks of the stage. Dickens' father had linguistic peculiarities—none of them resembling the "in short" mannerism—and it may be that his mother, like Mrs. Micawber, often protested that she would never leave her husband. Certainly the memory of the author was responsible for the famous advice Mr. Micawber gave young David before he left London, thus severing the last tie which might have kept the boy working indefinitely at the factory.

"My other piece of advice, Copperfield," said Mr. Micawber, "you know. Annual income twenty pounds, annual expenditure nineteen nineteen six, result happiness. Annual income twenty pounds, annual expenditure twenty pounds ought and six, result misery. The blossom is blighted, the leaf is withered, the god of day goes down upon the dreary scene, and—and, in short, you are for ever floored. As I am!"

To make his example the more impressive, Mr. Micawber drank a glass of punch with an air of great enjoyment and satisfaction, and whistled the College Hornpipe.[19]

Dickens had observed Fielding's ridicule of the grand manner of epics. Sudden changes from flowery heights to bare simplicity were part of that author's parody on the heroic style. This example was the germ which grew into Mr. Micawber's mannerism. Several other influences may have helped. Bulwer-Lytton had developed a style, now called *Bulwerese*, which sometimes reached proportions that remind one of the macabre Mr. Micawber. Bulwer at first did not understand that he was making his writing occasionally ridiculous by saying something in a verbose manner, then summing up in simple terms. In his revisions of his novels he eliminated most of the examples of Bulwerese in response to critical derision, and unless one has access to a first edition of *Paul Clifford* or *Eugene Aram*, the reader may have difficulty in finding good examples of this style.

Bulwer varied his contrasting language with "in short," "i.e.," "viz.," "in other words," and "to speak more plainly." For example Paul Clifford says to a fellow criminal, Long Ned:

"O longest of mortals . . . though the public may allow you to eat your mutton off their backs for a short time they will kick up at last and upset you and your banquet: in other words . . . the police will nab thee at last."[20]

This comparison is given to the recorded speech of one of his characters, and if it is an influence, it is easy to see Dickens' superiority in imagining the periods given to Mr. Micawber.

When the Micawbers leave London in search of something which might turn up, David is ready to run away to his aunt. Peggotty has mentioned her in one of the chapters which follow her first appearance, so the reader knows she is still alive.[21] For the boy's long trip to Dover on foot, Dickens invents as many circumstances as possible to increase David's difficulties and to bring him to Aunt Betsey's cottage in rags. There is the fellow who runs off with David's box and money, the pawnbroker who tries to cheat him and yells, "Oh, goroo, goroo!" and the tinker-tramp who robs him of what he has left.

At this point in the story, Forster began to feel the necessity of checking Dickens' tendency to farcical interludes. He protested definitely about Mr. Dick in the next episode. Dickens, in creating Mr. Dick, added another portrait to the list of harmless characters who are not in complete control of all their faculties, but whose simple goodness hardly qualifies them for insane asylums. Dickens replied to Forster's objections thus:

> Your suggestion is perfectly wise and sound. . . . I have acted upon it. I have also, instead of the bull and china-shop delusion, given Dick the idea that, when the head of King Charles the First was cut off, some of the trouble was taken out of it, and put into his (Dick's).[22]

The change, from this distance, seems infinitesimal. The point at which farce becomes "too farcical," to quote Forster, is difficult to locate. Nor does the substitution for the original passage (printed by Forster) alter the point that Mr. Dick has a ridiculous obsession. Many of Dickens' characters act as if they were a little mad in their peculiarities, so that Mr. Dick is no more insane than any individual who is observed only in his odd moments. But Forster apparently felt that the narrative was getting out of balance.

The first section draws to its climax in the fourteenth chapter when Aunt Betsey calls in the Murdstones to find out what to do about David's future. This scene illustrates forcibly the advantage in illusion which Dickens acquired by his use of the first person in narration. Melodramatic speech often accompanied similar scenes in earlier novels. David listens to his aunt and the Murdstones discussing him, and finally he has his own opportunity. He describes his feelings with natural restraint and lets Aunt Betsey supply the rhetoric. The point is that he speaks as Dickens himself might have spoken, not as an actor on the stage.[23]

The end of the fourteenth chapter provides the first break in Dickens' plan for the action of the novel. The panorama of persons and events up to this point has been subordinated to David. One fourth of the book is finished with David's settlement as the ward of his aunt. The most captious critic ought to be impressed by the author's accomplishment of intention. These chapters reach the highest degree of smooth and easy narration which Dickens was capable of accomplishing.

His plan now demanded new adventures. In the picaresque models, when one sequence is over and the hero is introduced to an entirely new set of characters, a new scene and what amounts to a new plot centering about the hero begins. In *Nicholas Nickleby,* at a parallel point in the narrative, Dickens sends Nicholas away to Vincent Crummles and his company, shifting the course of his tale completely.

He referred to his own life again. He thought of his work in Doctors' Commons, his love for Maria before they quarreled, and his marriage to Kate Hogarth. It was simple to elevate his own experiences and heighten his adventures. Instead of becoming a clerk, David would be articled at a cost of £1,000 on the way to becoming a real proctor, something which Dickens may have desired when he was young, but was never able to realize because of the lack of any such staggering sum in a family that had not long escaped the Marshalsea. The episode with Maria he also developed far beyond actuality. She was, as he imagined her and described her in the person of Dora, an empty-headed, impractical, lovable, cute, adorable, incompetent beauty—so good, so pure, so noble, and so stupid. But she had been physically attractive. Even though a casual acquaintance would have thought Dickens and his wife were perfectly happy—witness eight children already in evidence—their later separation is proof that he and Kate were not ideally mated. But his acute unhappiness grew in intensity after the creation of *David Copperfield.* His early affair with Maria had never reached marriage, but his history might have been more exciting if he had married her, then found out what the mature Dickens may have suspected in retrospect, that she would not have made a satisfactory wife, even if he had continued to love her. Sexual attraction had something to do with it, of course. Yet the tale could scarcely be complete if David should marry the attractive but unsatisfactory love of his youth and be stuck with her. The next step was obvious in Victorian times: one escapes from an unsatisfactory marriage by the death of one's partner. Dickens' wife did not oblige him in time, but Dora, like Nell, could die and leave David free to marry the girl he should have loved all along—the ideal who combined practicality with beauty and goodness. Wish fulfillment entered his mind again. Agnes is everything he hoped his real wife might be, perhaps part of what at that time she really had been to him.

The narrative problem was how to introduce the two girls into his story. David is approximately twelve when he comes to live with his aunt. Tom Jones had jumped from infancy to young manhood in a single section. But Dickens was publishing his tale in installments; he could not disrupt the interest of his readers by an extreme jerk in the continuity of his action. David could grow up rapidly, but time would have to be devoted to his development. Accordingly Dickens thought of sending David to school, the natural thing, and a good school this time. Since the boy would have to board with someone, Dickens supplies the girl David eventually marries after Dora's death. Enter: the school of Dr. Strong and the home of Mr. Wickfield who has a lovely daughter named Agnes. When David gets to Doctors' Commons he meets Dora.

So far, his invention moved easily and naturally. The autobiographical method had taken over his way of organizing his action. But his concept of Fielding's epic plan included a varied display of character and atmosphere, going into different parts of England and describing contrasting social spheres. Fortunately he could not lose the unity of style imposed by seeing everything through the eyes of David. In his next novel, *Bleak House,* he would avoid difficulties in following alternate threads of his complex tale by shifting from the first to the third person whenever he changed plots. To narrate several courses of action by means of the first person involves certain difficulties in shifting space and time. Dickens discovered that his first-person device and his general panoramic, multiple-plot practice might develop conflict. The only technical difficulties in *David Copperfield,* especially in the latter three fourths of the novel, result from this conflict.

He decided to make the unifying pattern for all his sequences true love or its antithesis, perhaps the need for controlling one's romantic emotions. Each of his plots illustrates the virtues or defects of attitude his characters express toward passion or romantic affection. His original plan of action had supplied a comparison between David and Steerforth. To this he now added several intrigues which would develop the unifying pattern. He constructed three main plots for this purpose.

The Steerforth-Emily-Ham triangle had been planned from the beginning. David's personal intrigue is now separated into two parts. When he goes to Doctors' Commons he meets, courts, and marries Dora, the daughter of the principal partner of the law firm to which he is articled. This is the first part. Dickens also invented a plot which would keep the reader interested in Agnes while David was elsewhere. This is the second part.

There was nothing in his own experiences to help him with Agnes. As he had done before, he had recourse to stage and romance tradition for a model. This called for a villain who would attempt to seduce or marry the heroine—well, go the whole way—the villain would get the girl's father in his financial and moral power, then try to force the girl to marry him by means of the hold he had on her father. This is the familiar "mortgage-on-the-home" plot of sentimental drama. Dickens introduces the "'umble" Uriah Heep, who writhes and fawns and who works for Mr. Wickfield. Dickens gave Mr. Wickfield the weakness of drink, caused by his mourning for Agnes' mother; this weakness provides the reason for Uriah's success in gradually getting control of Mr. Wickfield's business and involving him in apparent dishonesties so that the eventual power of the clerk over the master is complete. Mr. Wickfield invests money for various clients, including Aunt Betsey.

The three main streams of action can most easily be described from the fifteenth chapter on as concerning: David-Dora-Agnes, David-Agnes-Uriah Heep, and Steerforth-Emily-Ham. For the first two, since David is directly concerned with the action, the first-person point of view is satisfactory. The Steerforth-Emily plot is different, first, because David can scarcely be present in person frequently enough to tell the story adequately; second, because the distance from Yarmouth to Canterbury or London made it necessary for Dickens to find an excuse for David's going to visit Peggotty every time he wished to reveal anything about Emily's fatal passion.

He developed the love stories slowly, giving time for David to grow up. The author thought of everything he could to make the transition interesting. He invented adolescent love affairs and fights

172

with the butcher boy; he reintroduced the Micawbers and resurrected Traddles from the Creakles school. The installment plan forced him also to invent subplots and new conflicts of action in order to have something happening in every issue. Melodrama tempted him again.

His most important subplot derived from melodrama concerns the good old schoolmaster, Dr. Strong, and his young wife, Annie. This situation reminds the reader of Mr. Dombey's difficulties with a young wife, but in development it resembles the situation in *The Cricket on the Hearth* in which Mrs. Peerybingle returns to John after being attracted to a man her own age, the story implying that true love ought to be stronger than any difference of age or interest. The old professor combines fatherly affection and husbandly passion for his young wife. He also is so absent-minded and detached from the practical world that he never even suspects that his wife might love someone else until Uriah Heep disillusions him.

It appears to be Dickens' point that Annie should not have encouraged Jack Maldon at all. His intent in this subplot is open to the suspicion that he changed his plan in the middle. As the earlier scenes are presented, before Mr. Wickfield arranges to send Maldon away to India, the story shows a sympathetic study of a girl in a difficult situation, admiring and loving her elderly husband while fighting a passion which she knows to be wrong. But this interpretation is denied by the denouement. According to the conclusion, she asks the reader and her husband to believe that she never even considered loving Maldon, a conclusion which is hard to accept when one remembers her on her knees looking up at the old doctor on the night after Maldon departed for India. She says she had a childish attachment, but she is whitewashed, as Dickens purified Edith Dombey at the climax of the earlier novel.

There is another clearly incidental change of intention concerning Miss Mowcher, the volatile dwarf who carried her beauty shop on her person. Dickens described the eccentricities and deformities of this lady from a real-life model. After the chapter which introduced her appeared, he received a letter from the original protesting against what she considered a false and unpleasant presentation of her character. Dickens developed some compunction and felt it necessary to apologize in the course of the story, whitewashing her too.[24] This may have affected his plans, for Miss Mowcher could have been another Mrs. Gamp, and from the beginnings shown in the chapter in which she gives Steerforth a cosmetological treatment, Dickens must have intended to use her to narrate details of the Steerforth-Emily affair.

The part Miss Mowcher was intended to take in the novel is assumed by Martha, the prostitute who leaves Yarmouth for the big city to start life anew, and whose example should have warned Emily. It is Martha who eventually finds Emily and helps return her to her family. As an example of passion for sale Martha is rather colorless, and she suffers from being dragged into the story only to help along the intrigue. However, she listens at the door to hear news of Emily after her friend has left Steerforth. When she finds where Emily is, she hastens to tell David and Mr. Peggotty, thus setting up the climax of that plot.

The Steerforth-Emily situation is complicated by the presence of Rosa Dartle, the woman who should have been Steerforth's wife, but who is cast in the role of the woman scorned. Almost every appearance she makes in the story after her introduction comes at a moment which courts melodrama, and her stagey speeches, especially those to or about Emily, are in direct contrast to the manner David uses in first-person narration.

The pattern for presenting a number of characters and situations illustrating some degree of passion or love is clear. Most of these contrasting personalities are part of the blood stream of the story. One must recognize that the multiplicity of plot ideas occasionally turns the course of action from David. Dickens made the young David an interesting person; he continues to be attractive as he grows up, works in Doctors' Commons, falls in love with Dora, and learns to write novels. But the average reader naturally becomes interested in Steerforth and Emily too, or in the evil designs of Heep, rather than in what David is doing all the time. If it were not for the amusing and remarkable events which concern his courtship and marriage, David would become a pale narrator of interesting things which happen to other people. As it is, he becomes less important than the pattern.

In balancing and contrasting his action, Dickens often devotes a chapter in each installment to his three main plot sequences, or at least to two of them. The average reader, finding the story printed straight through in book form, is not aware of this practice. The fourteenth installment, for example (Chapters XL, XLI, and XLII), devotes the first chapter to Mr. Peggotty's account of Emily and Steerforth, the second to David's courtship of Dora under the auspices of her maiden aunts, and the third to Uriah's exposure of Annie's apparent lack of love for Dr. Strong. The forty-second chapter ends with a letter from Mrs. Micawber, complaining of her husband's deterioration since he has worked for Uriah Heep, a circumstance which brings in the third main plot and rouses the reader to renewed fears about Uriah's evil intentions concerning Agnes.

In some modern novels, those of Huxley particularly, when several courses of action are unfolding at the same time, a contrapuntal effect is secured which intensifies the eventual climax by doubling, tripling, or quadrupling the developing action.[25] Dickens reaches the best structural effect he has attempted in any of his novels by arranging his main sequences to reach their most interesting points at approximately the same time in David's life. This multiplies the emotional effect. In earlier novels his leaping from one scene to another had sometimes scattered the climaxes.

In the seventeenth installment (Chapters XLIX, L, and LI) the first chapter is devoted to Mr. Micawber's visit to David and Traddles and his decision to expose Uriah's villainy; the second concerns the finding of Emily by Rosa Dartle and Mr. Peggotty in successive scenes; the third finishes the action begun in the preceding chapter and prepares Mr. Peggotty and Emily for their emigration to Australia. In the eighteenth installment, Dickens achieves three contrasting climaxes. In Chapter LII, Heep is exposed; in LIII, Dora dies; in LIV, Aunt Betsey's fortune is restored, and the Micawbers get ready to emigrate to Australia in one of the funniest scenes Dickens devised for that remarkable family. In the first chapter of the nineteenth installment, the last climax is reached, the famous storm scene in which Ham tries bravely to save Steerforth from the slowly breaking ship, and both of these protagonists die. The result of this multiplicity of climactic interest shows Dickens at his narrative best. The contrasting pattern revolves perfectly.

Before this, however, Dickens ran into technical trouble. Part of it concerned the way in which the Steerforth-Emily plot had to be

175

narrated. Steerforth meets Emily through David. Before David makes up his mind what profession he will enter, he decides to spend a few days visiting Peggotty. On the way to Yarmouth, in London, he meets Steerforth for the first time since school days, is invited to his home, and becomes acquainted with Mrs. Steerforth and Rosa Dartle. Then he takes his friend down to Yarmouth with him, and the first step is taken for the seduction of Emily. David's character at this point retains some of its childish simplicity; he is easily imposed on, never looks for evil until the ugly reality is forced upon him, and is called "Daisy" by the sophisticated Steerforth. The two enter Mr. Peggotty's ship-home just as the engagement of Emily to Ham is announced, certainly the psychological moment.

From this point on Dickens was forced to tell by implication the growing attraction of Emily and Steerforth for each other. The only hints presented are from the point of view of one who looks back on it all years later, wishing he had known at the time, or had tried to do something to avert the tragedy. There is continual emphasis upon Steerforth's character and upon Emily's dissatisfaction with her social place. Dickens does not blame the caste system for her ruin. Striving for impossible heights merely adds to unhappiness, even if the system is wrong.

To make Emily's betrayal of Ham entirely clear, the reader must imagine that she was tremendously attracted to Steerforth. David himself was under the spell of his friend's personality, and passion constituted another phase of this fascination for Emily. All motivation for the seduction is in the story, but David can never witness a love scene. As Dickens thought of the character of David in contrast to that of Steerforth, any hint that David suspected the affair between Emily and his friend was impossible. What he attempted to do was to show the reader through David what was happening at the same time that David, as narrator, saw nothing. There was no other way for him to tell the story.

David gives Emily's explanation of her decision to run away with Steerforth. After she has gone, she writes letters back home. She says repeatedly: "I am too wicked to write about myself"; "I am so bad"; "Try to think as if I died when I was little, and was buried somewhere"; "Know no shame but me"; "My last tears, and my last thanks, for uncle!"[26] The modern reader, familiar with many stories of passion and of girls who should not have run away with men, instinctively feels that any girl who knows so clearly the error of her actions, and who never says she was carried away by love, is likely to be talking for the reader's benefit (and probably the Victorian reader at that) rather than for her own. One doubts that Ellen Ternan talked this way when Dickens came to see her not too many years after Emily's affair.

Steerforth takes Emily abroad. Wherever he might have taken her, David would not be present. This fact necessitates David's hearing what happened to Emily from the lips or writing of someone else. Mr. Peggotty decides to spend his time in search of her, and David hears part of the eventual story from him. Rosa Dartle and Littimer also give him information. But before this, David accompanies Mr. Peggotty to the Steerforth home in order to tell Mrs. Steerforth and Rosa about the elopement. The aristocratic mother points out haughtily that marriage is impossible, answering the question which was Mr. Peggotty's reason for coming. It is in this scene that Rosa attacks Emily violently in discourse which goes back to Dickens' melodramatic diction. She includes the whole Peggotty household in her wrath.

"I would trample on them all. . . . I would have his house pulled down. I would have her branded on the face, drest in rags, and cast out in the streets to starve. If I had the power to sit in judgment on her, I would see it done. See it done? I would do it! I detest her. If I ever could reproach her with her infamous condition, I would go anywhere to do so. If I could hunt her to her grave, I would. If there was any word of comfort that would be a solace to her in her dying hour, and only I possessed it, I wouldn't part with it for Life itself."

Even David's language takes on overtones. He says:

"Oh, shame, Miss Dartle! shame. . . . How can you bear to trample on his undeserved affliction."[27]

The best defense for this heightened scene is that it leaves the reader in sympathy with Emily, even if she is a sinner. Rosa also helps complete the pattern, illustrating her own variety of frustrated love.

Most of the rest of the story of Emily is narrated by someone other than David. Mr. Peggotty takes a residence in London, and one evening he tells of almost finding Emily on the Continent. This is the occasion when Martha listens at the door. Later, David stops at Steerforth's home in answer to a message from Rosa and hears from Littimer of Steerforth's desertion of Emily. Just why Rosa would summon David is problematical. Dickens asks us to believe that her purpose is to gloat over David, since he is a friend of Emily's.

When the sinner is found, Dickens puts her on the stage. This scene has all the atmosphere of the gas lights. But David has to be present in order to tell it. Dickens' technical difficulty was how to place David where he could hear Emily and Rosa together. He solved his problem by an extremely coincidental manipulation of motive and circumstance. First, Martha finds Emily, but cannot get in touch with Mr. Peggotty; she leaves a message and reaches David. When the two return to the house where Emily is, David goes into the next room, feeling that Mr. Peggotty should see her first; the fallen woman should not have to face anyone but her foster father. Unfortunately for her, Rosa Dartle has also discovered the place, and she arrives just after David. These coincidences put David in the next room with a paper-thin wall so that he can hear Emily told exactly what she is in the best Victorian castigation available for print. Dickens had a moral to drive home; this was his way of doing it. Passion without marriage will drive you to unhappiness and shame.

Whether or not one admires the presentation of this climax, the modern reader is unlikely to praise David for allowing Rosa to continue her torture of Emily for so long. David just listens:

> A frightened murmur was the only reply that reached my ears. I did not know what to do. Much as I desired to put an end to the interview, I felt that I had no right to present myself; that it was for Mr. Peggotty alone to see her and recover her. Would he never come? I thought, impatiently.[28]

David is not the only listener who is impatient. Perhaps one should be thankful that Rosa did not think of killing Emily.

Mr. Peggotty later tells David and the reader most of what had happened to Emily, and his simple, honest emotion returns her story to some degree of reality. Then Dickens shifts the scene and his manner again, capturing a new effect in contrast. He sends David down to Yarmouth for the storm scene by having him carry a letter from

Emily to Ham. Objectively and without sentimentality he describes Ham's emotion; with atmospheric clarity he builds up the tempest; rapidly and vividly he shows Ham's efforts to reach the stricken vessel; simply and sorrowfully he looks on the two dead bodies and realizes the injustice of Ham's sacrifice. The final paragraph shows David looking on the second body:

> And on that part of it [the shore] where she and I had looked for shells, two children—on that part of it where some lighter fragments of the old boat, blown down last night, had been scattered by the wind— among the ruins of the home he had wronged—I saw him lying with his head upon his arm, as I had often seen him lie at school.[29]

Dickens can never stop with a single effect. Contrast is always around the corner. In the next chapter David carries the news to Steerforth's mother and Rosa, and Rosa has another chance to tell someone off, the mother being the victim this time. Rosa's speeches are spiteful at all times, but at least she suggests the painful details of her unsatisfactory love affair with Steerforth. The two chapters furnish a remarkable difference in manner. The storm scene gives the illusion of tragedy; Rosa's passion is pure melodrama.

The plot sequence which Dickens balances against Emily and Steerforth through much of the novel is the one which concerns the designs of Uriah upon Agnes. This one is saved by Mr. Micawber. Working for Uriah, Mr. Micawber is just the type to be hired for this position, since his desperate need for money ought to make him willing to do almost anything for his employer. Uriah's plans are remarkably slow, a narrative circumstance which Dickens controls in order to build suspense. When David is in London this plot is brought to the attention of the reader by a series of visits, all of them natural. Uriah suspects David of being a rival for Agnes and observes him closely—a sufficient excuse for the appearances he makes in David's company.

When the time comes for Uriah to be exposed, Dickens calls on the windy rhetoric of melodrama, but the scene is one of the most convincing in the novel. This effect is secured by old-fashioned preparation or motivation. Mr. Micawber has naturally all the mannerisms of stage vocabulary; therefore when he reads his denunciation of Heep, the result is serious and comic at the same time. The speech is in Mr. Micawber's character; he has always talked this way. It may be argued that Rosa has always talked the way she does, too. But somehow heightened language is more effective when it is comic. Thousands of stage actresses have talked like Rosa; no one but Mr. Micawber talks like Mr. Micawber.

Whatever happened to the other plots, the most natural of them all is the one which concerns David himself. The reality of his own experiences makes the reader wish that the author had decided to continue the early style of the book and center everything about David. Even the propaganda about lawyers and Doctors' Commons becomes restrained in the telling, and the quiet sincerity of his feelings about this type of legal inefficiency and waste is much more forceful than the violent diatribes with which infestations of Carlyle's style sometimes imbued his earlier books.

David falls in love with Dora and courts her boyishly. His agonies of mind and extremities of emotion in love are portrayed delicately. When his aunt loses her money, he suffers horribly in trying to tell Dora that he is now poor and a beggar; he succeeds in getting her to use a cookbook, but only as an assistance to the tricks of Jip, her dog; he languishes in the best adolescent fashion, and he is completely human. The opposition of Dora's father to their marriage is quickly relieved by his sudden death—a fortuitous touch. The maiden aunts who supervise the later wooing are in the best tradition of Dickens personalities. The wedding ceremony is part of a chapter which utilizes simple reticence and, lacking any mention of passion or jesting about wedding nights, tells all that has to be told. Housekeeping difficulties are numerous and exquisitely revealed. This is all light farce. The pattern of all these plots praises true and unselfish love while it castigates selfish and immoral passion. The character who always behaves properly is Agnes. She says, at one point, that she trusts in simple love and truth to pull her through any difficulties. To illustrate Dickens' purpose, she deserves happiness in the end, so he portrays her as David's "good angel." She listens to his confessions of love for others and is always kind and sympathetic to Dora, even though she loves David. She takes care of her father in every trial and finds her faith in Truth and Justice rewarded when Mr. Micawber exposes Heep. She is present when Dora dies, and everyone except David knows she loves David. The narrator is self-conscious about admitting this, but he had to be faithful to Dora too.

If Agnes seems a little too good to be true, one must remember what happened to Dickens after he had finished this novel. It may have been his continued insistence upon the moral qualities of true love which put him in such an embarrassing position later. His published defense of his separation from Mrs. Dickens alienated many of his friends, but he did not want his personal life to illustrate a point which he had been careful to criticize in his novels. David marries Dora and makes the best of it. That she would realize her incapacity and give him to Agnes on her deathbed is fortuitous for the moral point. Since David takes several years to recover from Dora's death, not even the most puritanical of readers could object to his eventual marriage to Agnes. It is ironic that in real life Dickens changed in some degree from David to Steerforth. He had different reasons for his behavior, of course, but in the book David and Agnes ought to live happily ever after.

How close did Dickens come to accomplishing the epic intent which had been part of his ambition at the beginning? All art is dependent in some measure upon the tradition within which it works. Fielding's *Tom Jones* is real partially because it is frank as well as truthful; his times permitted him to be so. Dickens' *David Copperfield* exercises a certain ingenuity in avoiding part of the story of David and Steerforth; his times set such fashion. Since fashions change, the enduring judgment upon Dickens will rest upon an estimate of what he revealed, not what he concealed. The first fourth of the novel reveals a sensitive and attractive child; the entire story introduces character after character possessing interesting and entertaining mannerisms and qualities of speech; David's adolescence and youth, his growth, his love story—all reach great heights of inspired narration.

The technical weaknesses are present, but in relatively small number. The episodes featuring Rosa Dartle, the shift in intention which twists the Annie-Dr. Strong plot, the whitewashing of Miss Mowcher—these are matters whose importance varies with the reader. When Robert Graves rewrote the novel to eliminate the weaknesses, he managed to add others. Chesterton laments that the novel gradually turns into *Nicholas Nickleby,* but this seems to be a remarkably exaggerated judgment.

When one analyzes novels on this level of accomplishment, the air of opinion is rarefied. Way up there somewhere is *David Copperfield,* surely among the great English novels of all time. The book presents distinguished accomplishments in technical matters—first person narration, distinctive combination of a panoramic pattern with the autobiographical method, and considerable capacity in transposing issues of the deepest import into the varieties of human experience. There is more depth in some of the later novels, but this one looks forward to some of the most modern experiments with contrapuntal contrast. The standards of romantic love are Victorian standards, but the novel revolves its various strands of action around real human passion, whirling its world into a perspective which will always represent England, Age of Victoria, 1850.

THE MATURE DICKENS

CHAPTER X

The Collins Myth

VERY CRITIC who has devoted himself to the novels of Dickens has noticed that after *David Copperfield* the emphasis of his fiction shifts. This change has been described by various commentators in different ways. For some readers the early novels have some quality of spontaneous inspiration, of glorious fun-making, outrageous farce, and romantic action which is less evident in the later works. For others the plot-making becomes more complicated from *Bleak House* on; indeed, some say that the plot is imposed on the characters, rather than growing out of their characteristics. This feeling is particularly true if the critic does not relish Dickens' economic theories or his disgust with Victorian society. Forster was the first critic to express the general opinion that Dickens was at his best when his emphasis was upon characterization, therefore his last period marked a falling off in dramatic and fictional power.[1] Ley, speaking for The Dickens Fellowship, clarifies this view, which until recently has been that of the majority:

> The great novelist conceives a character first of all. The character points him along a certain road, takes him by the hand, as it were, and leads him along it. Then he becomes steadily conscious of—shall I say a destiny?—the destiny of that character. Is there any critic who does not agree that the influence of Wilkie Collins on Dickens was a stultifying influence on the whole? His marvellous creative genius could not be suppressed, but his greatest work was done when his creativeness was unhampered.[2]

Chesterton remarks that *Bleak House* is not Dickens' best *book*, but his best *novel*.[3] Apparently this implies that Dickens showed an increased grasp of the whole course of his action in the later novels, but had lost the spark which distinguished the earlier works.

183

Even if the modern critic does not accept this analysis of Dickens' accomplishment, a major question needs settling. Did Wilkie Collins cause a change in the art of Dickens? What was Collins' exact influence on the older novelist, if the change was so important? Why should emphasis on plan, organization, and a sense of unified effect weaken the novels of Dickens? The questions are important enough to demand special investigation.

One needs to look first at some biographical details. Collins' father was a painter, and his early environment was typical of prosperous middle-class culture, with an emphasis on artistic matters. The young man had studied two years in Italy, been an articled clerk in the tea trade, dabbled at law in Lincoln's Inn, written a biography of his father—whom he disliked—and published a bad first novel called *Antonina* when he met Dickens in 1851. Collins was twenty-five, Dickens thirty-nine; the younger man had decided to make literature his life work; the elder had just crowned a long list of successful novels with *David Copperfield,* a book which many would claim to be one of the masterpieces of English fiction in the middle of the nineteenth century.

Dickens was enjoying a vacation by helping present Bulwer-Lytton's play, *Not So Bad As We Seem,* and trying to find a sufficient number of authors to make up the amateur cast which would perform the play for his latest charitable interest. The artist Augustus Egg volunteered to bring Collins into the play to take a minor part, that of Dickens' valet, and so the two met. They became friendly immediately, partially because Collins got almost as much fun out of "splendid strolling" as did Dickens, and partially because Collins saw immediately that acquaintance with Dickens would be to his advantage in a literary sense. Dickens appears to have been fascinated with Collins from the first, perhaps because Wilkie was so *un*-Victorian, a man opposed to ordinary standards of behavior and thought, an individualist, and what Dickens would have called a "character." He invited Collins to his home, on vacations, and to many festive gatherings. After finishing *Bleak House* in 1853, Dickens joined Egg and Collins for a trip to Switzerland and Italy; they went to Paris together on several occasions; and there are innumerable records of short outings.[4]

In the four or five years after 1851 Collins began to acquire reputation as a novelist. Dickens looked upon his young friend as a protégé and spoke to everyone of his great promise. Wilkie worked hard at getting into the inner Dickens circle, particularly to make a place for himself on the staff of *Household Words,* Dickens' magazine. This project required close study of the magazine's style and learning to turn out the kind of work which Dickens would print. The tone of *Household Words* was deliberately fixed as kindly, optimistic, or "romantic"; Forster says, "with all familiar things, but especially those repellent on the surface, something was to be connected that should be fanciful or kindly; and the hardest workers were to be taught that their lot is not necessarily excluded from the sympathies and graces of imagination."[5] One of the staff, Percy Fitzgerald, later complained that everything in the magazine had to be exaggerated and colored for effect so that it bubbled like champagne.[6]

Collins' style was certainly at the opposite extreme from this description. He turned out three novels in this period, *Basil* (1852), *Mr. Wray's Cash-Box* (1852), and *Hide and Seek* (1854), in addition to a number of short stories. His early manner is solemn and roundabout. He found it difficult to get started on telling any tale directly. But most important, he was concerned with the morbid, the abnormal, and the grotesque. His talents at first were derived from Gothic influences, subjects which eventually turned in the direction of crime and punishment, and he eventually found his metier in the dissection of mystery and detection.

There was something special about Collins, however, and Dickens sensed it. He broke into the magazine with a fine short story, "A Terribly Strange Bed," in 1852, and this tale did show signs of extraordinary promise in the field of mysterious sensation. It is probably the best short story Collins ever wrote. Certainly it was the only thing Dickens would take for his "family magazine" for a period of two years. Collins eventually got in again with "Gabriel's Marriage," a tale he later turned into a Christmas play for Dickens under the title of *The Lighthouse.* He began to help with the annual special Christmas stories, and Dickens printed a series of tales based on the French Revolution, the best of which was called *Sister Rose.* Finally, by 1855, Collins had learned to attempt the gay, unaffected style of *Household*

185

Words, and he changed his slow-moving action to brisk and fast-moving materials in *A Rogue's Life,* which ran for five installments.

By 1856 Dickens found Collins so helpful that he offered him a position as assistant editor, on the regular payroll of the magazine. At that time he wrote to his subeditor Wills: "He is very suggestive, and exceedingly quick to take my notions."[7] By this time Dickens had already written *Bleak House, Hard Times,* and was in the middle of *Little Dorrit.* Surely there is no evidence here that Dickens received any influence at all from his young friend—at least up to this time. Everything points the other way. The indications also seem to show that very few people in Dickens' immediate circle of intimates liked Collins very much. The odd, witty little man with the large head and the bulging right temple was a cynic about everything but writing. He was reputed to be keeping a mistress, and the letters extant (one wonders about the nonextant ones) to Dickens and in reply indicate that he was a fast man on a party or a night out. It might be easier to make a case that Collins was influencing the morals of Dickens, but one recalls that Dickens had always argued that a man was responsible for his own deeds no matter what his environment.

The offer to Collins to join the magazine staff was probably made because he was preparing another play for a Christmas party, the last such festivity the united Dickens family was to enjoy. Collins was clever enough to deduce that the great man wanted a part which would dominate the stage, something he had supplied in *The Lighthouse.* In *The Frozen Deep* he came up with the idea of one man sacrificing his life for another, even though the other had won the girl beloved of both. Considering the fact that Collins had been working on stories about the French Revolution, and that he now had the idea of atonement in death which Dickens used in *A Tale of Two Cities,* definite signs of subject and plot source material for Dickens show themselves. The question we are concerned with is the influence on narrative style or technique. *The Frozen Deep* is not a very good play, but Dickens and Collins acted the two main roles. Dickens as the man who died for his rival (the eventual Sidney Carton role) made quite an impression on the assembled guests. There was a lot of snob appeal in attending a Dickens Christmas play, and in this case there was pressure to repeat the performance in various cities. It was necessary to hire some professionals for the female parts when they went "on tour," and the Ternans, mother and two daughters, appeared on the scene.

The events which followed are important in several ways. Naturally they concerned the personal happiness or unhappiness of Dickens, but from the standpoint of the novels he wrote, these events led to several years of close association with Collins in a personal as well as literary sense. The novels are *A Tale of Two Cities* and *Great Expectations,* and there is specific influence to be discerned in both these novels, from Collins in the direction of Dickens.

The performances of *The Frozen Deep* set off the events which led to the final break between Dickens and his wife Kate. Much of Dickens' seriousness of spirit, his "dark period," his acute unhappiness, arose from his relations with Mrs. Dickens. The attraction for the young actress, Ellen Ternan, provided the bomb which exploded the situation. When Dickens decided to make the break with Kate, he was faced with public sentiment. He had always stood for Victorian rules of morality; his novels had preached the values of true love; husbands and wives were supposed to be faithful to marriage, unless one member of the sacred compact could be shown to have broken the rules. Adultery had long been the only reason for divorce acceptable to official English church dogma, and whatever was wrong with Mrs. Dickens, it is clear that she was not associating with any man other than her husband. She may have felt that she had associated with him too much. Dickens was faced with an impossible situation as far as his public was concerned. He released a statement justifying himself at the expense of his wife and denying in effect that he had left her for another woman.

This statement does not show the great novelist in a very happy light. It alienated many friends of the family who were sure that Dickens must have transferred his affections to Kate's sister Georgina, who had long been a kind of housekeeper and foster mother for the younger children. There were rumors about the actress, too. Old friends like Forster disapproved heartily; they remained loyal to Dickens in most cases, but they shook their heads. At about this time Collins went to live with his mistress, Caroline Graves, openly flouting Victorian society and its feeling that these matters should at least be kept under cover. Dickens was naturally more at home with Collins than with anyone else in this situation, and one must assume that Collins replaced Forster as Dickens' most intimate friend. It seems also natural to observe that Forster would take a dim view of the younger man's influence and that in the biography he would imply that Dickens' later novels could not be as good as those he had written in happier and more moral days when he was listening to his good friend's advice and improving his technique by making the changes Forster had recommended.

A few ultimate facts must be recalled. Collins' brother, Charles, who was a Pre-Raphaelite painter, wooed and won Dickens' second daughter, Kate Macready Dickens, and married her in 1860. Wilkie dedicated a late novel, *Armadale,* to John Forster in 1867. Yet Forster in his biography mentions the name of Collins as rarely as possible. It has been suggested that he *disliked* Collins, and Wilkie is quoted rather grimly on the matter of the biography in later years, saying that it was "The Life of John Forster with occasional anecdotes of Charles Dickens."[8] From the days of *A Tale of Two Cities* (1859) on, the record shows that Dickens did not exactly ask Forster's opinion about how his novels should go. The days of Little Nell and commercial sentiment were long gone. But there are letters showing that he discussed his materials with Collins.[9]

The financial backers of *Household Words* objected to the publishing of Dickens' statement about his separation from Mrs. Dickens. Dickens rather imperiously arranged to abandon the project and start another magazine, which to all intents and purposes was the same one with different financial backing, called *All the Year Round.* He and Collins then dedicated their artistic efforts to establishing the new magazine's circulation. Dickens wrote *A Tale of Two Cities* for it; Collins came in with his first spectacular achievement in fiction, *The Woman in White;* Dickens followed with *Great Expectations,* and Collins supplied *No Name,* a novel which showed more Dickensian influence than any other book written by the younger man. *No Name* was naturally Dickens' favorite Collins novel. In 1862 he wrote to his friend about this story:

> I cannot tell you with what a strange dash of pride as well as pleasure
> I read the great results of your hard work. Because as you know, I was
> certain from the Basil days that you were the writer who would come

out ahead of all the field—being the only one who combined invention and power, both humorous and pathetic, with the invincible determination to work, and that profound conviction that nothing of worth is to be done without work, of which triflers and feigners have no conception.[10]

By this time Dickens was becoming more and more entangled in his great public reading tours, and Collins was entangled in his own private life. Collins' health deteriorated as time went on, and his bouts with what seems to have been the gout, his inflamed eyes, and his spells of depression produced an addiction to laudanum, huge quantities of which he consumed from the sixties on. His love life continued to be incredible, since he steadfastly refused to marry Caroline, even to legitimize her daughter Harriet (not his child), of whom he was genuinely fond. Caroline left him to marry a handsome plumber (Collins "gave her away" at the wedding ceremony), but came back after a time. Collins managed to console himself by having three children by another mistress named Martha Rudd. In the meantime— after *No Name,* specifically—the connection with Dickens grew more tenuous.

Nuel Pharr Davis, who has written a meticulous and excellent biography of Collins,[11] suggests that the great success of *The Woman in White* aroused the jealousy of Dickens to the point of fearing that his young friend would outdo him in public popularity. *Armadale* was sold to *Cornhill,* a rival magazine sacred to the name of Thackeray (1866), but *The Moonstone* came back to *All the Year Round* (1868). Just before publication of *The Moonstone* Dickens persuaded Collins to collaborate with him in a Christmas number which was entitled *No Thoroughfare.* Perhaps the friendship cooled, and one can deduce that the effect on Dickens' own writing might be in the direction of showing that whatever Collins did, he could do better. There is some indication of this in the fact that Dickens' last novel, *Edwin Drood,* was a direct attempt to surpass *The Moonstone,* a novel which is considered to be the first and best of the great English detective stories.[12]

Even a superficial glance at the connections between the two writers should serve to clarify the matter of influence. If Dickens' last period begins with *Bleak House,* Collins had nothing to do with whatever tendencies Dickens was illustrating in matters of technique. As far as his handling of plot or plots was concerned, Dickens merely completed and improved narrative tendencies which had been developing in his earlier novels. His seriousness of purpose, his concern with the doctrines of Carlyle, his dark and pessimistic perspective on life which came from his personal unhappiness—these matters have no connection with Collins.

But the preoccupation of both writers with mystery and suspense is another matter. Collins was always close to sensational sources and loved to study a spectacular crime. In his preface to *Basil* he says:

> I have not thought it either politic or necessary, while adhering to realities, to adhere to everyday realities only. In other words, I have not stooped so low as to assure myself of the reader's belief in the probability of my story by never once calling on him for the exercise of his faith. Those extraordinary accidents and events which happen to few men seemed to me to be as legitimate materials for fiction to work with—when there was a good object in using them—as the ordinary accidents and events which may, and do happen to us all.[13]

Mystery and suspense follow this theory in simple order. Collins was willing to spend much space in building up a sense of doom, or disaster, or impending tragedy. Some of these effects he may have learned from Dickens, for *Bleak House* is a good model. However, the narrative procedure which served him best in this process was the first person. He developed the habit of revealing his mysteries by multiplying the narrators, using letters, diaries, or the reminiscences of three, four, five, or six persons to tell the whole story. Dickens never availed himself of the multiple-first-person point of view.

Both writers were concerned with the particular ways in which mystery and suspense must be developed in narration. The matter of plot structure is particularly important. Collins has a great reputation as a master of plot, yet the evidence of the early novels is almost completely negative in this regard. *Basil,* for example, is an intensely melodramatic novel, full of false psychology, and distended by emphasis on the adultery and abnormal persecution themes. The most unconvincing and melodramatic of Dickens' early plot sequences cannot begin to approach Collins' in *Basil.* The next story, *Hide and Seek,* presents a mystery about the parentage of a deaf mute who had been adopted by some circus people. Collins' abilities in handling plot do not show to advantage here either. The tale is told "peculiarly"; characters and incidents surrounding them are introduced lamely and leisurely; you read till you meet a character who tells you his life story; further on somebody else enters who does likewise, and the whole narrative is incredibly roundabout.

The gap between *Hide and Seek* and *The Woman in White* was taken up by the short stories or "novelettes," most of which were printed in *Household Words*. By the time he wrote his first masterpiece Collins had learned to weave his various first-person narratives or autobiographical accounts so that the mystery and suspense were advanced to a sensational degree. Count Fosco is one of the best villains in fiction. His collection of canaries and the white mice which run in and out of his clothes add a Dickensian tone of grotesque menace to his character. His evil intentions toward Lady Glyde, his apparent accomplishment of her murder, are all opposed by Marian Holcombe, one of the narrators of the story by way of her diary. One of Collins' best touches is in showing her diary coming to a close when she is overcome by illness, then having Fosco append a postscript which informs the reader that he has accomplished his villainous purpose despite Marian's opposition.

Collins believed that suspense is effectively achieved when the reader is made acquainted in advance with the awful thing which is to happen. This must be told or implied early so that the tale encourages a sense of mounting horror as the reader sees the approach of something he does not want to happen. But Collins also believed that the best effect is secured when the author suddenly and unexpectedly fools the reader after all. In *The Woman in White* he gets this sudden substitution of sensation by the resemblance of Miss Fairlie to the "woman in white." This allows him to contrive a number of coincidences so that the wrong person (or the right one, for most readers) is murdered at the last. The climax has all the horror of killing off a heroine and all the joy of resurrecting her in as many breaths. His distinctive technique is: "Lead the reader to believe something is going to happen; then have something else more surprising occur."

Dickens wrote *Great Expectations* immediately after *The Woman in White* appeared. Here he invented the sensational incidents surrounding Miss Havisham and Satis House, a place kept as it had been when the mistress was deserted by her husband-to-be on her wedding day. Miss Havisham and the "woman in white" are both psychological case studies. Starting from this point Dickens shows the lady trying to revenge herself on all males. She apparently adopts Pip, and the suspense of the plot is woven around the idea that he "expects" to inherit her fortune. The real source of his expectations is carefully hidden from the reader and finally revealed suddenly in a surprise climax which exactly fits the Collins formula.

In the first days of his close association with Collins, Dickens was not convinced that a mystery should be disclosed early in the story. He saw that this effect can be successful only if the novel builds a tragic sense of inevitability. In one of the most interesting early exchanges between the two authors Collins argues that Dickens should have revealed the secret of Dr. Manette early in the course of *A Tale of Two Cities*. Dickens held off this disclosure until the second trial of Charles Darnay in Paris, the one which reverses Darnay's acquittal and sends him to the guillotine. Dickens accomplishes this reversal by having Defarge produce the letter written by the doctor in the Bastille, the letter which told of the reasons for his imprisonment and gave his curse on the whole St. Evremonde family, including Darnay. Up to this time the reader knows only that the doctor had suffered injustice, and from his behavior in connection with Darnay that the St. Evremonde family was involved in his past sufferings.

Collins wanted Dickens to tell this part of the tale earlier, then use this knowledge to gain suspense, making the reader fear the eventual suffering and death of Darnay because of this curse. All the doom of inescapable fate might be called upon to increase the reader's growing alarm as he watches Darnay drawn to Paris and the execution which his forgiving father-in-law has unwittingly prepared for him. Collins felt that having the document produced first at the trial would ensure surprise but lose suspense. Dickens rejected this suggestion firmly:

> I do not positively say that the point you put might not have been done in your manner; but I have a very strong conviction that it would have been overdone in that manner—too elaborately trapped, baited, and prepared—in the main anticipated, and its interest wasted. This is

quite apart from the peculiarity of the Doctor's character, as affected by his imprisonment; which of itself would, to my thinking, render it quite out of the question to put the reader inside of him before the proper time, in respect of matters that were dim to himself through being, in a diseased way, morbidly shunned by him. . . . I think the business of art is to lay all the ground carefully, not with the care that conceals itself—to show, by a backward light, what everything has been working to—but only to *suggest,* until the fulfillment comes. These are the ways of Providence, of which all art is but a little imitation.

"Could it have been done at all, in the way I suggest, to advantage?" is your question. I don't see the way, and I never have seen the way, is my answer. I cannot imagine it that way, without imagining the reader wearied and the expectation wiredrawn.[14]

One may say, in passing, that it would be pleasant to have a letter from Dickens to Forster illustrating rejection of change in narrative procedure.

In *No Name* Collins did what he had recommended to Dickens for the development of suspense in *A Tale of Two Cities.* He explained the mystery early in the story and tried to rouse "the reader's interest in following the train of circumstances by which these foreseen events are brought about."[15] For most readers this is not particularly successful, certainly not in the same degree as the surprising substitution climax he had manipulated in *The Woman in White.* The interesting Dickensian characters in the novel include the attractive scoundrel Captain Wragge, Mrs. Lecount, and Magdalen, who does female impersonations like the Mathews one-man performances, about which Collins had heard from Dickens.

Dickens must have felt that Collins' theories of suspense had some merit, for in *Our Mutual Friend* he developed two sequences which use, respectively, surprise and suspense. In one of them—the plot concerning the heir, Harmon, who returns to England expecting to disguise himself to find out whether he wants to marry the girl in order to accept the fortune left him by his father—Dickens tells the reader early what the situation is. Harmon is not really murdered; this we know, and we follow his behavior while in disguise with interest because we are expected to wonder whether or not Bella will choose him or money, whether she will marry for love or gain. This Dickens felt was legitimate suspense. The other plot, concerning Mr. Boffin's supposed degeneration into a miser, was intended to illustrate a sudden surprise, a denouement which the reader would not expect.

The final connection between novels by Dickens and Collins concerns *The Moonstone* and *Edwin Drood*. Collins' mystery story is narrated by several persons in accordance with his most expert practice, and the first narrators are wonderful people. Betteredge, the butler, and Miss Clack (Swinburne called her the "Evangelical Hag"), the tract-distributing Puritan, are typical Dickensian caricatures. Collins carries his theory of mystification into the realm of the detective story, the "whodunit." Obviously he does not disclose the mystery early, but he uses a variation of the suspense theory by leading the reader up a number of wrong roads. Who stole the Moonstone? Suspicion shifts from one character to another, even the detective being baffled. Casually, in Miss Clack's narrative, Franklin Blake is absolved of all responsibility. She shows how impossible it would be for him to commit the theft, in case the reader may be suspecting him. The conclusion, when everybody is cleared, is that nobody stole it. That Blake really did so under the influence of opium, unknown to himself, is the surprise which breaks the long-drawn and shifting effect of suspense.

The fact that Dickens did not finish *Edwin Drood,* leaving the conclusion of that mystery tale in the realm of *eternal* suspense because there is no certain evidence of exactly what he intended to do with the story, keeps us from being sure of the probable comparison with *The Moonstone*. But one may legitimately guess that he intended to write a novel which would be as sensational and mystifying as the one Collins wrote. He could lead the reader to expect that John Jasper murdered Drood, because all the signs pointing that way are in the tale. But if he were to surpass Collins, he would have to provide a sudden and surprising conclusion which would startle the reader as *The Moonstone* had done. It is therefore most likely that he intended to show Jasper, also under the influence of opium, thinking he had committed a murder, even confessing to it. The surprise would be that Drood had really escaped and disappeared. This solution will be examined in detail later, but the contention from the connection between Collins and Dickens is a strong one.

What, then, is the conclusion concerning the importance of the influence of Collins on Dickens? Dickens' first novels began with the presentation of characters who develop their own plots, and he had gradually changed his structure so that he presented a number of plots which alternate and contrast with each other as the novel progresses. He finally wove these plots around a central purpose, as he did around the theme of romantic love in *David Copperfield*. Collins in his best work showed a trend toward concentration. He tied all the strings of intrigue and action so that they contributed to the solution of a mystery. Dickens used multiple plots; Collins concentrated on *one*. Whenever Collins allowed several plots to clutter up his story, the reader can be sure he was missing his aims in narration.

In the matter of organizing the presentation of the action and choosing a point of view from which to tell the tale, the two authors are at opposite extremes. The Collins method may be summed up as the multiple-first-person approach, in which a number of different individuals take turns in revealing different parts of the mystery. Dickens never used this approach in any form. When he shifted his omniscient point of view, it was to develop a contrasting sequence of action. When he used the first person—as in *Great Expectations*— he told the entire story through the eyes of Pip.

In the matter of plot and episode, Dickens borrowed materials and developed several suggestions from Collins. The first such use of Collins as a source of inspiration is in *Hard Times,* for which the circus people were suggested by similar scenes in Collins' *Hide and Seek.*[16] Certainly the inspiration for *A Tale of Two Cities* derived from "Gabriel's Marriage," "Sister Rose," and *The Frozen Deep.* The fact that Franklin Blake and John Jasper both use opium may be mentioned as another resemblance in the subject matter treated by both authors.

There is no case for any important influence on narrative technique, therefore, except in the use of complex suspense and surprising climax, something which might be called *misdirection*. It is clear that when Collins showed how effective a story can be which leads the reader to a conclusion, then suddenly surprises him with a twist in the denouement, as in *The Woman in White,* Dickens would also utilize this device, as he did in *Great Expectations* and *Our Mutual Friend*. It is again clear—or probably so—that when Collins used a variation of this same effect in leading the reader to think that Blake

195

had not stolen the Moonstone, then showing that he had unconsciously done so under the influence of opium, Dickens would see how he could use a derived device in *Edwin Drood*.

Certainly the shift in emphasis after *David Copperfield,* the idea that Dickens began imposing characters on plots instead of vice versa, the idea that the whole tone of his fiction changed for the worse—that shift cannot be blamed on Collins, even if it were true. Dickens would have written *Bleak House, Hard Times,* and *Little Dorrit* pretty much as he did whether or not he had ever met Collins. His most important technical device, the revolving of his plots about a central theme, could have no connection with Collins. Therefore the long-existing impression that Wilkie was responsible for Dickens' obsession with plot structure and unified organization of his novels—that is the Collins myth, completely unjustified by the facts.

CHAPTER XI

The Social Microcosmic Pattern

s DICKENS advanced in wisdom and knowledge and in fictional vision, the problems of society began to weigh more heavily upon his creative conscience. With the completion of *David Copperfield* he was at the height of his creative powers. He was also very unhappy in his relationship with Mrs. Dickens. He was becoming more and more concerned with the economic and political problems of his day, and he began to attack social evils in his magazine. The combination of many influences produced in his fiction a seriousness of purpose and a breadth of perspective which overwhelmed all other considerations. *Bleak House, Hard Times,* and *Little Dorrit* represent a kind of dark period in his creative accomplishment, a period in which the serious issues of life came uppermost, in which his novels were completely suffused with a social microcosmic pattern.[1]

His narrative practice had developed many resources of effect. He had control of techniques like farce and caricature for humorous purposes; he could call upon dialogue and speech devices for dramatic reasons; he had a wide variety of plot situations at his command, and he was always finding new ones; he had reached into the depths and aspired to the heights of sentimental emotion; he knew the possibilities of the sensational and the terrible, the violent and the horrible; he had attacked error wherever he saw it, in human behavior and in social institutions; he had been tremendously impressed with the economic and political theories of Carlyle, and he had organized stories to convey his convictions to his reading audience. Artistically, he had used the many techniques at his command for contrast and alternation in his fiction. Gradually his habit of alternation had grown into a studied

197

theory of organizing his books around a purpose, a contrapuntal arrangement of various episodes, sequences, and techniques which were all related to a central thesis or idea. *Martin Chuzzlewit* is his first important accomplishment in this artistic development, and *David Copperfield* illustrates his control of the organization of a complex tale around a pattern.

Bleak House, Hard Times, and *Little Dorrit* all have a consuming purpose which follows a similar theme: an attack upon social institutions which interfere with human happiness. Dickens' intent was to make this widespread assault on many levels: from the incapacity of the legal system to the artificialities of caste; from the abuses of economic practice to the stupidities of religion, education, and politics; from the conditions which permit nauseous slums to the Victorian attitude which admired pyramiding capitalists and inefficient government. Above all was his growing sense that nothing could be done to make the world better unless the public saw what was wrong and used all its opportunities to better conditions for the future.

Pervasive obsession with social decay allied itself in a number of ways to Dickens' basic plan for *Bleak House*. He saw intense suffering around him; the widespread poverty of masses of people and the festering slums of London sickened him. But he wanted to make his case against causes rather than results. The focus of injustice in England seemed to him to be the very organization which was established to remove injustice—the law itself. Obviously the law, in its ideal intent, should aid and protect individuals against exploitation. But as legal institutions had developed in England, they had grown into an inextricable mass of red tape and inefficiency. To Dickens the law had come to stand for the exact opposite of its intention. This point has occasionally been misunderstood, as though the satire of *Bleak House* were concerned only with an isolated example of ridiculous legal procedure, exaggerated by Dickens and representative of conditions long since reformed. Beyond the law courts, the lawyers, the technicalities of muddling procedures, and the general inequities of justice stood fashionable society and Parliament itself. Society and its governing body were responsible for the laws and court procedure; assuredly society and Parliament were ultimately to be credited with the general state of England's health. Victorian England pretended to be extremely moral; the truth of the matter was that Victorian morality permitted and encouraged injustice and immorality. In Dickens' last novel, *Edwin Drood,* is perhaps the best statement of this point in all his writing. "It is not enough," says Mr. Sapsea, "that Justice should be morally certain; she must be immorally certain—legally, that is."[2] As Edgar Johnson remarks, "It [*Bleak House*] regards legal injustice not as accidental but as organically related to the very structure of that society."[3]

There are two main courses of action in *Bleak House.* The more prominent is Dickens' sulphurous attack on the practice of the Court of Chancery, the place where financial settlements are supposed to be judged. In the book, as it develops, this plot revolves around the Jarndyce will, which had left a great fortune in dispute. Endless legal technicalities and delays eventually eat up the fortune, and the heirs inherit nothing from the estate. There are several sources for this extraordinary example of Chancery entanglement, any of which could have supplied Dickens with the idea. The notorious Day case had involved £70,000 in costs from 1834 to the time the book was written. He cites the Jennings case, dating from 1789, which involved £1,500,000, and was still unsettled fifty years later. In fact, it carried on into the twentieth century.[4]

William Searle Holdsworth, one of England's recognized legal authorities, has written a book about Dickens as a legal historian. With typical judicial caution he says that if *Bleak House* is presumed to depict action which took place in the year 1826, its contentions are "wholly true."[5] He admits that if Dickens had set the action a quarter of a century later, "much of it was then still true."

> The physical fog amidst which *Bleak House* opens, which is so aptly made to typify the moral fog which enveloped the procedure of the Court of Chancery, is I think the finest piece of descriptive writing in the whole of Dickens' works. This moral fog had been produced by a variety of causes, operating through centuries; and its density had made the court the most crying abuse of an age in which there were many abuses.[6]

This opinion seems sufficient evidence for agreeing with Dickens' own statement in his Preface that his attack is "substantially true."

199

The point of his case was, however, not merely to call to the attention of his public a specific evil which might be rated with something like the bad boarding schools (exposed in *Nicholas Nickleby*) or the debtors' prisons (an abuse in punishment which had been altered by the time Dickens wrote *David Copperfield*)—therefore an evil which deserved criticism, but which had been essentially corrected—Dickens was also attacking the way Victorian England looked at laws and legal procedures. The Jarndyce case was a specific example, but the evil was not to be remedied by some slight change in court procedure so that future cases involving wills could be settled more promptly.

To get this broad social viewpoint into a novel Dickens followed his usual practice of devising several intrigues to develop the action. In this instance he evolved a number of narrative strands from the idea of showing how the Jarndyce case affected the fortunes of the people who were concerned with it. The general thesis was that Court of Chancery procedure ruined the lives of anyone dependent upon its procedures—and Dickens meant literally the word "ruin." First he shows the wise man, John Jarndyce, who knows enough to ignore the will, who lives as though the case or the money involved did not exist. Then he proceeds to Jarndyce's wards, Ada and Richard, who illustrate the main thesis, since Richard depends too much on his expected inheritance and comes to catastrophe, carrying Ada, who loves and marries him, along with him. Dickens then carefully plans a number of sequences which intensify this point and which show cumulatively the legal maleficence of Chancery procedure. There is Mr. Gridley, who suffers from Chancery injustice as do the principals in the Jarndyce case. Miss Flite is literally as well as figuratively mad because she expects results from the court. The slum sections of London, with all their astounding and horrible poverty, are shown as dependent upon the money tied up in cases like the Jarndyce affair. Jo, who dies of smallpox and neglect, the Necketts, and countless others are overwhelmed by their surroundings, by places like the shocking Tom-all-Alone's slum. A multitude of lawyers float through the story, from Conversation Kenge to Mr. Vholes to Mr. Guppy to the monstrous Tulkinghorn, each illustrating a different degree of perversity and evil. Mr. George borrows money and has his note taken up because a lawyer wants information from him. This circumstance brings his friends, the Bagnets, to distress because they are "on his note," and Dickens shows the inhuman partnership of moneylenders like Smallweed with the law in action.

It is interesting to discover that all these characters, from Ada and Richard down through the least important to the minor figures who suffer from the Court of Chancery, are drawn from life. Their experiences do not demand intrigue in the sense of a stage plot. But the contrasting course of action did derive from drama. The Dedlock plot has two parts. The essential situation depends upon the mystery of Lady Dedlock's past, the illegitimate child she had believed dead, and the gradual uncovering of her secret by the family lawyer, Tulkinghorn. The action then grows into what is the first fully developed mystery story in English fiction in the modern sense. Tulkinghorn is murdered, and a detective eventually unravels the mystery of how, why, and by whom it was done. Inspector Bucket is fiction's first detective in a full-length novel.

The story of Lady Dedlock was modeled consciously by Dickens from the eighteenth-century stage play, *Douglas*, by John Home. His manner of reshaping and adapting this original situation to his own purposes is one of his most suggestive borrowings from a source. The plot of *Douglas* is simple: Young Norval is the legitimate son of Douglas and Sir Malcolm's daughter; after the father's death, the mother married Lord Randolph, a leader of a rival clan. The child of the first marriage is believed dead, and Lord Randolph does not know of his existence, but Norval has been brought up by an old shepherd. Norval does not know the identity of his mother, but she discovers the relationship after the boy has grown to heroic manhood. Lady Randolph keeps the existence of her child secret from her husband, partially because the second marriage has produced no children, and in addition, her husband hates any reference to Douglas. There is a villain, Glenalvon, who persuades her husband that Lady Randolph is in love with the man she meets secretly, and the catastrophe follows. After Norval is killed by Glenalvon in a fight with Randolph, Lady Randolph commits suicide.

Dickens changed this plot idea in several essential places, adding and reshaping in order to fit the intrigue to his own times and his own purposes. Home's idea of tragedy was that it was an undeserved doom of destiny; Dickens shifted the story to make Lady Dedlock's fate a more deserved one. The erring woman who has an illegitimate child is substituted for the wife whose legitimate alliance has produced a child, so that when Lady Dedlock marries, thinking her child dead and her past buried, she will have a reason for attempting to keep her sin secret from her husband. The child is a daughter, not a son, in Dickens' story. Probably this shift was influenced by the fact that the author had just finished an experiment in telling a story in the first person; he wanted to try this narrative manner again, since he felt that *David Copperfield* had gained artistically from its point of view. Accordingly he proposed to narrate part of his new novel from the viewpoint of the illegitimate child. The female first-person technique would avoid repetition of David's male mannerisms. He saw that it would be difficult to develop his attack on the Court of Chancery through the first-person narration of Esther Summerson, and so he hit upon an alternate narrative manner. Esther tells whatever part of the story she can, and whenever it would be awkward to involve her in the Jarndyce action, Dickens returns to the third person—shifting between the first and third every two or three or four chapters with complete regularity.[7]

The shift of sex in the child is not significant in the plot, since Dickens wanted to stress something different from the idea of having the husband become jealous of his wife's relationship to the unrecognized son. The Oedipus complex did not interest him. The point was to satirize the artificial institution of society; Dickens did not want his intrigue to become lost in a melodramatic situation which would obscure his purpose. The action was intended to provide a skeleton in the Dedlock closet. Tulkinghorn, like Glenalvon in *Douglas,* undertakes to expose the skeleton, and it is the process of exposure which consumes much of the action. It is the general situation which derives from *Douglas,* not its development, but there are several extraordinary resemblances which merit attention here.

For example, one of the most interesting stage effects of the play is the peculiar attraction felt between Lady Randolph and her son when they meet without either knowing the existence of any relationship. The stage has helped foster the idea that mother and child are

attracted by some mystic power to each other. Lady Randolph acts so
peculiarly at the first sight of young Norval that her husband says:

LADY R.
>
> Ha! My Matilda! wherefore starts that tear?

> I cannot say: for various affections
> And strangely mingled, in my bosom swell.

Anna, her servant, notes:

> On him intent you gazed, with a look
> Much more delighted, than your pensive eye
> Has deigned on other subjects to bestow.[8]

When, in Act III, Lady Randolph finds out the truth from old Norval,
the shepherd, she says:

> 'Twas my child I saw! No wonder, Anna,
> That my bosom burn'd.

And Anna replies:

> How fondly did your eyes devour the boy!
> Mysterious nature, with the unseen cord
> Of powerful instance, drew you to your own.[9]

Mysterious nature shows itself in like fashion when Esther Summerson and Lady Dedlock first meet. They are in a summerhouse
watching a storm break. Lady Dedlock speaks, and her voice, never
before heard by Esther, stops the beating of her heart. Her face, says
Esther, "affected me in the same strange way."[10] Later, Esther talks
to herself about this peculiar attraction. When Lady Dedlock, who has
similar feelings, finally discovers that Esther is her daughter, she breaks
the news in the summerhouse where Esther is recovering from smallpox. Esther speaks:

> I was fluttered by her being unexpectedly so near . . . and would have
> risen to continue my walk. But I could not. I was rendered motionless.
> Not so much by her hurried gesture of entreaty, not so much by her
> quick advance and outstretched hands, not so much by the great
> change in her manner, and the absence of her haughty self-restraint, as
> by a something in her face that I had pined for and dreamed of when
> I was a little child; something I had never seen in any face. . . .[11]

In general Dickens rises above his more or less melodramatic source. The murder of Tulkinghorn is a well-developed mystery. The two courses of action, roughly speaking the Jarndyce plot and the Dedlock plot, are interlocked by as many connections as possible. Esther goes to live with John Jarndyce, the paternal and kindly guardian who makes her his housekeeper, falls in love with her, and eventually gives her up to the young doctor, Allan Woodcourt, with whom she is obviously in love. Esther naturally becomes friendly with Ada and Richard. She also catches smallpox from Jo, who is another link between the two courses of action. Tulkinghorn serves Sir Leicester Dedlock in his capacity as a lawyer and uncovers Lady Dedlock's secret by manipulations which concern the persons who suffer from the Court of Chancery's actions.

Weaving in and about the two plots are a great number of characters who achieve a remarkable amount of individuality. Each of these persons represents some part of Dickens' diagnosis of the infection he finds in the body of society in Victorian England. His attack is directed at the law and against society. The very name of Dedlock illustrates Dickens' symbolic point, for all of Sir Leicester's friends are dedicated to deadlock in social conflict. By a kind of narrative refraction, Dickens extends this indictment of social deadlock to the general disease which infects the caste system, Parliament, the economic system, and orthodox religion.

Mrs. Jellyby represents religious stupidity which devotes itself to foreign missions at the expense of the happiness of her own home. Her daughter, Caddy, tries to escape from this stultifying home atmosphere by way of marriage to Prince Turveydrop, a young man who has a leechlike father. Mrs. Rouncewell, the Dedlock housekeeper, has two sons, one of them a successful industrialist whose son wishes to marry Rosa, Lady Dedlock's second maidservant. The caste system stretches its tentacles into this love affair, for Sir Leicester resents Rouncewell's well-intentioned desire to educate Rosa and prepare her properly for marriage to his son. Several other sequences play upon the misunderstanding inherent in the older generation in connection with the love affairs of the younger generation. Mrs. Woodcourt thinks Esther Summerson is beneath her son, and certainly the elder Turveydrop does not look upon Caddy with enthusiasm. Mrs. Rouncewell's second son,

Mr. George, had run away to the army in his youth, and his efforts to establish himself in the world after an apparently misspent adolescence represent a rather appealing part of the novel. He is eventually restored to his mother.

Mrs. Jellyby has a contrasting foil in Mrs. Pardiggle, who completely misunderstands the basis of sincere charity. Harold Skimpole is an artistic representative of decayed society, artlessly preferring to depend upon anyone he can delude into helping support him. This is the portrait supposed to derive from the example of the poet, Leigh Hunt. Mr. Boythorn, based upon the model of Walter Savage Landor, is a boisterous, tempestuous character, definitely amusing in his eccentricities, but still representing an extreme of the caste system. Mr. Chadband is one of Dickens' most bitter caricatures of religious mannerism and hypocrisy. These and many other characters add their part to the case against some phase of social deadlock, dependent upon human stupidity and the absence of understanding tolerance or of old-fashioned brotherly love.

Parliamentary ineptitude comes in for special satire in the sections in which Dickens criticizes the Boodle-Coodle-Doodle clan, the ruling caste which approaches the job of running a country with complete inefficiency except for keeping in office. This attack finds more intensive attention in the Barnacle-Merdle episodes which heighten the satire of *Little Dorrit;* in *Bleak House* it underlines Dickens' feeling that the disease of the social structure of England goes from the slums to the law courts to the churches to the manor houses to the Houses of Parliament. It is a virulent pestilence, nowhere more nauseous than in high places.

Atmospheric symbolism accompanies Dickens' planned sequences of action, illuminating and intensifying the effect of his indictment. This device is a new development in Dickens' artistry. Over the pages of the book hovers an actual fog which effectively shrouds the spiritual darkness of the Court of Chancery and all its works. The rain and mist of England's foulest weather rot away the Dedlock mansion and all it stands for in fashionable decay. Fog, rain, and mist constitute atmospheric imagery, but the deepest symbolism is centered on Dickens' pictures of Chancery Court. This symbolism suffuses the shop of Mr. Krook, the illiterate secondhand dealer, who is facetiously called "the Chancellor" because his person and his shop represent accurately what the corresponding legal structure of the Court of Chancery really stands for.

The mad Miss Flite lives above Mr. Krook's shop, alongside Esther Summerson's father at the start of the tale. She keeps a collection of birds in cages: larks, linnets, and goldfinches.

> "I began to keep the little creatures," she said, "with an object that the wards will readily comprehend. With the intention of restoring them to liberty when my judgment should be given. Ye—es! They die in prison, though. Their lives, poor silly things, are so short in comparison with Chancery proceedings that, one by one, the whole collection has died over and over again. I doubt, do you know, whether one of these, though they are all young, will live to be free! Ve-ery mortifying, is it not?"[12]

Later Mr. Krook gives the names of these birds:

> "Hope, Joy, Youth, Peace, Rest, Life, Dust, Ashes, Waste, Want, Ruin, Despair, Madness, Death, Cunning, Folly, Words, Wigs, Rags, Sheepskin, Plunder, Precedent, Jargon, Gammon, and Spinach. That's the whole collection," said the old man, "all cooped up together by my noble and learned brother."[13]

When the Jarndyce case is dismissed because the costs have eaten up the fortune involved, and after the Tulkinghorn murder is solved, Miss Flite sets her birds free.

Mr. Krook's shop, full of odds and ends, uselessly cluttered, the bones of clients in the corner, is a symbolic Court of Chancery.

> "You see I have so many things here," he resumed, holding up the lantern, "of so many kinds, and all, as the neighbors think (but *they* know nothing), wasting away and going to rack and ruin, that that's why they have given me and my place a christening. And I have so many old parchments and papers in my stock. And I have a liking for rust and must and cobwebs. And all's fish that comes to my net. And I can't abear to part with anything I once lay hold of (or so my neighbors think, but what do *they* know?) or to alter anything, or to have any sweeping, nor scouring, nor cleaning, nor repairing going on about me. That's the way I've got the ill name of Chancery. I don't mind. I go to see my noble and learned brother pretty well every day, when he sits in the Inn. He don't notice me, but I notice him. There's no great odds betwixt us. We both grub on in a muddle."[14]

It is Mr. Krook who eventually dies of spontaneous combustion, and this incident takes on force because of its symbolic implications, not because it is a startling and sensational occurrence to be enjoyed for its realistic effect.

Dickens defends the authenticity of this most unusual type of death in his Preface and gives his authorities for its occasional appearance. There is apparent evidence for belief that he thought it could actually happen, but however one reacts to this mixture of fact and fantasy, it is an ideal judgment upon Chancery procedure. Dickens cites a number of sources for spontaneous combustion, but does not mention his main influence which is in a novel by Captain Frederick Marryat entitled *Jacob Faithful,* published in 1834.

Marryat was an early friend of Dickens, visiting at his home, and it is reasonable to suppose that he supplied Dickens with all the information later referred to in the Preface to *Bleak House.* In the novel Marryat tells of young Jacob, who was born and reared on a Thames River boat. At one point in the story, Jacob's mother and father are below in the cabin. His father rushes out and leaps in the Thames. Then:

> A strong, empyreumatic, thick smoke ascended from the hatchway of the cabin, and, as it had now fallen calm, it mounted straight up in the air in a dense column. . . . I went to the hatchway, and although the smell was still overpowering, I found that I could bear it. I descended the little ladder of three steps, and called "Mother!" but there was no answer. The lamp fixed against the after bulk-head, with a glass before it, was still alight, and I could see plainly to every corner of the cabin. Nothing was burning—not even the curtains to my mother's bed appeared to be singed . . . my mother was not there! But there appeared to be a black mass in the center of the bed. I put my hand fearfully upon it—it was a sort of unctuous, pitchy cinder. I screamed with horror. . . .[15]

Marryat continues by explaining that cases of this kind "present themselves but once in a century." *Bleak House* makes the second in the nineteenth-century. The cause is a good argument for prohibition: an immoderate use of spirituous liquors, "an inflammation of the gases generated from the spirits absorbed into the system."

Mr. Krook also drinks gin constantly, but Dickens does not seem concerned with any argument about immoderate indulgence. His thesis concerns Chancery, not liquor. And along with the symbolism of Miss Flite's birds and Mr. Krook's shop one finds the cat, Lady Jane, waiting like a lawyer ready to seize upon any bird that gets free from its cage. Each lawyer in the novel is accompanied by symbolic behavior of some kind, in "metaphors drawn from beasts of prey," as Edgar Johnson says.[16] The most notable illustration is Mr. Vholes's habit of skinning his black gloves from his hands as if he were in the process of flaying something—usually a victim. All through the novel one finds references to spiders, webs, and entangled flies. The imagery is cumulative.

The social microcosmic pattern is woven about the two interlocking strands of action, the Jarndyce case and the Dedlock mystery. The slums are at one end of the story, Chesney Wold at the other. The Court of Chancery affects the physical aspects of all England between these two extremes.

> It is but a glimpse of the world of fashion that we want on this same miry afternoon. It is not so unlike the Court of Chancery but that we may pass from the one scene to the other as the crow flies. Both the world of fashion and the Court of Chancery are things of precedent and usage: over-sleeping Rip Van Winkles, who have played at strange games through a deal of thundery weather; sleeping beauties, whom the Knight will wake one day, when all the stopped spits in the kitchen shall begin to turn prodigiously.[17]

But the novel is not named "Tom-all-Alone's" or "Chesney Wold" or "The Court of Chancery" or "Social Deadlock." It is called "Bleak House."

Bleak House is the home of John Jarndyce, the kindly guardian of Esther Summerson, who stands apart from the influences that are generated by the case which is mired in Chancery, who is affected by all the ill winds that blow from court, but who tries to aid all those who suffer from some form of exploitation. The word *bleak* supplies its own connotation. Shaw in a later day will use the same intent and substitute the word *heartbreak*. Dickens explains clearly what he meant by *bleak* and why he chose the title:

> "Bleak House: true. There is in that city of London there some property of ours [the Jarndyces], which is much at this day what Bleak House was then—I say property of ours, meaning of the Suit's, but I ought to call it the property of Costs; for Costs is the only power on

earth that will ever get anything out of it now, or will ever know it for anything but an eyesore and a heartsore. It is a street of perishing blind houses, with their eyes stoned out; without a pane of glass, without so much as a window-frame, with the bare blank shutters tumbling from their hinges and falling asunder; the iron rails peeling away in flakes of rust; the chimneys sinking in; the stone steps to every door (and every door might be Death's Door) turning stagnant green; the very crutches on which the ruins are propped decaying. Although Bleak House was not in Chancery, its master was, and it was stamped with the same seal. These are the Great Seal's impressions, my dear, all over England—the children know them!"[18]

How bleak is the house of Victorian society!

The modern reader finds that the novel poses a question. Did Dickens feel that the state of Victorian England was hopeless? Was everyone, from the slums to the mansions of fashionable society, so entangled in precedent and usage that there was no remedy but to have the social structure go up in spontaneous combustion? The characters in the novel who are presented as admirable possess certain stoic qualities which approach heroic resignation; they retain nobility because they fight against evil; they oppose their fate in whatever form circumstance devises; they are purified by tragic katharsis. Dickens hangs on to certain elements derived from his early Romantic beliefs, specifically his continuing assumption that the individual is responsible no matter what the difficulties of his environment. The only solution for man's difficulties with society is man himself. An explosion is appropriate and just, but reform is dependent upon human effort.

Carlyle had argued that man is purified by work. Richard illustrates the reverse of this thesis, for he allows himself to be ruined by his dependence upon his expectations. This concept recurs in later novels, finds a happy contrast in *Little Dorrit* with Arthur Clennam's successful attempts to escape from the effects of his environment, and reaches complete analysis in Pip's experiences in *Great Expectations.* Richard never works hard enough at anything to be successful, for he deludes himself into believing that his inheritance will eventually make up for what he should do for himself.

In contrast to Richard, Dickens studies a number of persons who achieve some measure of nobility by their efforts to fight against their surroundings, to make the best of a world beset by social and legal decay. Upon heroic individualism rests the hope of the world. Thus, Mr. George struggles toward regeneration from a wasted youth; Dr. Woodcourt serves all those who need help; Caddy fights against the influence of her mother, her husband's father, and the mischance of a deaf and dumb child to achieve respect and admiration; Esther continually strives against the blight of her birth and the tragedy of the disease which disfigures her face to find eventual happiness. Even Lady Dedlock, who had erred and had sold herself to wealth and fashion, reaches some measure of heroic stature in the end. Her death close to the grave of the man she had once loved represents her own recognition of the need for regeneration and atonement. Sidney Carton in *A Tale of Two Cities* finds a more spectacular way, but the judgment is similar.

Tragedy results when the individual is overcome by forces beyond his control. Lady Dedlock has some responsibility for her fate, but Jo does not. No matter how hard he struggles, he is doomed by his surroundings. This is the extreme statement of Dickens' case against Victorian society, for Victorian England allows its slums to kill those who must dwell in them; it allows the disease generated in those slums to infect everybody. What a horrible place is Tom-all-Alone's, says Dickens, and who can contradict him?

> It is a black, dilapidated street, avoided by all decent people; where the crazy houses were seized upon, when their decay was far advanced, by some bold vagrants, who, after establishing their own possession, took to letting them out in lodgings. Now, these tumbling tenements contain, by night, a swarm of misery. As, on the ruined human wretch, vermin parasites appear, so these ruined shelters have bred a crowd of foul existence that crawls in and out of gaps in walls and boards; and coils itself to sleep, in maggot numbers, where the rain drips in; and comes and goes, fetching and carrying fever, and sowing more evil in its every footprint than Lord Coodle, and Sir Thomas Doodle, and the Duke of Foodle, and all the fine gentlemen in office, down to Zoodle, shall set right in five hundred years—though born expressly to do it.[19]

Bleak House is incredibly complex in its action, but the action whirls about a dynamic core and achieves a coherent centripetal effect. Dickens uses all the technical effects with which he had previously experimented, attempting to heighten each small part of his story with the manner which was fitting.

For example, he calls upon farce and caricature, together with speech devices and mimicry, whenever he feels they are needed. It is true that pure farce is atmospherically out of keeping with the general over-all purpose of *Bleak House*. But in an ironic sense, farce under-lines his thesis, and for this reason he uses it, even though the reader can never laugh in the same reaction he experiences from the Pickwick-Bardell trial. Miss Flite and Mr. Krook are ironic eccentrics. Harold Skimpole speaks artificially at every appearance. Boythorn is ridiculous in his insistence upon fighting for a principle, being wildly unable to compromise with any neighbor, particularly Sir Leicester. Grandfather Smallweed, the moneylender, is nearly helpless in a physical sense; the exertion of throwing a cushion at the head of his wife whenever she mentions money thrusts him back into his chair like a broken toy, necessitating his being shaken up like a large bottle and poked and punched like a great bolster before he can recover.

Volumnia Dedlock uses too much rouge and wears an ugly pearl necklace which has the appearance of a rosary made of birds' eggs. Each of the lawyers has a distinct appearance and manner of speaking, from Kenge's mellow, rounded, meaningless rhetoric to Mr. Vholes's businesslike hypocrisy. Mrs. Badger impresses the memory of her previous husbands upon Mr. Badger to the extent that he will glory in his own comparative lack of conspicuous sufficiency. Perhaps the most obvious speech mannerism is given to the Reverend Mr. Chad-band, who uses the elocution of the pulpit in everything he says. Coming to the Snagsby household, he salutes the company typically:

> "My friends . . . peace be on this house!—on the master thereof, on the young maidens, and on the young men. My friends, why do I wish for peace? What is peace? Is it war? No. Is it strife? No. Is it lovely and gentle and beautiful and pleasant and serene and joyful? Oh, yes! Therefore, my friends, I wish for peace on you and yours."[20]

In other books certain incidents take on the effect of pure farce. Mr. Guppy's proposal to Esther is couched in legal forms, and his later desire to extricate himself from any responsibility to Esther is likewise lost in legal redundancy. Poor Mr. Snagsby is pursued by a wife who follows him around expecting to catch him out in some extramarital adventure. Mr. Boythorn and Harold Skimpole are presented in scenes which are outrageously heightened.

Dickens took great care with the details of the Dedlock-Tulking-horn plot. Tulkinghorn stands for the inhumanity of the law and as such is a symbolic personage as well as a lawyer. While he searches for the evidence which will reveal Lady Dedlock's past, he gradually un-covers her secret. Each fact connected with the mysterious Captain Hawdon who had died at Krook's house while working as a law writer is laboriously exposed. The search for incriminating examples of hand-writing leads him to hunt for letters in the possession of Mr. George and for those lost somewhere in the wastepaper that clutters Mr. Krook's shop. The connection of Mr. Guppy with this search is intricately developed, down to the machinations which put Jobling-Weevle on the Krook premises to search secretly for the documents.

The actual murder of Tulkinghorn is a tissue of contrived coinci-dental manipulation. The maid, Mademoiselle Hortense, is a symbol of abnormality. Her mouth is feline, her face tight, she sees out of a corner of her eyes, and she is fascinated by knives. Tulkinghorn uses her to get information about her mistress, then neglects to reward her when she is dismissed. After Jo sees Lady Dedlock visiting the grave of Captain Hawdon, Tulkinghorn dresses Hortense in the same clothes as her mistress in an experiment which will allow Jo to identify her and add another fact to the lawyer's collection of data about Lady Dedlock's past. This masquerade adds its bit to the confusion about the identity of the murderess when Tulkinghorn is killed.

Lady Dedlock's remorseful flight from Chesney Wold and from her husband coincides with the murder. Inspector Bucket turns up all the evidence, and the suspicions of the reader shift from Mr. George (who is caught by coincidence) to Lady Dedlock to Hortense. The inspector also has to uncover Lady Dedlock's secret in order to solve the mystery of her flight, and so the whole story comes to light. The gradual solution of the murder leads the novel to a climax which gains from suspense and the sensational unraveling of carefully pre-pared complications. Dickens had never previously produced a plot so well developed and so artfully revealed at the last. Most of his earlier intrigues are journeyman's work to this. In *Bleak House* he is long past a melodramatic situation which is either sensational for its own sake or imposed on characters who are interesting for other reasons. Nor is there any change in intention in the middle or before the end, as in the flight of Edith Dombey from her husband. Lady Dedlock, Tulkinghorn, Hortense—all the characters are consistent from first to last. The plot supports the thesis of fashionable and legal decay; it adds mystery and suspense to its part in the total effect.

Appropriate sensation and horror accompany the death of Mr. Krook. The only undeniable artistic weakness in the story derives from sentimentality. Esther tells half the tale, and despite the fact that she represents qualities which Dickens admired, she often descends to the verge of such sweetness that she may in some measure remind the reader of Little Nell. She is naturally noble, but so is Oliver Twist. The point at which an ideal escapes reference to reality is hard to pin down exactly. Esther, like David Copperfield, sees many people and many happenings and often expresses judgments one might expect from the author himself. In the case of David this is appropriate. Further, Dickens is not consistently successful in identifying himself with the female point of view necessary to make Esther completely convincing. There was a reasonable narrative excuse for David's telling his story: he was a novelist, supposedly relating the interesting story of his own life. But Esther has no particular reason for writing her adventures. At the end she says:

> Full seven happy years I have been mistress of Bleak House. The few words that I have to add to what I have written, are soon penned; then I, and the unknown friend to whom I write, will part forever. Not without much dear remembrance on my side. Not without some, I hope, on his or hers.[21]

The novel has been consistently praised by many modern readers for its unified effect and for its atmospheric impact. Strangely enough this conclusion, by the implications of craftsmanship, ought to conflict with the shifting manner in which the tale is told. The alternation between first- and third-person narration normally achieves contrast rather than unity. But in this novel, alternation is carefully turned to a kind of double vision as the story unfolds. The reader sees different specimens of diseased Victorian society from two points of view. The essential satire is doubled rather than separated. The revolving reflection of Dickens' social microcosmic pattern comes from two mirrors, each presenting its picture in narrative contrast. The effect is therefore not contradiction but intensification. If the reader is not distracted or annoyed by Esther's heightened qualities of sentimental goodness, this technical effect is completely satisfactory. The story departs from the mannerisms of melodrama, and even the effect of Jo's death is most likely to appeal to the right kind of sentiment in the modern reader because of its convincing relation to Dickens' thesis. If you are impressed by the pattern, you must be shocked by what life does to people. You also must be shocked by what happens to Esther when Jo's smallpox is communicated to her. In the chapter in which she goes blind, the reader can hardly feel that the effect is mawkish or artificial. Esther is not Little Nell, nor is she the sister of Paul Dombey even though the critical reader may notice some very distant relationship.

In the final analysis, *Bleak House* achieves universal appeal because of Dickens' intensity. The truth becomes more true as each element in his technical arsenal combines with all the others to add weight to his thesis. The emotional power of this thesis overcomes his narrative obstacles, and the revolving techniques play their parts in driving home his indictment of Victorian society. *David Copperfield* achieves mastery on a different level of attainment; the effect of *Bleak House* must be judged as deeper, as probing the depths of human behavior, as searching out the essential characteristics of society itself. It is a "bleak" masterpiece, but it is a powerful one.

The second novel in Dickens' dark period continues his indictment of Victorian society. Since *Hard Times* is—of all his books—the clearest in its statement of his economic beliefs, it naturally holds the attention of all those readers who find this phase of Dickens' fiction to be the most stimulating in our times. Yet for years this was the novel most easily dismissed by traditional Dickensians, since it represents few of the narrative qualities they were accustomed to praise. It it tempting for the modern critic to say that the traditional Dickensian has been wrong and that *Hard Times* is an underrated novel. Its thesis is challenging, it contributes materially to Dickens' total study of the social microcosm, but it is something less than a great novel for several reasons. Since it has been enthusiastically praised by George Bernard Shaw, and since a critic of the stature of F. R. Leavis thinks it is Dickens' greatest book—"a completely serious work of art"[22]—one needs to look closely at the reasons for finding it less effective than *Bleak House* or *Little Dorrit*.

Several factors must be taken into account in judging *Hard Times*. It was not meticulously planned; it was written somewhat hurriedly to fill a blank in the schedule of *Household Words;* and it was constructed in the weekly and constricted installments with which Dickens had last contended in *The Old Curiosity Shop* and *Barnaby Rudge*. Despite the fact that the thesis of *Hard Times* is an integral part of his narrative intentions in this creative period, he found less room for developing his contrasting plot sequences. He also had difficulty in focusing all his narrative technical resources on his subject, so that the novel does not call upon many of his best devices. One needs a relatively large scope for many contrasting plots in action. The sequences which interlocked the large monthly parts of *Bleak House* had no similar opportunity in the smaller pieces which were required by the magazine's weekly issues. The novel sometimes gives the effect of choppy episodes, of undeveloped contrasts, of unfinished business, and this kind of effect is not exactly characteristic of Dickens' last period of creation.

Dickens was hampered by several other considerations in writing this novel. He evidently intended to discuss unions and strikes at more length, but he had contracted to print a novel by Mrs. Gaskell immediately after his own. He had read her manuscript before he began *Hard Times*. She was using the same subject matter, as anyone who wishes to examine *North and South* can see. Mrs. Gaskell read the installments of *Hard Times* with growing uneasiness, and even seems to have been suspicious (apparently with good reason) that Dickens was stealing her thunder as well as appropriating her material.[23] Her protests must have bothered Dickens.

Hard Times retains force because of its purpose. It is influenced materially by Carlyle's economic ideas; it follows naturally Dickens' attack on legal and social maleficence in *Bleak House,* since economic exploitation was another phase of his case against Victorian society.

As the novel stands, its thesis is a satire on utilitarian economy. Dickens felt that a dependence upon capitalistic *practicality* without reference to *sympathy* and *brotherly understanding* causes continued difficulties in the relations of capital and labor. His scene was Manchester or Leeds or some such center of England's industrial revolution, and he called the place Coketown.

Dickens planned three separate plot sequences for his novel, each of them presenting opportunities for development and contrast. His main action was to center around Thomas Gradgrind, a retired wholesale hardware merchant who had become a member of Parliament. Gradgrind is Mr. Utilitarian, "a man of realities; a man of facts and calculations; a man who proceeds upon the principle that two and two are four, and nothing over."[24] Mathematically speaking, with no allowances for the tender or susceptible emotions, Mr. Gradgrind conducts all the business of life *practically,* because this is the way one gets ahead, makes money, and becomes financially and socially successful according to Victorian standards. Mr. Gradgrind bows to Carlyle's God of Cash-Payment, and he intends to conduct his life and bring up his children according to his philosophy.

The plot divisions show how this utilitarian philosophy works out. There are four children in the family, plus the adopted Sissy Jupe. Two of the children (named Adam Smith and Malthus) are mentioned, then dismissed from the tale. But Louisa, Tom, and Sissy carry the main action. Louisa is given in marriage to the capitalist, Mr. Bounderby, and is tempted to escape from her resulting unhappiness by an affair or elopement with Mr. Harthouse, a handsome dilettante who offers her admiration and some degree of excitement. The temptation of Louisa is the first complication in the Gradgrind plot; Dickens handles it as he had occasionally done in the past, by showing his heroine on the verge of succumbing to temptation, but successfully resisting it at the last moment. Certainly Louisa's upbringing and her father's philosophy are of no help to her. This sequence is a typical intrigue borrowed from the tradition of sentimental drama.

In contrast, young Tom is ruined by his environment. He is presented as selfish, ill-natured, sensual, and completely mercenary. He is employed as a clerk in a bank owned by his sister's husband, Mr.

216

Bounderby, and eventually steals money from the bank in order to cover his debts contracted in dissipation and idleness. He contrives a scheme to throw the blame on Stephen, a workman in Mr. Bounderby's factory, and the resulting action which establishes Stephen's innocence and fixes the blame properly on Tom brings the novel to its conclusion.

Sissy Jupe is the daughter of a clown, who deserts her and runs off from the circus which is playing in Coketown. The father had grown so old and stiff that he had lost his ability to amuse his audiences. Thinking his daughter well-situated at the Gradgrind school, he disappears, and Mr. Gradgrind decides to provide for her. Sissy, like a character in a morality play, illustrates all the ideas opposite from the utilitarian philosophy taught at school. If any special intrigue was to have been developed around her, it never finds place in the novel. However, she does shame Mr. Harthouse into leaving the neighborhood just as Louisa seems on the verge of joining him, and she helps Tom escape when he is about to be arrested for stealing, sending him to the circus where Mr. Sleary, the owner, conceals him and gets him safely abroad.

The second division of action centers about Mr. Bounderby, who is an even more vicious portrait of the hardhearted capitalist than was Scrooge or Mr. Dombey. Mr. Bounderby is part of the Louisa-Harthouse triangle, but he also has a separate course of action, based upon his relationship to his housekeeper, Mrs. Sparsit. This lady is from a higher caste and presumably brings social distinction to the home of a man who had made his own money. Since she is destitute, she accepts money from Mr. Bounderby. She nurses an unrequited affection for him which shows itself in jealousy of the young wife he brings home. Bounderby also has a mother he is ashamed of, and there is a small intrigue which shows her visiting Coketown on occasion just to look at her son from a distance. Bounderby thus illustrates false pride as well as a lack of filial affection. He is exposed at the end as having fabricated much of the story he tells about his youth and the lack of opportunities afforded him in his climb to fortune and power.

The third division of action concerns the power-loom weaver, Stephen Blackpool. Stephen is tied to an impossible wife who has drunk herself into a state which defies marital happiness. Stephen loves another woman, Rachael, wants a divorce from his wife, but finding it impossible to secure one, he and Rachael live in a state of frustration. Since it is Stephen who is used by Tom Gradgrind in his scheme to shift responsibility for the theft from the bank, Stephen is connected with the Gradgrind sequence. He refuses to join the union of working-men, suffering ostracism because of this, but he insists on defending his fellow workers when Mr. Bounderby asks him about the union. He is accordingly fired and blacklisted. Dickens then shows him leaving Coketown at the time when he is coincidentally suspected of stealing. He tries to return to defend himself, but falls into an abandoned mine shaft on the way back. He is discovered just before he dies.

These three plot sequences illustrate Dickens' general plan for revolving his action around his thesis. The thesis is broader than the attack on utilitarian economy, since it also encompasses criticism of the educational system, the caste system, and divorce laws. Mr. Gradgrind's school, conducted by M'Choakumchild, stresses hard facts and resembles in many respects the forcing school of Dr. Blimber in *Dombey and Son*. Mr. M'Choakumchild knows a little about everything, but has never learned how to communicate anything but knowledge for its own sake. Sissy reports to Louisa her difficulties in understanding him in a particularly suggestive passage:

> "And he said, Now, this school room is a Nation. And in this nation there are fifty millions of money. Isn't this a prosperous nation? Girl number twenty, isn't this a prosperous nation, and an't you in a thriving state?"
>
> "What did you say?" asked Louisa.
>
> "Miss Louisa, I said I didn't know. I thought I couldn't know whether it was a prosperous nation or not, and whether I was in a thriving state or not, unless I knew who had got the money, and whether any of it was mine. But that had nothing to do with it. It was not in the figures at all," said Sissy, wiping her eyes.[25]

The caste system finds satiric emphasis through the story of Mrs. Sparsit, whose ambition and position in the social scheme are at variance. Mr. Harthouse shows the decay which comes from rank without character. The criticism of the divorce law is quite modern, because it is obvious that one cannot get a divorce in England without luck, influence, or money. Since Stephen's wife is an impossible matrimonial companion, since she has not even enough personality to give him reason for divorcing her according to the law which fixes adultery as the only legal excuse, and since Stephen has not enough money to circumvent the law, happiness is out of reach. Dickens had some feelings about his own marital unhappiness which related to the opinions expressed in the novel.

The plot sequences of *Hard Times* are not so complex as those of *Bleak House,* nor are they so fully developed. There is a reasonable amount of motivation in the details of Louisa's abortive attraction for Harthouse, and there is careful preparation for Tom's theft. Mr. Gradgrind is shown as a man with a heart underneath his philosophy, for he aids Sissy, and he sees the error of his ways after his children experience unhappiness or ruin because of his utilitarian philosophy. Louisa is studied with care, and the reader is likely to sympathize with her difficulties. There is mystery and suspense in the circumstances of Tom's theft, and there is sensation in Stephen's death in the mine pit.

But the humor is absent; the caricature technique fights a losing battle; the speech devices are less effective than usual. The shadowy ghost of caricature shows itself in the early description of Gradgrind and of M'Choakumchild. Mrs. Sparsit has a Coriolanian nose and dense black eyebrows. Her great-aunt, Lady Scadgers, is an immensely gross woman who loves meat and possesses a leg which has refused to get out of bed for fourteen years. Probably the best characters in what is usually an effective Dickensian technique are the circus people. Mr. Sleary, the proprietor, is a fat man with one fixed and one loose eye, a voice like a broken bellows, a head which is never either completely sober or sufficiently drunk, and a manner of speaking which is affected by his asthma and comes out in a lisp which makes his speeches difficult to read. Mr. E. W. B. Childers is a horseman with the troupe and is described extravagantly as resembling a centaur "compounded of the stable and the playhouse. Where the one began, and the other ended, nobody could have told with any precision." Master Kidderminster is a dwarf who assists Childers, being carried on the palm of Childers' hand, feet upward, while the daring vaulting act goes on.

The best speech device is given to Slackbridge, the union organizer. He talks in an oratorical manner which capitalizes on all the rhetoric and elocution usually accompanying hypocrisy. He addresses the Coketown hands in this manner:

> "But, oh, my friends and brothers! Oh, men and Englishmen, the downtrodden operatives of Coketown! What shall we say of the man—that working-man, that I should find it necessary so to libel the glorious name—who, being practically and well acquainted with the grievances and wrongs of you, the injured pith and marrow of this land, and having heard you, with a noble and majestic unanimity that will make Tyrants tremble, resolve for to subscribe to the Funds of the United Aggregate Tribunal, and to abide by the injunctions issued by that body for your benefit, whatever they may be—what, I ask you, will you say of that working-man, since such I must acknowledge him to be, who, at such a time, deserts his post and sells his flag; who, at such a time, is not ashamed to make to you the dastardly and humiliating avowal that he will hold himself aloof, and will *not* be one of those associated in the gallant stand for freedom and for Right?"[26]

The symbolic atmosphere which distinguishes the total effect of *Bleak House* is much less important in *Hard Times*. In its place is the rhetorical, exclamatory manner of Carlyle, explaining Dickens' effects instead of implying them. It is true that a smoky haze hovers over Coketown, and elsewhere the workers are described as rising in protest and falling in defeat like the sea. Stephen falls into a pit, and Dickens explains the significance of the pit in Stephen's dying speech:

> "I ha' fell into th' pit, my dear, as have cost wi'in the knowledge o' old fok now livin', hundreds and hundreds o' men's lives—fathers, sons, brothers, dear to thousands an' thousands, an' keepin' 'em fro' want and hunger. I ha' fell into a pit that ha' been wi' th' Fire-damp crueler than battle. I ha' read on 't in the public petition, as onny one may read, fro' the men that works in pits, on which they ha' pray'n the lawmakers for Christ's sake not to let their work be murder to 'em, but to spare 'em for th' wives and children that they loves as well as gentlefok loves theirs. When it were in work, it killed wi'out need; when 'tis let alone, it kills wi'out need. See how we die an' no need, one way an' another—in a muddle—every day."[27]

Edgar Johnson and several other critics have found effective symbolism in *Hard Times*, but it is difficult to rank this symbolism in the same class with the fog, mist, rain, and spontaneous combustion of *Bleak House,* or with the prison atmosphere of the following novel, *Little Dorrit.* Surely *Hard Times* should be judged on its artistic merits, a statement which means that it should not be underestimated because of its narrative insufficiency, nor overestimated because its thesis appeals to the reader who is concerned with weaknesses in the capitalistic system. Even George Bernard Shaw descends to a judgment which he would normally ridicule in the writings of anyone else. He says:

> Here he begins at last to exercise quite recklessly his power of presenting a character to you in the most fantastic and outrageous terms, putting into its mouth from one end of the book to the other hardly a word which could conceivably be uttered by any sane human being, and yet leaving you with an unmistakable and exactly truthful portrait of a character that you recognize at once as not only real but typical.[28]

The least one can say in response to this kind of praise is that it is special pleading. Furthermore, it does Dickens' case little good.

Dickens' criticism of the economic system is quite plain. He is obviously opposed to the excesses of selfish capitalism; he knows that too many workers are underpaid. If something is not done to organize our economy so that laborers have a fair chance to make a reasonable living, he states, there will be trouble. These opinions he holds in common with Carlyle. He says:

> Utilitarian economists, skeletons of schoolmasters, Commissioners of Facts, genteel and used-up infidels, gabblers of many dog-eared creeds, the poor you will have always with you. Cultivate in them, while there is yet time, the utmost graces of the fancies and affections, to adorn their lives so much in need of ornament; or, in the day of your triumph, when romance is utterly driven out of their souls, and they and a bare existence stand face to face, Reality will take a wolfish turn, and make an end of you.[29]

This comment indicates that Dickens is aware of the threat of revolution or other violence. Yet Stephen, a sympathetic character, does not join the union. The organizer Slackbridge, in *Hard Times,* is given a most offensive mannerism of speech, and the general impression of the union is that it forms because foolish capitalists will make no concessions to reality. Workers join a union in an effort to protect themselves. Dickens says, in describing the Coketown hands, that when they rise "like a sea," they do harm chiefly to themselves. This is their

221

dilemma. The implication is that strikes and violence do not help in the long run.

Most of the critics who argue that Dickens is a conscious or unconscious radical either ignore Slackbridge or belittle his importance in relation to Dickens' economic views. Edgar Johnson apparently is one of this group:

> Such a description is a piece of sheer ignorance, not because union leaders cannot be windbags and humbugs as other politicians can, but because labor organizers are not like Slackbridge and do not talk like him, and did not do so in Dickens' day any more than in ours.[30]

It would be possible for ministers to argue that no preacher talks like Chadband, or for servants to argue that no one talks like Sam Weller, or for Dickens' mother to insist that no woman talks like Mrs. Nickleby. It all depends on whose ox is being gored. One must either assume that Dickens did not mean what he was saying in heightened form, or else he was bowing to the opinions of his readers. If either is true, his entire picture of Victorian society loses force, and the reader might as well discount whatever part of the picture he disagrees with.

There is some further evidence which bears upon the problem. In *Household Words* Dickens says that laborers have the same right to organize that their employers have.[31] In another issue he asks workingmen to force reforms from the Government.[32] On the occasion when he read *A Christmas Carol* to an audience composed entirely of workingmen and their wives, he made an introductory address in which he said that it was necessary and right for workers to take a share in the management of industry. Cooperation would make an end of exploitation.[33] This view would not startle a Fabian Socialist or a member of England's Labour party, but it would hardly satisfy Lenin.

One last quotation from *Hard Times*. Stephen speaks for Dickens:

> Sir, I canna, wi' my little learning an' my common way, tell the genelmen what will be better aw this—though some workingmen o' this town could, above my powers—but I can tell him what I know will never do 't. The strong hand will never do 't. Vict'ry and triumph will never do 't. Agreeing for to mak' one side unnat'rally awlus and forever right, and t'oother side unnat'rally and forever wrong, will never, never do 't. Nor yet lettin' alone will never do 't.[34]

This is usually taken as an attack upon the laissez-faire system of letting business do what it pleases. But Dickens says that neither side can be always and forever right without reference to the other side. He is arguing for what he conceives to be justice to both capital and labor; he is arguing for cooperation; he is saying that Victorian society does not award justice to labor; he is saying that something drastic needs to be done, or revolution will erupt and ruin all.

This conclusion is also the moral of the later *Tale of Two Cities.* In what is perhaps the most rewarding essay written about Dickens, George Orwell says:

> Revolution, as he sees it, is merely a monster that is begotten by tyranny and always ends by devouring its own instruments. In Sidney Carton's vision at the foot of the guillotine, he foresees Defarge and the other leading spirits of the Terror all perishing under the same knife—which, in fact, was approximately what happened.[35]

This novel, as well as *Hard Times,* contributes its evidence to show how deep was Dickens' "horror of revolutionary hysteria."

In the final analysis *Hard Times* has a kind of fictional importance which transcends its effect as a work of art. Reading it helps explain what Dickens did more subtly in *Bleak House, Little Dorrit,* and *Our Mutual Friend.* When Leavis praises *Hard Times* in *The Great Tradition* as being the only novel of Dickens which he is willing to put with the works of the "greatest English novelists"—Jane Austen, George Eliot, Henry James, and Joseph Conrad—he does so for deceptive but perfectly genuine reasons.

> The Adult mind doesn't as a rule find in Dickens a challenge to an unusual and sustained seriousness. . . . It [*Hard Times*] has a kind of perfection as a work of art that we don't associate with Dickens—a perfection that is one with the sustained and complete seriousness for which among his productions it is unique.[36]

Further reasons for praising *Hard Times* are all based on Leavis' interest in the kind of art which is significant because it is profoundly serious. He finds in all the other novels too much that is merely entertaining or falsely melodramatic.

In disputing this view one is placed in a peculiar position. The critic may find himself in more or less complete agreement with Leavis' general premises and judgments, but for what seem almost exactly the same reasons cited may find *Bleak House, Little Dorrit,* and *Our Mutual Friend* to be better illustrations of all that Leavis praises in *Hard Times.* One supposes that many modern readers besides this incisive critic ought to be able to use *Hard Times* as a springboard to enjoyment and appreciation of Dickens' other profoundly serious and greater novels.

The third of the dark period novels, *Little Dorrit,* is Dickens' deepest masterpiece. The climactic penetration of his analysis of the Victorian social microcosm reaches an ultimate meridian in this book, which was relatively unappreciated in his own time, but which has grown steadily in importance with the passing of the years. This is the novel which Shaw says made him a revolutionist. He is quoted also as remarking that it is more seditious than *Das Kapital.*[37] The term *seditious* requires examination and definition, but there is no question about the fact that this novel epitomizes Dickens' criticism of his times and his country.

Artistically, *Little Dorrit* represents the most complex of Dickens' narrative patterns, for each of the plots in the novel serves as a spoke in the searing wheel of fire which lights up his denunciation of the fools and the idiots, the exploiters and the usurers, the proud and the selfish, the bigoted and the evil members of society who make up most of our world. The narrative speculum which reflects this pattern illustrates all his technical devices, each falling into place in regular contrast, each providing its alternative vivification of his central theme. The result is the most perfect use of counterpoint in his power.

The focal point from which he began planning the novel was the debtors' prison, the Marshalsea, which he remembered from his own childhood. He had developed a phobia about prisons and had treated them in scene after scene in his earlier novels. He had even touched upon the Marshalsea itself in his picture of the Micawbers in *David Copperfield.* Now he decided to do a full study of the effect of that prison upon the Dorrit family, and particularly on William Dorrit, the man who spent years behind locked gates. Imprisonment for debt was representative of the way English law had missed the point of proper punishment and proper regeneration. England had already abandoned this part of the criminal code by the time of *Little Dorrit*, but the basic institution of English law and injustice remained. In imagining contrasting plot sequences to go along with the story of the Dorrits, Dickens conceived the idea of showing the prison taint in a number of related episodes. Gradually the symbolic pattern of prison atmosphere took form in his creative consciousness, and he saw how he could use it as the central image of his coordinating plan.

Society, as he viewed it, is constricted by prison walls, by custom, tradition, and ignorance, by economic bonds, by religious fetters, by the chains of caste, by the locked doors of fashionable society, and by the stone walls and barred windows of political inefficiency. He began to see in his mind's eye the possibilities of his symbol. He saw Rigaud and Cavaletto in the Marseilles jail: "A prison taint was on everything there. The imprisoned air, the imprisoned light, the imprisoned damps, the imprisoned men were all deteriorated by confinement."[38] He saw the slum-ridden dwellers in Bleeding Heart Yard: "Everything was bolted and barred that could by possibility furnish relief to an over-worked people."[39] He saw the prison of puritanical restriction in old Mrs. Clennam. He saw the confining restraint of the business system, of Mr. Casby, the strictures of economic manipulation, of pyramiding capitalism, of Mr. Merdle, the prisoners of poverty at one end of the system and the jailors of wealth at the other. He saw the government struggling in the bonds of political red tape, the Barnacles, and the solitary confinement of ignorance and selfishness in the Halls of Parliament itself. The symbol fascinated him.

In a world which has decided to live behind bars, what is man's destiny? He is subject to the heroic necessity for struggling to escape from his bondage. Admirable human beings get out or go down fighting; the evil and the weak succumb. Dickens visualized the way in which he could show a number of characters in conflict with their prisons, in whatever predicament they found themselves. Man's struggle with existence could be related to comparable themes. He could be shown fighting against his heredity and environment, against the social system and the rigid customs of caste, against economic handicaps, against political insufficiency, and against the bars of religious bigotry. It was at this point in planning, one supposes, that Dickens considered calling his projected novel "Nobody's Fault," a kind of satiric statement of his opposition to the idea that prison bars and the confinement of environment constrict a man's life so that he is not responsible for his behavior. He planned in his basic plot sequence to show the Dorrits in prison and out, behind the walls of poverty and then still imprisoned by the symbolic barriers of fashionable society after they inherited great wealth. He divided his novel into two sections and planned to show that the Dorrits behaved in exactly the same manner whether they were in prison or out. Each member of the family would have to be judged, in the final analysis, by what he was, not by how much money he had or under what conditions he existed. Dickens then saw how he could broaden this theme to his other sequences of action and to the other characters in his tale.

Dickens devised six distinct plot sequences to develop his thesis and to "weave his pattern," as he says in his Preface. The first is the Dorrit story, presenting William Dorrit, "the Father of the Marshalsea" because he has been there longer than anyone else, with his brother Frederick and his three children, Fanny, Edward, and Amy. The full-length study of William Dorrit becomes Dickens' most penetrating character portrayal. Frederick is a patient, suffering man who plays the clarinet in a small theater orchestra and lives under the spell of William. Fanny is a gold-digger; Tip, as Edward is called, tires of everything he tries and manages to be consistently worthless; Amy, the Little Dorrit of the title, represents all a good woman can be, working tirelessly and uncomplainingly, caring always for her father, doing the best she can no matter what fate sends her.

The first part of the novel shows the life of the Dorrits in prison; after they inherit their fortune, they live mostly on the Continent, and several intrigues develop about them. Amy falls in love with Arthur Clennam; Fanny sells herself in marriage to Edmund Sparkler, the son of Mrs. Merdle by her first husband, thus gaining the social stature she had always desired; Mr. Dorrit is on the point of marrying the frozen-faced governess, Mrs. General, when he suffers a stroke and dies.

The second plot concerns the Clennams. As the story opens, Arthur, Mrs. Clennam's son, comes home from the Orient on the death of his father. His mother has directed their business from the old mansion where she has been confined (hysterical paralysis or arthritis?)

for years. Mrs. Clennam combines the excesses of her Puritan creed with utilitarian ruthlessness, which makes her home the scene of dark and mysterious happenings. She says:

> "If I did not know that we are, every one, the subject (most justly the subject) of a wrath that must be satisfied, and against which mere actions are nothing, I might repine at the difference between me, imprisoned here, and the people who pass that gateway yonder."[40]

But she never passes the gateway of love and sympathy until the end of the story. Around her and the old house Dickens builds an atmosphere which compares in some degree with Krook's shop in *Bleak House*. The Clennam house collapses at the end of the story, just as Krook himself disintegrated.

Arthur is one of the central figures who illustrate Dickens' thesis about individual responsibility and freedom of the will. At the beginning he feels that he is a man whose character has been imprisoned by his heredity and rigid environment. He says:

> "I have no will. That is to say," he colored a little, "next to none that I can put in action now. Trained by main force; broken, not bent; heavily ironed with an object on which I was never consulted and which was never mine; shipped away to the other end of the world before I was of age, and exiled there until my father's death there, a year ago; always grinding in a mill I always hated; what is to be expected from *me* in middle-life? Will, purpose, hope? All those lights were extinguished before I could sound the words."[41]

Yet Dickens devises action which will show Arthur gradually but surely achieving force of character, will, purpose, and hope. He will separate himself from his mother, though giving her filial respect; he will try to find his real place in life by working with Mr. Doyce; when he loses his money in Merdle enterprises he will go to the Marshalsea, but he will eventually escape and marry Little Dorrit. The prison bars will not hold him forever.

Dickens invents an old-fashioned intrigue about Arthur's birth, eventually showing him to be the son of a woman other than Mrs. Clennam; he invents a suppressed will; he introduces Rigaud, a murderer and a blackmailer, who will attempt to extort money from Mrs. Clennam by possession of her secret. Rigaud (or as he is known by the alias, Blandois) represents Dickens' theme that vice on the criminal

227

level is morally the same as vice on a business or fashionable level. Rigaud says:

> "If you try to prejudice me, by making out that I have lived by my wits—how do your lawyers live—your politicians—your intriguers— your men of the Exchange?"[42]

Like Mrs. Clennam, or Mr. Casby, or Mr. Merdle, he is a man of business. He gets money at other people's expense.

Dickens puts Jeremiah Flintwinch and his wife Affery in the Clennam house. These characters are semicomic caricatures, who add grotesque detail to the intrigue but also build up the atmosphere of gloom and horror which spreads through the creaking old mansion where the reader may suspect strange happenings, exaggerated visions, and secret passageways.

The third sequence concerns Dickens' attack on the government. He invented the general term "Circumlocution Office" to symbolize the various divisions of official red tape, the alphabet agencies of his day. In the Circumlocution Office he placed the Barnacle tribe, the name clearly explaining his satire. The tangled mass of procedural red tape effectively constricts any action at all on whatever would be to the benefit of the country, for all these officials have learned "how not to do it." This sequence contains Dickens' bitterest satire. Edgar Johnson has described the bureaucracies in pungent terms which can hardly be improved upon:

> It is the imprisonment of habit, custom, convention, established forms swollen to more importance than the uses for which they were invented, and confined by inertia, profit, selfishness, and privilege. It is rigidity grown supreme.[43]

The ruling caste in Victorian times had discovered a method by which they could evade all responsibility. The organization of government under the parliamentary system was caught in the toils of inefficiency and inactivity, from the Civil Service to the Home Office to the Foreign Service. It was all talk, no action, and complete circumlocution. Says Dickens:

> "Have you ever known it to be beforehand in the adoption of any useful thing? Ever known it to set an example of any useful kind?"[44]

Lord Decimus Tite Barnacle, the leader of his caste, represents the last degree of uselessness:

> On this sublime discovery, in the great art how not to do it, Lord Decimus had long sustained the highest glory of the Barnacle family; and let any ill-advised member of either House but try How to do it, by bringing in a Bill to do it, that Bill was as good as dead and buried when Lord Decimus Tite Barnacle rose up in his place, and solemnly said, soaring into indignant majesty as the Circumlocution cheering soared around him, that he was yet to be told, My Lords, that it behooved him, as the Minister of this free country, to set bounds to the philanthropy, to cramp the charity, to fetter the public spirit, to contract the enterprise, to damp the independent self-reliance, of its people.[45]

The Barnacle clan float through the story, absorbing constant scorn. They resemble too many servants of government in a free democratic society, says Dickens. Who—examining the history of political action since his day—can find his picture exaggerated? One-sided, says the modern reader; it ignores the existence of leaders who fought for positive action; but one always recognizes the Barnacles.

It is the Circumlocution Office that has lost the records of the debt which put William Dorrit in the Marshalsea. Clennam tries to find out about the case, but never gets the slightest satisfaction from his inquiries. Mr. Doyce, the inventor and engineer, tries to give his masterwork to the government, but is unable to find anyone in the Circumlocution Office who can understand him, much less accept his invention. This sequence of action is tied to the other two main plots when Clennam becomes the business manager for Doyce's enterprises and falls in love with Amy.

The fourth sequence winds itself around the economic fortunes of the great banker and financier, Mr. Merdle. The prisoner of money and power, Mr. Merdle stands for the extreme of financial manipulation which is based on forgery and sharp dealing on the highest level. Here Dickens presents the man we have seen so many times in capitalistic society, the robber baron, the pyramiding capitalist, the man who builds one speculation on another, who uses credit through interlocking corporations, who twists cartels around his fingers, whose manipulations are so complicated that no one can discover their intricacies until they all collapse and ruin the investors who have been sure that anything the genius of finance touches is as good as gold.

Merdle buys social and political privilege. He arranges a title and a sinecure for his wife's stupid son, Sparkler. The Barnacles and Stiltstalkings flock to his parties and beg for favors. Merdle suffers from a peculiar malady, obviously his conscience, which puzzles his doctor. Dickens shows him committing suicide when his economic house of cards collapses, and it collapses as completely as does the old Clennam house.

The fifth sequence concerns Mr. Casby and his servant Pancks. Mr. Casby is the landlord of Bleeding Heart Yard; his appearance and reputation are benevolent and upright. His hireling collects the rents and squeezes the tenants, taking upon himself the reputation for inflexible business dealings. Mr. Casby's daughter, Flora, is the girl Arthur Clennam had loved before he went to China, and she decorates the story with her incoherent speech—surely a symbolic daughter of Mrs. Nickleby or Mrs. Gamp. It is Pancks who finds the Dorrit inheritance, and it is Pancks who at the end unmasks Mr. Casby for the hypocrite he is.

The sixth sequence is devoted to the Meagleses. Mr. Meagles is a utilitarian but kindly father who spoils his daughter, Pet. At first Arthur Clennam thinks himself in love with Pet, but she marries Henry Gowan, a charming offshoot of the Barnacle clan. Gowan represents the fashionable idler who tolerantly criticizes and accepts everybody and everything, finding great virtue in the greatest fools. Since he will not work hard enough to amount to anything, he can bring nothing but unhappiness to Pet. As a foil to Clennam, he is the man who never escapes from the prison of his environment and heredity, but remains chained to the consequences of fashionable society. His jail is, of course, a state of mind or of caste.

A minor sequence attached to the Meagles plot concerns the servant Tattycoram, adopted by the Meagleses, but always resenting the favors given to Pet by her parents. Tattycoram feels that the accident of birth has deprived her of proper recognition in the world and that she is as good as Pet. Her ungovernable temper drives her into tantrums whenever she feels herself beaten down by unfair circumstance in comparison to her young mistress. Tattycoram falls under the

230

spell of a certain Miss Wade, who is also a prisoner of heredity and environment. There is the suggestion of abnormality in the picture of Miss Wade and her relationship to Tattycoram; the young girl leaves the Meagles family to run away with her. At the end Tattycoram returns, seeing the error of her ways.

These six major courses of action are inextricably interwoven in Dickens' pattern. Arthur Clennam gets acquainted with Little Dorrit because she works for his mother and for Flora Casby. He tries to find out the details of the Dorrit case in the Circumlocution Office. There he becomes acquainted with Mr. Doyce, who is trying to give a patent to the government. He becomes the partner of Mr. Doyce. He meets Pancks because the Doyce factory is close to Bleeding Heart Yard, and Pancks persuades him to invest his and Doyce's capital in Merdle enterprises. He goes to the Marshalsea until he is rescued by Doyce, who returns from a distant land with enough money and honor to start them off again in business. He had met the Meagles family abroad, had thought himself in love with Pet, so that sequence is also tied to his story. Even Miss Wade has information which Rigaud uses to blackmail Mrs. Clennam. Here and there are other connections: Fanny marries Sparkler; Mr. Dorrit invests money in Merdle enterprises; Gowan knows Rigaud; and so on.[46]

Often in earlier novels Dickens had used his varying narrative devices for expressive contrast. In this novel, his farce-caricature technique and the speech devices appear with some regularity, relieving and intensifying his somber effects, marking off the moments when his feelings about the Circumlocution Office or Mr. Merdle become violent. The Flintwinches could have appeared in an earlier novel as straight farce characters. Jeremiah has a twisted neck, his cravat is usually under one ear, and his swollen features give the effect of his just coming from being hanged. Affery lives in a sleepwalking state and is a browbeaten wife. Jeremiah is always threatening her with a physic, "I'll give you such a dose, old woman,—such a dose!" Their presence in the Clennam house lightens the darkness and relieves the Gothic evil which hovers over it.

The description of the Marshalsea also shows the fine skill of contrast. Mr. Dorrit begins as a caricature and mellows into a remarkable portrait. His position as Father of the Marshalsea is a satire on the caste system, even in a debtors' prison. His lofty airs, his dependence upon charitable gifts, his despicable pretences, his bland misunderstanding of all that Little Dorrit does for him—all these things contribute to an incisive study which cuts deep into the whole man. Mr. Dorrit appears in a number of extraordinary scenes. Perhaps the best of the early ones is that in which he allows himself to suggest that Amy marry the son of the turnkey, since such an alliance would be of social advantage to him in the prison. The last scene in the novel, in which he suffers a stroke and imagines himself back in the Marshalsea even though he is at a fashionable dinner in Italy, is one of Dickens' most poignant episodes.

The prison contains a number of eccentrics. Most challenging are the Chivery father and son. The turnkey:

> Locked himself up as carefully as he locked up the Marshalsea debtors. Even his custom of bolting his meals may have been a part of an uniform whole; but there is no question, that, as to all other purposes, he kept his mouth as he kept the Marshalsea door.[47]

His son John is weak in appearance, gentle in intention, great in soul, poetical, and faithful. His love for Amy is ridiculous, and he suffers through much of the tale. Yet the reader eventually comes to hold a degree of affection for him, as one feels sorry for and laughs at any hopeful, languishing young lover. Maggie, who adores Amy, is a light but deft study of the person who is not in complete control of all her faculties.

Bleeding Heart Yard provides more caricatures. The most interesting is Mr. Pancks:

> He was dressed in black and rusty iron grey; had jet black beads of eyes, a scrubby little black chin, wiry black hair, striking out from his head in prongs, like forks or hair-pins, and a complexion that was very dingy by nature, or very dirty by art, or a compound of nature and art. He had dirty hands and dirty broken nails, and looked as if he had been in the coal; he was in a perspiration, and snorted and sniffed and puffed and blew like a little laboring steam-engine.[48]

Although he serves the falsely benign Mr. Casby, he is a generous man underneath his necessities, and at the last he is given a wonderful scene in which he cuts the hair of the old sinner for whom he works, exposing the blooming hypocritical face for what it is.

The remarkable pair, Flora Casby Finching and her dead husband's aunt (known only as Mr. F's Aunt), have two of Dickens' most
distinctive speech devices. Flora (who is always mentioned as being
suggested by Dickens' impression of Maria Beadnell in middle age)
follows in the incoherent mixed-reference habit of speaking which had
earlier made Mrs. Nickleby and Mrs. Gamp incomparable, never-ending gabblers. Mr. F's Aunt has a generally damaged countenance and
an alarming habit of interrupting people with some completely inappropriate remark, delivered in a deep, warning voice. This usually
effectively stops the conversation.

Fashionable society and the higher castes furnish their share of
caricatured eccentrics. Mrs. Merdle, like Mrs. Skewton in *Dombey
and Son,* admires natural goodness while she illustrates artificiality. The
Barnacle tribe are all fools. Mrs. Merdle's son, Edmund Sparkler, has
no brains to speak of, and he proposes to every girl he meets. He always
refers to these women, after he has been detached from their clutches,
by saying, "She was a doosed fine gal, well educated too, with no big-
godd nonsense about her." The dignified and imposing Mrs. General,
who is engaged by Mr. Dorrit in the second part of the novel to "form
the mind" and manners of his daughters, is tremendously genteel, with
a floury countenance and clothes that never wrinkle: "A cool, waxy,
blown-out woman, who had never lighted well." Henry Gowan
(charged with being a caricature of Thackeray) is a man of tolerance
and of no settled principles:

> It appeared, before the breakfast was over, that everybody whom this
> Gowan knew was either more or less of an ass, or more or less of a
> knave; but was, nothwithstanding, the most lovable, the most engaging,
> the simplest, truest, kindest, dearest fellow that ever lived.[49]

This congregation of characters is as entertaining a group as any
Dickens has managed to put in a single novel. Nevertheless, the
general result is more in keeping with the effect gained by a comic
satirist like Molière than by an author who is amusing an audience
for the sake of generating pure laughter. Each of these caricatures
carries some quality to the extreme, and the extremes occasionally exceed the bounds of humor and enter the dangerous territory of vice or
degeneracy. Like Molière's Miser, they begin by being funny and often

end by being vicious or horrible. The intensity of Dickens' thesis has lifted them from general farce and caricature to symbolic irony.

The interwoven plots depend upon intrigue. If there is melodrama in the story, it centers on the character and machinations of the blackmailer, Rigaud. The mysterious story of Clennam's parentage and the suppressed will are the only parts of the tale that derive from complicated intrigue. The interpolated story of Miss Wade's parentage and early life is presented by Dickens, as he says in a letter to Forster, with the intent of intensifying his thesis.[50] There is constant reference to the best devices of Gothic horror and sensation in the scenes which center on the old Clennam house.

Little Dorrit herself suffers from an excess of goodness, as did so many of Dickens' female heroines, from Little Nell to Esther Summerson. Like Agnes, she is a "legless angel." The main interest of the tale does not depend upon her, even though the novel is named for her. In an allegorical sense she illustrates Dickens' positive thesis, that one must stand out against destiny and do one's best no matter what the circumstances. She succeeds in becoming sentimentally heroic, and she is naturally rewarded with marriage to Arthur Clennam.

In this murky masterpiece, what is Dickens' positive purpose? Will England's economic house fall to pieces as does the Clennam mansion? Will the manipulations of Victorian business reach the black days of collapse, as did the Merdle enterprises? Will the Government or Parliament ever have sense enough to remedy the crying defects of Victorian society? Will society escape from its prisons?

Dickens is not very sanguine. Carlyle had argued for a benevolent dictator. Dickens does not bring any specific proposals into *Little Dorrit* or the other novels. Whatever remedies are to improve the social microcosm must depend upon human will and wisdom. Dickens sarcastically points out that nations other than England seem to encourage inventors and scientists like Doyce; nor do they run their offices in terms of circumlocution. When Arthur Clennam is talking to Ferdinand Barnacle about the collapse of Mr. Merdle's financial empire, he expresses the hope that people will be wiser in the future.

> "My dear Mr. Clennam," returned Ferdinand, laughing, "have you really such a verdant hope? The next man who has as large a capacity and as genuine a taste for swindling will succeed as well. Pardon me,

but I think you really have no idea how the human bees will swarm to the beating of any old tin kettle; in that fact lies the complete manual of governing them."[51]

Against this fear, Dickens sets the words of Doyce to Clennam at the end:

"First not a word more from you about the past. There was an error in your calculations. I know what that is. It affects the whole machine, and failure is the consequence. You will profit by the failure, and will avoid it another time. I have done a similar thing myself, in construction, often. Every failure teaches a man something, if he will learn; and you are too sensible a man not to learn from this failure."[52]

Escape from the prison of false social standards rests mainly upon individual desire and capacity for improving the world as a result of experience. Dickens thinks an incompetent governing class must be replaced; conditions must provide justice for all; worn-out institutions must come down as must prison walls; the caste system, hypocritical Puritanism, economic exploitations must vanish or fall to pieces as did the Clennam house. Human brains and will power are our only hope. Otherwise why write such a novel?

Little Dorrit is Dickens' darkest, most powerful, most furious novel. In it he scorns Victorian society; he laughs at it angrily; but he is not hopeless or resigned. He is a liberal who is "generously angry," as George Orwell says.[53] He loves people but hates fools. This is not exactly "seditious," whatever Shaw meant by the word. Nor is it treasonable, as a jingoistic fanatic would understand the term. But it is certainly rebellious, belligerent, and unorthodox. It demands freedom and justice for all mankind. In the sense of power and purpose, all artistry arranged around theme, this is Dickens' most concentrated novel; it was as far as he could go.

CHAPTER XII

Recalled to Life

HE WRITING of novels provides a legitimate means of making a living, certainly far removed from any ethical problems raised by buying cheap and selling dear. Dickens made a fortune by writing, and he added immeasurably to his financial resources by the public readings which he began to give in the latter period of his life. The problem faced by critics in estimating Dickens' eventual accomplishment is complicated by the necessity for taking his life, character, experiences, and need for making money into serious account when examining the reasons for his writing as he did. In the middle of the twentieth century there has been great temptation to interpret Dickens' novels by direct reference to the man himself, this tendency being accentuated by the discovery of Dickens' relationship with Ellen Ternan. Since Dickens long had a reputation for encouraging Victorian morality, this apparent defection from virtue has been taken as a major psychological factor in his artistry. Put another way: If he did not behave as he urged his characters to behave, why should we take his novels seriously?

An extreme tendency to judge Dickens' creative accomplishment by his life will obscure the effect of his novels, which must stand by themselves as works of art. The critic needs to be reminded of T. S. Eliot's symbol of the catalyst. Dickens has often endured "impure" criticism, as if his characters were important *because* they resemble people he has known, or derive their behavior from his *own* psychological fixations. It is quite obvious that one may be interested in the influences exercised by the author's experiences on his planning of his novel, but an interpretation of the novel itself on this basis leads the reader into strange and sometimes inconsequential regions.

Yet Dickens is not the kind of writer who can be completely removed from his writing. He lived inside his novels as well as outside. His characters often speak for him. Some of the most important interpretations of his writing have come from greater knowledge of the man. For example, in *Little Dorrit* Arthur Clennam seems to be motivated by a feeling of guilt when he tries to find out from his mother whether the family fortune depends upon some evil manipulation or business trickery which has robbed some deserving person of his fair inheritance. This feeling leads him to an attempt to discover the circumstances which confine the Dorrit family to the Marshalsea. Lionel Trilling is much interested in the author's own guilt complex because of this incident.[1] One remembers that although Dickens hated the laissez-faire system, he became very wealthy by it. Edmund Wilson interprets many of the novels in terms of the psychological wound suffered by Dickens in his early days, beginning with his reactions to his family's experiences in the Marshalsea and his job in the bottling factory.[2] Jack Lindsay sees much of the writing through the dark glasses of Freudian theory, thus explaining Dickens' objections to Victorian society by means of his personal unhappiness and discontent.[3] Julian Symons goes so far as to make Dickens a manic-depressive type in his latter days.[4] This kind of analysis is supposed to be particularly helpful in explaining such matters as Dickens' "day-dream psychosis," which Lindsay says allowed the author to lose himself in the parts of his stories in which his hero loves a beautiful, young, and "little" woman. Presumably Dickens' fascination for Kate's sister explains his portrayal of Little Nell, Little Dorrit, and the innumerable other heroines who are reminiscent of Mary Hogarth, all of whom must be sentimentalized, even falsified, because of his idealization of the dead "dream-girl."[5] The important point is, of course, whether Little Nell is a well-conceived character or not.

The traditional omniscient point of view commonly used by Dickens has the effect of adding to the illusion that the author is part of the action, at least an observer and commentator who sometimes tells the reader what events imply. Dickens as a person is very close to his action. There is no question but that his artistry accentuates its dark tinge in the fifties because of certain family circumstances. His use of the Marshalsea prison atmosphere in *Little Dorrit* takes on force because of his own early experiences. His difficulties with a lawsuit which he won in the days after he had first reached fame gave him a phobia about the Court of Chancery, since he won the suit, but lost money.[6] These things are important if they illuminate the circumstances of artistic creation. When the words are on paper, the novels speak for themselves.

Between the writing of *Little Dorrit* and of *A Tale of Two Cities* several important personal experiences affected Dickens' creative attitude. *A Tale of Two Cities* is a completely different kind of novel from any he had previously attempted, to a certain extent unlike his usual composition. It is odd that because this is the Dickens work that has been generally assigned for reading, generations of high school students have known Dickens mainly through this untypical novel. *Great Expectations* is also representative of experimental narrative technique, somewhat unlike his previous custom. One must look to Dickens' life for some light on this shift from the complex, interlocking-plot method and the careful dependence on symbolic reference he had developed in the great novels of his dark period.

When he broke with his wife and got involved in disagreement with the backers of *Household Words*, he decided to start a new magazine. *All the Year Round* needed to establish itself in the public eye, and it had to attract subscribers. It was natural for him to feel commercial pressure and to desire to re-establish his reputation with the reading public. He decided to write a novel for the new magazine which would "sell," and he wanted a subject which would attract attention. He would have to write it in weekly installments, and he recalled how much trouble he had experienced with his panoramic plan in *Hard Times*. Therefore he abandoned the multiple-plot technique and chose a subject completely different from his usual concerns. Accordingly, he did not aim at anything like the breadthwise cutting attempted by Tolstoi in *War and Peace* or by Thomas Hardy in *The Dynasts*, as one might have expected from the example of *Bleak House* and *Little Dorrit*.

His usual rule for aiming at commercial success in fiction was to emphasize excitement, sentiment, and humor. Yet nothing was certain, and you could not foretell success or failure. He had reached sudden fame with *Pickwick,* had sold in the neighborhood of 100,000 copies for each issue of *The Old Curiosity Shop,* had dropped down to 20,000 for *Martin Chuzzlewit,* had gone back up with *Dombey and Son,* had fallen with *David Copperfield,* and had reached about 35,000 for *Bleak House* and *Little Dorrit.* Several conclusions derive from these figures. One of them is that his public did not comprehend the theses of his novels; his violent attacks on Victorian society did not materially affect his popularity and the money he received. A second conclusion is that his mature artistry was not generally understood or appreciated, since his most popular books sold best for reasons which were ephemeral or illogical. *Martin Chuzzlewit* and *David Copperfield* made him the least money of all his novels in monthly part form. From a commercial standpoint it is easy to see that Dickens might have been puzzled about his relationship to his audience. It is certain that his language, his tone, and his choice of material were influenced many times by his efforts to adjust his fiction to his readers, not only from a financial but from an artistic standpoint. Therefore he wrote *A Tale of Two Cities,* his latest attempt to compose a "popular" novel.

The new book was to be "historical." His only previous experimentation with history had been in *Barnaby Rudge.* But this time he was vitally interested in the history and convinced of its importance in relation to his own times. A number of sources supplied the inspiration for his story of the French Revolution. In the background for these influences was Carlyle's *French Revolution,* which Dickens claimed to have read over and over. In this book he felt he had a perfect source book for the primary historical scenes and events he would need.

His basic plot idea derived from the play written by Wilkie Collins, *The Frozen Deep.* The action of this play centers upon rivalry in love, one man at the last sacrificing himself to save the life of the other, who has won the girl. The main characters are Richard Wardour, Frank Aldersley, and Lucy Crayford. When Lucy decides to marry Frank, Richard volunteers for a dangerous sea voyage to the frozen North, and later Frank is assigned to the same expedition. When the exploring party is shipwrecked and marooned, two of the survivors are chosen by lot to attempt to get back to civilization and bring aid. Richard and Frank are—naturally—the two chosen. Frank becomes exhausted, and it appears that Richard may leave him to die. The final scene, however, shows Richard carrying his rival to safety, after which Richard collapses and dies. Dickens acted the role of Richard, and Collins was Frank in the performance which brought Ellen Ternan eventually into Dickens' life.

The idea of one man sacrificing himself for another who had won the girl beloved of both also implied that the better man deserved the girl. Dickens had often studied the character who did not make the most of his capacities: Martin Chuzzlewit, Steerforth, Richard Carstone, and Henry Gowan show weakness in overcoming their environmental obstacles. Out of this type evolved Sidney Carton, man of great ability and charm, drifting with the tide, but atoning for his weaknesses by a grand gesture at the last—sacrificing himself that the girl he loves might be happy with the man she marries, the man whose life he saves at the cost of his own. Dickens was correct; this kind of story would sell.

The Frozen Deep does not resemble *A Tale of Two Cities* except for the central triangle-sacrifice theme. Dickens took this idea and set it in the time and events of the French Revolution. His main inspiration for the transposition was a novel by Bulwer-Lytton called *Zanoni*, which had been published in 1845. *Zanoni* is full of Rosicrucian dogma and concerns the initiate who has achieved earthly immortality; he lives for centuries. One of the requirements for reaching this magical state is the renunciation of all earthly passions, including love. Zanoni falls in love with a beautiful singer, Viola, and is faced with the choice between temporary happiness and earthly immortality. The theme of the novel is Zanoni's passion; he eventually sacrifices his own life to save Viola's, although she dies too and makes his attempt unavailing.

The early events of *Zanoni* take place in Italy, but the action moves to Paris and the Revolution for its climax. Here Viola is sentenced to the guillotine, and all efforts to help her prove abortive. Suspense rises as Zanoni realizes that the only way to save her is to die for her. Since he is theoretically able to live forever if he will abandon her, he has to make the supreme gesture to prove his love. His substitution for her in the condemned group is relatively simple. The number to die is eighty. Zanoni takes Viola's place and attempts to arrange the disguise and forged passports for her escape with Glyndon, a young man who also loves her. Zanoni then goes to his death by guillotine:

> On to the Barrière du Trone. It frowns dark in the air,—the giant instrument of murder! One after one to the glaive,—another and another and another! Mercy! Oh, mercy! is the bridge between the sun and the shade so brief,—brief as a sigh? There, there! *His* turn has come. "Die not yet; leave me not behind. Hear me, hear me!" shrieked the inspired sleeper. "What! and thou smilest still!" They smiled—those pale lips— and *with* the smile, the place of doom, the headsman, the horror vanished! With that smile, all space seemed suffused in eternal sunshine. Up from the earth he rose; he hovered over her,—a thing not of matter, —an IDEA of joy and light! Behind, Heaven opened, deep after deep; and the Hosts of Beauty were seen, rank upon rank, afar; and "Welcome," in a myriad melodies broke from your choral multitude, ye People of the Skies,—"Welcome, O purified by sacrifice, and immortal only through the grave,—this it is to die." And radiant amidst the radiant, the IMAGE stretched forth its arms, and murmured to the sleeper, "Companion of Eternity! This it is to die!"[7]

Comparison with Dickens' eventual death scene for Carton is interesting indeed; the younger author must have wanted to surpass this stylistic monstrosity, and he rose to the occasion.

The Frozen Deep and *Zanoni* combined to provide in the creative mind of Dickens the sacrifice of one lover for another, with the French Revolution and the guillotine providing the scene for death. When Dickens began planning the action which would lead up to this climax, he must have felt that a more dramatic means of substituting one lover for the other would have to be worked out. Previous novelists, including Collins, had written stories in which one main character resembled the other, resulting in confusion. Collins had just done this in *Hide and Seek,* and he was to do it in *The Woman in White* soon afterward. So Dickens seized upon the idea of having Darnay and Carton resemble each other.

The fact that Collins had been writing stories about the French Revolution had something to do with turning Dickens to this historical background. Two of these tales, *Gabriel's Marriage* and *Sister Rose,* were printed in *Household Words.* The latter tale introduces characters named Trudaine and Sister Rose who are denounced by Rose's villainous husband because they aided the escape of a victim of the revolutionary party. They are tried, sentenced, and would have gone to their deaths but for the help of a certain Lomaque, a worthless character who atones for his shameless life by saving them. He does it by painting an erasing liquid over their names on the death list, timing this to coincide with the fall of Robespierre, when all prisoners were released. Lomaque is a spy, and like Barsad in *A Tale of Two Cities,* he is in a position to effect a substitution of prisoners before the march to the guillotine. Dickens got Barsad into his novel early, because he knew he would have to supply a convincing way of putting Carton in Darnay's place at the climax. The general nature of this inspiration from Collins is apparent.

With a broad sketch of his proposed novel securely set in his mind, Dickens had a few definite ideas for narration: sacrifice of one lover for another; substitution before the guillotine; the French Revolution as his scene. He needed a reason for his hero's being sentenced to die. Those who died were generally aristocrats; Darnay becomes an aristocrat, but a good one. He accordingly disagrees with the evil principles of his class, principles which Carlyle had categorically insisted caused the Revolution, and long before the Terror, Darnay emigrates to England. This allowed Dickens to balance the action between the two countries, and his idea for his title followed naturally. Darnay could fall in love in England, win his suit for Lucy against Carton, and later be caught in the Terror's net in Paris, setting up the closing scenes.

At what point his actual reference to Carlyle occurred does not matter for our purposes. Perhaps it was previous to some of the points discussed or coincident with them. Carlyle does not tell lurid stories of the atrocious deeds of the aristocrats in the days before the Revolution. Dickens understood the conclusions of Carlyle very well. Lack of concern, pity, brains, understanding, and leadership among the aristocrats had driven the downtrodden lower classes to rise in desperation. Any ruling class needed to pay more than it was *forced* to pay in wages or living conditions for its underlings, or it courted revolt. This point had been the essence of Carlyle's warnings in *Chartism* and *Past and Present.* But for his story Dickens needed a striking example of the criminal incapacity and intolerance of the ruling classes.

When he asked for help in discussing his proposed tale with Carlyle, the latter confused his own scholarly practice with Dickens' simple needs and sent down a cartload of books which he had used in preparing *The French Revolution.*[8] These books must have looked very imposing and uninviting to the novelist, but he selected from them the ones he thought would do him the most good. Forster says that Dickens found Mercier's *Tableau de Paris* a useful source for many incidents and ideas incorporated in the novel. Actually, all Dickens got from it was an atrocity or two.

Mercier provided a meticulous rendition of the years which preceded the Revolution. His several-volume history covered the entire story and gave Carlyle important parts of his data. Among Mercier's facts and rumors of fact were instances of the feudal privileges once held by the lord over his serfs. These included the notorious custom which permitted the lord to take temporarily any woman in his domain from her family or husband, the so-called *droit du seigneur.* Many tales have been founded on this custom, particularly when some rebellion occurred against it. The man who refused to give up his newly wed wife was often roughly treated, sometimes tortured or killed when he resisted or attempted vengeance. Dickens decided to use this spectacular example of evil aristocratic privilege in his novel.

Forster pointed out later, when Dickens had supplied it as the reason for Dr. Manette's confinement in the Bastille, that such feudal customs had disappeared long years before the time Dickens covered in *A Tale of Two Cities.* The author seems somewhat nettled in his reply:

> I had of course full knowledge of the formal surrender of the feudal privileges, but these had been bitterly felt quite as near to the time of the Revolution as the Doctor's narrative, which you will remember dates long before the Terror. With the slang of the new philosophy on the one side, it was not unreasonable or unallowable on the other, to suppose a nobleman wedded to the old cruel ideas, and representing the time going out as his nephew represents the time coming in. If there be anything certain on earth, I take it that the condition of the French peasant generally at that day was intolerable. No later inquiries or provings by figures will hold water against the tremendous testimony of men living at that time. There is a curious book printed at Amsterdam, written to make out no case whatever, and tiresome enough in its literal dictionary-like minuteness; scattered up and down the pages of which is full authority for my marquis. This is Mercier's *Tableau de Paris.*[9]

In Carlyle's history, as part of his description of the fall of the Bastille, there is reprinted a letter found in the paper archives of the old prison. Dated October 7, 1752, it reads:

> If for my consolation Monseigneur would grant me, for the sake of God and the Most Blessed Trinity, that I could have news of my dear wife; were it only her name on a card, to show she is alive! It were the greatest consolation I could receive; and I should forever bless the greatness of Monseigneur.[10]

This letter intrigued Dickens. It became his device for revealing the secret of Dr. Manette's imprisonment, elaborated into an account of the whole story of the woman appropriated by Monseigneur, brought to death along with her protesting brother. Dr. Manette, called in a medical capacity to attend the dying woman and her brother, later writes a letter to the King about what he had seen, and is therefore put in the Bastille by Monseigneur through a *lettre de cachet*. The letter quoted by Carlyle furnishes the ending of Dr. Manette's document, found by Defarge in Manette's empty cell in the Bastille when it is stormed:

> If it had pleased God to put it in the hard heart of either of the brothers, in all these frightful years, to grant me any tidings of my dearest wife—so much as to let me know by a word whether alive or dead—I might have thought that He had not quite abandoned them.[11]

Mention of the prisoner's wife suggests the existence of a child. Dickens needed the girl for whom Carton would die. What better idea than that she should be Dr. Manette's child, sent to England after her mother's death and her father's imprisonment, ignorant of his fate? That Darnay, nephew of Monseigneur and son of the brother who was involved in the affair which led to Dr. Manette's imprisonment, should also go to England, love and marry Lucy Manette, appealed to Dickens as another dramatic source of emotion. This circumstance would set the stage for Manette's Parisian and revolutionary friends to take revenge on all the descendants of Monseigneur for his past evil deeds, and it would provide the excuse for Darnay's death sentence.

In planning his novel, Dickens also took account of the difficulties he had previously encountered in the shorter installments. His solution was a simple one, but he had never tried it before: long novel—complex plots; short novel—one plot. All he really needed was the Darnay-Manette-Carton intrigue, with a dependent subplot to provide for the detail of exchanging his principals in prison before the guillotine. This is where Barsad came in, the spy whose scheme to fake the death of his fellow spy, Roger Cly, would be discovered by Jerry Cruncher, the body snatcher. Later in Paris this information is used by Carton to put pressure on Barsad and force his help in replacing Darnay with Carton on the guillotine list. A further narrative device occurred to Dickens in adapting his tale to shorter installments. This idea was to eliminate excessive dialogue, change his practice of developing his story by conversation, and describe more of the action. Forster did not like this idea at all. He says:

> To rely less upon character than upon incident, and to resolve that his actors should be expressed by the story more than they should express themselves by dialogue, was for him a hazardous, and can hardly be called an entirely successful experiment.[12]

The result, however hazardous it seemed to Forster, did contribute one thing to the final effect: It automatically eliminated many opportunities for melodramatic excesses, and by substituting description Dickens produced a tighter, faster-moving story than usual. What he lost was characteristic humor and entertaining speech. He had difficulty in selecting the scenes he wished to use from the many which occurred to him. He did not like restraint. He complains in his letters, "the small portions drive me frantic," but he was interested in the story and in the possibilities of his tragic action: "Nothing but the interest of the subject, and the pleasure of striving with the difficulty of the form of treatment . . . could else repay the time and trouble of the incessant condensation."[13]

To the modern reader Dickens' way of developing all his novels is dramatic, since he normally uses dialogue more than any other device and designs his scenes as if for the stage. For *A Tale of Two Cities* he planned the course of action in direct imitation of the way it would be done for the theater, even though he had resolved to limit his dialogue. He says: "How as to a story in two periods—with a lapse of time between, like a French Drama?"[14] The reference to French drama is significant. He was thinking of the type of French tragedy which started its action with a prologue before the main acts, the conflict of

motives being seized at some interesting point, back action thereby revealed, and the stage prepared for the main intrigue. The action which
followed was usually in two acts which were carefully balanced in
effect. Dickens decided to use as a kind of prologue the journey of
Mr. Lorry to France to bring to England the recently released prisoner,
Dr. Manette, to restore him to his daughter who had grown up in
safety in England while he was confined in the Bastille. This opening
scene introduced the mystery of what the doctor had done to cause
his confinement. Then Dickens was ready to leap into his main story.
A Tale of Two Cities is divided into three books as it is printed, but
the first is really the prologue, shorter than the other two, which are
balanced in length and action.

The practice of the historical novelist requires some specific
knowledge of the history involved. Carlyle is Dickens' authority for
the scenes in Paris before and during the Terror. There are three kinds
of inspiration in the references Dickens makes to Carlyle. These are
direct borrowings of description and scene, indirect use of characters
and events, and suggestions which Dickens transfers to different characters or combines into new forms for fictional purposes.

For example, in the section in which the Bastille is stormed
Dickens transposes many of Carlyle's own words:

> . . . the living sea rose, wave on wave, depth on depth, and overflowed
> the city to that point. Alarm-bells ringing, drums beating, the sea
> raging and thundering on its new beach, the attack begun . . .[15]

> . . . behold, . . . how the multitude flows on, welling through every
> street; tocsin furiously pealing, all drums beating the *générale*: the
> Suburb Saint-Antoine rolling hitherward wholly, as one man! . . .[16]

The second example is Carlyle's. The historical source gives many
details which Dickens omits or concentrates, but the entire description
is quite similar up to Defarge's journey to Dr. Manette's old cell to
hunt for the document hidden there—the document which will later
doom Darnay at the time of his trial.

Further direct borrowings are evident in the following chapter,
which tells of continued killings and hangings to the *lanternes*.[17] The
murder of old Foullon who had once been injudicious enough to say
of the third estate, "Let them eat grass!" is similar in both books.[18]
Smaller resemblances are numerous. Carlyle always talks of the suburb

of Saint-Antoine as a sort of symbol of the third estate. It is here that the worst rioters, known as Brigands, operate. Dickens naturally puts the Defarges and their wine shop in this section. The conduct of the trials, prison procedures, the tumbrils, and the guillotine come from Carlyle.[19] The dancing of the Carmagnole finds its place in the novel as Lucy watches the prison where her husband lies.[20] When Darnay is temporarily released he puts his name over the door of his residence in accord with the custom noted by Carlyle.[21] The third volume of *The French Revolution* was an extremely convenient source book for all the details Dickens needed, and the novel gives the effect of authenticity for this reason.

Defarge and his wife come indirectly from Carlyle. The history presents Santerre, a brewer, living in Saint-Antoine, who became a leader of the revolt, and Carlyle makes casual mention of the president of the Jacobin Society, whose name was Lafarge.[22] A certain Usher Maillard was active in the storming of the Bastille, doing most of what Defarge did in Dickens' narrative. "Defarge" combines from these originals whatever the novelist needed for his action. Carlyle also devoted eleven chapters in his history of the early rioting to "The Insurrection of the Women."[23] One of his female leaders, a black Joan of Arc, was Demoiselle Théroigne, a striking and spectacular mob captain. In the fight at the Tuileries, Carlyle describes her as *Sibyl* Théroigne: "Vengeance, *Victoire ou la mort!*" Mme. Defarge is not "small-waisted," but she performs as mob leader, being much more ruthless than her husband. Dickens also invents a character, a companion of Mme. Defarge, whom he designates only as The Vengeance. He took what he wanted from Carlyle, changed and concentrated it, and dressed up the details of his story from the historical record.

Carlyle attributes the worst excesses of the mob to the Jacobins, or the *Jacquerie*. Dickens creates types of revolt leaders from the lowest classes, giving them the names of Jacques One, Jacques Two, Jacques Three. The insignia of the French Revolution was patterned in threes—witness the tricolor and the slogan, "Liberty, Fraternity, and Equality." The Jacobin women were especially prominent at the guillotine, too, and the stories of their knitting while watching the executions were famous. Carlyle describes them at the executions,[24] and Dickens applies this graphic bit of data to Mme. Defarge's knitted record of victims, handwork in which the names of the doomed were entwined with vengeance in her own variety of shorthand. The women are there knitting when Carton dies.

Names occasionally wander from one book to the other, perhaps in some entirely different connection from the original, showing merely that the name remained in Dickens' mind and was appropriated because the novelist needed some kind of cognomen. The hated *gabelle,* France's salt tax, turns up as the name of Darnay's agent on Monseigneur's estate, the man whose letter to Darnay begging his assistance in his trial is the excuse for tempting Darnay back to France and his capture. Carlyle casually mentions Thelusson's Bank, where the great Necker was once a clerk.[25] Dickens, needing a name for the agency which served to bring Lucy Manette and later her father from France to England, shifted the establishment to Tellson's Bank, with branches in Paris as well as London.

Carlyle's description of the butchery which went on outside La Force Prison in the September Massacres of 1792 is about as horrible as anything in his chamber of hyperbolic horrors.[26] Wanton and brutal slaying in the streets with axe and sword is much more forthright than death under the guillotine. Dickens describes the great grindstone in the yard outside the quarters of Tellson's Bank in Paris where the mob, shirts and clothing dripping with the blood of their victims, comes to sharpen weapons blunted in the awful slaughter.[27]

Much of this transposition is the routine custom of the historical novelist, taking his details from a reputable source and supplying his facts where they are needed in his story. Of more interest to the critic of narrative technique are the instances in which only a suggestion is in the source, Dickens' expansion adding to the picture or the characterization which becomes an important part of his story. Dr. Manette, for example, lost his mind in the long years of confinement.[28] He learned the shoemaker's trade in prison, and although nursed back to health and sanity upon coming to England, he suffers lapses of memory and reverts to his prison occupation whenever he is seriously troubled. This regression happens when Lucy marries Darnay and again when all seems lost and Darnay is sentenced to die.

Louis XVI was the king who mismanaged the governmental treatment of all parties in the days before the Terror. Without ability at the proper moment, he was often a pitiable figure as he became more and more enmeshed in problems beyond his scope. Occasionally he escaped from the world of his troubles with the tools of a smith, finding perfect release and forgetfulness while fashioning something purely mechanical. The leap from this account in Carlyle to Dickens' brilliant use of the shoemaker's tools by Dr. Manette shows his genius in action; it is the trait which makes Dr. Manette the unforgettable person he is.

The whole picture of Carton's death is traceable to bits of inspiration from Carlyle. Maton de la Varenne tells of his own narrow escape from death when the haphazard trials were at their height. His terror and the wild events during the time he spent in prison are recounted in a pamphlet called "Ma Résurrection."[29] Dickens seized upon the idea of the resurrection as a symbol for Carton's death and intensified it in other parts of the story. The connection with Christ's death and the doctrine of the atonement was an easy transference. Dickens prepares for his use of the resurrection theme by having Carton remember, on the night before Darnay is sentenced, how he had followed his father to the grave, and the preacher had read: "I am the resurrection and the life."[30]

Mme. Roland, a brave and noble lady, was another individual sentenced to die. Carlyle tells her story:

> And now, short preparation soon done, she too shall go her last road. There went with her a certain Lamarche, "Director of Assignat-printing"; whose dejection she endeavoured to cheer. Arrived at the foot of the scaffold, she asked for pen and paper, "to write the strange thoughts that were rising in her": a remarkable request; which was refused. Looking at the Statue of Liberty which stands there, she says bitterly: "O Liberty, what things are done in thy name!" For Lamarche's sake, she will die first; show him how easy it is to die: "Contrary to the order," said Samson.—"Pshaw, you cannot refuse the last request of a Lady"; and Samson yielded.[31]

That Dickens referred to this passage is clear from his epilogue, where he records what Sidney Carton might have been thinking had he been able to do what Mme. Roland wanted to do. Says Dickens:

> One of the most remarkable sufferers by the same axe—a woman—had asked at the foot of the same scaffold, not long before, to be allowed

to write down the thoughts that were inspiring her. If he had given utterance to his, and they were prophetic, they would have been these: . . .

The thoughts follow, ending with the lines:

"It is a far, far better thing that I do, than I have ever done; it is a far, far better rest that I go to than I have ever known."[32]

Mme. Roland's friend Lamarche had been timid about dying. The inspired idea of giving Carton the little seamstress to comfort—a completely new character in the story—follows from this hint. There is one other influence. It comes from the account in Carlyle of the manner in which Elizabeth, sister of Louis, and the "once timorous" Marchioness de Crussol went to the scaffold. They embraced before they walked up the steps to the guillotine.[33] And so the little seamstress waits her turn, and as she goes to her death, "she kisses his lips, he kisses hers."

A Tale of Two Cities is the one book of Dickens in which the student can see his artistry in some detail, since the sources can be compared more accurately and completely than usual. His practice of noting and transforming anything he could use shows also to advantage. His climactic chapter depicting the death of Carton is his best experiment with sensation, and it reaches tragic intensity. The curtains of trite melodrama have fallen away; dissection of his narrative devices shows how far he had come from the pure sentimentalism of Little Nell's death.

The novel, excellent as it is in certain respects, presents a number of problems. It is different from Dickens' usual narrative style, and this difference does not utilize every resource which we are accustomed to associate with his artistry. Farce and caricature are either absent or underplayed. The only effective farce character is Jerry Cruncher, the body snatcher who robs graves and objects to his wife's praying while he is at work. Mr. Lorry is described in the old manner of caricature, Mr. Stryver is a stupid ass, and Miss Pross as Lucy's maid has some eccentric moments. No remarkable speech mannerisms are given to any of the characters, unless Jerry may be considered to have one. In a sense Dr. Manette's "far away" voice is such a device, and it is appropriate to his long confinement in the Bastille. The development of action by dialogue is not completely replaced by description, for there are a few rare moments when Dickens reverts to his old habits. Examples are the scenes in which Jerry talks to his wife, or Carton almost proposes to Lucy.

The development of the plot is generally expert. In Book Two Dickens alternates action between England and France, managing to balance the events which introduce the Defarges and the scene in which Monseigneur is assassinated after he has run over a child, with the story of Lucy and Dr. Manette in London, building up to Lucy's marriage with Darnay. Dickens also carefully contrasts the two trials for Darnay's life, the first showing him acquitted on the false charge of spying brought by Barsad and Cly. Carton saves him by calling attention to the remarkable resemblance they have for each other, and thus confuses the witness and the jury. The second trial, in Book Three, gives Carton another opportunity for saving Darnay, but only after sentence is passed.

The weaknesses of the novel derive partially from Dickens' need to have something exciting happen in each installment. It is a shock to read the Bastille chapter and find the authentic surging action come to its crest when Defarge goes to Dr. Manette's cell. It is almost as if, for the purposes of the plot, the whole taking of the Bastille is important only because a fatal private document is hidden there. This is a question of emphasis, yet the novel is the tale of Carton, Darnay, and Lucy, not of the larger implications of the Revolution itself. In his dark novels Dickens had used his plots to illuminate the largest issues he could imagine. In this book he does not try to make the story of the Manettes symbolize the deepest meanings of French history.

Wilkie Collins was not quite satisfied with the way in which Dickens handled his plot. In addition to suggesting that the story of Dr. Manette might be revealed early, he apparently felt that the device of the document which leads to the conviction of Darnay was weak or unlikely. Perhaps the doctor might have been able to write such a detailed and lengthy account of his wrongs and secrete it in his cell; it is improbable that the entire record would be read in the trial at this date in Paris. Dickens certainly imitated the practice of French drama in his alternating trial sequence, in which the hero's concerns prosper at first, then are suddenly reversed. Stage and motion-picture versions of the double trial usually combine events of the two days and speed up the action. In this and in several other moments which develop Dickens' intrigue there is the suggestion of overelaborate complication.

A few sequences have little motivation. Why does Carton go to Paris? Darnay goes to help Gabelle escape a death sentence, although what happens to Gabelle is lost in Darnay's own difficulties. Carton supposedly goes because Lucy is in trouble. Of course, Darnay spends a long time in prison before his trial, Dickens rapidly passing over months in his narrative. Carton could hardly know when he leaves London that he will be called upon to sacrifice his life for Darnay. In this kind of novel, such coincidence is generally accepted by the average reader, but it must be taken into account by the particular and critical ones.

The substitution of Carton for Darnay calls for more manipulation. Dickens' readers would hardly retain respect for Darnay if he easily permitted Carton to die for him; therefore he must be tricked into escaping. Dickens solved this problem by having Darnay drugged with some form of anesthetic so that he will be far from Paris before he wakens to learn what has happened. The exact nature of the anesthetic remains doubtful, since such drugs were not in general use at the time.[34] Dickens reached into the misty realm of alchemy to find the mysterious potion which could secure the necessary effect. This point is easily accepted by the modern reader because he is used to the general properties of anesthesia and knows about Mickey Finns from modern detective novels.

The symbolism used by Dickens in this novel is of a different order from the fog of *Bleak House* and the prison atmosphere of *Little Dorrit*. It centers about the "recalled to life" hint in Carlyle and extends itself to the general implication of resurrection. Dr. Manette's release is a form of resurrection, and "Recalled to Life" is the password of the Prologue or Book One. Jerry Cruncher introduces a grotesque variation of this theme when he steals bodies to sell to medical students. Carton's death is a form of spiritual resurrection at the same time that Darnay's release is to life from the sentence of

252

death. Carton also carries some sense of atonement into his sacrifice, and the symbol works its way into the great climax.

This climax is prepared for and built up in a more concise fashion than in any other novel. The last three chapters are chronologically adjusted for this effect. In Chapter XIII Carton substitutes himself for Darnay, and the drugged man is hurried from the city by Mr. Lorry, Lucy, and Dr. Manette. Enough is told to assure the reader that they escape, and then they are lost to the narrative. Chapter XIV recounts the death of Mme. Defarge at the hands of Miss Pross, then goes on to show that she and Jerry Cruncher escape too. In Chapter XV Carton goes to the guillotine, and that is the end. In other novels Dickens had sometimes added chapters and incidents to take care of the future of almost every character in the story. In *A Tale of Two Cities* Carton dies, and the story is finished except for his imaginary thoughts at the scaffold.

The thesis of the novel is: *Revolution can happen in England too!* The aristocrats in France were stupid and hardhearted; they were responsible for spurring the people to revolt; England's ruling classes were also being stupid and hardhearted. Dickens joins with Carlyle in showing the reasons for what had happened in France, although he does not try to bring in a panoramic view of historical characters like Mirabeau, Lafayette, Robespierre, or Napoleon. Nor is there any attempt to do what Tolstoi might have attempted: show the struggles of the government for money in time of depression, the difficulties of parliament, the pathetic story of Marie Antoinette, the philosophical thinking behind the movement. Dickens centered on saying of the French Revolution just what he had said concerning the economic crises which were happening in England. In the first part of his novel he sympathizes with the downtrodden people; but at the last these people are the villains. Extreme injustice leads to violence; see what happened in the days of the Terror. If British employers insist upon the selfish laissez-faire doctrine, workers will eventually rise to protect themselves. A catastrophe like the French Revolution could easily happen elsewhere.

The implied comparison is not quite valid. Modern research shows that the French Revolution was a much more complex affair than Carlyle and Dickens judged. But the effect of Dickens' novel is intentionally limited in scope. The book is not *War and Peace.* His tale remains the account of one small group of characters who suffered in the course of the cataclysm which surged about them and went on to historical, political, and economic developments completely beyond the purposes of the tale. On a small and relatively selective scale within the limits defined it is a dynamic historical novel, even though it does not call upon all the technical resources at Dickens' command. He sacrificed solidity for the spectacular, the large scene for the single vivid flash, but he got it.

The following novel, *Great Expectations,* is another experiment in narrative technique. It draws upon most of the resources in Dickens' possession, its close texture achieves an admirable degree of design and unity, and it provides Dickens' most convincing study of a round or developing character in Pip. The central thesis reverts again to Carlyle—the doctrine of work, the philosophical contention that man is happiest when he produces something important to himself and to society. Carlyle argued also that the political, economic, and social structure of society should reward a man properly for his industry. Dickens was continually aggravated by the false returns awarded by the caste system, by economic manipulation, by education, religion, law, and every unjust accident which man encounters in the existing social system. There is more than casual resemblance to some of the arguments of Thorstein Veblen at a later date—that unearned increment ruins the leisure class, which exists because it has money it does not deserve and has not worked to get. Dickens thought that all classes could be ruined by undeserved expectations and unearned resources. It is interesting that he took as his hero a representative of the working class rather than an aristocrat or a capitalist.

Dickens had created many characters who develop from incapacity to capacity, who start wrong and learn better, who eventually discover how to depend on themselves rather than upon luck, or heredity, or environment. Part of the fascination he felt for the picaresque hero had been this opportunity for showing a youth in the process of gradual development to maturity. Nicholas Nickleby and

Martin Chuzzlewit are his earliest studies in this kind of character; David Copperfield continues the type. But these characters develop suddenly or spasmodically. They are more flat than round. His idea of Pip was a boy around whom the whole story revolves, a young man who could be interpreted in detail as his character deteriorates under the stimulus of "great" or "undeserved" expectations of wealth and position. Dickens invented a series of events which would let Pip come close to ruin as a person because of his expectations, reach a climax of disappointment when they turn out to be "false" (false in the sense of caste and prestige), achieve maturity in the experience, then find gradual regeneration by learning to work for proper rewards in life. *Great Expectations* is planned on this concept of character, and all the action revolves around it. Dickens also decided to tell the story in the first person, but completely differentiated it from *David Copperfield* in the development.

When the novel was in its first planning stage he wrote to Forster:

> The book will be written in the first person throughout, and during these first three weekly numbers you will find the hero to be a boy-child, like David. Then he will be an apprentice. You will not have to complain of the want of humour as in *A Tale of Two Cities*. I have made the opening, I hope, in its general effect exceedingly droll. I have put a child and a good-natured foolish man, in relations that seem to me very funny. Of course I have got in the pivot on which the story will turn too—and which, indeed, as you remember, was the grotesque tragi-comic conception that first encouraged me. To be quite sure I have fallen into no unconscious repetitions, I read *David Copperfield* again the other day, and was affected by it to a degree you would hardly believe.[35]

The "grotesque tragi-comic conception" was that Pip would expect his money from the wrong source—wrong in the sense that it would not contribute to his desired social postion. The author's plan was to have Pip unintentionally befriend an escaping convict who would later make a fortune in Australia and decide to give it all to Pip, but do it secretly so that Pip would not know the source of his expectations.

Dickens felt rightly that it was tragicomic for Pip to expect a fortune from a source he would not be proud of. At the end he loses all the money anyway, since it is forfeit to the Crown. Because nothing in Pip's character or accomplishments merits any inheritance at all, he is sobered by getting his money from Magwitch, a person who cannot help him to the social standing he admires. This effect demanded that Pip and the reader should both be surprised at the real source of Pip's expectations, so Dickens invented another plot to provide the false trail. As Wilkie Collins had done in *The Woman in White,* he decided to create as much suspense as he could, then suddenly shock the reader with the real truth. The supposed source of the inheritance was from Miss Havisham.

Miss Havisham is imagined as a woman who would lead the boy to the wrong standards of manhood. She is, by this necessity, a warped individual. When Dickens had been in Paris several years before, he had noted the strange story of a duchess whose eccentricities were revealed at her death. He relayed the account to Forster as an example of his continual discovery of truths which were stranger than fiction and which would be charged as impossible against any author inventing them:

> The Duchess who is murdered lived alone in a great house which was always shut up, and passed her time entirely in the dark. In a little lodge outside lived a coachman (the murderer), and there had been a long succession of coachmen who had been unable to stay there, and upon whom whenever they asked for their wages, she plunged out with an immense knife, by way of an immediate settlement. The coachmen never had anything to do, for the coach hadn't been driven out for years; neither would she allow the horses to be driven out for exercise. Between the lodge and the house, is a miserable bit of garden, all overgrown with long rank grass, weeds and nettles; and in this the horses used to be taken out to swim—in a dead green vegetable sea, up to their haunches.[36]

This strange suggestion grew into Miss Havisham. Dickens' desire for a pattern which would intensify the "great expectations" theme led him to supply a story for her which would show her misanthropy dependent upon expectations of her own which had proved false. Miss Havisham stops her clocks, leaving everything in her house exactly as it was on the day when she expected to be married—

one shoe on and one off, the decayed wedding cake on the dining-room table, the garden weed-choked, the whole house packed with blackness. Her disappointment has led her into a fixation which expresses itself in revenge on all men to retaliate for the suffering caused by the man who cheated her and deserted her. She will hurt Pip, along with the others, if she can.

Pip's degeneration involves many things. Most people, like Dickens, could imagine him falling in love with the wrong girl. Accordingly Miss Havisham adopts Estella, beautiful and willful, in order to help lead astray as many men as possible through her up-bringing as a heartless flirt. Miss Havisham (a female Volpone) also attracts a number of fawning relatives who pretend great affection for her in order to inherit money from her when she dies. These sycophantic characters, the Pockets, add to the theme of expectations based on undeserving inadequacy. Miss Havisham knows what the avowals of her relatives are worth and eventually rewards them in kind.

Dickens knew from his experience with the first person in *David Copperfield* that he had to develop all his plots where Pip could observe and narrate them properly. He planned to center his several courses of action so close to his narrator that they would revolve directly about him. His only real difficulty came in the third sequence. This involves Compeyson, the man who swindled and deserted Miss Havisham, and Dickens has difficulty keeping this character from resembling a typical Victorian stage villain. It is Compeyson who also leads Magwitch astray, and Dickens thus connects his three main courses of action. Dickens devised an intrigue which makes Magwitch and Compeyson develop violent antipathy, rising first in Magwitch because Compeyson double-crosses him at their trial in order to get a lighter sentence. This enmity then continues to the time when Magwitch returns from Australia to see Pip, contrary to the terms of his sentence, and contributes to the final scenes in which Pip tries to get Magwitch safely out of the country, and Compeyson manages to expose him to the authorities.

Dickens' desire to tie the plots together also led him to make Magwitch the father of Estella. The details of the Havisham-Compeyson-Magwitch intrigue and the rare appearances of Compeyson in Pip's company keep this sequence cloudy. Compeyson appears on the scene in the first chapters when he escapes from the prison barge and is recaptured along with Magwitch; he sits behind Pip at Wopsle's performance of *Hamlet* at the theater; he arrives at the climax to intercept Magwitch's escape and dies in the ensuing struggle. Just as David had trouble being at the scene of Steerforth's actions, so does Pip miss connections with Compeyson.

In order to add sensation, Dickens invented Orlick, a dull, oafish apprentice who strikes down Pip's sister, wants to marry Biddy, and eventually tries to murder Pip and put his body in a limekiln. The last incident is contrived so that it happens while Pip is trying to help Magwitch escape; the two escape episodes come together, and Dickens intended that they should intensify the climax. The Orlick scenes provide an additional, relatively minor sequence, and generally speaking, all the sequences involve Pip.

Great Expectations gives the effect of following a rather exact outline. It is true that no such outline has been preserved in Dickens' papers. The expectations theme is doubled and redoubled. Joe Gargery and Biddy have no false expectations and accept their humble station in life as proper and necessary. The Pockets want to inherit their expectations from Miss Havisham or somebody. Pumblechook would like to share in Pip's good fortune. Mr. Wopsle expects to improve the condition of serious drama and has no ability to provide any assistance. The lawyer, Jaggers, plays upon the hopes and expectations of all those who try to escape the legal consequences of their unlawful activities. Even Wemmick expects "portable property" when he marries. Compeyson expects to get whatever money he can steal or confiscate from his victims. Magwitch expects to atone for a worthless life by setting up Pip in wealth and comfort. John Hagan says, in his brilliant analysis of this novel: "Dickens manages to display a whole range of the different effects 'great expectations' can have upon the human spirit."[37] Few of the characters deserve what they expect.

The development of the action illustrates an intricate balance and design. In the first six chapters Pip has his first meeting with Magwitch; in the next twelve he is exposed to Miss Havisham and

Estella; in Chapter XX he goes to London after being told of his expectations; for eighteen chapters his character degenerates as he lives beyond his means and tries to learn to be a gentleman; in the thirty-ninth chapter Magwitch appears, and Pip is shocked to find the true source of his expectations; in Chapter XLII Magwitch tells of his past and his relationship with Compeyson; in Chapter XLVIII Pip learns of Estella's parentage; in Chapter XLIX he saves Miss Havisham from the fire; in Chapter LIII he escapes from Orlick; in Chapter LIV Magwitch is captured. Hagan points out the many examples of mathematical organization and neat development which can be deduced from this outline. Pip meets Magwitch in the first six chapters; then in the third stage of Pip's development, Magwitch appears again in the six chapters which stretch from XL to XLVI. Chapters VII to XI introduce Miss Havisham and Estella; Chapters XLVII to LI resolve this relationship and end with Miss Havisham's belated regeneration. Chapters XII to XVII expose Pip's gradual decline in snobbery; Chapters LII to LVI show him in the process of character rebuilding through his unselfish devotion to Magwitch. Chapters XVIII and XIX show him leaving the old forge; Chapters LVII to LIX reveal him returning to it a chastened and mature man ready to work for what he gets in the world.[38]

Dickens assured Forster that he would not have to complain of the lack of humor in this book, and there is justification for this claim. Joe Gargery is a good-natured, illiterate man whose simple affection protects Pip from Joe's wife, who is also Pip's sister. Mrs. Gargery browbeats her husband and brings Pip "up by hand." Mr. Pumblechook is a pompous and silly fool. Mr. Wopsle is eccentrically elocutionary in his dramatic efforts. Mr. Jaggers is one of Dickens' most convincing lawyers, washing his hands when he is through business and displaying on the walls of his office the death masks of the convicts he has unsuccessfully defended. Mr. Wemmick lives a double life, changing character completely between office and home. His home is also inspired by Commodore Trunnion's ship-house in *Peregrine Pickle;* it is constructed and managed like a medieval castle. The Pocket family are all caricatured. Herbert has grandiose expectations of his own, and the girl he marries, Clara Barley, is afflicted with a gout-ridden father who might easily have inhabited the pages of *Pickwick Papers* or *Nicholas Nickleby*. There is no Sam Weller, or Mrs. Nickleby, or Mr. Micawber, or Flora Finching in the novel, but the average of caricature is high.

Miss Havisham's Satis House is an authentic Gothic structure, and there is sensation in the sequences which end with Pip's escape from Orlick and Magwitch's capture. Magwitch's death is handled with due regard for its sentimental opportunities without being grossly exaggerated. In general Dickens utilized all of his technical resources and centered them about a well-constructed story which contains a number of interesting courses of action. Of all his shorter novels written in weekly installments, this is the finest example of concentration where several plots are involved. He had limited himself in *A Tale of Two Cities* to one plot and had reduced his dramatic dialogue. In *Great Expectations* he returned to his usual practice, but planned his action more effectively than in the earlier, short-installment, panoramic novels.

The particular appeal of the story lies in the development of Pip's character, revealed tellingly in the first person. Pip goes wrong for a time, but learns to do right. The reader is in sympathy with him even when he is behaving badly. The revelation of his decline is gradual, and the reader always hopes that he will improve. Dickens expected to draw a moral with Pip. He insists, as he had done previously, that improvement in our world must come when we see our mistakes and profit from them in the future. This is made clear in passages like the one in which Pip reviews his past:

> How much of my ungracious condition of mind may have been my own fault, how much Miss Havisham's, how much my sister's, is now of no consequence to me or to any one. The change was made in me; the thing was done. Well or ill done, excusably or inexcusably, it was done.[39]

Because Pip understands this ungracious quality, he must be expected to reverse it. Back at home after his sister has been hit on the head with the convict's leg-iron, he muses:

> As I had grown accustomed to my expectations, I had insensibly begun to notice their effect upon myself and those around me. Their influence

upon my character I disguised from my recognition as much as possible, but I knew very well that it was not all good. I lived in a state of chronic uneasiness respecting my behaviour to Joe. My conscience was not by any means comfortable about Biddy. When I woke up in the night—like Camilla—I used to think, with a weariness of my spirits, that I should have been happier and better if I had never seen Miss Havisham's face, and had risen to manhood content to be partners with Joe in the honest old forge. Many a time of an evening, when I sat alone looking at the fire, I thought, after all, there was no fire like the forge fire and the kitchen fire at home.[40]

Dickens did not mean that classes should be static in the caste system, that where a man was born, there he should stay. Abilities are subject to no law of class, and he had depicted many aristocrats who did not deserve their rank or responsibility. Pip later shows that he has capacities, and he uses them to achieve modest success in the business world. Hard work for everyone, whatever was appropriate to his talents and abilities, supplied the answer. As Pip reforms and changes through the shock of learning the true story behind his expectations, he turns to the solid foundations of conscientious effort and labor. Then he merits Dickens' idea of true heroism, a term which he defined as force of character. This thesis influenced somewhat his change of the novel's ending. The compressed scope of his tale did not permit him to study in detail Pip's later change for the better. The author implied this change and hoped that the reader would accept it from the story. But few readers are completely aware that Dickens says Pip should have married Biddy instead of pursuing Estella with an affection which matched his false expectations. When Biddy marries Joe, Pip is shocked by the realization of what he might have had in the way of happiness. It is clear that Dickens did not originally intend that Pip should finally marry Estella, the girl who stands for everything in life which is beyond the place and position he deserves.

The original ending left Pip a bachelor, and the story concluded on a melancholy note. Maybe he has changed, says Dickens in effect, but even so, Pip does not deserve the usual happy fate for heroes. The thesis was to be more impressive because he received a *lasting* reminder in the way of punishment. Dickens wrote this ending, but happened to visit Bulwer-Lytton just afterward. They discussed the matter while they were considering the business which had brought Dickens to Bulwer's home. Forster records the sequel:

> "You will be surprised," he wrote, "to hear that I have changed the end of *Great Expectations* from and after Pip's return to Joe's and finding his little likeness there. Bulwer, who has been, as I think you know, extraordinarily taken with the book, so strongly urged it upon me, after reading the proofs, and supported his view with such good reasons that I have resolved to make the change. You shall have it when you come back to town. I have put in as pretty a little piece of writing as I could, and I have no doubt the story will be more acceptable through the alteration."[41]

It is hard to see how he could have altered the endings of *Bleak House* or *Little Dorrit* without damaging his purpose. He must not have felt so deeply about this novel. It is probable that Bulwer's "good reasons" were not completely commercial. He could have argued that Pip had changed and that his fortunes should change also. It would be an inadequate moral point to deny Pip any reward after he had shown growth of character. Eleven years might change Estella too. Give the two eventual happiness because they eventually deserve it.

Forster records that the new ending was popularly received. Since that time Shaw has brought out a version for The Limited Editions Club which substitutes the original ending. The Rinehart edition prints both endings.[42] Does the new conclusion interfere with the force of the thesis on which the entire structure of the novel was based? One must say, sadly, that the novel is injured in some measure. *David Copperfield* would have suffered if Steerforth had been saved to marry Little Emily at the last because he had changed, but of course *he* did *not* change and Pip did. On the other hand, the reversed ending cannot alter the convincing effect of Pip's story of degeneration and regeneration. It merely keeps the final pages from complete harmony with what had already been accomplished.

Great Expectations includes excellent examples of almost every narrative device in Dickens' possession. It has farce-caricature, amusing speech mannerisms, an exciting plot or two, restrained sentiment, Gothic atmosphere, a moral dependent upon the philosophy of Carlyle, and a carefully developing and changing central character. The texture of the novel is tight, and the contrasts are nicely balanced. The use of the first person adds simplicity and naturalness to the narrative manner at the same time that it avoids any melodramatic excesses. The "false expectations" symbols add their force to the impact of the novel. For many readers *Great Expectations* is the most satisfactory of Dickens' novels in the sense expressed by T. S. Eliot in his remarks about *Bleak House,*[43] that it often shows the author to advantage and rarely at his worst. It does not reach exuberant heights, as some of the early novels do, it does not have the intense personal charm of *David Copperfield,* and it misses the solid social criticism on a grand scale that one finds in *Bleak House* or *Little Dorrit*. But in the canon of Dickens' novels, it deserves a high place.

CHAPTER XIII

Inferno

ICKENS' bitterest attack upon his world is in his last completed novel, *Our Mutual Friend*. After his technical experimentations in *A Tale of Two Cities* and *Great Expectations,* he went back to the schematic structure of *Bleak House* and *Little Dorrit,* the panoramic plan which organized the novel around a pattern and fashioned every character and episode around interlocking symbols. *Our Mutual Friend* was written in the old monthly installment way, thus allowing for the play of all his resources and the development of his tale by dialogue—a form which afforded the best opportunity for his genius to display itself.

Critics like to use a touchstone for emphasis. It is far-fetched to suggest that *David Copperfield* was Dickens' *Odyssey* or that *Little Dorrit* was his *Hamlet;* it is more nearly exact to say that *Our Mutual Friend* was his *Inferno.* In this novel he sees London, England, Age of Queen Victoria, fashionable society, the economic and political structure of the middle nineteenth century wallowing in Hell. It is his sardonic disgust which gives his last great novel its character and tone. Many critics have completely missed the point of *Our Mutual Friend,* blaming its effect upon his health or his state of mind, arguing that he was losing his grip, that the railway accident and the strain of his public readings combined to lead him closer to the stroke which eventually killed him. Some part of this argument is coincidentally true, for Dickens was drinking the dregs of his cup. He had reached fame and fortune, but he was disgusted with much of his own life. His marriage had gone from frustration to unhappiness to separation; Ellen Ternan was at best a temporary substitute for what he had always wanted; the standards of Victorian England repelled him; his children were a constant drain on his spirits and his aspirations; life was continually falling short of what he hoped for. The result was that he sarcastically planned a novel in which he could *entertain* the reading public with a picture of Victorian society struggling in Hell. Late in life he had come to understand his readers. His contemptuous concept of his public made him recognize that most of his audience would take his book as another interesting story, but he had his share of eternal hope: He believed that some of the effect of his book would sink into parts of the Victorian consciousness, and he must have thought that future generations might see his point more clearly.

The starting place for the planning of his novel was in the symbol of the dust heap. In 1867 the collection of refuse in London was still in private hands. The trash-and-garbage business was a dirty one, but it was profitable. In the great mounds of the so-called dust heaps were valuable segments of bones, rags, cinders, refuse, discarded odds and ends—everything one puts in a trash barrel or a garbage can. In the dumping grounds of London great heaps were piled up, and scavengery occasionally paid extra dividends when one found something valuable that had been accidentally or ignorantly thrown away. London's sanitary system had come a long way from Elizabethan days and the great drainage ditch which separated the two sides of the city, but the Thames was still the main way to get rid of London's sewage. Dickens, in seizing upon the theme of trash and refuse, immediately saw that his parallel action should involve scavengers of both sorts—the dust and trash collectors and the water-front boatmen who looked for valuable leavings in the filth and slime of the Thames. Hell is a place where one encounters refuse and sewage.

Dickens' titles for his novels have often unintentionally aided misunderstanding of his themes or his purposes. He began by naming his stories for his characters, using some complicated alliteration in given names after the manner of Smollett. His themes are rarely helped by his titles. Certainly "Our Mutual Friend" gives no real hint as to Dickens' purpose in his picture of Victorian Hell in dust, trash, and sewage. His exquisite and sustained disgust, his sewage-smear fixation might have found expression in the twentieth century in some title like "A Moundful of Dust," "Disposal," "The Wasteland," "Ashes to Ashes," "Trash Collection," "All the Queen's Horses," "Garbage-ways," "The Slime of Time," "The Organs of Defecation," "Cloaca

Revisited," "Scavengers' Wake," or even (if one supposes some expansion of the time machine to an era which would accept complete frankness) a title limited to a single, vulgar, four-letter word.

The symbol around which his theme revolves illustrates all of his objections to what was wrong with his world. That anyone would value above all else whatever drips from the body of society seemed to him to rouse the incarnate infernal. In horrified dismay he observed society seeking nothing that lives eternally, but all that is preserved to decay. Economically speaking, his world could see no difference between unearned increment and diffused excrement. From Parliament to wealthy mansions to filthy business houses to narrow streets to slums, in every part of London he saw mankind straining and struggling over a dung heap trying desperately to produce money or whatever could be measured in pounds and shillings. The quintessence of his symbol was dust and trash; its parallel form was the cesspool of the Thames, draining off the slime and ooze from the wasteland of life. His pen became an excretory organ spouting out a sizzling cover for all the organic corruption which lay festering in the values that money set, the awful offal of Victorian standards.

He planned three courses of action to develop his symbol. Forster describes these faithfully. The first was to center about the longshoremen who make a living by salvaging the wreckage of the Thames and who sometimes rob the bodies of the drowned; the second was to involve "a man, young and perhaps eccentric, feigning to be dead, and *being* dead to all intents and purposes external to himself, and for years retaining the singular view of life and character so imparted"; the third was to describe a man and woman who married, each expecting to live off the money possessed by the other—neither having any—and this last plot was to introduce a number of rich people with completely false economic and moral values.[1]

It is interesting to trace the source of the first of these plot ideas. In his wanderings around London while searching for local color for some of the water-front scenes in *Great Expectations,* he had seen handbills posted describing persons drowned in the Thames. There flashed into his mind, then or soon after, the remembrance of a play by Sheridan Knowles, *The Daughter,* which he had seen in 1836 or 1837, and which had been based upon the "wreckers" or salvagers of dead bodies. The first scene of the play showed these men picking up float-ing bodies, and the suspicion is voiced that someone may be providing the victims these wreckers discover. Marian, the heroine, is ashamed of her father's trade and attempts to dissuade him from practicing it. She occasionally follows him, fearing that he might be tempted to murder live bodies in addition to robbing dead ones. Another wrecker, Black Norris, proposes a partnership with Marian's father, and with an ac-complice named Wolf he plans a murder, fabricating evidence for a charge against Marian's father of murdering one of the dead men he brings in.

Norris does all this to get the father in his power, since he wants to marry the daughter. The play shows his apparent success, for he exonerates the father in return for marriage with Marian. The climac-tic scene reveals the wedding in progress when the long but sure arm of melodrama intervenes. The accomplice, Wolf, has a conscience; he confesses in time to stop the wedding, implicating Norris. Marian's long-absent lover returns from distant lands to marry her. Incidental sensational items include the fact that Norris really stabbed his own father and that Marian was forced at the trial to testify against her father because she thought she saw him wield the knife, and besides she could not tell a lie.

Dickens used this source as inspiration for the main theme of his first plot. He gives Gaffer Hexam a daughter Lizzie, a villainous part-ner named Rogue Riderhood, and he retains all the paraphernalia of the original situation in which suspicion is generated about the possible murder of the body recovered; Riderhood eventually accuses Gaffer of the deed. The name "Rogue Riderhood" is a truly Dickensian evolu-tion from the "Wolf" of Knowles's play and the fairy tale association. In his story Riderhood informs against Gaffer for a reward, and Dickens wisely abandoned the melodramatic development of the play which included the villain's designs upon the virtuous daughter.

One wonders whether remembering one play by Knowles led to recall of another. Knowles reached perhaps his greatest success with *The Hunchback,* seen by Dickens in 1832 with Fanny Kemble in the leading feminine role.[2] The plot of this play concerns a hunchback who returns after long years of absence to test the character of a daughter who does not know him. Walter adopts Julia without telling her their relationship and then attempts to force her to marry a pretended Lord Rochdale instead of Clifford, the man she really loves. Clifford had thought, up to the discovery of the so-called Lord Rochdale, that he was the holder of the title himself. He becomes secretary to this impostor, while his ladylove struggles with the decision to marry for love or for money. She decides for love, of course, and having demonstrated the true worth of her character, her father reveals himself as the real lord and shows that he was testing her. She marries Clifford with Walter's blessing and gets the money too.

For his second plot Dickens used the complications of this source, adapting them to his central symbolic intention. He abandoned the hunchback characteristic and changed the relationships of the characters slightly. Reading in the newspaper of a dust collector who left a sizable fortune upon his death, Dickens seized upon this incident and combined the details of his two sources to work out an interlocking intrigue. Thus, his plan relates that: eccentric dustman dies, leaving money to faithful servant and to his son if the son will marry a certain woman; son having quarreled with father and lived in the colonies comes home desiring to find out whether he really wants to marry the girl bequeathed to him with his fortune; son prepares stratagem to disguise himself and find out about the girl; stratagem works too well, and he is thrown in the river for dead by villainous companions, but manages to save himself; having changed clothes with the hero (the plot creaks here), one companion quarrels with his fellow conspirators, is murdered, thrown in the river, and eventually identified as the missing heir, whose clothes he wears; Gaffer Hexam and Rogue Riderhood bring in *The Daughter* plot sequence at this point, Rogue being the real murderer; meanwhile, the supposedly dead heir finds living quarters at the home of Bella Wilfer, the girl he is supposed to marry; he eventually becomes secretary to Mr. Boffin, the servant who succeeded to the entire dust fortune upon his (Harmon's) reported death; it is at this point that Harmon is casually referred to as "Our Mutual Friend"; the Boffins adopt Bella, carrying out the *Hunchback* plot, and aid her by Mr. Boffin's pretense that he has become a miser to choose true love instead of great wealth; Bella chooses to marry the poor secretary for love and receives her ideal reward by eventually getting love, the man, and the money too. That Bella should show all the signs of being a spoiled beauty at first, willfully selfish, intensifies her moral struggle. Dickens intended a study in the round, following her development from weakness, as he had done with Pip. His general arrangement and manipulation of the two sources, combining them in his plan, shows again his mastery of this kind of complicated intrigue. It also allowed him to develop the twin symbolic themes which were dependent upon his central purpose—for one plot involved the dust-and-trash collection; the other depended upon the scavengery connected with the body-robbing on the Thames.

The third plot is less complicated. It presents a group of social snobs, the newly rich Veneerings and company. Among the snobs are the Lammles, who married each other for money and are equally disappointed. After their mistake they aim to recoup their fortunes by preying on others; they try to arrange a marriage between the silly but rich Georgianna Podsnap and the moneylender Fledgeby; later they attempt to oust Bella and Harmon-Rokesmith from the good graces of the Boffins, hoping to substitute themselves.

Dickens intended to reinforce his theme and symbols by constructing many streams of action. The Lammles follow the symbolic intention of his theme in that they try to live off the leavings of other people. Dickens invented several minor sequences, each of which illustrates some additional variation on this theme. Wegg is the man who sells odds and ends in the street, who is hired by Mr. Boffin to read *The Decline and Fall of the Roman Empire* to him. Wegg has a wooden leg and spends most of his waking hours trying to figure out how to make money out of other people. He eventually tries and is for a time apparently successful in blackmailing Mr. Boffin. Wegg examines the dust heaps for unexpected fortune, and when he finds a new Harmon will he thinks he has the power to deprive Boffin of the money he has inherited—unless he is paid off. A characteristic Dickensian touch concerns his leg—the one which has been amputated. It was preserved and sold to Mr. Venus, the articulator of bones, skeletons, and stiffs for medical research. Mr. Wegg feels some sentimental attachment for his detached member and eventually buys it from Mr. Venus to keep it from being mistreated or defiled. This episode gives a sardonic twist to the main symbol, for Wegg is always valuing overmuch all those things which are discarded by the body as well as by the soul.

Fledgeby, like Mr. Casby in *Little Dorrit,* is a moneylender who stays behind the scenes and prospers from the misfortunes of other people, hiding under the cover of the old Jew, Riah, and wringing his victims dry while he pretends to sympathize with them. Fascination Fledgeby is one of Dickens' most unpleasant characters, tied into the other plots by way of the Lammles, who try to arrange the marriage between him and Georgianna Podsnap for financial reasons. Fledgeby becomes a symbol of laissez-faire capitalism squatting over the helpless victims who borrow money from him.

Another sequence concerns Lizzie Hexam, who finds herself with two lovers. One is Eugene Wrayburn, a ne'er-do-well lawyer from a good family, of the Carton stamp, a man who lives on the allowance or leavings of his father, never gets much business, and seems a part of the leisure-class *merde* which gathers at the home of the Veneerings. Eugene has good intentions, but has never done anything about them. He is fascinated by Lizzie, but cannot make up his mind whether to seduce or marry her. The other lover is Bradley Headstone, victim of social standards which relegate the teacher to a position at the bottom of society, in the outhouse of the caste system. He reacts psychologically to his condition so that he develops an obsession against Eugene. Headstone thinks that teaching ought to lift him out of his depths and resents in a manic-depressive sense the fact that he has to stay where he is. He eventually plots to murder Eugene, attacks him, and throws him into one of London's sewage canals. Even in this detail Dickens brings in another variation upon his theme. Poor Lizzie tries to run away from her problem, since she loves Eugene and thinks he will not marry her. After she saves his life he decides on his deathbed to marry her and recovers after all.

Two other minor sequences introduce Jenny Wren and Betty Higden. Jenny is a dolls' dressmaker, cursed with a deformed, twisted body and an alcoholic father. Lizzie lives at Jenny's home after Gaffer drowns, and it is Jenny who serves as a sadistic instrument of justice in the scene in which Lammle beats Fledgeby. Jenny helps Fledgeby dress his wounds and puts pepper on the bandages. The connection with the central theme is tenuous, but it is there. Jenny buys "damage and waste" from Riah to dress her dolls, and thus ekes out a living. The old Jew explains:

> "Our waste goes into the best of company, sir, on her rosy-cheeked little customers. They wear it in their hair, and on their ball dresses, and even (so she tells me) are presented at Court with it."[3]

Betty Higden is the rugged old lady who has kept herself out of the Workhouse by hook and crook. Dickens thus makes his last assault on the kind of charity which takes pride in helping others with one's discards. He had made his first attack on Poor Houses in *Oliver Twist*. Betty achieves stature by refusing all charity, preferring to live in utter poverty to accepting help from others. She wants to deserve what she gets and does not want help. Her struggles to raise her family, plus Sloppy whom she has adopted, keep her barely alive, and she eventually dies trying to make a desperate living. But she manages to stay out of the Poor House, and she dies independent. Dickens considers her admirable because she would not accept the leavings of hypocritical charity—a kind of charity which purges itself by depositing what it does not need on those who must accept it.

Every incident in the novel depends upon the symbolic idea that the world has managed to transform its possibilities of Heaven into the actual condition of Hell. And Hell is full of dust, garbage, slime, excretion—all that is foul. Dickens' narrative techniques are all present in contrast and alternation, each one casting a new infernal light by its juxtaposition. The reader goes from the scavengers of the river front to the dust and garbage mounds to the tepid leavings of the Veneering parties to Wegg to Headstone to Lizzie to Jenny Wren to Riah to Betty Higden to Venus to the Wilfers to Riderhood to Fledgeby, each character writhing in filth or struggling to get out. At the bottom of all is money, the love of money at the cost of everything else. It is the overweening desire for money which lands most people in the filth of Hell.

Dickens' attitude toward money needs some explanation. It is apparent that he felt it to be a medium of exchange rather than something valuable in itself. He thought that Adam Smith's concept of economics allowed the economic system to use money to breed more money. Further, it permitted the wealthy, and the lucky, and the scheming crooks of our world to profit beyond any possible ideal of justice, if one presumes that a fair day's work deserves but rarely gets a fair return in money. Dickens' definition of money as a symbol of exchange, not value, resembles the elaborate theories of the modern exponents of Social Credit.[4] It implies that living from dividends, interest, and from owning things which make money without producing anything is usury. Usury is the foundation for Dickens' picture of evil, since usury exists to deprive its victims of what they have rightfully worked for and should have themselves. Dickens explains this:

> As is well known to the wise in their generation, traffic in Shares is the one thing to have to do with in this world. Have no antecedents, no established character, no cultivation, no ideas, no manners; have Shares. Have Shares enough to be on Boards of Direction in capital letters, oscillate on mysterious business between London and Paris, and be great. Where does he come from? Shares. Where is he going to? Shares. What are his tastes? Shares. Has he any principles? Shares. What squeezes him into Parliament? Shares. Perhaps he has never of himself achieved success in anything, never originated anything, never produced anything? Sufficient answer to all; Shares. O mighty Shares! To set those blaring images so high, and to cause us smaller vermin, as under the influence of Henbane or opium, to cry out night and day, "Relieve us of our money, scatter it for us, buy us and sell us, ruin us, only, we beseech ye, take rank among the powers of the earth, and fatten on us!"[5]

All the company that gathers at the Veneering table lives from an inherited or manipulated income. They have no virtues of any kind except that they derive money from direct or indirect preying upon others.

> Buffer says that another of them hadn't a sixpence eighteen months ago, and, through the brilliancy of his genius in getting those shares issued at eighty-five, and buying them all up with no money and selling them at par for cash, has now three hundred and seventy-five thousand pounds—Buffer particularly insisting on the odd seventy-five, and declining to take a farthing less.[6]

What is the essential difference, asks Dickens, between living from dust, garbage, and floating corpses and living from the misfortunes of others? Our economic system values the filth of usury above all else. It rewards sharp dealing and ignores honest endeavor.

Dickens takes great pains to show the apparent degeneration of Mr. Boffin through his acquiring fortune. Mr. Wilfer discusses this with Bella:

> "But Mr. Boffin is being spoiled by prosperity [says Bella], and is changing every day."
>
> "My dear Bella, I hope and trust not."
>
> "I have hoped and trusted not too, Pa; but every day he changes for the worse, and for the worse. Not to me—he is always much the same to me—but to others about him. Before my eyes he grows suspicious, capricious, hard, tyrannical, unjust. If ever a good man were ruined by good fortune, it is my benefactor. And yet, pa, think how terrible the fascination of money is! I see this, and hate this, and dread this, and don't know but that money might make a much worse change in me. And yet I have money always in my thoughts and my desires; and the whole life I place before myself is money, money, money, and what money can make of life!"[7]

Mr. Boffin, in the beginning of the story, hires Wegg to read Gibbon's *Decline and Fall of the Roman Empire* to him, and Dickens shows subtly the effect of the comparison between ancient Rome and modern England, as Mr. Boffin learns the old story from history. The next step is reading the lives of famous misers and usurers, and Boffin seems particularly interested in the tale of one who found his treasures in a dunghill.

The portrayal of the Veneering circle is of technical interest, since Dickens uses the conversation of this group as a kind of hellish chorus, commenting on the values of our society. Veneering buys his way into Parliament; Boots and Brewer are fashionable toadies; the Lammles are fortune hunters; Podsnap is pompous, stuck-in-the-mud England, completely satisfied with the *status quo* as long as he profits by it and dictates to it; Lady Tippins is an aged coquette who keeps a list of lovers, a giggling, stupid representative of the nobility whose face resembles the bloated corpse Lightwood has to identify; Twemlow is a poor relation of Lord Snigsworth, living uncomfortably from an allowance, but with some pretentions to character, even if he is usually in a mental fog; Lightwood and Wrayburn are younger sons of wealth, existing with no purpose, existing because there is nothing better to do, but capable of better things. The conversation of this group gives the effect of continual straining over a vacuum of intellectual constipation. Thus must the devils converse in Hell.

The wide scope of Dickens' contrapuntal arrangement gave him adequate opportunity for displaying his technical resources in narration. Caricature, farce, and speech mannerisms abound in the tale. Mr. Boffin might go back as far as Toby Weller:

> A broad-shouldered, one-sided old fellow . . . dressed in a pea overcoat, and carrying a large stick. He wore thick shoes, and thick leather gaiters, and thick gloves like a hedger's. Both as to his dress and to himself, he was of an overlapping, rhinoceros build, with folds in his cheeks, and his forehead, and his eyelids, and his lips, and his ears, but with bright, eager, childishly inquiring gray eyes under his ragged eyebrows and broad-brimmed hat. A very odd-looking old fellow altogether.[8]

Mrs. Boffin is, in the words of her husband, "a high-flyer at fashion." Fascination Fledgeby is described as possessing small talk, jerky manners, and a face which confidently expected whiskers some day. Bradley Headstone is "decent" in appearance, mechanically stiff in his clothes and his knowledge. Alfred Lammle has too much of everything in his looks, from nose to ginger whiskers to torso to the sparkle of his studs, his eyes, his buttons, his talk, and his teeth. Miss Peecher, who nurses an unrequited love for Headstone, is "a little pincushion, a little house-wife, a little book, a little work-box, a little set of tables of weights and measures, and a little woman, all in one." Miss Georgianna Podsnap is all high shoulders and low spirits, "who seemed to take occasional frosty peeps out of childhood into womanhood, and to shrink back again, overcome by her mother's head-dress, and her father from head to foot." Sloppy, the love child, is ungainly and awkward, "too much of him longwise, too little of him broadwise, and too many sharp angles of him anglewise." Lady Tippins has an immense, obtuse, drab, oblong face, like a face in a tablespoon, "and a dyed long walk up the top of her head, as a convenient public approach to the bunch of false hair behind." The Veneerings are "bran-new" in all features and characteristics.

The Wilfer household steps into the realm of farce at every opportunity. Reginald, the father of Bella, is a cherub, never possessing a whole new suit of clothes at the same time. Browbeaten and henpecked by his wife, he ekes out an unhappy existence as a chubby, smooth, and innocent old-young clerk. Mrs. Wilfer is a stately, impressive woman, who ties up her head in a pocket handkerchief knotted under her chin. Her speech mannerism consists of constant protests against misfortune, and she wears her complaints like her gloves as she laments her difficulties. Bella's sister, Lavinia, is what used to be called saucy, an irrepressible example of sharpness and jealousy. Conversation in the Wilfer household is usually illustrative of what in earlier Dickens novels would be comic relief for its own sake.

Silas Wegg and Mr. Venus are a precious pair, too. Wegg is described thus:

> A knotty man, and a close-grained, with a face carved out of very hard material, that had just as much play of expression as a watchman's rattle. When he laughed, certain jerks occurred in it, and the rattle sprung. Sooth to say, he was so wooden a man, that he seemed to have taken his wooden leg naturally, and rather suggested to the fanciful observer that he might be expected—if his development received no untimely check—to be completely set up with a pair of wooden legs in about six months.[9]

Mr. Boffin finds Wegg at his fruit stall, near Cavendish Square, where Wegg also sells and sings ballads. When he is hired to read to Mr. Boffin, the discussion takes on a whimsical turn:

> "Half a crown," said Wegg, meditating. "Yes. (It ain't much, sir.) Half-a-crown."
> "Per week, you know."
> "Per week. Yes. As to the amount of strain upon the intellect now. Was you thinking at all of Poetry?" Mr. Wegg inquired, musing.
> "Would it come dearer?" Mr. Boffin asked.
> "It would come dearer," Mr. Wegg returned. "For when a person comes to grind off poetry night after night, it is but right he should expect to be paid for its weakening effect on his mind."[10]

Wegg, in the course of his readings, is often talked into singing a ballad or two, and one must admit that his kind of poetry—even without the music—might weaken the ear as well as the mind.

Mr. Venus' shop is out of Smollett's collection of models intended to nauseate the reader. In it are skeletons in all processes of articulation, animals being stuffed, unborn babies in jars, all the paraphernalia of a man who makes a living from that which is dead or liable to decay. Mr. Venus joins Wegg in the blackmail attempt on Mr. Boffin, but eventually shows a better nature by disclosing the plot to the victim. Mr. Venus suffers from melancholy throughout the novel, since his ladylove objects to his business and refuses his hand. That he should eventually marry Pleasant Riderhood, the daughter of Rogue, seems gruesomely fitting to the theme of the novel.

The Podsnaps are especially annoying in their caricatured stupidity. Mrs. Podsnap is so artificial, so externally lacquered, so full of dusty stuffings that she is likened to a rocking-horse. Mr. John Podsnap is so pompous, so self-satisfied, so ready to patronize all his acquaintances that he becomes a model for all the jackasses that have ever graced society. An insurance man, he began with inherited money, married money, and was quite satisfied with money. He makes money from the clients who insure themselves against death or loss. Anything that bothers him he dismisses from the discussion: "I don't want to know about it: I don't choose to discuss it; I don't admit it!" he says, and these phrases become a kind of tag. A peculiar flourish of his right arm helps clear the world of all difficult problems, since the motion sweeps them all behind him and out of existence. Podsnap is supposed to be modeled on John Forster, but one instinctively feels that this identification is exaggerated. Dickens could not possibly have hated his friend as he hated Podsnap, for Podsnap is the stuffiest devil in the limbo of Victorian society.

Our Mutual Friend also presents a number of planned crosscurrents in characterization. The admirable characters are those who strive to find redemption from the lust for money. Mr. Boffin refuses to succumb despite his pretense of degeneration. Harmon-Rokesmith, the young man who carries his disguise throughout the elaborate intrigue of the story, values sincere love more than his fortune, and it is his effort to find out whether Bella is worth the money left him that precipitates most of the mystery in the novel. Bella chooses love over money after a hard struggle. Old Betty Higden prefers to work rather than succumb to charity. Wrayburn decides not to marry money, but to turn instead to Lizzie Hexam, although it takes a murderous attack by Headstone to force him over the right edge of decision. The Reverend Frank Milvey, the first religious figure in a

Dickens novel to be presented favorably, is a young curate turned social worker who devotes his life to those that need help. The old Jew, Riah, is created as a contrast to Dickens' earlier picture of Fagin, and Dickens points out that Jews are like all other people, good, bad, and indifferent. Riah is of a generous, noble nature, forced to be a front for Fascination Fledgeby in the moneylending business, but doing whatever he can for his friends.

As the action develops, Dickens awards praise to those who strive to get out of Hell—or at least for those who are unhappy in it. Real values emerge out of the dust heap and the refuse piles—even from the slime of the Thames. Boffin's transformation from supposed miserliness shows that he rises above his surroundings. Bella is transformed from a selfish, money-loving brat to a loving, understanding wife. Eugene is changed from idleness and lack of energy to strength of character by his true love for Lizzie. Even some of the lesser persons tend toward regeneration. Mrs. Lammle at the last cannot bear to see Georgianna sold to an unhappy married life, and little, ineffectual Mr. Twemlow has the courage to insist that Wrayburn's marriage to Lizzie is the act of a true gentleman, despite the difference in caste involved.

Dickens intended to use the opposite techniques of surprise and suspense in developing his two main mysteries. He says in his epilogue:

> To keep for a long time unsuspected, yet always working itself out, another purpose originating in that leading incident, and turning it to a pleasant and useful account at last, was at once the most interesting and the most difficult part of my design. Its difficulty was much enhanced by the mode of publication: for it would be very unreasonable to expect that many readers, pursuing a story in portions from month to month through nineteen months, will, until they have it before them complete, perceive the relations of its finer threads to the whole pattern which is always before the eyes of the story-weaver at his loom.[11]

What he intended to "keep unsuspected" is Mr. Boffin's pretended change to miserliness. The reader is supposed to think that Boffin is caught in Wegg's blackmailing toils, and the surprise of Boffin's change is to be complete. However, from the beginning of the contrasting plot he casts hints that Harmon is really alive, and he makes that mystery completely clear so that the reader's interest is in learning how it will become apparent to the other characters in the tale. The illusion of Boffin's degeneration is similar to the effect Dickens had planned in *Great Expectations,* in which the reader is led to think Pip's money will come from Miss Havisham and is as surprised as Pip to find it originates with Magwitch. But Dickens uses the opposite device with the Harmon intrigue, and discloses its secret almost at the beginning, preferring to build suspense in contrast to the surprising Boffin mystery.[12]

Melodrama, sentiment, and Gothic horror also find their places in the novel, although their potential excesses are controlled by the theme. The old mannerisms of stagey and unreal dialogue are in the main discarded. When the Lammles arrange a meeting between Fledgeby and Georgianna Podsnap, the melodramatic possibilities of the scene are completely covered by farce, since neither of the "lovers" has anything to say, and the Lammles must invent all the discourse. When Bella decides to leave the Boffins, her language reproduces the accents of reality rather than of the stage. Comparison of the dialogue in this novel with almost any used in *Nicholas Nickleby* at climactic moments will illustrate this judgment.

One must admit that the complicated Harmon intrigue which allows the heir to seem dead although alive resembles the trappings of melodrama. Rogue Riderhood might have inhabited an early Dickens novel as he tries to collect the reward by accusing Gaffer of killing Harmon. Yet the contrasting study of Bradley Headstone is a psychological casebook example of a neurosis which had to end in an attempt at murder. The water front scenes are also authentic rather than distorted. The discovery of Gaffer's body is an exciting episode, and when Riderhood is rescued from drowning and brought back to life, one lives on the real Thames, not on a make-believe stage. The illusion of evil is never more horrible than when Headstone carries Riderhood with him into the slimy water, and both men drown. Those who live with filth should die in it, and the force of Dickens' thesis carries over from the page into life. The novel is fiction, but Dickens achieves the illusion of actuality in scene after scene. He is not depicting Hell in make-believe, but in real Victorian society.

Gothic or sensational atmosphere is adapted to the purposes of the tale. The dust heaps are unique in literature; they are not derived from Mrs. Radcliffe or Monk Lewis. Venus' shop is an eerie place, generating horror and disgust. Headstone's murder takes place with atmospheric overtones. The most forceful of all the settings is the Thames itself, under fog and mist, dead things floating on the tide, and the sinister boatmen picking their way through the gloom to find reward in the bloated, floating bodies they rob as they rescue. When Lightwood and Wrayburn go down with the Inspector and Riderhood to get Gaffer, they spend a chilling night trying to locate the man whose body is already floating with the slime. Dickens' experience with black horror stood him in good stead in this scene, but it is more than traditional technique. The shadowy and sinister castles of Mrs. Radcliffe are gone with the misty Thames, nor are there any references to heroines trapped in dark rooms awaiting mysterious visitors of evil intent during the night. If this is Gothic, it is good Gothic. We are never asked to look in on Lizzie Hexam's bedroom as Headstone climbs in a window to molest her. Nor are we asked to believe that she is miraculously saved in the nick of time. Headstone is a real devil, not a make-believe one wearing a stage costume.

Dickens gives his sentimental sympathy to several characters in the story. Lizzie Hexam is a heroine from the lowest classes, and she may claim some kinship with Little Nell and Little Dorrit. Like the other examples of a type that Dickens always loved and admired, she struggles to overcome her heredity and her environment, meaning to do what is right and hoping that sincere and honest virtue will carry her through. But Lizzie never weeps in the fashion of Florence Dombey. Dickens retains his excesses for Betty Higden; even when he says, "hearts may count in heaven as high as heads," his sentiment achieves restraint, if one remembers how he talked about the death of Little Nell. When her grandson Johnny dies, Dickens is outraged at society for letting such things happen. Sloppy is a briefly pictured Oliver Twist, brought up in the Poor House and eventually adopted by the Boffins. Whatever sentiment appears in these portrayals appears in

279

proportion to Dickens' own intense feelings, and in the light of his thesis his sentiment avoids maudlin excess. The only touches which seem doubtful concern his references to the "Boofer lady" and his delight in Bella's "inexhaustible baby."

All in all, it is the peculiar fitness of Dickens' symbolic imagery which raises *Our Mutual Friend* above the common effect of traditional fiction. Dust pile and sewage, economic misery and social standing based upon filth, stolid and stupid complacency with a world which permits all that is evil under heaven—truly Dickens' Inferno is a horrendous place. Furthermore, it exists among us who live, not as a punishment after death. Dickens retains his deepest scorn for a world which is satisfied to remain in its filth:

> My lords and gentlemen and honorable lords, when you in the course of your dust-shoveling and cinder-taking have piled up a mountain of pretentious failure, you must off with your honorable coats for the removal of it, and fall to the work with the power of all the queen's horses and all the queen's men, or it will come rushing down and bury us alive.[13]

It is the peculiar quality of what is now Dickens' cosmic pessimism that he could always urge the possibility of escape from conditions which induced it. The purpose of fiction is to teach a lesson—or so he had always believed. He had grown suspicious of schemes for easy improvement of the world, but he believed in the hope for release, for Heaven on earth. Even with his great disgust for Podsnappery, his intense hatred of false money values, his explosive excretion on Victorian society, he could hold up for praise and for happy rewards those characters who escape the slime and the dust in spirit. In such individuals lies our hope for the Kingdom of Heaven. In effect Dickens is saying, "If this be pessimism, make the most of it. There is no other way to improve the world." The best quotation in all the novels to illustrate this eternal hope comes from one of the Veneering table conversations:

> "There is not," said Mr. Podsnap, flushing angrily, "there is not a country in the world, sir, where so noble a provision is made for the poor as in this country."

The meek man was quite willing to concede that, but perhaps it rendered the matter even worse, as showing that there must be something appallingly wrong somewhere.

"Where?" said Mr. Podsnap.

The meek man hinted, Wouldn't it be well to try, very seriously, to find out where?

"Ah!" said Mr. Podsnap. "Easy to say somewhere; not so easy to say where! But I see what you are driving at. I knew it from the first. Centralization. No. Never with my consent. Not English."

An approving murmur arose from the heads of tribes; as saying, "There you have him! Hold him!"

He was not aware (the meek man submitted of himself) that he was driving at any ization. He had no favorite ization that he knew of. But he certainly was more staggered by these terrible occurrences than he was by names, of howsoever so many syllables. Might he ask, was dying of destitution and neglect necessarily English?

"You know what the population of London is, I suppose," said Mr. Podsnap.

The meek man supposed he did, but supposed that had absolutely nothing to do with it, if its laws were well administered.

"And you know; at least I hope you know," said Mr. Podsnap with severity, "that Providence has declared that you shall have the poor always with you?"

The meek man also hoped he knew that.

"I am glad to hear it," said Mr. Podsnap with a portentous air. "I am glad to hear it. It will render you cautious how you fly in the face of Providence."[14]

The meek man, otherwise unidentified, speaks for Dickens. Clearly Mr. Podsnap is willing to lay the blame for everything that is wrong with our world on Providence. Dickens felt that God must be disgusted with our world, that He is not dictating its sufferings. Surely too, God must be punishing us for our false dependence on Providence by what He has allowed our world to become. But God leaves destiny and escape to man. Dickens does not depend upon any particular panacea or ization or "ism" to bring things right. The regeneration of man is a personal, an individual responsibility. Otherwise we shall stay in Hell under whatever system of government we favor.

Our Mutual Friend has had an unusual history. It is generally considered to be a novel which illustrates much of Dickens' genius, but in meager proportions. The old inspiration is supposed to lag in it, even though it shows flashes of his greatness. No novel he wrote has been more underestimated; it ranks along with *Bleak House* and *Little Dorrit* as a masterpiece. The symbolic theme is even more forceful than the prison imagery which shines through his other great book. It is only in recent years that readers have begun to see its exceptional worth. Edmund Wilson, Jack Lindsay, and Edgar Johnson have praised it highly, and the general understanding of its significance has begun to find expression.[15] It was Dickens' final attack on Victorian society, and in it he reached a savage intensity which previous novelists had never touched. As he wove all his plots, all his characters, and all his technical resources around his theme, he raised his gigantic dust heap and probed his slimy sewage to a reflection of infernal tragedy. Fiction and sublime artistry coincide in *Our Mutual Friend*.

CHAPTER XIV

Dead or Alive?

HEN A novelist dies and leaves a book unfinished, his admirers feel a natural curiosity about how the work might have developed if it had been completed. When the novel contains a mystery, speculation is increased a thousandfold, especially when there is no completely convincing evidence of the author's intentions. *The Mystery of Edwin Drood* presents the most challenging example of this situation in literary history, for Dickens wrote exactly half of his novel, died suddenly, and left the story with its important complications unresolved. Hearsay provides some aid as to his intentions, but the mystery is real. Because the novelist was Dickens, and because the situation in the story presents several alternate possibilities, *Edwin Drood* may be called the world's greatest mystery story. The fact that it can never be solved to every reader's satisfaction adds an extra fascination for mystery and detective story fanatics.

Any novel Dickens might have written after *Our Mutual Friend* was likely to illustrate some reaction from the measured disgust he had poured into his final attack on Victorian society. After *Little Dorrit* he had turned to the historical challenge of *A Tale of Two Cities* and had written a different kind of novel. Dickens' shift to the fabrication of a complex mystery was caused partially by the sudden interest of the reading public in such tales in the late 1860's. Detective stories derive historically from the Gothic tradition, with horror as the original basic ingredient. Edgar Allan Poe had bridged the narrative gap between horror and detection with his *Murders in the Rue Morgue, The Purloined Letter,* and *The Mystery of Marie Roget,* short stories which introduced the deductive exploits of Dupin, the first real detective in fiction (1841). Although no one imitated Dupin for a number of years, interest in crime as subject matter for fiction grew. Then Wilkie Collins used several of the Poe tales as sources for short stories in the 1850's. Dickens had explored the East End of London with Police Inspector Field in 1850 in order to get material for some articles in *Household Words*. He had used his information to create Inspector Bucket for *Bleak House* and to show this police officer solving the murder of Tulkinghorn. This is the first important appearance of a detective in British fiction, although the mystery is not presented in the Sherlock Holmes manner, all clues being given to the reader who is challenged to match wits with the detective and the author in solving the crime.

Inspector Bucket was only one of several characterizations interesting to Dickens as furnishing subject matter for his multiple-plot scheme; the Inspector does not represent the beginning of a detective-story trend or emphasis in his narrative art. Like Balzac and Sue, Dickens found that crime occasionally afforded good material for entertaining storytelling. His first experiment with a mysterious killing had been in *Barnaby Rudge,* in which a supposedly dead murderer turns up alive. There is another mystery in *Martin Chuzzlewit,* in which novel Jonas thinks he killed his old father. The later novels of Dickens furnish the solution of a robbery in *Hard Times* and of a murder in *Our Mutual Friend.* In the latter novel another detective, Mr. Inspector, helps discover the criminal. In the 1860's other writers besides Dickens experimented with crime-and-punishment fiction. Drama also provided one interesting example, for Tom Taylor wrote a play called *The Ticket-of-Leave Man* (1863), introducing the detective Hawkshaw, who preceded Sherlock Holmes in the public consciousness as England's traditional literary detective. But before 1866, the appearance of a detective to solve the crime was generally coincidental, not a vital narrative ingredient. In that year Gaboriau published the first full-length detective novel.

The father of the modern detective-mystery novel is thus French rather than English. Gaboriau published four such novels before the publication of *Edwin Drood,* and he antedates Collins slightly. In *L'Affaire Lerouge* (1866), *Le Dossier 113* (1867), *Le Crime d'Orcival* (1868), and *Monsieur Lecoq* (1869), he created a type of tale which presented a crime, its solution by a detective, a suspect entangled in a web of circumstantial evidence, suspicion running on a false trail, and baffling disguise on the part of the detective. Collins wrote a great mystery story in *The Woman in White* (1860), but the only one of his novels which exactly fits the Gaboriau and *Edwin Drood* type is *The Moonstone,* which appeared in *All the Year Round* in 1868, just about a year before Dickens started on *Edwin Drood.* There is no detective in *The Woman in White,* but Sergeant Cuff appears in *The Moonstone,* and Datchery (in disguise) comes into *Edwin Drood* to help solve the crime.

Dickens' first inspiration for his new novel does not seem to have involved a detective or even a crime. It concerned the situation which confronted Edwin and Rosa. He wrote to Forster:

> What should you think of the idea of a story beginning in this way?— Two people, boy and girl, or very young, going apart from one another, pledged to be married after many years—at the end of the book. The interest to arise out of the tracing of their separate ways, and the impossibility of telling what will be done with that impending fate.[1]

This was in July, 1869. In August he wrote again:

> I laid aside the fancy I told you of, and have a very curious and new idea for my new story. Not a communicable idea (or the interest of the book would be gone), but a very strong one, though difficult to work.[2]

Since so many readers have made guesses and deductions concerning Dickens' intentions in *Edwin Drood,* it is necessary to be extremely careful in drawing any conclusions which are not based directly upon evidence. Several things are, however, beyond disagreement. First, Dickens planned a short novel—not to be issued in weekly installments, but limited to twelve instead of twenty monthly numbers. With the shortened scope of his proposed book, he decided to limit himself to the development of one plot rather than to create several sequences of action revolving around a central purpose and a symbolic theme. There is only one plot in *Edwin Drood,* and it is the basic one he suggested to Forster. Second, as Dickens developed his story, one can set some limitations to the "curious and new idea" he says he had, but which he did not communicate.

285

The plot he devised began with the boy, Edwin, and the girl, Rosa, who are promised to each other by their parents—parents who are dead. Edwin Drood is then given an uncle, John Jasper, not much older than himself, and Jasper becomes the central figure in the novel. Jasper is a choir director in the cathedral at Cloisterham (obviously based on Rochester), is addicted to opium smoking, has a split personality, loves Rosa with a neurotic fixation, and is tempted to murder his nephew and ward in order to clear the way to the girl for himself. Rosa is afraid of Jasper, who seems to exert a kind of hypnotic power over her at times. Dickens works out the relations of Edwin and Rosa so that they eventually decide to be "brother and sister" rather than to marry each other. But Jasper does not find this out until after Edwin disappears on Christmas Eve.

The mystery centers on what happened to Edwin. Jasper certainly intends to kill him, and it is also indicated that afterwards he has a guilty conscience.[3] From the evidence presented in the novel as far as Dickens went, the following facts emerge: Jasper frequents an opium den run by a character called the Princess Puffer, talks of his plans in his opium dreams, and rouses her suspicions so that she follows him on two occasions to find out where he lives. The simplest reason for her following him is that she intends to blackmail him. Jasper also lays the ground for the implication of someone else when Drood disappears, so that Neville Landless will be suspected of killing him.

Neville and Helena Landless, twins, come to England from Ceylon as orphans. Both arrive in Cloisterham, Neville to study with Canon Crisparkle and Helena to be educated at Miss Twinkleton's school for girls, where Rosa also is. Neville likes Rosa at first sight and resents Edwin Drood's cavalier treatment of her. Neville and Edwin quarrel, since Neville is hotheaded and impulsive. Jasper drugs their drinks so that their quarrel becomes more violent on the first occasion they meet. Jasper records his fears of Neville in his diary, tells Crisparkle of his concern, and puts suspicion of Neville in everyone's mind. As Crisparkle tries to aid Neville to control his temper, he arranges that Neville and Edwin apologize to each other, and Jasper asks them both to dinner on Christmas Eve in order to resolve their quarrel. It is from this dinner that Edwin disappears, although Neville says he left Edwin at the door around midnight, and Jasper says Edwin never came home from the walk he took with Neville.

Neville starts on a vacation the next morning and is caught and brought back after a fight with his pursuers which leaves blood on him and his walking stick. Since Edwin's body is never discovered, Neville is eventually released, but he is forced to leave Cloisterham and go to London to study. He remains under a cloud of suspicion, and Dickens leaps forward six months in the novel to show him hoping to clear himself eventually. Helena is presented as a stronger, more dependable person than her brother. She sees through Jasper from the beginning, becomes very friendly with Rosa, and spends the time from Christmas to June at Miss Twinkleton's school. She then goes to London to live near her brother.

Jasper's behavior in preparing for the crime also seems pretty clear. He explores the old cathedral from burial vaults to tower in the company of the custodian Durdles, an elderly drunkard who knows every tomb and the location of all the bones. On one of their excursions Jasper drugs Durdles by tampering with his jug, and there is some hocus-pocus with the keys Durdles carries. Jasper apparently secures a duplicate of the key he wants, and since Edwin disappears, the assumption of all readers is that Jasper intended to put Edwin's body in one of the tombs, probably Mrs. Sapsea's. Mrs. Sapsea was the wife of the auctioneer-mayor, a pompous ass who furnishes comic relief in the tale. Durdles also calls attention to a limekiln in the yard, and every reader knows that lime will destroy a dead body very rapidly.

An additional complication throws light on what may have happened. A lawyer, Mr. Grewgious, is Rosa's guardian. He had once loved her mother, and her mother's ring was left him for Edwin to use as an engagement ring, providing Rosa and Edwin went through with their marriage. Their inheritances do not depend upon their marrying, so that Edwin and Rosa do not lose anything material by their decision not to follow their parents' desires. But before the actual decision is made, just before Christmas, Mr. Grewgious gives Edwin the ring. Our attention is called to the fact that Edwin also owns and wears a gold watch and tiepin. After his disappearance, the watch and tiepin are discovered in the weir by Crisparkle, who is mysteriously drawn to the exact place apparently at the hypnotic suggestion of Jasper. But the ring never shows up. Since Jasper does not know of its existence, one is justified in thinking that it will eventually serve some purpose in clearing up the mystery. For example, if the body is discovered, but almost completely destroyed by lime, the ring will identify the body. In fact, Forster says this was to happen.

In the last chapters of the written part of the novel, a disguised person who calls himself Datchery arrives in Cloisterham and devotes himself to investigating the murder or disappearance, although he does not explain to the townspeople what he is doing. He watches Jasper constantly and makes the acquaintance of Deputy, the urchin who is paid by Durdles to throw stones at him to get him home when he is stupefied by drink. Deputy may have seen Jasper do something suspicious, and Datchery will probably acquire some information from him—or so one supposes. But better evidence is on the point of being discovered when Datchery meets the Princess Puffer as she follows Jasper from one of his opium sprees at her dive. Datchery keeps the score of his progress with chalk on his closet door, and from the marks the reader can tell that he is getting somewhere in working up a case against Jasper. To all intents and purposes Datchery is a detective.

Now this is the main action which is disclosed by the first half of the novel. What does Dickens mean by saying that he had a "curious and new idea" for the story? Jasper is not mentioned in his first letter to Forster, and the new idea certainly concerns Jasper. Part of it must have been that Jasper would murder or intend to murder Edwin. Further, this idea might have included the part to be played by the lime, the ring, the opium, or something else not revealed in the sections which were written by the time Dickens died.

The key to any explanation of the mystery must take Collins into account. The relationship between Dickens and Collins had been close, but there are signs that Dickens would balk at being surpassed by his friend. He was pleased when *The Woman in White* boosted the sales of *All the Year Round,* but when it sold more copies than *A Tale of Two Cities,* he was startled. The critical reception of *The Moonstone* also must have galled him a little. The only way to interpret this reaction is to say that Dickens thought of Collins as the writer he had helped along the road to fame, but whose accomplishment ought never to equal or surpass that of his master. In a letter to Wills he allows some of this feeling to come to light when he says of *The Moonstone,* "The construction is wearisome beyond endurance."[4]

How much Dickens and Collins discussed plots and ideas for stories is arguable. During the fifties, especially when Collins was on the staff of *Household Words,* they must have talked over many possible subjects for tales. Collins' library included at his death many books of criminal trials, celebrated cases from French records, and all the novels of Gaboriau.[5] In the early days he had reworked or borrowed a number of short stories from Edgar Allan Poe.[6] One cannot help wondering whether Collins at some time or other did not mention some case or plot situation which inspired whatever Dickens was intending to do in *Edwin Drood.* Only two years before the death of Dickens the two had been alternating in writing *No Thoroughfare* together. It would have been most natural for Collins to have finished *Edwin Drood.* There were rumors after Dickens died that Collins would complete the unfinished mystery, but his publishers issued public statements denying this rumor. What seems to have happened is that Collins wrote a story of his own, starting fresh from another source entirely, but using exactly the same ingredients as Dickens. This long tale or novelette was published in America late in 1873, and is entitled *The Dead Alive, or John Jago's Ghost.* The resemblances of this story to *Edwin Drood* are so remarkable that one must conclude that they either represent what Collins thought Dickens' intentions were, or else they may be studied as evidence that this is the way Collins would have finished *Edwin Drood* if he had been writing it.[7]

The Dead Alive was ostensibly inspired by one of America's famous criminal cases, the Boorn Trial, which had occurred in 1819. As it actually happened, a certain Russel Colvin had disappeared. He had been married to the sister of the two Boorn brothers, and since there had been quarrels, the townspeople in Vermont had gossiped about his disappearance. An uncle of the brothers eventually told of having dreams in which Colvin appeared to him and led him to where his body was buried. Then a dog dug up some bones on the farm. The bones turned out to be animal bones, but in the meantime the brothers were arrested. The police examined the remains of a cellar under a burned barn and found buttons and a penknife belonging to Colvin. There was no clear evidence of murder, only suspicion, when one of the brothers suddenly accused the other of killing Colvin. After recrimination and contradiction, one brother confessed, and both were sentenced to hang. The surprising conclusion was the discovery of Colvin—alive—in New Jersey. He was trying to get away from his wife; he seems to have had no intention of helping her brothers escape hanging, but the undeniable fact of his existence freed them.

As Collins reworks this tale he makes some interesting changes which compare with the situation Dickens had stressed in *Edwin Drood*. He presents two brothers, Ambrose and Silas Meadowcroft, who attempt to kill John Jago. When Jago disappears and they are under suspicion of murder, Silas accuses Ambrose of destroying the body in a limekiln. Investigation discloses remnants of bones and some metal buttons identified as belonging to the dead man's coat. The brothers confess the crime in separate statements. Jago had loved a girl coveted by the brothers (in the source he had been married to their sister), and this rivalry had precipitated the quarrel. Jago comes back voluntarily in Collins' tale, partially in the hope that Naomi will marry him as a reward for his gesture. His story is that he had been kept captive by the brothers, and since they had really intended to kill him, each thinks the other actually committed the crime. He escaped his bonds, put animal bones and his coat in the limekiln (where his body was supposed to go), then left the country in terror to save himself further trouble from the Meadowcrofts. He loses the girl anyway.[8]

The resemblances of *The Dead Alive* to *Edwin Drood* seem a little too close to be accidental, considering the close relationship between their authors. One can say that Collins derived his individual touches—the ones which compare with *Drood* rather than with his source—from Dickens, rather than the opposite. But if one substitutes Jasper for the two brothers, Drood for Jago, Rosa for Naomi, changes the relationships around to fit Dickens' idea concerning two young people who had been destined to marry each other by their parents, sets the whole story in Cloisterham, pretends to put a body in a limekiln, has the villain confess to a murder he thought he committed, then one has a story like that which Dickens wrote. Collins' tale supposes that the Meadowcroft brothers did not know their victim escaped, and each thought the other did the actual killing. How could a single murderer think he had committed his crime, confess his deed, and still be innocent of it? This is indeed a complication which would be, in Dickens' words, "difficult to work."

As the story of Drood stands, half-finished, there is only one way out, if Edwin really escaped. In *The Moonstone* the hero steals a famous gem while under the influence of opium, and is completely unaware that he had done so. It is this circumstance which creates the mystery and fools the reader. Both Collins and Dickens were using opium or laudanum in the 1860's, although Dickens' addiction was minor, resembling the use of tranquilizers in our time. Both men were naturally curious about the possible effects of laudanum, and Collins was sure that under its influence a man might do things he could not remember. He exploited this opinion in *The Moonstone*.

Dickens explains his idea of the subconscious in a passage in *Edwin Drood* as he describes Miss Twinkleton:

> As, in some cases of drunkenness, and in others of animal magnetism, there are two states of consciousness which never clash, but each of which pursues its separate course as though it were continuous instead of broken (thus if I hide my watch when I am drunk, I must be drunk again before I remember where), so Miss Twinkleton has two distinct and separate phases of being.[9]

It is no great step from this assumption concerning schizophrenia to suppose that a man could imagine he committed murder—or could actually do so—but could not remember the exact circumstances unless he was drunk on opium again. If he intended to commit the murder, if bones were in the lime and evidence in the tomb, he would naturally suppose that he had done what he intended to do, even though his memory of his exact behavior is in a separate state of consciousness. If Jasper actually committed the crime, why did Dickens invent all this business about the subconscious and dress it up with the opium dreams?

If one accepts the reasonable assumption that Dickens decided to write a detective story which would emulate or surpass those of Collins and probably of Gaboriau, and that he mixed his original plot idea of two young people destined by their parents to marry with his "curious and new idea" of a murder that was supposed to be committed, several conclusions emerge. Gaboriau had evolved a pattern for such stories, and this pattern always presented a crime, a suspect who is apparently guilty, caught in a situation in which circumstantial evidence points to him as the criminal, and finally a detective who disguises himself and eventually discovers the truth, which is suddenly and surprisingly revealed at the end. It would seem clear that Dickens' invention of a disguised detective in Datchery has to derive from the model of Gaboriau, so that the rest of Gaboriau's formula might also reasonably be cited. Collins in *The Moonstone* had presented a puzzle in which suspicion shifts from one person to another. The story ends with a surprising solution by which the least likely person is discovered to be unconsciously guilty. Dickens in *Great Expectations* and *Our Mutual Friend* had built sequences through which the reader is brought to expect a certain conclusion, then the author substituted an unexpected ending. It can be argued that he was following the technique of suspense instead of surprise, as he had done with the Harmon-Rokesmith mystery in *Our Mutual Friend*. But there is no *mystery* unless Dickens leads the reader to believe that Jasper murdered Edwin, then fools everyone by showing that Jasper only thought he did, and because of an opium haze was under the illusion that he was a murderer as he intended to be.

Dickens would have to imagine some scene in which Edwin was drugged, but regained consciousness. His return to consciousness would take place while Jasper had either left him or had gone into some form of trance. If Edwin were to act as John Jago in Collins' story, he would become conscious, be horribly shocked at discovering what his uncle was trying to do, would put bones (there were plenty of bones around in the vault), his coat (and the ring, either purposely or accidentally) in the tomb with the lime, then disappear. Edwin intends to go to Egypt as an engineer. His state of mind can easily be imagined. He and Rosa have decided not to marry; there is nothing to hold him in England; perhaps he believes he could not prove that Jasper tried to murder him; perhaps he does not wish to bring such an accusation; he would be terrified at finding out the real character of his uncle who might try again to murder him if he escapes; the easiest thing to do in his shocked condition might be to counterfeit the success of Jasper's intention and disappear.

If Edwin is really murdered and Neville Landless is to be framed for the crime, why does the body have to be put in a limekiln and destroyed? Why all the business of opium and the disappearing body if no surprising and unexpected climax is to develop? The ordinary story of a murderer whose conviction is drawn out through a number of installments is exceedingly simple in comparison with the practice of Gaboriau and Collins. It is too simple if Dickens was trying to equal and surpass Collins, and who, reading the record of the relationship between the two men, can doubt that Dickens would not attempt to outdo his friend in his friend's own field?

Everyone who reads *Edwin Drood* has his own favorite explanation. Whether or not one accepts the contention presented here is of little moment. My experiences in observing Dickens' reworking of his sources plus the astonishing resemblances of Collins' *The Dead Alive* to *Edwin Drood* make the conclusion stated above appear the most likely to me. But Dickens added an unintentional touch to his practice of leading the reader to believe one thing before he disclosed another solution: He died before he got to the surprise, and he never told anyone what his ending was to be. In fact, one must assume that he deliberately misled his family and friends. Normally, he discussed his plots with Forster, but their close collaboration and discussion grew less about the time of *A Tale of Two Cities*. The extant letters about *Edwin Drood* (those cited) are very vague. He must have told something to Forster, for the biographer says (with his usual omniscience, real or assumed) that he knows the conclusion. Forster would *have* to insist that he knew how the book was to end. He says that the originality of the plot:

> . . . was to consist in the review of the murderer's career by himself at the close, when its temptations were to be dwelt upon as if, not he the culprit, but some other man, were the tempted. The last chapters were to be written in the condemned cell, to which his wickedness, all elaborately elicited from him as if told of another, had brought him. Discovery by the murderer of the utter uselessness of the murder for its object, was to follow hard upon the commission of the deed; but all discovery of the murderer was to be baffled till towards the close, when, by means of a gold ring which had resisted the corrosive effects

of the lime into which he had thrown the body, not only the person murdered was to be identified but the locality of the crime and the man who committed it.[10]

This evidence presents another problem which we must delay discussing, but it is obvious that Dickens could have told Forster this solution, even though he intended to surprise his friend and his public with an ending which showed Jasper had not really committed the crime he thought he had. There is still more hearsay evidence that Jasper was really a murderer. The immediate family have little to say about it, but what they do tell indicates that they all thought that Jasper murdered Drood. Sir Luke Fildes, whose drawings accompanied the six printed issues of the novel, states positively that Dickens told him to draw a large, loose, black scarf for Jasper, because Jasper was going to use it to strangle Drood. The scarf is mentioned in the story, of course. Fildes also says that Dickens told him that one illustration was to show a condemned cell.[11]

In contradiction to this evidence we know that Dickens considered several titles for his novel before deciding on "The Mystery of Edwin Drood." These include: "The Loss of Edwin Drood," "Edwin Drood in Hiding," "The Disappearance of Edwin Drood," and "Dead or Alive?" These titles could be construed as being based on the intention of Dickens to keep his readers in suspense about a murder that had actually been committed, the point of suspense depending on the fact that no body would be discovered until the climax. But they would seem to imply that Drood was not dead.

One must also consider the cover drawn by Charles Collins for the monthly issues of the novel. Charles—Wilkie's undependable artist brother and Dickens' son-in-law—was first supposed to do all the drawings, but apparently had trouble meeting deadlines. His cover pictures several scenes. The unimportant ones show Edwin walking with Rosa, Jasper in robes marching with the choir, a woman (perhaps an allegorical figure) looking at a placard which reads "Lost," the Princess Puffer holding a smoking pipe, a Chinese smoking a pipe, and a scene in a garden where a young man is kissing Rosa's hand. Two additional scenes are more important. One of them shows three men climbing steps (which must be in the cathedral) to a tower. They are in a hurry and are in search of something or are chasing someone.

One of them is pointing upwards. The second picture shows a man, apparently Jasper, holding a lantern high to confront a young man wearing a soft hat and a coat buttoned to his chin. Jasper has one hand on the knob or lock of an opened door. Both of these last pictured scenes, plus the one in which the young man is kissing Rosa's hand, concern incidents not in the finished section of the novel. They can be most logically interpreted as showing the incidents in which Jasper is exposed and pursued before being caught. The confrontation scene must supply someone who is in the tomb when Jasper opens it—for some reason or other—either Drood himself or someone like Helena Landless masquerading as Drood, as part of a device to surprise Jasper and make him confess because he sees a ghost.

Any solution to the mystery must take into account the black scarf, the scene in which Jasper with a lantern is confronted by some unexpected person in a room where he has just unlocked a door (this must be the tomb with the lime), and the chase up the stairs of the cathedral (after Jasper?). In addition, the ending must include Jasper's confession in the condemned cell, so that he must be charged with murder. These necessities surely derive from the evidence. Further, the solution ought to disclose the identity of the disguised detective, Datchery. There is no evidence for this last mystery except what one can guess from the finished part of the novel. Forster did not know or claim to know, and no one else says that Dickens told him who Datchery is.

The candidates for the detective mentioned by Dickens interpreters are Grewgious, his clerk Bazzard, Edwin Drood himself, Helena Landless, or someone not yet mentioned in the tale. The requirements for identification include some special reason for wanting to expose Jasper. Grewgious, the lawyer who loved Rosa's mother and feels a fatherly interest in the young girl, fulfills the main requirement. Besides he has been shown just after Christmas telling Jasper that Edwin and Rosa had decided not to get married. We have seen him looking with an expression of grave suspicion on Jasper's fit of emotion as he hears this news. One has to suppose, if Datchery is Grewgious, that his disguise is complete, since Jasper knows the lawyer. Besides, in the chronology of the story as it is printed, Grewgious is in London when Datchery seems to be in Cloisterham. Several critics have urged arguments to overcome these difficulties, and one must conclude that Datchery could be Grewgious.[12]

An ardent Dickensian, J. Cumings Walters, reasons that Datchery is Helena Landless, and his case has convinced a critic of the stature of Edmund Wilson, plus many other readers.[13] One suspects that there is some purpose connected with the plot for Helena and Neville to be twins. She looks like a man, her speaking voice is low, and early in the story we are told that she has masqueraded as a male in the past. She would want to expose Jasper in order to clear her brother. Since Datchery does not appear in Cloisterham until the school term at Miss Twinkleton's is over, and Helena is then supposed to be in London, this circumstance can be turned to account in explaining why six months elapse before the detective appears on the scene. The arguments against this identification rest on the perfectly normal feeling of many readers that no woman could masquerade so convincingly, especially since Datchery gives the impression of some bulk and of middle age. In addition, Helena is in London when Rosa gets there, fleeing from the attentions of Jasper. It is true that she does not see Rosa till the morning after the younger girl gets to Mr. Grewgious' apartment, and she could have been sent for. Other reasons may occur to the reader who likes this solution, but most of us will continue to believe that Dickens would never ask the reader to accept such an impersonation, on the grounds that in real life somebody would recognize her either as herself or as a woman. Dickens, not long before, had written to Wills about the manuscript of *The Moonstone,* saying:

> It is a very curious story—wild, and yet domestic—with excellent characters in it, great mystery, and nothing belonging to disguised women or the like.[14]

There are too many difficulties in the theory that Datchery might be Drood himself. One must suppose that he had suffered from some form of amnesia to justify his coming back to check up on Jasper; his disguise would have to be extraordinary to fool everyone who had previously known him. The simplest identification is Bazzard, Grewgious' clerk. If Datchery is Bazzard, he would have the same general reasons as his employer for trying to discover the truth. From the little we know of him, as the story stands, he is an eccentric person who has written an unperformed play. Further, Grewgious tells Rosa when she gets to London that Bazzard is away without explaining where. Someone interested in the stage could easily manage the wig and simple make-up which distinguish what we are told of Datchery's face, and no one in Cloisterham knows Bazzard. Perhaps such an identification does not seem so exciting or enticing as one of the others that have been suggested, but it could most easily be the answer. Surely no specific identification can be proved to everyone's satisfaction.

Coincidentally, it is of interest to note that Jack Lindsay has probably found the reason why Dickens chose the name of Datchery.[15] Lady Lytton wrote a novel known to Dickens and entitled *Cheveley,* which was published in 1839. In it an old man and the heroine named Mary are arrested and put on trial, then are suddenly vindicated in court by the arrival of a character called Datchet, who brings in evidence enough to convict the real villain and exonerate the innocent. Dickens' choice of names for his characters often indicates his unconscious reminiscence of a similar person from a novel he had read or a play he had seen. Unfortunately, *Cheveley* does not throw any light on the real mystery of *Edwin Drood.*

An extraordinary amount of speculation about this mystery has been printed. One of the most illuminating articles was written by Aubrey Boyd.[16] In it he sums up the case for explaining Jasper's powers as a hypnotist. In the sections finished by Dickens there are a number of incidents which cannot be understood unless one supposes that Jasper is practicing some variety of mesmerism or "animal magnetism," as hypnotism was then called. The main scenes include the one in which Jasper is accompanying Rosa at the piano, and she struggles under some spell as she tries to sing. She later is frightened by hearing the sound of the organ as Jasper plays, and she tells Helena that Jasper can reach her through a wall. In the scene in which Jasper declares his love to her, she is thoroughly terrified and tries several times to get away from him, but is detained against her will. Jasper exerts this power on other people, too, since he silently urges Edwin and Neville on to quarrel when they are in his rooms. After

Edwin disappears, Crisparkle leaves Jasper and goes—without knowing why—to the weir where he finds Edwin's watch and stickpin.

Students of Dickens' biography will remember that he experimented with hypnotism himself. On his first trip to America he succeeded in hypnotizing his wife several times. On later occasions he tried his powers on friends to relieve pain or some illness. This worked on John Leech, and a certain lady he met in Genoa in 1844 had delusions and strange dreams which he was able to banish or control by continued and repeated experiments with what he called mesmerism. Dickens surely intended to use mesmerism or hypnotism in the uncompleted sections of his novel. There are several possibilities, the most obvious of which involves Jasper's designs on Rosa. Jasper must have thought that he could eventually cast a spell on her so that she would marry him whether she loved him or not. Helena Landless senses this power in Jasper and apparently has the capacity to destroy it or overcome it. In the singing scene Edwin Drood talks to Helena:

> "Pussy's not used to an audience; that's the fact," said Edwin Drood. "She got nervous, and couldn't hold out. Besides Jack, you are such a conscientious master, and require so much, that I believe you make her afraid of you. No wonder."
>
> "No wonder," repeated Helena.
>
> "There, Jack, you hear! You would be afraid of him under similar circumstances, wouldn't you, Miss Landless?"
>
> "Not under any circumstances," returned Helena.[17]

Later when Rosa tells Helena how she feels about Jasper and how frightened she is, Dickens includes one of his foreshadowing commentaries which is aimed partly at the reader and partly at some future action in the novel:

> The lustrous gypsy-face drooped over the clinging arms and bosom, and the wild black hair fell down protectingly over the childish form. There was a slumbering gleam of fire in the intense dark eyes, though they were then softened with compassion and admiration. Let whomever it most concerned look well to it![18]

It is Boyd's contention that Helena will hypnotize Jasper in the condemned cell—in the ending described by Forster—so that he will enter his separate state of being and tell "as if told by another" what he himself tried to do to Edwin Drood. The only other possibility which is suggested by the written parts of the tale is that Jasper will finally gain access to Rosa, even though she has fled to London to escape him, that he will try to exert the full power of his intended spell—something he has experimented with up to now—and that Helena will defend Rosa and rescue her by exerting her own powers against him, eventually freeing Rosa from the influence which is "malicious." The evidence for one or both of these scenes is strong.

Another remarkable article about *Edwin Drood* concerns the black scarf worn by Jasper, which Fildes reports Dickens to have said will strangle Drood. Howard Duffield, in "John Jasper, Strangler,"[19] builds an extraordinarily interesting case for believing that Jasper belongs to the Indian sect of Thugs, or had done so before he came to England. At first glance, this theory sounds as wild as anything which could be suggested. But there are a remarkable number of facts to support the theory—so many that they cannot be completely coincidental. The novel contains many references to the Orient, and this is unique in Dickens' novels. The Landlesses come from Ceylon. Many readers, trying to examine every possible clue to the mystery, have considered this fact and wondered what can possibly be deduced from it. What is the nationality of the Princess Puffer? Chinese smoke pipes in her den, and lascars frequent it. Jasper dreams of elephants, sultans, and dancing girls when he is under the influence of opium. Edwin Drood, in his first meeting with Neville Landless, insults him with a reference to his background:

> "You may know a black common fellow, or a black common boaster, when you see him (and no doubt you have a large acquaintance that way), but you are no judge of white men."[20]

Jasper has "thick, lustrous, well-arranged black hair and whiskers"; his voice is described as "womanish"; his background is never explained, where he came from, why he contracted the habit of smoking opium, why he is schizophrenic. The Thugs were believers in Kali, a Hindu goddess of destruction, and their ritual murders followed a prescribed formula. If Jasper is a Thug, he obeys this formula to the last minute detail. Each murder was supposed to be committed by means of a fold of black cloth which was a fragment of the goddess' gown—at least symbolically understood to be so. This cloth had to be worn; Jasper wears his black scarf. A secret burial place was to be selected beforehand; Jasper selects Mrs. Sapsea's tomb in his tour of the cathedral with Durdles. A certain number of omens have to be fulfilled, and the call of a rook is always interpreted as a favorable sign for the murder; the rooks which hover over Cloisterham are part of Dickens' description when Jasper looks over the ground. A number of minor points also fit exactly. Thugs murdered travelers; Edwin Drood is preparing to go on a journey to Egypt. Jasper, in his second dream under the influence of opium talks of his proposed murder, and his vision is entirely in terms of a journey and someone who travels with him. The Thug is exceedingly kind to his victim, often using exaggerated terms of endearment—as Jasper does to Edwin.

The exact process of the actual murder is also followed in the case of Edwin. The Thug invites his victim to his own home, gives him a drug in his food or drink, persuades him to leave a little after midnight, then strangles him outside the house, depositing the body in the prepared hiding place. There is a Thug superstition that the man to be murdered must have no gold in his possession, otherwise disaster to the plan will result. Edwin carries the gold ring he was to have used for an engagement ring; his other jewelry is evidently taken from him, since Crisparkle finds it in the weir. Forster says that the ring was to be discovered later in the quicklime with the bones. By missing the ring, Jasper slips up in following the ritual.

Several questions follow. Did Dickens know about the Thug practices and ritual? If he did, how was he going to bring about this revelation in the story, that is, if one is convinced that he planned to utilize this strange history for Jasper's attempt at murder? Dickens knew Eugene Sue's *The Wandering Jew,* in which there is a Thug strangler who could have supplied everything necessary for the Jasper-Drood crime. Collins had introduced into *The Moonstone* a band of Hindu fanatics who commit a secret murder in trying to retrieve the Moonstone. Dickens therefore had access to the proper information, and Collins had already used somewhat similar material in the novel Dickens was trying to surpass.

How were all these facts to be revealed? Since Datchery's part in the novel is to expose Jasper, he would have to discover *something.* As the novel breaks off, he has just encountered the Princess Puffer and hired Deputy to follow her so he can find her again. If Jasper has babbled enough in his opium dreams, Datchery may be able to get sufficient information from the old hag to put him on the right track. The Landlesses ought to know about Thugs—perhaps that is the point of their having come from Ceylon—and they can fill in whatever gaps the Princess Puffer leaves.

If one accepts for the moment all the contentions that have been advanced, how would the plot development have been arranged? This solution includes Drood alive, Jasper's thinking he is a murderer, Bazzard as Datchery, the hypnotism and Thug suggestions. Suppose that Datchery has dug up the facts about Thuggery and Jasper's intentions; what proof of crime could be produced which would stand up in a court of law? Dickens planned to have Jasper confess, so something was to spur him to confessing. There is some indication in the novel that it will reach its conclusion on the anniversary of Edwin's disappearance, on the next Christmas Eve. Suppose that Grewgious, who has put Datchery on to the case, plants in Jasper's mind the knowledge that Edwin had the telltale ring; suppose that Jasper goes back to the tomb to get it, realizing that it would give away the identity of the body he thinks is there; suppose that Edwin returns to England from Egypt and goes to Grewgious for advice; suppose that they arrange for Edwin to be in the tomb when Jasper goes there; or, alternately, someone like Helena masquerades as Edwin; suppose that the other interested parties are in hiding nearby, including Neville Landless, Crisparkle, and Lieutenant Tartar. This last character was apparently introduced to provide a love interest for Rosa. But he also swings about from window to window by way of vines and is extraordinarily active in climbing, his experience in the rigging of ships being responsible for his ability. How would Dickens use this?

The scene which follows these suggestions would explain the drawings made by Charles Collins for the monthly covers: Jasper opens the door of the tomb, and encounters the apparition of Edwin Drood alive; he flees madly up the stairs to the cathedral tower; Neville Landless follows him in the lead of the pursuit, reaches him and struggles with him, then is thrown off the tower to his death; Jasper climbs out on the roof or along the walls; Tartar swings after him and catches him, knocking him senseless. This would set up the later scene in prison

301

during which Helena Landless hypnotizes Jasper and he confesses to murdering Edwin.

The basic appeal of a novel of this type is in trying to outguess the novelist. Whatever the real solution, it would have to be complex to explain the opium, the schizophrenia, the scarf, the ring, the hypnotism scenes, the Collins cover, and the identity of Datchery. If the story was really to contain nothing but the murder of Drood by Jasper, it does not promise to outdo Collins in his *Moonstone,* much less Gaboriau. Nor does the scene suggested by Forster in the condemned cell supply enough of the sensational which one expects to find in a good mystery story or detective tale. It is true that such a solution might have been used by Dickens in the days of Jonas Chuzzlewit or Barnaby Rudge. The Thug material and the hypnotism episodes would certainly make the novel different. In whatever fashion Dickens intended to develop his conclusion, the best evidence is for a startling denouement and the sudden reappearance of the supposedly murdered man. John Jago and Collins argue for such a conclusion, too. Certain matters like the absolute identification of Datchery can never be solved.

How good is the book as it stands, and how might it have stood up as a novel in comparison with Dickens' other books? Well, the story is half of a good mystery story. It contains many of the traditional devices of Dickens and typical technical accomplishments. Edmund Wilson gives high praise to the analysis of the character of Jasper.[21] The description of Cloisterham is infinitely precise and photographic in detail. The wonderful atmospheric picture of the storm which shakes the cathedral town on Christmas Eve is as striking as any Gothic effect in Dickens' other novels. Everything about the old cathedral transcends the Gothic horror tradition, even as the novel makes use of practically every typical mannerism of the genre.

Dickens does not depart from his farce-caricature technique in the novel. Mr. Sapsea, the pompous mayor, and Mr. Honeythunder, the booming, boring philanthropist, are typical fools, supplied by their author with wonderful speech devices and mannerisms. Miss Twinkleton is an extremely funny school principal, and the scene in which she converses by way of Rosa with the landlady, who is known as the Billickin, is worthy of an earlier novel devoted to comedy for its own sake. Edwin's first meeting with Rosa reminds one of some of the scenes in David Copperfield's courtship of Dora, even though it results differently. Crisparkle is caricatured pleasantly—the second member of the clergy to emerge from a Dickens novel unscathed; the old Dean does not fare so well. Grewgious, Bazzard, Durdles, and several other characters are described and developed in the usual Dickensian manner, their best eccentricities carefully noted and their individual mannerisms providing incidental amusement. The unwritten ending probably would allow Rosa to marry Tartar, and Crisparkle ought to win Helena Landless.

There is probably no intense social, philosophical, or moral purpose in the novel, except that murder is not a good idea, and one should not smoke opium. Both Edgar Johnson and Edmund Wilson find deeper meanings, but no remarkable symbolic pattern distinguishes *Edwin Drood*. It is basically an extremely ingenious puzzle. One can only remark something about the ways of Providence: If any Dickens novel had to be stopped half-finished, is it not fortunate that this was the one?

CHAPTER XV

Fire from Flint

HE STATURE of Dickens the novelist is based upon a foundation of artistry and a structure of analysis which reaches great heights of creative invention. Study of his craftsmanship reveals how high he built and what he accomplished for later ages as well as his own. The ability to describe characters, events, and ideas so that they are fascinating in themselves is the main task of the novelist; the selection and arrangement of these materials is the special work of the artist; to symbolize simultaneously the deepest meanings of life is the particular accomplishment of genius. From the eternal flint comes the flame.

The view of Dickens as a master of caricature, farce, and gusto is an accurate one; he is lord of the creative world of comic eccentricity. The estimate of Dickens as a Romantic genius approaches the truth; he dipped deep from the wellsprings of inspiration and unfathomable invention. The notion of Dickens as a commercial author who depended upon sensation, sentiment, and melodrama to attract and satisfy a low public taste is no figment of the critical imagination; he wrote novels to sell. The judgment of Dickens as a humanitarian reformer and a proletarian liberal comes closest to essential analysis; he valued issues and ideals above all other narrative ends. The concept of Dickens as a psychological neurotic is a fascinating guess at the circumstances of catalysis; no author is completely normal in the sense of resembling everybody else. Each of these attitudes is a glimpse at truth. Historical criticism must take them all into account.

The fluctuations of Dickens' reputation as a great novelist depend upon partial vision, upon the phase of his artistry which has most impressed the critic and reader. Swinburne could refer to Little Nell as being "monstrous as a baby with two heads."[1] Oscar Wilde used to say that one must have a heart of stone to read the death of Little Nell—long dramatic pause—without laughing.[2] Henry Miller could dismiss Dickens' commercialism with a reference to "the harmless rose water vaporings of the back pages of Charles Dickens."[3] The hero of Evelyn Waugh's novel, *A Handful of Dust,* ends his days confined to the jungle so that he can read aloud the works of Dickens to his illiterate and half-mad patron.[4] James Joyce plays punfully upon the titles of Dickens' novels in *Finnegans Wake,* suggesting "the old cupiosity shape" and "dove-eyed covetfilles" to the linguistic imagination.[5] Graham Greene calls the mature style of Dickens "a secret prose which gives the sense of a mind speaking to itself with no one there to listen."[6] Will future ages interpret the secrets and amplify the sound?

The whole Dickens was the sum of his parts. From the study of his craftsmanship definite conclusions emerge. He is more than a buffoon of gusto, a creator of caricatured eccentrics, a well-meaning but Romantic humanitarian, a liberal believer in economic reform, a commercial dabbler in melodrama and sentiment. He is an artist who raised fiction to the concept of an art form. He developed from experimentation in contrasts to mastery of symbolic and panoramic fictional pattern. Those who praise or blame him for his melodrama, his sentimentality, his sensation for its own sake have distorted his accomplishment. Because he began writing with a fully developed gift of comedy he unintentionally misled even his most fanatical followers. Appreciation of his growth from casual and commercial optimism to a controlled pessimistic pattern suffered from the implications of his early success. Forster and Chesterton contributed materially to the illusion that his first novels were his best.

The growing awareness of Dickens' accomplishments in developing his artistry has also been obscured by the vogue of Henry James. The fact that the heritage of James contributed to many of the most remarkable accomplishments in modern fiction does not alter its effect on Dickens' artistic reputation. Exploration of the ways in which an author can center on one character and limit himself to one point of view was carried to vital and complete analysis in the work of James. One may or may not prefer his artistry to that of Dickens, but the scope of fiction is not limited to microscopic perfection. It also permits the panoramic pattern as an artistic end. It is this view of fiction which explains why Dostoevsky recommended the reading of Scott, Pushkin, Gogol, and Cervantes, and "all Dickens' works without exception."[7] It shows the reason for Tolstoi's admiration of the overall effect of Dickens' novels, which he calls a combination of subjective and objective treatment.[8] The large-scale picture of life coincides with the important aims of both these novelists.

Consider Dickens, for the moment, from the standpoint of Henry James, concentrating on point of view and narrative perspective. Dickens began by using the omniscient third person to narrate his action, describing his characters with heightened and caricatured details. He carried on his comic action by dialogue and filled the gaps between description with whatever action was necessary to get his characters to a farcical situation or into the next development of the episode. As he widened his purposes from humor to sensation and sentiment, he used the third person to describe more and more of the action, although he always relied basically upon reporting conversation to advance the movement of the story. Like an announcer who describes what he sees to an audience listening over a fictional radio, he reproduced the effect of theatrical action on a fictional stage.

He used the third person to create the background and atmosphere necessary to give the illusion of reality for his scenes. In this style he was meticulously accurate and detailed. Occasionally, as in the chapters which return to the third person from the first person narrative of *Bleak House,* he described this atmosphere with heightened intensity, creating an effect of immense importance. He also used the third person to explain the implication and meaning of his stories, a form of rhetorical comment which underlines the action. His interpretive commentary ran the scale from philosophical speculation to stylized exclamation. In only one novel, *A Tale of Two Cities,* did he attempt to develop his action without basic reference to dialogue.

He used the first person in three novels, through the entire course of *David Copperfield* and *Great Expectations,* and in half of *Bleak House,* in which he alternated the first and third persons. He achieved the effect of natural communication in the two novels in which his narrator is male, and even when he assumed the first-person-female point of view in *Bleak House,* his action gains a high degree of reality from its manner of telling. In general he was more sure of automatic narrative effectiveness in the first than in the third person, since the omniscient point of view presents the opportunity for more variables in purpose and more possibilities for slips in approach than does the first person. He could err when using the third person. Yet *Little Dorrit* and *Our Mutual Friend* are written in the third person.

The variables with which Dickens experimented in the third person include soliloquy. Sometimes soliloquy takes on the aims which later authors would call stream-of-consciousness, as in the long imaginary speech of Sidney Carton at the guillotine. Occasionally a character will express ideas which normally would be voiced by the author himself, and Dickens usually used this device for sarcastic or satiric purposes. The monologues of certain characters assume unconscious or psychologically revelatory properties. Flora Finching in *Little Dorrit* is such a character, and all the persons who gabble for humorous reasons reveal themselves to some extent, beginning with Mrs. Nickleby and concluding with Mrs. Lirriper. Dickens even attempted the effect of hallucination in *Our Mutual Friend* with Lizzie Hexam's imagining she hears her father calling her at the time that Gaffer's body is already floating on the Thames.

However, the artistic devices used by Dickens in narrative technique are not confined to point of view. They are primarily related to the planning, the atmosphere, and the over-all effect of the action. These devices have been described in terms of caricature and farce, speech mannerisms and mimicry, action derived from stage models, sentimental effect, and sensational horror. Dickens planned to use all his technical resources in some form of alternation, contrasting one effect with another after he had advanced beyond *Pickwick Papers*. This aim in craftsmanship depends upon a multiple concept of narrative technique and is at the opposite pole from Henry James's concentration on the single and unified effect.

When Dickens sat down to write, he followed a more or less regular habit of creative process. He said to himself (probably unconsciously), "How did someone else achieve the narrative effect I want in this scene? How can I use similar methods and materials to get better effects? What people and places do I know that I can put into this story? What ideas from books and plays can I use?" It is for this reason that a study of his sources has proved so fruitful. The plots and situations which inspired him were transformed into terms of his own times, with the exception of his two excursions into historical epochs, *Barnaby Rudge* and *A Tale of Two Cities*. He peopled his episodes with characters he had encountered and put these characters into the towns and cities, the streets and houses and inns he knew. He arranged his action to appeal to the emotions of laughter, suspense, sympathy, horror, and excitement. He hoped that some readers would also reflect. He constantly experimented with the devices which he admired in the writings of others, combining, changing, and transforming his sources to reach completely unique and individual ends in his best writing.

It is not really illuminating to say concerning any work of art that it has genius—and to stop there. The audience which sees a Shakespearean play has always in the background somewhere the realization that the great dramatist is working perforce with the art of a theater that dates from the days of Queen Elizabeth. If Hamlet feigns madness because Shakespeare's source had it that way rather than because the situation demands it, is the essential emotional effect lost? It is not the ghostly trappings of Shakespeare's plays, nor is it the limitation of the Elizabethan theater which explains the fascination Shakespeare has for us today. But a knowledge of the trappings and the theater explains why Shakespeare wrote as he did.

In like manner Dickens followed a tradition which occasionally exposed him to weak or false effects. He fought his way through the mists of melodrama and sentiment to authentic tragedy and sincere emotion. This conclusion allows us to see that his early novels are spotty, full of the extraordinary and the good, but occasionally containing the weak and the indifferent. Insofar as these novels depended on farce, caricature, and the humors of monologue, they are remarkably satisfactory on the level of entertainment. In other technical effects they present varied realization. The Dickens admirer is always tempted to explain away his failures, because they are set side by side with triumphs. Contrast and alternation produce the illusion of mirage. This fact is the only possible explanation for any reader's inability to see that Dickens reached artistic maturity with *David Copperfield*, and that his later novels are his most enduring masterpieces. It is Shaw who makes this point succinctly: "When Dickens became a serious master of his art, his progress was on a road that leads away from sentimental, cowardly, sweet-toothed lying to sympathetic, courageous, nutritious truth."[9]

Not only did Dickens mirror the creative past, he reflected it into the future. His innovation made by inventing a new concept of fictional art lies in his development from multiple, contrasting techniques in narration to a panoramic pattern with an accompanying and suffusing symbolism. Beginning with *Martin Chuzzlewit,* he arranged his narrative effects around a theme and a pattern. This purpose derived from his desire to improve the world, to give a deeper meaning to his stories than mere entertainment. From the relatively simple purpose of attacking hypocrisy and pride he grew to the overwhelming concept of drawing all social malevolence into his narrative net.

So he came to reveal inner realities by outer oddities, the truth by what is forceful and challenging rather than by minute copying of the actual, the eternal by the ephemeral. His great characters become at once individuals and symbolic images. They combine with their actions and their surroundings to imply a total comment upon the meaning of human existence. It is the social microcosm which creates the effect, not the individual story, not the flat and fleeting show of life that passes into oblivion with the last page of the tale. The technical pattern he invented to accomplish this end was an organization of his typical plots around a thesis, with contrasting individual narrative techniques playing their part in supplying diversity and stimulus to the reader's attention.

The development of a narrative pattern which proceeds from alternative and contrasting effects to synthesis and intensification reaches its height in *David Copperfield,* in *Bleak House,* in *Little Dorrit,* and in *Our Mutual Friend.* These are the novels in which his characters and events stand for many things, the characters as individuals in a story, the events as happenings in life, the background and atmosphere as a reproduction of reality—but each division representing society, the problems and conflicts of man's relationship to his reasons for existing and struggling with the forces that made him and surround him. Jack Lindsay has put it clearly when he says:

> Dickens' greatness as a novelist lies in the way in which he can define
> general tendencies in terms of personal relations and create his over
> life-size figures who are simultaneously fantasy projections, social
> emblems, and intensely individualized entities.[10]

The pattern allows character after character, situation after situation, and plot sequence after plot sequence to intensify its fellows in achieving the total effect. The use of symbols in *Bleak House, Little Dorrit,* and *Our Mutual Friend* drives home the artistry.

Yet above all Dickens used his new concept of fiction as an art form to intensify his comment upon his world and all the worlds that follow the Victorian Age. The creative artist whose work grows in importance as the years go by is the man whose genius forces him to foresee that which is vital to the future through his knowledge of the past. He floats on the stream of recurrent fluctuation in human history. Dickens said savagely that his world was an inferno of intolerance, a privy of pride, a graveyard of greed, a sewer of selfishness, a pit of privilege, a dungeon of caste, a wasteland of filth, a rat-warren of lawyers, a paradox of preachers, an abscission of teachers, and a parliament of fools. But he still saw Paradise within reach. Eternal Hope was ever ready to get up on her knees and crawl if she could. Dickens was everlastingly jabbing the sharp pin of personal responsibility into the quiescent torpor of human lassitude. He was forever tugging at the reins of volition, pulling reluctant sensibility into action. He was evermore urging fallen warriors to get up and fight again.

The miracle of Dickens' accomplishment is that an absorption with essential human conflict grew out of narrative techniques which were developed to the ends of entertainment for its own sake. One can still read him for the story alone, for the plot, for the escape from boredom. But the pattern is also there for the man who sees it; the symbol hovers over the page. For years the pattern and the symbol were relatively unnoticed. This circumstance explains his original popularity, for thousands of readers could enjoy him without realizing that they were the butts of his underlying purpose.

His purposes were so compelling that they did not die with him. Perhaps it took a later generation to see the disgust which would make Dickens name two characters Murdstone and Merdle after the implications of the French *merde*. The relationship between Faulkner's

Emily and Dickens' Miss Havisham could become apparent only after the advent of Faulkner. Just as Dickens delved into the deepest implications of the law in *Bleak House,* so did Kafka reach into the depths of bewildering legal muddle in *The Trial,* but the comparison depends upon the years that follow, not upon the time that created *Bleak House.* Just so, historical criticism justifies its being and directs new attention to the past which lives on into the future.

Those who say Dickens was a moral writer spoke more wisely than they knew. His voice was pitched always on the note of human hope. He lived for man's redemption from selfishness, from hypocrisy, from the love of money for itself, from the evasion of personal responsibility for one's brother man. He devoted his techniques, his narrative capacities, his fictional pattern to a noble purpose. From the sign came the symbol; from the flint came the flame. Genius is destiny in action. The flame is still alight and blazing.

Notes

References to Forster's biography are to the J. W. T. Ley edition and are marked "Forster." References to the novels and reprinted pieces are indicated by chapter, with specific page notation from the Nonesuch edition of Dickens' complete works. The letters are identified by volume and page from the Nonesuch edition. The titles of the novels are abbreviated as follows:

SkB	*Sketches by Boz*
PP	*Pickwick Papers*
OT	*Oliver Twist*
NN	*Nicholas Nickleby*
OCS	*The Old Curiosity Shop*
BR	*Barnaby Rudge*
MC	*Martin Chuzzlewit*
CC	*A Christmas Carol*
Ch	*The Chimes*
D&S	*Dombey and Son*
DC	*David Copperfield*
BH	*Bleak House*
HT	*Hard Times*
LD	*Little Dorrit*
T2C	*A Tale of Two Cities*
GE	*Great Expectations*
OMF	*Our Mutual Friend*
ED	*Edwin Drood*

CHAPTER I

TOWARD A FRAME OF REFERENCE

1. Lionel Trilling, "The Measure of Dickens," *The Griffin*, II (1952), I.

2. G. K. Chesterton, *Appreciations and Criticisms of the Works of Charles Dickens* (1911), p. xv. The Romantic Genius approach can be checked also in J. B. Priestley's *The English Novel* (1927); Sir Osbert Sitwell's *Dickens* (1932); Algernon Swinburne's "Charles Dickens," *Quarterly Review* (July, 1902); Paul Elmer More's *Shelburne Essays*, Vol. V (1908); George Santayana's *Works*, Vol. II: *Dickens* (1936); and Stephen Leacock's *Charles Dickens, His Life and Works* (1933).

3. "Who Wrote Dickens' Novels?" *Cornhill Magazine*, n.s. XI (1888), 114.

4. See George Bernard Shaw, *Introduction to Hard Times* (1912).

5. London *Times*, December 27, 1845, p. 6. For further examples, note *Times* for June 1, 1846, p. 7, and January 2, 1847, p. 6.

6. See George H. Lewes, "Criticism in Relation to Novels," *The Fortnightly Review*, III (1866), 325-61. Saintsbury's opinions can most easily be examined in *The Cambridge History of English Literature*, Vol. XIII; Roberts' in *This Side Idolatry;* and Kingsmill Lunn's in *The Sentimental Journey*.

7. T. S. Eliot, "Wilkie Collins and Dickens" (1927), *Selected Essays* (1932).

8. Robert Graves, *The Real David Copperfield* (1933).

9. George Gissing, *Charles Dickens* (1898), or *The Immortal Dickens* (1925).

10. A proper distinction ought to be made between appreciation and scholarship without depreciation or exaggeration of the value of either approach. Reference can profitably be made to laudatory and investigative books like E. Beresford Chancellor's *Dickens and His Times* (1937), or *The London of Dickens* (1924); Thomas Parsons Cooper's *The Real Micawber* (1920); W. Walter Crotch's *Charles Dickens: Social Reformer* (1913); Bernard Darwin's *Dickens* (1933); H. C. Dent's *The Life and Characters of Charles Dickens* (1933); Walter Dexter's *The England of Dickens* (1925), together with his other books about the Kent and London of Dickens; Humphry House's *The Dickens World* (1941); James L. Hughes's *Dickens as an Educator* (1900); Frederic G. Kitton's *Charles Dickens; His Life, Writings, and Personality* (n.d.), together with seven other books about phases of Dickens; Rudolph C. Lehmann's *Charles Dickens as Editor* (1912); J. W. T. Ley's *The Dickens Circle* (1919); André Maurois' *Dickens* (1935); Edwin Pugh's *Charles Dickens: The Apostle of the People* (1908); Ralph Strauss's *Charles Dickens* (1928); Edward Wagenknecht's *The Man Charles Dickens* (1929), or even Alexander Woollcott's *Mr. Dickens Goes to the Play* (1922).

11. See F. D. Wierstra, *Smollett and Dickens* (Den Helder, De Boer, 1928); Frank W. Wilson, *Dickens in Seinen Beziehungen zu den Humoristen Fielding und Smollett* (Leipzig: O. Schmidt, 1899); J. B. Van Amerongen, *The Actor in Dickens* (1927).

12. Dame Una Pope-Hennessy's *Charles Dickens* (1946); Hesketh Pearson's *Dickens: His Character, Comedy, and Career* (1949); Jack Lindsay's *Charles Dickens: A Biographical and Critical Study* (1950); Julian Symons' *Charles Dickens* (1951); and Edgar Johnson's *Charles Dickens: His Tragedy and Triumph,* 2 volumes (1952).

13. Edmund Wilson, "Dickens, the Two Scrooges," *The Wound and the Bow* (1941), and George Orwell, *Dickens, Dali, and Others* (1946).

14. Lindsay, *op. cit.*

15. Chesterton, *op. cit.* References to books and authors mentioned by Dickens are difficult to count with complete accuracy, but there are more than 170 to Shakespeare's plays, 150 to chapbooks and fairy tales, 40 to Defoe, 40 to Smollett, 25 to Fielding, 25 to Goldsmith, and from 10 to 20 each to Scott, Sheridan, Cervantes, Swift, Addison, and Sterne.

16. *DC,* chap. iv, p. 55.

17. Trollope so jibes at Dickens in *The Warden.*

18. G. Santayana, "Dickens," *Dial,* November, 1921, p. 542.

19. *DC,* chap. xi, p. 167.

20. Forster, p. 553.

CHAPTER II

HUMOR IN MOTION—THE FARCE-CARICATURE TECHNIQUE

1. Letter to Frank Stone, May 30, 1854, Nonesuch, II, 560.
2. Smollett, *Peregrine Pickle,* chap. iv.
3. *PP,* chap. xxiii, p. 311.
4. *PP,* chap. lii, p. 730.
5. *PP,* chap. xvi, p. 208.
6. *Peregrine Pickle,* chap. xlviii.
7. *PP,* chap. xxx, pp. 406-7.
8. *PP,* chap. xxxi, p. 432.
9. *NN,* chap. xv, pp. 176-77.
10. Smollett, Dedication to *Ferdinand Count Fathom.*
11. Percy Lubbock, *The Craft of Fiction,* p. 129. This observation is made concerning *David Copperfield.*
12. See Letter to Forster, June 1856, Nonesuch, II, 776, in which Dickens says that he thought of "making the introduced story so fit into surroundings impossible of separation from the main story, as to make the blood of the book circulate through both." This comment concerns the story of Miss Wade in *Little Dorrit,* Bk. II, chap. xxi.
13. *PP,* chaps. vi, ix, and x.
14. *PP,* chaps. xxii, xxiii, xxiv, and xxv.
15. *PP,* chaps. xii, xviii, xx, xxvi, xxxi, and xxxiv.
16. Henry Fielding, *Joseph Andrews,* Bk. IV, chap. viii.
17. Henry Fielding, *Tom Jones,* Bk. XVI, chap. v.
18. *OT,* chap. ii, pp. 12-13.
19. *OT,* chap. vii, p. 47.
20. *NN,* chap. xvi.

CHAPTER III

MIMICRY: THE TECHNIQUE OF MONOLOGUE

1. The best extant editions are:
   Mathews' Theatrical Budget; or the Actor's Multum in Parvo (London: Hodgson, n.d., 1823?).
   The London Mathews: Containing an Account of This Celebrated Actor's Memorandum Book (London: Cole, 1825).
   Mr. Mathews' New Entertainment for 1826, Called Invitations (London: Cole, 1826).
2. Forster, pp. 59-60.
3. Forster, p. 380.

4. Mamie Dickens, *My Father as I Recall Him* (1897), pp. 47-48.
5. See *Mathews in America* (London: Hodgson, n.d.), p. 36.
6. Collected by Fitzgerald, *The History of Pickwick*, pp. 136 ff.
7. See my article, "Dickens and the Evolution of Caricature," *PMLA*, LV (1940), pp. 231-40.
8. Holcroft, *The Road to Ruin*, Act II, scene 1.
9. *Mathews' Theatrical Budget*, pp. 116-17.
10. *Mathews at Home: Home Circuit; or Cockney Gleanings* (London: Cole), pp. 7-8.
11. *PP*, chap. ii, p. 12.
12. *PP*, chap. ii, p. 11.
13. *Mathews' Comic Annual for 1830* (London: Cole), p. 4.
14. *NN*, chap. xli, pp. 533-34.
15. *MC*, chap. xl, p. 629.
16. *LD*, chap. xxiv, p. 294.
17. *Mrs. Lirriper's Legacy*, chap. i (*Reprinted Pieces*, pp. 617-18).
18. *The London Mathews*, p. 16.
19. *Mr. Mathews' New Entertainment*, p. 9.
20. *Mathews' 1825 Memorandum Book* (London: Cole), p. 5.
21. *OMF*, chap. ii, p. 11.
22. *DC*, chap. xi, pp. 155-56.
23. *DC*, chap. xii, p. 173.
24. See Charles Kent, *Charles Dickens as a Reader* (1872), p. 261. See Johnson, II, 937, where Dickens' habit of editing copy for reading is described.
25. See Mrs. Anne Mathews, *The Life and Correspondence of Charles Mathews the Elder*, p. 203.
26. George Gissing, *Charles Dickens, a Critical Study*, pp. 116-17.

CHAPTER IV

CONFLICT IN ACTION: THE TECHNIQUE OF PLOT ARRANGEMENT

1. *The Village Coquettes, The Strange Gentleman*, and *Is She His Wife, or Something Singular* (all 1836 and 1837).
2. Letter to Macready, February 27, 1851, Nonesuch, II, 274-75.
3. Forster, p. 348.
4. The following plays are referred to by Dickens in his novels:
   Shakespeare (170 references to almost all the plays)
   Beaumont and Fletcher, *The Maid's Tragedy*
   Massinger, *A New Way to Pay Old Debts*
   Otway, *Venice Preserved*

315

Rowe, *Jane Shore*
Addison, *Cato*
Van Brugh-Cibber, *The Provoked Husband*
Fielding, *Tom Thumb*
Lillo, *George Barnwell*
Moore, *The Gamester*
Home, *Douglas*
Goldsmith, *The Good-Natured Man, She Stoops to Conquer*
Sheridan, *The Rivals, School for Scandal, The Critic*
Kotzebue, *The Stranger, Pizarro*
Colman the Younger, *Ways and Means, Heir-at-Law, The Poor Gentleman, John Bull*
Holcroft, *The Road to Ruin*
Reynolds, *How to Grow Rich*
Morton, *A Cure for the Heart-Ache, Speed the Plough*
Tobin, *The Honeymoon*
Anonymous, *Thirty Years of a Gambler's Life*
Knowles, *Virginius, William Tell, The Hunchback, Alfred the Great, The Daughter, The Love Chase*
Jerrold, *Black-Eyed Susan, Rent Day, Nell Gwynne*
Byron, *Werner*
Talfourd, *Ion, The Athenian Captive*
Bulwer-Lytton, *The Lady of Lyons, Richelieu, Money*
The letters, of course, add more titles.

5. The clearest modern statement about the difference between melodrama and tragedy is in a speech by the Chorus in Jean Anouilh's *Antigone* (the Lewis Galantière English edition), pp. 37-38 (Samuel French, 1946).

6. Chesterton, *op. cit.,* introduction to *Edwin Drood.*

7. Actually spoken by Tyrrel to the worthy Hawkins in Godwin's *Caleb Williams.*

8. *NN,* chap. xix, p. 243.

9. *NN,* chap. xx, p. 255.

10. *NN,* chap. xxix, p. 376.

11. *NN,* chap. xxxiii, p. 420.

12. *NN,* chap. liv, p. 722.

13. *OT,* chap. lii, p. 414.

14. *OT,* chap. xvi, p. 114.

15. *OT,* chap. xxii, p. 163.

16. Douglas Jerrold, *Black-Eyed Susan,* Act I, scene 3.

17. *NN,* chap. xxvii, p. 355.

18. *MC,* chap. xxx, p. 486.

19. *BR,* chap. xvii, p. 140.

20. Stefan Zweig, *Three Masters, Balzac, Dickens, Dostoevsky,* p. 74.

21. *NN,* chap. xxiii ff.

22. Walter Dexter, *Some Rogues and Vagabonds of Dickens,* p. 59.

23. *OT,* chap. li, p. 400.

24. *NN,* chap. xliv, p. 573.

25. *OT,* chap. xlii, pp. 381-82.

26. Letter to Forster, August, 1859, Nonesuch, III, 117.

27. These scenes are numerous. Examples occur in *NN,* chaps. xxxii, xlvii, xlii, lvii; *OCS,* chap. xlii; *OT,* chap. xlvi; *D&S,* chap. lii; *DC,* chap. xl.

28. *DC,* chap. xiv, pp. 210-11.

CHAPTER V

TEARS AND TERROR:

THE TECHNIQUES OF SENTIMENT AND SENSATION

1. Laurence Sterne, *The Sentimental Journey* (Yorick edition, Taylor), p. 382.

2. J. M. S. Tompkins, *The Popular Novel in England 1770-1800,* p. 95.

3. Act V, scene 1.

4. *PP,* chap. xi, p. 132.

5. *The Recollections of Sir Henry Dickens,* p. 42.

6. *BR,* chap. lxvi, pp. 548-49.

7. *D&S,* chap. xviii, p. 255.

8. Smollett, *Peregrine Pickle,* chap. xxvii.

9. *Ibid.,* chap. lxxxvi.

10. Forster, p. 151.

11. *OCS,* chap. lxxii, pp. 575-76.

12. *DC,* chap. liii, p. 762.

13. *Ibid.*

14. *DC,* chap. liv, p. 763.

15. *T2C,* Bk. III, chap. xv, p. 362.

16. William Harrison Ainsworth, *Rookwood,* Preface.

17. See Mrs. Anne Radcliffe's *The Mysteries of Udolpho,* Vol. II, chap. i.

18. See Scott's description of Ravenswood in *The Bride of Lammermoor,* chap. vii.

19. *OT,* chap. xxxviii, p. 281.

20. *BR,* chap. xiii, p. 110.

21. *BR,* chap. ii, p. 20.

22. *ED,* chap. xiv, pp. 162-63.

23. *OCS,* chap. xxx, p. 240.

CHAPTER VI

DIALECTIC ROMANTICISM: TECHNIQUES IN FUSION

1. *OT,* chap. xxxii, p. 238-39.
2. *OCS,* chap. xii, p. 99.
3. *OCS,* chap. xxiv, p. 191.
4. *OCS,* chap. vi, p. 58.
5. *BR,* chap. xxv, p. 202.
6. *BR,* chap. liii, p. 436.
7. *BR,* chap. lxxvii, p. 640.
8. William Godwin, *Caleb Williams,* chap. vii.
9. *D&S,* chap. xxvii, p. 389.
10. *OCS,* chap. xxxii, p. 254.
11. *LD,* Bk. I, chap. xx, p. 251.
12. "The Noble Savage," *Reprinted Pieces,* pp. 133-38.
13. *BR,* chap. xi, p. 94.
14. Letter to Macready, March 22, 1842, Nonesuch, I, 413.
15. *MC,* chap. xxi, p. 353.
16. *MC,* chap. xxxiv, p. 538.
17. *D&S,* chap. xxi, p. 291.
18. *D&S,* chap. xxi, pp. 295-296.
19. Godwin, *Caleb Williams,* chap. ix.
20. Bulwer-Lytton, *Paul Cilfford,* chap. vii.
21. *Ibid.,* Preface to 1840 edition.
22. *Ibid.,* chap. xviii.
23. *OT,* Preface to Third Edition (1841), ix.
24. Ainsworth, *Rookwood,* Bk. I, chap. ix.
25. Ainsworth, *Jack Sheppard,* Bk. III, chap. v.
26. *MC,* Preface to First Cheap Edition (1849), xi.

CHAPTER VII

ECONOMIC THEORY

1. T. A. Jackson's *Charles Dickens: The Progress of a Radical* (1938), sums up all these arguments. It is illuminating to examine George Orwell's rejection of this point of view in *Dickens, Dali, and Others* (1946), since Orwell's interest in revolt against the evils of capitalism is highly regarded.

2. Emery E. Neff's *Carlyle and Mill* (1924), is still the most dependable source for Carlyle's opinions and influence. See also Julian Symons' *Thomas Carlyle, the Life and Ideas of a Prophet* (1952).

3. Forster, p. 227.
4. *CC,* chap. i, p. 6.
5. Carlyle, *Chartism,* chap. vi.
6. *CC,* chap. i, p. 10.
7. *CC,* chap. i, p. 19.
8. Carlyle, *Past and Present,* Bk. III, chap. ii.
9. Carlyle, *Chartism,* chap. ii.
10. Dickens intended to use as the third character a "Young England" gentleman, but Forster objected to him. Obviously Forster toned down part of Dickens' attack on laissez-faire attitudes. See Forster, p. 355, concerning his "filing away at Filer."
11. *Ch,* chap. ii, 116.
12. Friedrich Engels, *The Condition of the Working-Class in England* (1844).
13. Charles Gavan Duffy, *Conversations with Carlyle,* pp. 74-76.
14. *D&S,* chap, v, p. 60.
15. *D&S,* chap. xxxviii, pp. 543-44.
16. *D&S,* chap. xi, p. 143.
17. *D&S,* chap. xi, pp. 143-44.
18. Letter to Forster, September, 1854, Nonesuch, II, 585.
19. Letter to Macready, October 4, 1855, Nonesuch, II, 695.
20. Letter to J. H. Chamberlain, November 17, 1869, Nonesuch, III, 751.
21. Monroe Engel's "The Politics of Dickens' Novels," *PMLA,* LXXI, 5 (December, 1956), 945-74, has the best summary of Dickens' political opinions available to the scholar.

CHAPTER VIII

FROM ALTERNATION TO PATTERN: THE TECHNIQUE OF CONTRAST

1. *OT,* chap. xvii, p. 119.
2. *OT,* chap. xii ff.
3. *OT,* chap. xxvii, p. 203.
4. See Forster, p. 604.
5. *OCS,* chap. xxxviii, p. 299.
6. Alfred Ulrich, *Studien zu Dickens' Roman "Barnaby Rudge"* (Jena, 1931), presents a working study of the source material for the historical part of this novel.
7. Gashford is Dickens' invention. Gordon's real secretary was named Watson, a man who was not a traitor or villain. See Ulrich for other changes.
8. Forster, pp. 169-70.
9. Forster, p. 168.

10. Philip Dormer Stanhope, 4th Earl of Chesterfield, *Letters Written by the Earl of Chesterfield to His Son.*

11. Forster, p. 170.

12. Forster, p. 291.

13. Forster, p. 290.

14. *MC,* chap. xxviii, p. 463.

15. F. J. H. Darton, chap. xvi in *The Cambridge History of English Literature,* Vol. XI, is probably the best source of information on chapbooks. James Orchard Halliwell-Phillips compiled a *Catalogue of Chap-Books, Garlands, and Popular Histories* in 1849. These sources list enough subjects to account for innumerable references in Dickens' works to the titles listed. Dickens tells of finding these books in "A Christmas Tree" in *Household Words* (*Reprinted Pieces,* pp. 262-77).

16. Forster, pp. 471-73.

17. *Ibid.*

18. Forster, p. 473.

19. Forster, p.423.

20. *D&S,* chap. xi, p. 139.

21. *D&S,* chap. xxvii, p. 397.

22. Forster, p. 484.

CHAPTER IX

FIRST PERSON: DAVID COPPERFIELD

1. Forster, p. 479.

2. Forster, pp. 522-23.

3. Preface to *David Copperfield,* 1869 edition, p. xiii.

4. Forster, pp. 523-24.

5. See Ley's note (No. 10), Forster, pp. 17-19, for the evidence of Dickens' relations with his mother.

6. Preface to *David Copperfield* (1869).

7. *DC,* chap. i, p. 1.

8. *The Holly Tree,* Christmas story for *Household Words,* 1855.

9. *The Uncommercial Traveller,* chap xxxiv, is devoted to an attack on *Sandford and Merton.*

10. See Paul C. Kitchen, "Holcroft, Dickens, and *David Copperfield,*" *Schelling Anniversary Papers* (1923).

11. Forster, Life of Oliver Goldsmith, chap. vi.

12. Robert Langton, *The Childhood and Youth of Dickens* (1883), p. 83.

13. Forster, *Goldsmith,* chap. vi.

14. *DC,* chap. vii, pp. 95-96.

15. Smollett, *Roderick Random,* chap. ii.
16. *DC,* chap. v, p. 78.
17. *DC,* chap. viii, p. 120.
18. *DC,* chap. ix.
19. *DC,* chap. xi, pp. 155-56.
20. Bulwer-Lytton, *Paul Clifford,* chap. vi.
21. *DC,* chap. viii.
22. Forster, p. 503.
23. See discussion of this in Chapter IV.
24. See Forster, p. 548.
25. See Aldous Huxley's multiple climax in *Eyeless in Gaza* for this particular technical effect.
26. *DC,* chap. xxxi, presents these examples of Emily's letters.
27. *DC,* chap. xxxii, p. 467.
28. *DC,* chap. l, p. 712.
29. *DC,* chap. lv, p. 789.

CHAPTER X

THE COLLINS MYTH

1. Forster, p. 731, says specifically that Dickens was at his best when he relied upon character. After *Bleak House,* he expresses less and less enthusiasm in his critical summaries of the later novels, and the traditional Dickensian follows this line.
2. J. W. T. Ley, "Victorianism," *The Dickensian,* XXVIII (1932), p. 66.
3. Chesterton, *op. cit.,* p. 148.
4. J. W. T. Ley, *The Dickens Circle,* chapter on Collins, especially p. 339. The Johnson biography and the letters bring this study up to date.
5. Forster, p. 512.
6. Percy Fitzgerald, *Memories of Charles Dickens* (1913), pp. 170-71.
7. Letter to W. H. Wills, September 16, 1856, Nonesuch, II, 800.
8. This remark seems to have been attributed to a number of people. It was first given to Collins by S. M. Ellis, *Wilkie Collins, Le Fanu, and Others* (1931). Note that Kenneth Robinson, *Wilkie Collins,* pp. 258-60, prints some of the annotations Collins made in his copy of Forster's biography, all of them extremely critical.
9. *Letters of Charles Dickens to Wilkie Collins, 1851-1870,* edited by Laurence Hutton, puts this correspondence in a compartment that can be easily examined. Note that Collins and Dickens argue, attack, and defend matters of narrative technique. Forster was usually deleting or toning something down.

10. Letter to Collins, September 20, 1862, Nonesuch, III, 304. This is the letter which also explains to Wilkie that he must not say his characters "laid down."

11. Nuel Pharr Davis, *The Life of Wilkie Collins* (1956). Also available for study is Kenneth Robinson's *Wilkie Collins* (1952). The Robinson biography put in print a great deal of material concerning Collins, whose life had contained much which was as mysterious as his books for many years.

12. Davis, *op. cit.,* pp. 257-58.

13. Preface to *Basil* (July, 1862).

14. Letter to Collins, October 6, 1859, Nonesuch, III, 124-125.

15. Preface to *No Name* (1862).

16. Davis, *op. cit.,* p. 153.

CHAPTER XI

THE SOCIAL MICROCOSMIC PATTERN

1. Edgar Johnson says (II, 744), "The grimmer and more comprehensive vision Dickens brought to his enlarged purpose fills these novels with somber hues." The seriousness and gloom of Dickens in this period leads Lionel Stevenson to write about "Dickens' Dark Novels, 1851-1857," *Sewanee Review*, LI (1943), 398-409.

2. *ED,* chap. xviii, p. 205.

3. Johnson, II, 762.

4. *Ibid.,* 771.

5. William Searle Holdsworth, *Charles Dickens as a Legal Historian* (1928), p. 81.

6. *Ibid.,* p. 85.

7. The breaks in point of view, jumping from first to third person, are, by chapters:
   33111131133311131133331133333113331111333311133331113333131111 31131.

8. John Home, *Douglas* (1756), Act II.

9. *Ibid.,* Act III.

10. *BH,* chap. xviii, pp. 248-49.

11. *BH,* chap. xxxvi, p. 506.

12. *BH,* chap. v, p. 55.

13. *BH,* chap. xiv, p. 199.

14. *BH,* chap. v, pp. 51-52.

15. Captain Frederick Marryat, *Jacob Faithful,* chap. i.

16. Johnson, II, 770.

17. *BH,* chap. ii, p. 8.

18. *BH,* chap. viii, pp. 95-96.

19. *BH*, chap. xvi, p. 219. The Boodle-Coodle-Doodle names are suggested by Fielding's *Tom Thumb*.
20. *BH*, chap. xix, p. 261.
21. *BH*, chap. lxvii, p. 871.
22. F. R. Leavis, *The Great Tradition*, p. 273.
23. Johnson, II, 797. Mrs. Gaskell must have thought it odd that Dickens would begin writing a novel so much like hers in theme when he was contracting to print hers afterwards. Note his letter to her, April 21, 1854, Nonesuch, II, 554. One may conjecture that Dickens liked the theme very much and thought it ought to be handled properly by a good novelist, namely Dickens.
24. *HT*, Bk. I, chap. ii, p. 490.
25. *HT*, Bk. I, chap. ix, p. 541.
26. *HT*, Bk. II, chap. iv, pp. 617-18.
27. *HT*, Bk. III, chap. vi, p. 739.
28. Shaw, Introduction to *Hard Times*.
29. *HT*, Bk. II, chap. vi, p. 638.
30. Johnson, II, 811.
31. "Strike," *Household Words*, February 6, 1858, pp. 169-72.
32. "To Working Men," *Household Words*, October 7, 1854.
33. Jack Lindsay, *Charles Dickens*, p. 300.
34. *HT*, Bk. II, chap. v, p. 627.
35. George Orwell, *Dickens, Dali, and Others*, p. 14.
36. Leavis, *op. cit.*, p. 32.
37. Shaw, Preface to *Great Expectations*.
38. *LD*, Bk. I, chap. i, p. 4.
39. *LD*, Bk. I, chap. iii, p. 31.
40. *LD*, Bk. I, chap. xxx, p. 369.
41. *LD*, Bk. I, chap. ii, pp. 22-23.
42. *LD*, Bk. I, chap. i, p. 12.
43. Johnson, II, 893.
44. *LD*, Bk. I, chap. x, p. 111.
45. *LD*, Bk. I, chap. xxxiv, p. 417.
46. The six plots are followed in a pattern which does not revolve in exact mathematical division, of course. Numbering them as they have been described, they are treated as follows, the commas standing for chapter divisions:
Book I. 2A, 2B-4, 2B, 2A, 2-1, 1, 1, 1, 1, 3, 2A, 1, 6-2BA, 1, 2A, 3-4AB, 4A, 1, 1, 1-5, 5, 1, 3-6, 1-6, 6-2A, 3-4A, 4B, 4A, 2A, 2A, 1, 1, 5, 3-4A, 1, 1.
Book II. 1, 1, 1, 1, 1, 1, 1, 3-4A, 4AB-6, 2A, 1, 5, 6-3-2B, 1, 1, 1-5, 1-2A, 1, 1, 4B, 4B, 3-2A, 2A, 5, 5, 2B, 2B, 2BA, 1-2B, 2A, 2A, 6, 4AB, 2B-1-3.

47. *LD,* Bk. I, chap. xxv, p. 307.
48. *LD,* Bk. I, chap. xiii, pp. 153-54.
49. *LD,* Bk. I, chap. xvii, pp. 211-12.
50. Forster, p. 626.
51. *LD,* Bk. II, chap. xxviii, pp. 763-64.
52. *LD,* Bk. II, chap. xxxiv, pp. 849-50.
53. Orwell, *op. cit.,* p. 75.

CHAPTER XII

RECALLED TO LIFE

1. Lionel Trilling, Introduction to *Little Dorrit.*
2. Wilson, *op. cit.*
3. Lindsay, *op. cit.*
4. Symons, *op. cit.*
5. Lindsay, pp. 170-75.
6. Johnson, I, 492-94.
7. Bulwer-Lytton, *Zanoni,* chaps. vii-xvii.
8. See Curt Böttger's *Charles Dickens' Historischer Roman "A Tale of Two Cities" und seine Quellen* (Konigsberg, 1913). This is incomplete, but has a fine listing of the influence of Carlyle's *French Revolution* on the Dickens novel.
9. Letter to Forster, August, 1859, Nonesuch, III, 117.
10. Carlyle, *The French Revolution,* Vol. I, Bk. V, chap. vii.
11. *T2C,* Bk. III, chap. x, p. 320.
12. Forster, p. 731.
13. Forster, p. 730.
14. Forster, p. 749.
15. *T2C,* Bk. II, chap. xxi, p. 207.
16. *Fr. Rev.,* Vol. I, Bk. V, chap. vi.
17. *Fr. Rev.,* Vol. I, Bk. V, chap. ix.
18. *Ibid.*
19. *Fr. Rev.,* Vol. II, Bk. I, chap. vii.
20. *Fr. Rev.,* Vol. III, Bk. V, chap. iv.
21. *Ibid.*
22. *Fr. Rev.,* Vol. III, Bk. I, chap. i.
23. *Fr. Rev.,* Vol. I, Bk. VII, chaps. i-xi.
24. *Fr. Rev.,* Vol. III, Bk. II, chap. v.
25. *Fr. Rev.,* Vol. I, Bk. II, chap. v.
26. *Fr. Rev.,* Vol. III, Bk. I, chap. iv.
27. *Ibid.*

28. Louis Sebastian Mercier, *Tableau de Paris,* goes into great detail, pp. 239 ff, telling of the man who was released after long years in the Bastille and his difficulties in readjustment. The "nouvelle edition" (Amsterdam, 1783), has the "recalled to life" phrase on p. 168.

29. *Fr. Rev.,* Vol. III, Bk. I, chap. v.

30. *T2C,* Bk. II, chap. ix, pp. 302-3.

31. *Fr. Rev.,* Vol. III, Bk. V, chap. ii.

32. *T2C,* Bk. III, chap. xv, p. 363.

33. *Fr. Rev.,* Vol. III, Bk. VI, chap. iii.

34. Anesthetics came into use about the middle of the nineteenth century, having been discovered years after the French Revolution. The first operation under ether was performed in 1842.

35. Letter to Forster, October, 1860, Nonesuch, III, 186.

36. Forster, p. 620.

37. John H. Hagan, Jr., "Structural Patterns in Dickens' *Great Expectations,*" *Journal of English Literary History (ELH),* XXI, 1 (March, 1954), 61-62.

38. Hagan, *op. cit.,* pp. 55-56.

39. *GE,* chap. xiv, p. 104.

40. *GE,* chap. xxxiv, p. 270.

41. Forster, p. 737.

42. Ley's notes to Forster print the original ending, pp. 737-38. The Limited Editions Club version (1937), with Shaw's Introduction, prints the novel with the substituted first version of the conclusion. The Rinehart edition (1948), with Earle Davis' Introduction, prints both endings alternately so that the reader may make his choice.

43. T. S. Eliot, "Wilkie Collins and Dickens."

CHAPTER XIII

INFERNO

1. Forster, p. 740.

2. L. H. Meeks, *Sheridan Knowles and the Theatre of His Time* (1933), gives the details of Knowles's connection with Macready and the latter's acting in his plays. Dickens owned a copy of *The Hunchback,* autographed with date, July, 1832. There are manuscript notes and the copy is well-worn, *Catalogue of the Library of Dickens* (Henry Sotheran and Company, 1878). There was some contemporary opinion among the Macready coterie to the effect that Knowles was among the great dramatists. Obviously Dickens saw all the Knowles productions, and he refers to six of the plays in his novels.

3. *OMF,* Bk. II, chap. v, p. 314.

4. "Moneysworth," *Household Words,* XIII, May 31, 1856, pp. 461-64, is the clearest statement of Dickens' beliefs about money in his magazine articles. In this one he argues that value is a function of labor and time, and that currency must be based on work rather than upon metal which is considered valuable in itself. This opinion is at odds with the concept of a gold or silver standard, since money in this sense ought to be used to facilitate exchange rather than represent wealth in itself. See also Monroe Engel, "The Politics of Dickens' Novels," *PMLA,* LXXI, 5 (December, 1956), 945-74.

5. *OMF,* Bk. I, chap. ix, p. 127.

6. *OMF,* Bk. III, chap. xvii, p. 706.

7. *OMF, Bk.* III, chap. iv, pp. 520-21.

8. *OMF,* Bk. I, chap. v, pp. 51-52.

9. *Ibid.*

10. *OMF,* Bk. I, chap. v, p. 56.

11. *OMF,* Postscript, p. 926.

12. This practice of surprise versus suspense is discussed in the chapter on the influence of Collins on Dickens.

13. Johnson, II, 1031, quotes this and more from the Forster Collection, Dickens' original MS notes.

14. *OMF,* Bk. I, chap. xi, pp. 157-58.

15. See Wilson, *op. cit.,* pp. 76-84, and Johnson, III, 1041-45. Lindsay, *op. cit.,* p. 380, says, "A work which vindicates Dickens' right to stand, as no other writer can stand, at the side of Shakespeare."

CHAPTER XIV

DEAD OR ALIVE?

1. Letter to Forster, July, 1869, Nonesuch, III, 732.

2. Letter to Forster, August 6, 1869, Nonesuch, III, 735.

3. *ED;* see end of chap. xv.

4. Letter to W. H. Wills, July 26, 1868, Nonesuch, III, 660.

5. *Library of Wilkie Collins,* Catalogue by Puttick and Simpson, January 20, 1890.

6. "The Stolen Letter" and "The Yellow Mask" imitate "The Purloined Letter," "Lygeia," and "The Masque of the Red Death."

7. See N. P. Davis, *op. cit.,* p. 265. Probably no one asked Wilkie to finish the novel. It is possible that if he felt some ownership of the original plot idea, he would rather use it in a story completely his own.

8. Wilkie Collins, *The Dead Alive, or John Jago's Ghost* (1873).

9. *ED,* chap. iii, p. 20.

10. Forster, p. 808.

11. Forster, p. 815.

12. Richard M. Baker, *The Drood Murder Case* (1951), makes the best case for Grewgious as Datchery.

13. J. Cumings Walters, *The Complete Mystery of Edwin Drood,* states the argument for Helena as Datchery.

14. Letter to W. H. Wills, June 30, 1867, Nonesuch, III, 534.

15. Lindsay, pp. 408-9.

16. Aubrey Boyd, "A New Angle on the Drood Mystery," *Washington University Studies, Humanistic Series,* October, 1921.

17. *ED,* chap. v., p. 64.

18. *ED,* chap. v, p. 69.

19. Howard Duffield, "John Jasper, Strangler," *Bookman,* February, 1930.

20. *ED,* chap. viii, p. 77.

21. Wilson, p. 101.

CHAPTER XV

FIRE FROM FLINT

1. Quoted by Ford, *Dickens and His Readers,* p. 61.

2. Quoted by Hesketh Pearson, *Oscar Wilde,* p. 208.

3. Henry Miller, *The Colossus of Maroussi,* p. 115.

4. Evelyn Waugh, *A Handful of Dust;* see concluding chapters.

5. James Joyce, *Finnegans Wake* (Viking Press, 1943), p. 434, line 26 ff.

6. Graham Greene, *The Lost Childhood and Other Essays,* pp. 52-53.

7. *Letters of Dostoevsky,* p. 241.

8. Quoted by Aylmer Maude, *The Life of Tolstoy* (1929), I, 177.

9. George Bernard Shaw, "Ibsen's New Play," *Pen Portraits and Reviews,* p. 153.

10. Lindsay, p. 281.

INDEX

329